C.W. James

1987

HISTORY OF
Ancient Philosophy

W. WINDELBAND

Translated by Herbert Ernest Cushman

DOVER PUBLICATIONS, INC.

NEW YORK

Published in Canada by General Publishing Company, Ltd., 30 Lesmill Road, Don Mills, Toronto, Ontario.

Published in the United Kingdom by Constable and Company, Ltd., 10 Orange Street, London WC 2.

This Dover edition, first published in 1956, is an unabridged and unaltered republication of the authorized English translation of the second German edition, as originally published by Charles Scribners' Sons circa 1900.

Standard Book Number: 486-20357-3
Library of Congress Catalog Card Number: 57-14418

Manufactured in the United States of America
Dover Publications, Inc.
180 Varick Street
New York, N.Y. 10014

TRANSLATOR'S PREFACE

PROFESSOR WINDELBAND'S *Geschichte der Alten Philosophie* is already well known to German philosophical readers as one of the famous Müller series of hand-books, and yet to that wider circle of English readers it is still a foreign book. In many quarters technical scholars of Greek philosophy have already commended its important innovations, and to these its erudition and scholarship are patent. In its translation, however, under the title of "The History of Ancient Philosophy," it will reach the general reader and serve as an introduction to the beginner in philosophy. I have personally never been able to see why the approaches to the study of philosophy have been made as difficult and uninviting as possible. In other hard subjects all sorts of helps and devices are used to allure the beginner within. Into philosophy the beginner has always had to force his way with no indulgent hand to help. In the past the history of thought has too often been entirely separated from the history of affairs, as if the subjective historical processes could have been possible without the objective concrete events. Professor Windelband has gone far to lead the general reader to the history of thought *through* the history of the affairs of the Greek nation. This is, to my mind, the difficult but absolutely necessary task of the historian of thought, if he wishes to reach any but technical philosophers. This work occu-

pies a unique position in this respect, and may mark the
beginning of an epoch in the rewriting of the history of
philosophy.

I am indebted to many friends for help in my translation of this work. The reader will allow me to mention in
particular Professor George H. Palmer, of Harvard, my
friend and former teacher, for introducing me to the work ;
and my colleagues, Professor Charles St. Clair Wade for
much exceedingly valuable assistance, and especially Pro-
fessors Charles E. Fay and Leo R. Lewis, whose generous
and untiring aid in the discussion of the whole I shall
ever remember. Whatever merits the translation may
have, are due in no small measure to their help; for
whatever defects may appear, I can hold only myself
responsible.

So complete are the bibliographies here and elsewhere
that I have found it necessary to append only a list of such
works as are helpful to the English reader of Ancient
Philosophy.

HERBERT ERNEST CUSHMAN.

TUFTS COLLEGE, *June*, 1899.

PREFACE

HAVING undertaken to prepare a résumé of the history of ancient philosophy for the *Handbuch der Klassischen Altertumswissenschaft*, it seemed expedient to offer to my trained readers, not an extract from the history of the literature of the Greeks and Romans, which can be found elsewhere; but rather a short and clear presentation, such as would awaken interest and give an insight into the subject matter and the development of ancient philosophy. The necessity of a new edition gives evidence that this presentation has won itself friends far beyond the circle of those most nearly interested. This, moreover, would not have happened had I not abandoned the idea of presenting a collation from the data usually furnished, and had I not given to the subject the form which my long personal experience as an academic teacher had proved to be most available. As a result I found myself in the somewhat painful position of being compelled to present didactically many very considerable deviations from the previous conception and treatment, without being able in the limitations of this résumé to advance for experts my reasons save in short references. I should have been very glad if I could have found time to justify my innovations by accompanying detailed discussions. But, unfortunately, the execution of my whole purpose has been postponed up to this time through more important and imperative tasks. The new edition, therefore, finds me again in the same position of being compelled to trust more in the force of the general relations of the subject matter and in the emphasis briefly laid upon important moments, than in a leisurely extended polemical presentation, which would otherwise have been usual in this particular field.

For the chief matters in which I have gone my own ways — the separation of Pythagoras from the Pythagoreans and the discussion of the latter under " Efforts toward Reconciliation between Heracleitanism and the Theory of Parmenides," the separation of the two phases of Atomism by the Protagorean Sophistic, the juxtaposition of Democritus and Plato, the conception of the Hellenic-Roman philosophy as a progressive application — first ethical and then religious — of science, to which I have also organically connected Patristics, — all this the reader finds unchanged in its essentials. My treatment of these questions has found recognition in many quarters, but in many also an expected opposition ; and the reader may be assured that I have always been grateful for this latter, and have given it careful consideration. This weighing of objections was the more needful since I had occasion in the mean time to deal with the same questions in a larger connection and from a different point of view. The trained eye will not fail to recognize in this second edition the influence of the objections of experts, even where these have not convinced me, in the numerous small changes in the presentation, and in the choice of bibliography and citations. Here, again, the revising hand needed to follow many a kindly suggestion in the discussions of this book, and accept many a gratifying explanation in the works that have appeared during the past five years.

The only change in the external form of the book is in the very desirable addition of an index to the philosophers discussed.

Then may my brief treatise continue to fulfil its task: to solicit friends appreciative of a noble cause, to preserve alive the consciousness of the imperishable worth which the creations of Greek thought possess for all human culture.

WILHELM WINDELBAND.

STRASSBURG, *April*, 1893.

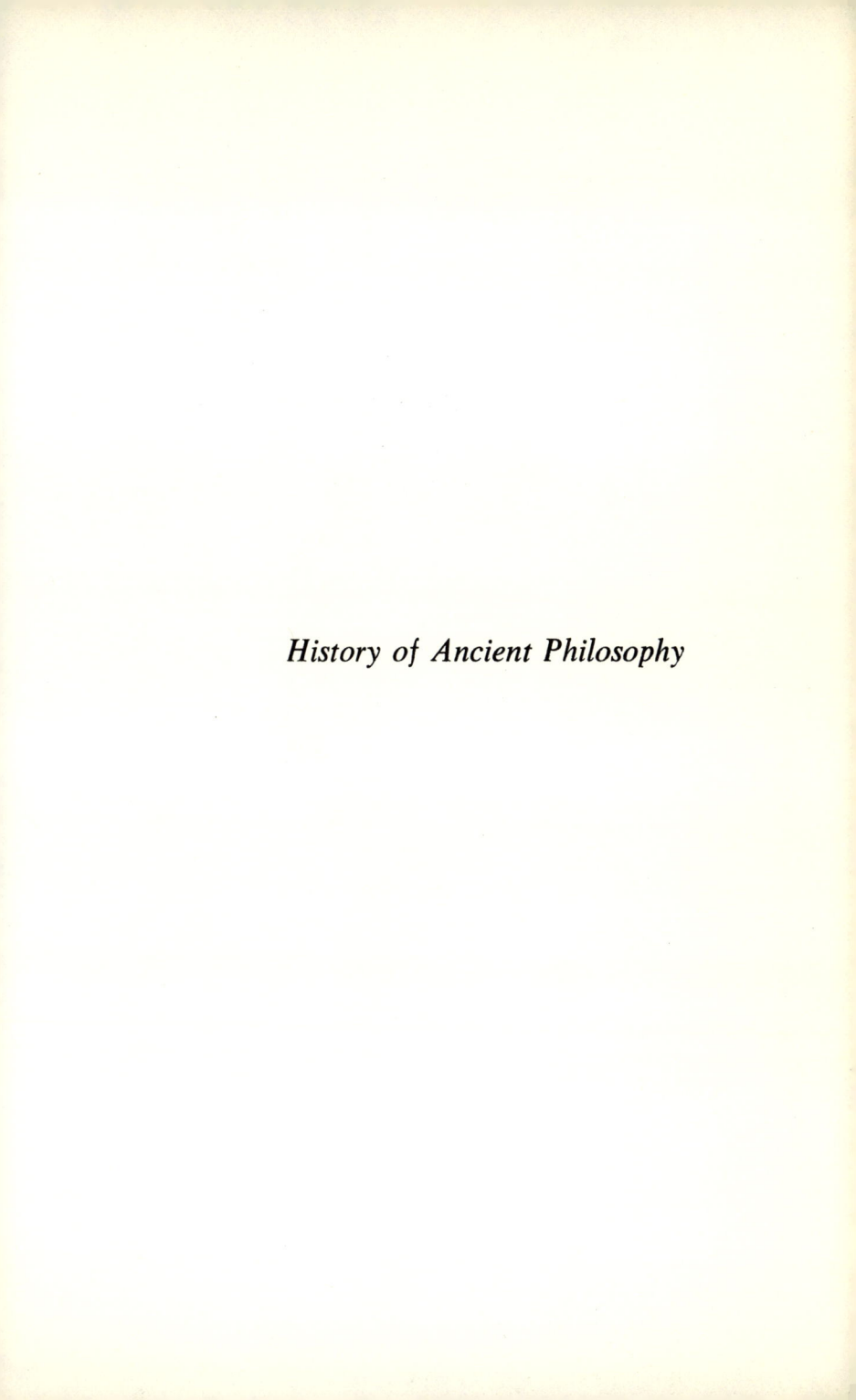

History of Ancient Philosophy

TABLE OF CONTENTS

B. — HELLENIC–ROMAN PHILOSOPHY

HISTORY

OF

ANCIENT PHILOSOPHY

INTRODUCTION

1. Scientific interest in ancient, especially in Greek, philosophy, is not confined to the value that it possesses as a peculiar subject for historical research and for the study of the growth of civilization. But it is also equally concerned in the permanent significance that the content of ancient thought possesses by reason of its place in the development of the intellectual life of Europe.

The emphasis falls primarily upon the lifting of mere knowing to the plane of systematic knowledge, or science. Not content with his storing of practical facts, and with his fantastic speculations born of his religious needs, the Greek sought knowledge for its own sake. Knowledge, like art, was developed as an independent function from its involvement in the other activities of civilization. So, first and foremost, the history of ancient philosophy is *an insight into the origin of European science in general.*

It is, however, at the same time the history of the birth of the separate sciences. For the process of differentiation, which begins with distinguishing thought from conduct and mythology, was continued within the domain of science itself. With the accumulation and organic arrangement of its facts, the early, simple, and unitary science to which the Greeks gave the name φιλοσοφία, divided into

1

the special sciences, the single φιλοσοφίαι, and these then
continued to develop on more or less independent lines.

Concerning the history and meaning of the name of " philosophy," see especially R. Haym, in Ersch and Gruber's *Encyklopädie*, III. division, vol. 24 ; Ueberweg, *Grundriss*, I. § 1 ;
Windelband, *Praeludien*, p. 1 ff. The word became a technical
term in the Socratic school. It meant there exactly what science means in German. In later time, after the division into
the special sciences, the word philosophy had the sense of
ethico-religious practical wisdom. See § 2.

The beginnings of scientific life that are thus found in
ancient philosophy are most influential upon the entire
development that follows. With proportionately few data,
Greek philosophy produced, with a kind of grand simplicity,
conceptual forms for the intellectual elaboration of its facts,
and with a remorseless logic it developed every essential
point of view for the study of the universe. Therein consists the peculiar character of ancient thought and the high
didactic significance of its history. Our present language
and our conception of the world are thoroughly permeated
by the results of ancient science. The naïve ruggedness
with which ancient philosophers followed out single motives
of reflection to their most one-sided logical conclusions,
brings into clearest relief that practical and psychological
necessity which governs not only the evolution of the
problems of philosophy, but also the repeated historical
tendencies toward the solution of these problems. We
may likewise ascribe a typical significance to the universal
stages of development of ancient philosophy, in view of the
fact that philosophy at first turned with undaunted courage
to the study of the outer world ; thwarted there, it turned
back to the inner world, and from this point of view, with
renewed strength, it attempted to conceive the World-All.
Even the manner in which ancient thought placed its
entire apparatus of conceptual knowledge at the service of

social and religious needs has a peculiar and more than historical value.

The real significance of ancient philosophy will be much exaggerated if one tries to draw close analogies between the different phases of modern philosophy and its exponents, and those of the ancients. Read K. v. Reichlin-Meldegg, *D. Parallelismus d. alten u. neuen Philosophie*, Leipzig and Heidelberg, 1865. A detailed parallelism is impossible, because all the forms of the modern history of civilization have so much more nearly complete presuppositions, and are more complicated than those of the ancient world. The typical character of the latter is valid in so far as they have " writ large " and often nearly grotesquely the simple and elemental forms of mental life, which among moderns are far more complicated in their combinations.

2. The total of that which is usually designated as ancient philosophy falls into two large divisions, which must be distinguished as much in respect to the civilizations that form their background as in respect to the intellectual principles that move them. These divisions are, (1) Greek philosophy, and (2) Hellenic-Roman philosophy. We may assume the year of the death of Aristotle, 322 B. C., as the historical line of demarcation between the two.

Greek philosophy grew out of an exclusive national culture, and is the legitimate offspring of the Greek spirit. The Hellenic-Roman philosophy came, on the other hand, out of much more manifold and contradictory intellectual movements. After the days of Alexander the Great a culture that was so cosmopolitan that it broke down all national barriers, increased in ever-widening circles among the nations upon the Mediterranean Sea. The fulfilment of these intellectual movements was objectively expressed in the Roman Empire, subjectively in Christianity ; and, be it remarked, the Hellenic-Roman philosophy forms one of the mightiest factors in this very process of amalgamation.

Moreover, there is a not less important difference in the scientific interest of the two periods. Greek philosophy

began with an independent desire for knowledge. It was
ever concerned in the quest for knowledge that was free
from all subordinate purposes. It perfected itself in Aristotle, partly in his logic, which was a universal theory of
knowledge, and partly in the scheme of a developed system
of sciences. The energy of this purely theoretic interest
was gradually extinguished in the following time, and was
only partly maintained in unpretentious work upon the
objective special sciences. The practical question how the
Wise Man should live entered into " philosophy," however,
and knowledge was no longer sought on account of itself
but as a means of right living. In this way the Hellenic-
Roman philosophy fell into dependence upon the general
but temporary changes in society, — a thing that never
happened in purely Greek philosophy. Then later its
original ethical tendency changed entirely into the effort to
find by means of science a satisfaction for religious aspira-
tion. In Greece, philosophy, therefore, was science that
had ripened into independence; in Hellenism and the
Roman Empire, philosophy entered with a full possession
of its consciousness into the service of the social and
religious mission of man.

It is obvious, from the elasticity of all historical divisions,
that this antithesis is not absolute, but only relative. The post-
Aristotelian philosophy is not entirely lacking in endeavors
for the essentially theoretical, nor indeed among the purely
Greek thinkers are there wanting those who set for philosophy
ultimately practical ends, — the Socratics for example. However, comparison of the different definitions which in the course
of antiquity have been given for the problem of philosophy,
justifies, on the whole, the division we have chosen, which takes
the purpose of philosophy in its entirety as the *principium
divisionis*.

These divisions approach most nearly among later writers
those of Ch. A. Brandis in his shorter work, *Gesch. d. Entwick.
d. griechischen Phil. u. ihrer Nachwirkungen im römischen
Reiche* (2 vols., Berlin, 1862 and 1864), although he distinguishes formally three periods here, as in his larger work.

These periods are: (1) pre-Socratic philosophy; (2) the development from Socrates to Aristotle; (3) post-Aristotelian philosophy. Yet he unites the first two divisions as " the first half," and distinctly recognizes their inner relationship in contrast to the third division, which forms " the second half." Zeller and Schwegler also employ these three periods as the basis of their work upon the Greeks, while Ritter puts the Stoics and Epicureans also in the second period. Hegel, on the other hand, treats the entire Greek philosophy until Aristotle as the first period, to which he adds the Græco-Roman philosophy as the second and the neo-Platonic philosophy as the third. Ueberweg accepts the divisions of Ritter, with this variation, — he transfers the Sophists from the first period to the second.

We purposely desist from dividing here the two chief periods of philosophy into subordinate periods. The demand for comprehensiveness, which alone would justify further divisions, is satisfied with the simple general divisions, while a comprehensive view of the steps in development is provided for in another manner by the treatment of individual doctrines. If a completer subdivision should be insisted upon, the following might be adopted : —

(a) Greek philosophy into three periods : —

(1) The cosmological, which includes the entire pre-Socratic speculation, and reaches down to about 450 B. C. (§§ 1–3);

(2) The anthropological, to which belong the men of the Greek Enlightenment, i. e., the Sophists, Socrates, and the so-called Socratic schools (§ 4);

(3) The systematic, which by its uniting the two preceding periods is the flowering period of Greek science.

(b) Hellenic-Roman philosophy into two sections : —

(1) The school-controversies of the post-Aristotelian time, with the accompanying essential ethical tendency, critical skepticism, and retrospective erudition (§§ 1 and 2).

(2) Eclectic Platonism, with its bifurcation into the rival systems of Christian and neo-Platonic religions (§§ 3 and 4).

3. The scientific treatment of the history of philosophy or of a part of that history, as in this treatise, has a double task. On the one hand it must determine the actual number of those concepts which are claimed to be " philosophic," and must conceive them in their genesis, particularly in their relation to each other. On the other

hand, it must determine the value of each individual philosophic doctrine in the development of the scientific consciousness.

In the first regard the history of philosophy is purely an historical science. As such, it must without any predilection proceed, by a careful examination of the tradition, to establish with philological exactness the content of the philosophic doctrines. It must explain their origin with all the precautionary measures of the historical method. It furthermore must make clear their genetic relations, on the one hand, to the personal life of the philosophers, and, on the other, to civilization as a whole. In this way it will be plain how philosophy has attained to an actual process of development.

From this historical point of view, however, there arises for the history of philosophy the critical task of determining the results which the various systems of philosophy have yielded for the construction of the human conception of the world. The point of view for this critical study need not be the peculiar philosophical attitude of history. Nevertheless it must, on the one hand, be that of inner criticism, which tests the teaching of a philosophical system by logical compatibility and consistency; it must, on the other hand, be that of historical generalization, which estimates philosophical teaching according to its intellectual fruitfulness and its practical historical efficacy.

The history of ancient philosophy as a science has to meet very great and sometimes insuperable difficulties in the fragmentary character of the literary sources. On the other hand, in its critical problem, it is fortunate in being able, after a development of nearly two thousand years, to judge the value of individual teaching with no personal bias.

The different points of view taken in investigating the history of philosophy are as follows : —

(1) The naïve point of view of *description*. According to this the teachings of the different philosophers are supposed to be reported with historical authenticity. So soon, however, as any report is claimed to be of scientific value, the tradition must be criticised; and this, as all other historical criticism, can be accomplished only by investigating the sources.

(2) The *genetic* point of view of *explanation*, which has three possible forms, —

(*a*) The psychological explanation. This represents the personality and individual relations of the respective philosophers as the actual causes or occasions of their opinions.

(*b*) The pragmatic method. This is an attempt to understand the teaching of each philosopher by explaining the contradictions and unsolved problems of his immediate predecessors.

(*c*) The *kultur-historisch* view. This sees in the philosophical systems the progressive consciousness of the entire ideal development of the human mind.

(3) The speculative attitude of *criticism*. Starting from a systematic conviction, this seeks to characterize the different phases of philosophical development by the contributions thereto which they have severally furnished. (Compare Hegel, in *Vorlesungen über d. Gesch. d. Phil., Complete Works*, Vol. XIII. 19 ff.; Ueberweg, *Grandriss*, I. § 3; Windelband, *Gesch. d. Phil.*, Freiburg i. B., 1892, §§ 1 and 2.) Until within the previous century enumeration of the *placita philosophorum*, with some little application of the pragmatic method, essentially predominated in the history of philosophy. Hegel, with all the exaggeration of this speculative point of view, was the first to raise philosophy from a mere collection of curiosities to a science. His constructive and fundamental idea — that in the historical order of philosophical theories the categories of true philosophy repeat themselves as progressive achievements of humanity — involved an emphasis upon the *kultur-historisch* and the *pragmatic* explanations, and this required only the individualistic *psychological* supplementation. On account of Hegel's speculative conception, on the other hand, historical criticism fell with the disappearance of faith in the absolute philosophy. By this historical criticism the mere establishment of the facts and their genetic explanation are changed into a complete philosophical science. Hegel created the science of the history of philosophy according to its ideal purposes, but not until after his day was safe ground presented for achieving such a science by the philological method of getting the data without presuppositions. Upon no territory has this method since recorded such far-reaching success as upon the field of ancient philosophy.

4. The scientific helps to the study of ancient philosophy fall into three classes : —

(*a*) *The Original Sources*.   Only a very few of the writings of ancient philosophers have been preserved. As to complete single works in the purely Greek philosophy, they are to be found only in Plato and Aristotle. The original sources, however, are richer in the Hellenic-Roman period.   The writings of the ancient Greek thinkers are preserved in only a fragmentary way through incidental citations of later literature.

The most comprehensive collection not especially mentioned hereafter, is that of F. W. A. Mullach, *Fragmenta philosophorum Græcorum* (3 vols., Paris, 1860–81).   Yet it satisfies to-day neither the demands for completeness nor for accuracy.

Nevertheless the works that have come down to us are by no means to be accepted *in toto* and on trust.   Not alone unintentionally, but also from its desire to give to its own teaching, so far as possible, the nimbus of ancient wisdom, later antiquity substituted in many instances its own compositions for the writings of the ancients, or interpolated their texts.   The sources of Greek philosophy in particular are not only in a very fragmentary but also in a very uncertain state, and we are still limited to a conjecture of a greater or less degree of probability in regard to many very weighty questions.   The philological-historical criticism, which seems indispensable under these circumstances, requires a safe criterion for our guidance, and this criterion we possess in the works of Plato and Aristotle.

Opposed to the easy credulity with which in the previous century (according to Buhle) tradition was received, Schleiermacher had the especial merit of having begun and incited a fruitful criticism.   Brandis, Trendelenburg, Zeller, and Diels were likewise the leaders in this direction.

5. (*b*) *The Corroborative Testimony of Antiquity*.   Early (according to Xenophon) in ancient literature we find tes-

timony on the life and death of notable philosophers. Of importance for us, moreover, are the passages in which Plato and Aristotle — especially in the beginning of his *Metaphysics* — linked their own teaching to the early philosophy. At the time of Aristotle there arose a widely spread, partly historical and partly critical literature, concerning what was then ancient philosophy. Unfortunately, this has been lost, excepting a few fragments. Especially deplorable is the loss of the writings of this character of Aristotle and his immediate disciples, — Theophrastus in particular. Similar works, likewise no longer extant, issued from the Academy, in which, moreover, commentating also had its beginning at an early time. So, also, the historical and critical works of the Stoics have gone forever.

This historiography of philosophy, the so-called doxography, with its commentating and collating, developed enormously in the Alexandrian literature, and had its three philosophical centres in Pergamus, Rhodes, and Alexandria. These voluminous and numerous works in their original form are in the main lost. Yet with all recognition of the erudition that doubtless permeated them, it must still be maintained that they have exercised a bewildering influence in various ways upon succeeding writers, who took excerpts directly out of them. Besides this almost unavoidable danger of reading later conceptions and theories into the old teaching, there appear three chief sources of error, —

(1) In the inclination to fix the succession of ancient philosophers after the manner of the later successions of scholarchs.

(2) In the fantastic tendency to dignify ancient Greece with the miraculous and the extraordinary.

(3) Finally, in the effort that sprang out of an undefined feeling of the dependence of Grecian upon Oriental culture. Encouraged by a new acquaintance with the East, some scholars have tried to knit every significant fact as closely as possible with Oriental influence.

Statements at only third or fourth hand are left over to us from the Roman period. The historical notes in the fragments of Varro, in the writings of Cicero (Rud. Hirzel, *Untersuch. zu C. philos. Schriften*, 3 parts, Leipzig, 1877–1883), as well as of Seneca, Lucretius, and Plutarch, are valuable, but must be used with care. The philosophical-historical writings of Plutarch are lost. The compilation preserved under his name, *De physicis philosophorum decretis* (in Dübner's edition of the *Morals*, Paris, 1841), is, according to Diels, an abstract of the Placita of Aëtius, dating back to Theophrastus, and was made perhaps in the middle of the second century. The spurious book περὶ φιλοσόφου ἱστορίας, which is falsely ascribed to Galen, is in the main identical with it (published in the nineteenth volume of *Kühn'schen Gesamtausgabe*). Many later excerpts of Favorinus are included among the uncritically collected reports; so, also, those of Apuleius and of Gellius (*Noctes atticæ*, ed. Hertz, Leipzig, 1884–85; see also Mercklin, *Die Zitiermethode u. Quellenbenutzung des A. G.*, Leipzig, 1860). Lucian's writings must also be mentioned in this connection. Those numberless historical accounts in the writings of Galen (especially *De placitis Hippocratis et Platonis*, separately published by Iwan Müller, Leipzig, 1874) and of Sextus Empiricus (*Op.* ed. Bekker, Berlin, 1842 : πυρρώνειοι ὑποτυπώσεις and πρὸς μαθηματικούς) are philosophically more trustworthy. Out of the same period grew the work of Flavius Philostratus, *Vitæ sophistarum* (ed. Westermann, Paris, 1849), and of Athenæus, *Deipnosophistæ* (ed. Meineke, Leipzig, 1857–69). Finally, there is the book which was regarded for a long time almost as the principal source for a history of ancient philosophy ; viz., that of Diogenes Laertius, περὶ βίων, δογμάτων καὶ ἀποφθεγμάτων τῶν ἐν φιλοσοφίᾳ εὐδοκιμησάντων βιβλία δέκα (ed. Cobet, Paris, 1850).

Another kind of secondary sources is furnished by the

writings of the church fathers, who have polemical, apologetic, and dogmatic aims in reproducing the Greek philosophy. This is especially true of Justin Martyr, Clement
of Alexandria, Origen (κατὰ Κέλσου), Hippolytus (*Refuta-
tio omnium hæresium*, ed. Duncker, Gött., 1859, the first book
of this being formerly supposed to be a work of Origen
under the title φιλοσοφούμενα), Eusebius (*Præp. evang.*, ed.
Dindorf, Leipzig, 1868), and in certain respects also Tertullian and Augustine. The importance of the church fathers
as sources for the study of ancient philosophy has attained
recently to a completer and more fruitful recognition,
especially since the impulse given by Diels to their study.

Finally, the activity in commentating and historical research was carried on in a lively fashion in the neo-
Platonic school. The chief work indeed, that of Porphyry,
is not preserved (φιλόσοφος ἱστορία). On the other hand,
the writings of the neo-Platonists in general offer numerous
historical data ; and, as already the earlier commentaries
of Alexander of Aphrodisias (*zu Arist. Met.*, ed. Hayduck,
Berlin, 1891, and *zu Arist. Top.*, M. Wallies, Berlin, 1891 ;
smaller works by Ivo Bruns, Berlin, 1893), — so the commentaries of Themistius, and especially Simplicius, contain
many carefully and intelligently compiled excerpts from
the direct and indirect sources of earlier times. Among
the latest writers of ancient literature ·the collections of
Stobæus and Photius, and those also of Hesychius, appear
useful for the history of philosophy.

Compare Diels, *Doxographi Græci* (Berlin, 1879). An excellent and, for a beginning, an extraordinarily instructive
collection of the most important passages from the primary and
secondary sources is that of Ritter and Preller in their *Historia
philosophiæ Græco-romanæ ex fontium locis contexta* (7 ed. is
brought out by Schulthess and Wellmann, Gotha, 1888).

6. (*c*) *The Modern Expositions.* Scholarly treatment
of ancient philosophy was in modern literature con-

12   HISTORY OF ANCIENT PHILOSOPHY

fined at first to a brief criticism of the latest works of antiquity. Thus, the occasional historical collections concerned with ancient philosophy which we find in the Humanistic literature, in the main led back to neo-Platonic sources. The very first work, the *History of Philosophy*, by Thomas Stanley (London, 1665), scarcely more than reproduced the reports of Diogenes Laertius. Bayle in his *Dictionnaire historique et critique* (1 ed., Rotterdam, 1697), gave a powerful impulse to critical treatment.[1]

Later appeared the writings of Brucker, thoroughgoing, industriously compiled, but in point of fact not equal to the task: *Kurze Fragen aus der philosophischen Historie* (Ulm, 1731 f.), *Historia critica philosophiæ* (Leipzig, 1742 f.), *Institutiones historiæ philosophiæ* (Leipzig, 1747 ; a compendium for a school manual).

With the formation of the great schools of philosophy, particularly in Germany, the history of philosophy began to be treated with reference to its single directions and systems. In the front D. Tiedemann came with his empirical-sceptical *Geist der Philosophie* (Marburg, 1791 ff.). Then followed, from the Kantian point of view, J. G. Buhle with *Lehrbuch der Geschichte der Philosophie* (Gött., 1796 ff.) ; Tennemann, *Geschichte der Philosophie*, 1798 ff.) ; then the *Grundriss der Geschichte der Philosophie* (5th ed.), Amad. Wendt, Leipzig, 1829, a much used epitome, commending itself by its careful literary data ; and J. F. Fries, *Geschichte der Philosophie* (1 vol., Halle, 1837). From the Schellingen point of view, there are Fr. Ast's *Grundriss einer Geschichte der Philosophie* (Landshut, 1807) ; E. Reinhold, *Geschichte der Philosophie nach den Hauptpunkten ihrer Entwickelung* (Jena, 1858). From the point of view of Schleiermacher, are his own notes for his lectures on the history of philosophy in a collection

[1] Upon which a philosophical article of value in part even to-day has been published in German by H. Jacob (1797–98, Halle).

of three parts, four volumes (Berlin, 1839): H. Ritter, *Die Geschichte der Philosophie* (Hamburg, 1829 ff.); F. Ch. Pötter, *Die Geschichte der Philosophie in Umriss* (Elberfeld, 1873).[1] From the Hegelian point of view, are Hegel's lectures upon the history of philosophy in his complete works, XIII. ff.; J. E. Erdmann, *Grundriss der Geschichte der Philosophie* (3 ed., Berlin, 1878). From the Herbartian point of view, is Ch. A. Thilo, *Kurze pragmatische Geschichte der Philosophie* (Cöthen, 2 ed., 1880). With especial reference to the factual development of problems and concepts, ancient philosophy has also been treated by W. Windelband, *Geschichte der Philosophie* (Freiburg i. Br., 1892). Of the other numerous complete presentations of the history of philosophy, that of J. Bergmann (Berlin, 1892) may be finally mentioned. Of the presentations in other languages than German which also give valuable contribution to the study of ancient philosophy, may be here mentioned: V. Cousin, *Histoire générale de la philosophie* (12 ed., Paris, 1884); A. Weber, *Histoire de philosophie européenne* (Paris, 5 ed., 1892); A. Fouillée, *Histoire de la Philosophie* (Paris, 3 ed., 1882); R. Blakey, *History of the Philosophy of Mind* (London, 1848); G. H. Lewes, *A Biographical History of Philosophy* (London, 4 ed., 1871, German ed., Berlin, 1871).

The completest literary data for the historiography of philosophy, and particularly ancient philosophy, are found in Ueberweg, *Grundriss d. Philos.*, a work which presents also in its remarkable continuation by M. Heinze (7 ed., Berlin, 1886) an indispensable completeness in its annotations. The texts furnished by Ueberweg himself were at first only superficially systematized by him, and were given an unequal, confused, and, for beginners, untransparent character by his later additions, interpolations, and annotations.

[1] An inspiring statement of the development of ancient philosophy is also that of Brandis's *Geschichte der Philos. seit Kant*, 1 Part (Breslau, 1842).

The profounder philological studies at the beginning of
the nineteenth century were advantageous to the history
of ancient philosophy, since a critical sifting of tradition
and a philological and methodical basis for historical-
philosophical research was facilitated (compare Zeller, *Jahrbücher der Gegenwart*, 1843). The greatest credit for such
a stimulus is due to Schleiermacher, whose translation of
Plato was a powerful example, and whose special works
upon Heracleitus, Diogenes of Apollonia, Anaximander,
and others have been placed in Part III. book 2, of his collected works. Among the numerous special researches are
to be mentioned A. B. Krische's. *Forschungen auf dem
Gebiete der alten Philosophie* (Gött., 1840); also A. Trendelenburg, *Historische Beiträge zur Philosophie* (Berlin,
1846 f.), the author of which deserves credit for his stimulation of Aristotelian studies; H. Siebeck, *Untersuchungen zur
Philosophie der Griechen* (2 ed., Freiburg i. Br., 1888);
G. Teichmüller, *Studien zur Geschichte der Begriffe* (Berlin,
1874 ff.); O. Apelt, *Beiträge zur Geschichte der griechischen
Philosophie* (Leipzig, 1891); E. Norden (the same title),
Leipzig, 1892.

As the first product of these critico-philological studies,
we may consider the praiseworthy work of Ch. A. Brandis,
*Handbuch der Geschichte der griechisch-römischen Philoso-
phie* (Berlin, 1835–60), by the side of which the author
placed a shorter and especially finely conceived exposition,
*Geschichte der Entwickelungen der griechischen Philosophie
und ihrer Nachwirkungen im römischen Reiche* (Berlin, 1862
u. 1864). With less exhaustiveness, but with a peculiar
superiority in the development of the problems, Ludw.
Strümpell (2d part, Leipzig, 1854, 1861), K. Prantl
(Stuttgart, 2 ed., 1863), and A. Schwegler (3 ed., especially, by Köstlin, Freiburg, 1883) treated the same subject.
All these valuable works, and with them the numerous
synopses, compendiums, and compilations (see Ueberweg,

above mentioned, pp. 27–29), are overshadowed beside that masterpiece and, for many reasons, final word upon ancient philosophy: E. Zeller, *Die Philosophie der Griechen* (Tübingen, 1844 ff.: the first book is published in the fifth edition, the second in the fourth edition, the others in the third edition).[1] Here, upon the broadest philological-historical foundation and upon original sources, a philosophical, authoritative, and illuminating statement is given of the entire development. Zeller has published a clever summary of the whole in *Grundriss d. Gesch. der Alten Philos.* (4 ed., Leipzig, 1893).

The special sides of ancient philosophy have been presented in the following notable works: —

Logic: K. Prantl, *Gesch. d. Logik im Abendlande* (vols. 1 and 2, Leipzig, 1855 and 1861); P. Natorp, *Forschungen z. Gesch. des Erkenntnissproblems im Altertum* (Berlin, 1884); Giov. Cesca, *La teoria della conoscenza nella filos. greca* (Verona, 1887).

Psychology: H. Siebeck, *Gesch. d. Psy.* (vol. 1, Gotha, 1880 and 1884); A. E. Chaignet, *Histoire de la psy. des grecs* (Paris, 1887–92).

Ethics: L. v. Henning, *D. Prinzipien d. Ethik,* etc. (Berlin, 1825); E. Feuerlein, *D. philos. Sittenlehre in ihren geschichtlichen Hauptformen* (Tübingen, 1857 and 1859); Paul Janet, *Histoire de la philosophie morale et politique* (Paris, 1858); J. Mackintosh, *The Progress of Ethical Philosophy* (London, 1862); W. Whewell, *Lectures on the History of Moral Philosophy* (London, 1862); R. Blakey, *History of Moral Science* (Edinburgh, 1863); L. Schmidt, *D. Ethik d. al. Griechen* (Berlin, 1881); Th. Zeigler, *D. Ethik d. Gr. u. Römer* (Bonn, 1881); C. Köstlin, *Gesch. d. Ethik* (1 vol., Tübingen, 1887); especially compare R. Eucken, *D. Lebensanschauungen d. grossen Denker* (Leipzig, 1890).

The following particularly treat special topics: M. Heinze, *D. Lehre v. Logos* (Leipzig, 1872); *D. Lehre d. Eudaemonismus in griech. Philos.* (Leipzig, 1884); Cl. Bäumcker, *Das Problem d. Materie in d. griech. Philos.* (Münster, 1890); J. Walter, *Gesch. d. Aesthetik im Altertum* (Leipzig, 1893).

[1] Referred to in this work usually as I[5]., II[4]., etc. — TR.

A. GREEK PHILOSOPHY

INTRODUCTION

The Preliminary Conditions of Philosophy in the Greek Intellectual Life of the Seventh and Sixth Centuries B. C.[1]

7. The history of the philosophy of the Greeks, like the history of their political development, requires a larger conception of the geography of the country than the present conception of its political relations would imply. Our usual present idea of ancient Greece is of a country wherein Athens by its literature overshadowed the other portions, and by the brilliancy of its golden age eclipsed its earlier history. Ancient Greece was the Grecian sea with all its coasts from Asia Minor to Sicily and from Cyrene to Thrace. The natural link of the three great continents was this sea, with its islands and coasts occupied by the most gifted of people, which from the earliest historical times had settled all its coasts. (Homer.) Within this circle, the later so-called Motherland, the Greece of the continent of Europe, played at the beginning a very subordinate rôle. In the development of Greek culture, however, leadership fell to that branch of the race which in its entire history was in closest contact with the Orient, the Ionians. This race laid the foundation of later Greek development, and by its commercial activity established the power of Greece. At first as seafarers and sea-robbers in the train of the Phœnicians, in the ninth and eighth centuries the Ionians won an increasing independence, and in the seventh century they commanded the world's trade between the three continents.

Over the entire Mediterranean, from the Black Sea to the Pillars of Hercules, the Greek colonies and trade cen-

[1] Reference should be made to corresponding sections in historical parts of this book for details.

tres were extended. Even Egypt opened its treasures to
the enterprising Ionian spirit. At the head of these cities
of commerce, and at the same time the leader of the Ionian
League, Miletus appeared in the seventh century as the
most powerful and most notable centre of the Greek genius.
It likewise became the cradle of Greek science. For here
in Ionia of Asia Minor the riches of the entire world were
heaped together; here Oriental luxury, pomp, material
pleasure held their public pageants; here began to awaken
the sense of the beauty of living and the love of higher
ideals, while rude customs still ruled upon the continent of
Europe. The spirit became free from the pressure of daily
need, and in its play created the works of noble leisure, of
art, and of science. (The cultured man is he who in his
leisure does not become a mere idler.)

8. Thus, while wealth acquired from trade afforded the
basis for the free mental development of the Greek, so, on
the other hand, this same wealth led to changes of political and social conditions which were likewise favorable to
the development of intellectual life. Originally, aristocratic families had ruled Ionian cities, and they were
probably descended from the warlike bands that in the so-
called Ionian migration from the continent of Europe had
settled the islands. But in time, through their commerce,
there grew up a class of well-conditioned citizens, who restricted and opposed the power of the aristocracy. On the
one hand bold and ambitious, on the other thoughtful and
patriotic men took advantage of these democratic tendencies, and after destroying the power of the oligarchy
tried to set up monarchies and equalize, as far as possible,
the interests of all classes.

The tyranny based on democratic principles is the typical
governmental rule of this time, and extended its power,
although not without vigorous and often long partisan
struggles, from Asia Minor across the islands even to

European Greece. Thrasybulus in Miletus, Polycrates in Samos, Pittacus in Lesbos, Periander in Corinth, Peisistratus in Athens, Gelon and Hiero in Syracuse, — these men had courts that at this time constituted the centres of intellectual life. They drew poets to them; they founded libraries; they supported every movement in art and science. But, on the other hand, this political overthrow drove the aristocrats into gloomy retirement. Discontented with public affairs, the aristocrats withdrew to private life, which they adorned with the gifts of the Muses. Heracleitus is a conspicuous example of this state of affairs. Thus the reversed relations favored in many ways the unfolding and extending of intellectual interests.

This enrichment of consciousness, this increase in a higher culture among the Greeks of the seventh and sixth centuries, showed itself first in the development of lyric poetry, in which the gradual transition from the expression of universal religious and political feeling to that which is personal and individual formed a typical process. In the passion and excitement of internecine political conflict, the individual becomes conscious of his independence and worth, and he " girds up his loins " to assert his rights everywhere. In the course of time satirical poetry grew beside the lyric, as the expression of a keen and cleverly developed individual judgment. There was, moreover, still more characteristic evidence of the spirit of the time in the so-called Gnomic poetry, the content of which is made up of sententious reflections upon moral principles. This sort of moralizing, which appeared also in fable-poetry and in other literature, may be regarded as symptomatic of the deeper stirring of the national spirit.

9. Now, any extended reflection upon maxims of moral judgment shows immediately that the validity of morality has been questioned in some way, that social consciousness has become unsettled, and that the individual in his growing

independence has transcended the bounds authoritatively
drawn by the universal consciousness. Therefore it was
entirely characteristic of this Gnomic poetry to recommend
moderation ; to show how universal standards of life had
been endangered by the unbridled careers of single persons, and how in the presence of threatening or present
anarchy the individual must try to re-establish these rules
through independent reflection.

The end of the seventh and the beginning of the sixth
centuries in Greece formed, therefore, an epoch of peculiar
ethical reflection, which is usually called, after the manner
of the ancients, the Age of the Seven Wise Men. It was an
age of reflection. The simple devotion to the conventions
of the previous age had ceased, and social consciousness was
profoundly disturbed. Individuals began to go their own
ways. Notable men appeared, and earnestly exhorted [1]
society to come back to its senses. Rules of life were
established. In riddle, in anecdote, in epigram, the moralizing sermon was made palatable, and " winged words "
passed from mouth to mouth. But, let it be remembered,
these homilies are possible only when the individual op-
poses the vagaries of the mob, and with independent judgment brings to consciousness the maxims of right conduct.

Tradition selected early seven of such men, to whom it
gave the name of the Wise Men. They were not men of
erudition, nor of science, but men of practical wisdom, and
in the main of remarkable political ability.[2] They pointed
out the right thing to do in critical moments, and therefore

---

[1] With this conception about the Seven Wise Men, it is conceivable
that Plato (*Protag.*, 343 a) should characterize them as forerunners of
the old strong Dorian morality in contrast to the innovations of the
Ionian movement: ζηλωτ.ὶ καὶ ἐρασταὶ καὶ μαθηταὶ τῆς Λακεδαιμονίων
παιδείας·

[2] Dicaiarchus called them οὔτε σοφοὺς οὔτε φιλοσόφους, συνετοὺς δέ
τινας καὶ νομοθετικούς. Diog. Laert., I. 40.

in public and private matters were authorities to their fellow-citizens. The spirit of Gnomic poetry was prominent in the apothegms, the catchwords, which they are supposed to have uttered. Nothing was repeated by them so often and with so many phrasings as the μηδὲν ἄγαν !

Tradition is not agreed as to the names of " the Seven." Four [1] only are mentioned by all: Bias of Priene, who upon the invasion of the Persians recommended to the Ionians a migration to Sardinia; Pittacus, who was tyrant of Mitylene, about 600 B. C.; Solon, the law-giver of Athens and the Gnomic poet; Thales, founder of the Milesian philosophy, who advised the Ionians to form a federation with a joint council in Teos. The names of the others vary. The later age ascribed to the Seven all kinds of aphorisms, letters, etc. (collected and translated into German, but without critical investigation, by C. Dilthey, Darmstadt, 1835). [2]

While in this way, through political and social relations, the independence of individual judgment was educated first on its practical side, and the propensity was formed for expressing such judgment, it was an inevitable consequence that a similar emancipation of single individuals from the ordinary way of thinking should take place within the domain of theory. Independent judgment naturally appeared at this point, and formed its own views about the connection of things. Nevertheless this propensity could manifest itself only in a revision and reconstruction of those materials, which the individuals discovered partly in the intellectual treasures accumulated previously in the nation's practical life, and partly in the religious ideas.

10. The practical knowledge of the Greeks had increased to very remarkable dimensions between the time of Hesiod's Works and Days and the year 600 B. C. The inventive, trade-driving Ionians undoubtedly had learned very much from the Orientals, with whom they had inter-

---

[1] Compare Cic. *Rep.*, I. 12.   Also Lael., 7.
[2] Brunco, *Aet. Sem.-Erl.*, III. 299 ff.

course and of whom they were rivals. Among these, especially among the Egyptians, Phœnicians, and Assyrians, there existed knowledge that had been garnered through many centuries, and it is incredible that the Greeks should not have appropriated it wherever opportunity offered.

The question how much the Greeks learned from the Orient has passed through many stages. In opposition to the uncritical, often fantastic, and untenable statements of the later Greeks, who tried to derive everything important of their own teaching from the honorable antiquity of Oriental tradition, later philology, in its admiration for everything Greek, has persistently espoused the theory of an autochthonic genesis. But the more the similarities with the Oriental civilization, and the relations between the different forms of the old and the Greek culture have been brought to the light by acquaintance with the ancient Orient, dating from the beginning of this century; and the more, on the other hand, philosophy understood the continuity of the historical moments of civilization; so much the more decided became the tendency to refer the beginnings of Greek science to Oriental influences, particularly in the history of philosophy. With brilliant fancy A. Röth (*Gesch. unserer abendländischen Philos.*, Mannheim, 1858 f..) attempted to rehabilitate the accounts of the neo-Platonists, who by interpretation and perversion had read into the mythic narratives, which were introduced from the Orient, Greek philosophical doctrines ; he then rediscovered these doctrines as primeval wisdom. With a forced construction, Gladisch (*D. Religion u. d. Philos. in ihrer weltgesch. Entwick.*, Breslau, 1852) tried to see in all the beginnings of Greek philosophy direct relations to individual Oriental peoples; and he so conceived the relationship that the Greeks are supposed to have appropriated in succession the ripe products of all the other civilizations. This appears from the following titles of his special essays: *Die Pythagoreer und die Schinesen* (Posen, 1841); *Die Eleaten und die Indier* (Posen, 1844); *Empedokles und die Egypter* (Leipzig, 1858); *Heracleitos und Zoroaster* (Leipzig, 1859) ; *Anaxagoras und Israeliten* (Leipzig, 1864). Besides the fact that they first found many analogies through an artful interpretation, both Röth and Gladisch fell into the error of transmuting analogies into causal relations, where equally notable disparities might also have been found. Moreover, where, as usual, religion is concerned, that of the Greeks, which has influenced the beginnings of science in so many ways, was found to be in genetic and historical relationship with that of the Orient.

Such exaggerations are certainly censurable. But, on the other hand, it would be denying the existence of the sun at noontide to refuse to acknowledge that the Greeks in great measure owe their information to contact with the barbarians. It is here even as in the history of art. The Greeks imported a large amount of information out of the Orient. This consisted in special facts of knowledge, particularly of a mathematical and astronomical kind, and consisted perhaps besides in certain mythological ideas. But with the recognition of this situation, which recognition in the long run is inevitable, one does not rob the Greeks in the least of their true originality. For as they in art derived particular forms and norms from Egyptian and Assyrian tradition, but in the employment and reconstruction of these used their own artistic genius, so there flowed in upon them too from the Orient many kinds of knowledge, arising out of the work and practical needs of many centuries, and various kinds of mythological tales, born of the religious imagination. But nevertheless they were the first to transmute this knowledge into a wisdom sought on account of itself. This spirit of science, like their original activity, resulted from emancipated and independent individual thought, to which Oriental civilization had not attained.

Principally in mathematics and astronomy do the Greeks appear as the pupils of the Orientals. Since economic needs compelled the Phœnicians to make an arithmetic, and from early times led the Egyptians to construct a geometry, it is probable that in these things the Greeks were pupils rather than teachers of their neighbors. A proposition like that concerning proportionality and its application to perspective, Thales did not communicate to the Egyptians, but derived from them.[1] Although there are further ascribed to him propositions like that concerning the halving of the circle by the diameter, the isosceles triangle, the vertical angles, the equality of triangles having a side and two angles equal, yet it may be safely concluded in every instance that these elementary propositions were generally known to the Greeks

[1] See § 24.

of his time. It is likewise a matter of indifference whether Pythagoras himself discovered the theorem named after him or whether his school established it, whether the discovery was the result of pure geometrical reasoning or was an actual measurement with the square and by an arithmetical calculation, as Röth says. Here, again, the reality of such knowledge at that time is rendered certain, and its suggestion, at least, from the Oriental circle is probable. In any case, however, these studies in Greece soon flourished in a high degree. Anaxagoras was reported, for instance, to have busied himself in prison with the squaring of the circle. Astronomical thought had a similar status, for Thales predicted an eclipse of the sun, and it is highly probable that he here availed himself of the Chaldæan Saros. On the other hand, the cosmographical ideas ascribed to the oldest philosophers point to an Egyptian origin, especially that view, authoritative for later time, of concentric spherical shells in which the planets were supposed to move around the earth as a centre. From all reports it appears that the questions concerning the constitution of the world, of the size, distance, form, and rotation of the planets, of the inclination of the ecliptic, etc., keenly interested every one of the ancient thinkers. The Milesians still thought the earth to be flat, cylindrical, or plate-shaped, floating upon a dark, cold atmosphere and in the middle of a world sphere. The Pythagoreans seem to be the first independently to discover the spherical shape of the earth. In the physics of this time the interest in meteorology is dominant. Every philosopher felt bound to explain the clouds, air, wind, snow, hail, and ice. Not until later did an interest in biology awaken, and the mysteries of reproduction and propagation called forth a multitude of fantastic hypotheses (Parmenides, Empedocles, etc.).

Deficiency in physiological and anatomical knowledge obviously delayed for a long time the progress of medical science. Therefore we are safe in saying [1] that medical science was inherited in its original tradition entirely independently of all other sciences as the esoteric teaching of certain priestly families; and that philosophy also hardly had any connection with medicine down to about the time of the Pythagoreans. Medicine consisted simply in empirical rules, technical facts, and a mass of data accumulated during the experience of centuries. It was not an ætiological science, but an art practised in the spirit of religion. We have still the oath of the Asclepiades (a priestly order of this sort, which however had also lay brethren), who as well as the gymnasts practised the art of healing. Such medical orders or schools existed notably in Rhodes, Cyrene, Crotona, Cos, and Cnidus. Rules for the treatment of the sick were partly codified in documents, and Hippocrates knew two versions of the γνῶμαι Κνίδιαι (Cnidian sentences), the more valuable of which (ἰατρικώτερον) came from Euryphon of Cnidus.

Likewise the geographical knowledge of the Greeks had reached a high degree of completeness about this time. The broad commercial activity whereby they visited the Mediterranean Sea and all its coasts had essentially transformed and enriched the Homeric picture of the world. It is stated that Anaximander drew up the first map of the world. The statement of Herodotus [2] is interesting, that Aristagoras, by showing such a chart in Lacedæmon, sought to awaken the continental Greeks to a realizing sense of the menaced geographical situation of Greece by the Persian Empire.

Historical knowledge too was beginning to be accumulated at this time, — yet strikingly late for a people like the Greeks. From the old epic had issued the theogonic poetry, on the one hand, and the heroic on the other.

[1] Häser, *Lehrbuch d. Gesch. d. Medizin,* 2 ed., §§ 21–25.
[2] V. 49.

Collections of saga and of the histories of the founding of cities, as they had been gathered by the logographers, were added to these for the first time in the Ionian cities of Asia Minor. Men, who after long journeys gave to their logographies greater extent and variety of interest, introduced then that form of historical presentation which we may still recognize in Herodotus. At the same time, however, this was pressed into the background by the grouping of all accounts around the important event of the Persian wars. In place of fantastic fables about strange people in the form that Aristeas of Proconnesus related them, we now have the more sober reports of the logographers. Of these there appeared, in the sixth century, Cadmus, Dionysius, and especially Hecateius of Miletus, with his περιήγησις, in which geography and history are closely interwoven. In these men realistic considerations had taken the place of æsthetical, and their writings therefore have the prose rather than the poetic form.

About 600 B. C. the intellectual circle of the Greeks was replete with this manifold and important knowledge, and it is clear that there were men, otherwise favorably conditioned in life, who took a direct and immediate interest in knowledge which had hitherto been employed for the most varied practical ends. They planned how to order, classify, and extend these acquisitions. It is likewise comprehensible how scientific schools for the same purposes were formed, as it might happen, around distinguished men, and how in these schools by co-operative labor a kind of scholastic order and tradition maintained itself from one generation to another.

After the investigations of H. Diels (*Philos. Aufsätze z. Zellerjubiläum*, Berlin, 1887, p. 241 f.) it can scarcely be doubted that in this very early time the scientific life of the Greeks constituted itself into closed corporations, and that the learned societies already at that time carried all the weight of judicial-religious associations (θίασοι) which v. Wilamowitz-Möllendorf

(*Antigonos von Karystos*, p. 263 f.) has already proved for the later schools. The Pythagoreans were undoubtedly such an association. The schools of physicians were organized on the same principle, — perhaps still more rigorously in the form of the priestly orders. Why, then, should this not be the case with the schools of Miletus, Elea, and Abdera?

11. Likewise, in the religious notions of the Greeks lay certain definite points of departure for the beginnings of their philosophy, especially since those religious notions were in the liveliest fermentation about the time of the seventh and sixth centuries. This is accounted for by the great vitality which from the beginning characterized the religious existence of the Greeks by reason of their unparalleled development. Out of the early differentiation of originally common ideas, out of the capricious formation of local cults within families, tribes, cities, and provinces, incidentally also out of the introduction of distinctive foreign religious ceremonies, there grew up a rich and, as it were, confusingly iridescent variety of religions. Standing over against this, epic poetry had already created its Olympus, its poetic purification, and its human ennobling of the original, mythical forms. These products of poetry came to be the national religious property of the Hellenes. But along with the veneration of these products there were the old cults that shut themselves up only the more closely in the Mysteries, in which now as ever the peculiar energy of religious craving expressed itself in a service of expiation and redemption. With the advance of civilization, however, the æsthetic mythology succumbed to a gradual change in two directions which had been blended indistinguishably in the Olympian forms. The first direction was toward mythical explanation of nature ; the second was toward ethical idealizing.

The first tendency showed itself in the development of the cosmogonic out of the epic poetry. Cosmogonic poetry shows how the individual poets with their peculiar fancies studied the question of the origin of things, and in addition mythologized the great powers of nature in a traditional or freely creative form. Two groups can be distinguished among them, corresponding to the different interpretations of Homeric poetry. Such of the Orphic theogonies, which go back thus far, belong, with the sole exception of Hesiod, to one group, and Epimenides and Acusilaus are among its better defined historic names. Whether they presuppose only Chaos or Night as the original powers, or whether with these Air, Earth, Heaven, or something else, — they appear reasonably enough in Aristotle as οἱ ἐκ νυκτὸς γεννῶντες θεόλογοι. For it is always some dark and reasonless primeval ground from which they evolve material things, and they may be considered as representatives of the evolutionist idea. Likewise in this respect Milesian science followed immediately in their wake, and had in part the same principles but with greater clearness of thought (§§ 14–16). Over against these was the later tendency whose representatives were regarded by Aristotle as standing between the poets and philosophers (μεμιγμένοι αὐτῶν). By these the Perfect was supposed as the forming (creative) principle at the beginning of time. To them belongs, besides the entirely mythical Hermotimus of Clazomenæ,[1] the historical Pherecydes of Syrus, a contemporary of the earliest philosophers and a man who wrote his conceptions in prose. He presupposed Zeus as the personality giving order and reason to the world, and that Time[2] and Earth act with Zeus as original principles (χρόνος, χθών). He appears to have represented in grotesque images the "five-fold" development of individual things out of the rational principle.

[1] Whom some try to identify with Anaxagoras. See Carus, *Nachgelassene Werke*, 4 vols., 330 f.; Zeller, I⁴. 924 f.

[2] χρόνος may mean something else. Zeller, I⁴. 73.

Sturz (Leipzig, 1834) has published the fragments of Pherecydes. Röth, out of most uncertain data, *Gesch. unserer abendlandischen Philos.*, II. 161 f., tried to attribute to Pherecydes the introduction into Greece of Egyptian metaphysics and astronomy. J. Conrad (Coblenz, 1857), R. Zimmermann, *Studien u. Kritiken* (Vienna, 1870, 1 f.), also treat the " philosophy" of Pherecydes. See H. Diels, *Arch. f. Gesch. d. Philos.*, I. 11.

These later cosmogonies were apparently already under the influence of the ethical movement, which had pressed into the circle of religious ideas, and, as against the nature-mythical interpretation that ascribed æsthetic character to the different gods, sought to embody in them the ideal of moral life. The second tendency comes to light in the Gnomic poetry in particular. Zeus is thus (Solon) honored less as creator of Nature than as ruler of the moral world. The fifth century, in following out this idea, saw the Homeric mythology expressed completely in ethico-alle-gorical terms (especially ascribed to Metrodorus of Lamp-sacus, a pupil of Anaxagoras). Three moments especially in the ethicizing of religious ideas appear : (1) the gradual stripping off of naïve anthropomorphism from the gods, which led to a violent opposition to æsthetic mythology on the part of Xenophanes, who was a direct descendant in this respect of the Gnomic poets ; (2) necessarily connected with the above, the development of the monotheistic germs contained in the previous ideas; (3) the emphasis on the thought of moral retribution in the form of faith in immor-tality and transmigration. So far as the last two thoughts belonged with a greater or less degree of clearness also to the Mysteries, they were in some degree the centre of an ethical reaction against the pantheon " constructed by the poets."

12. In this direction tended the great movement which shook the western part of civilized Greece about the end of the sixth century, and in many ways influenced the devel-

opment of science. This movement is the *ethico-religious reformation of Pythagoras.*

It is absolutely necessary, in the interest of historical clearness, to distinguish Pythagoras from the Pythagoreans, and the practice of the former from the science of the latter. The investigations of modern time have more and more led to this distinction. The accounts of the later ancients (neo-Pythagorean and neo-Platonic) had gathered so many myths about the personality of Pythagoras, and had so ascribed to him the ripest and highest thoughts of Greek philosophy through direct and indirect falsification, that he became a mysterious and entirely inconceivable form. But the fact that the cloud of myths should thicken from century to century in ancient time around him, makes it necessary [1] to go back to the oldest and, at the same time, most authoritative accounts. Therein it appears that neither Plato nor Aristotle knew anything about a philosophy of Pythagoras, but simply make mention of a philosophy of the " so-called Pythagoreans." Nowhere is the "number theory" referred to the "Master" himself. It is also to be regarded as highly probable that Pythagoras himself wrote nothing. At any rate, nothing is preserved which can be confidently attributed to him, and neither Plato nor Aristotle knew of anything of the sort. On the other hand, the first philosophical writing of the school is that of Philolaus, [2] the contemporary of Anaxagoras, and therefore of Socrates and Democritus. This philosophic teaching will be set forth in the place which belongs to it chronologically in the development of Greek philosophy (§ 24). Pythagoras himself, however, in the light of historical criticism, appears only as a kind of founder of religion, and a man of grand ethical and political efficiency. His work had an important place among the causes and the preliminary conditions of the scientific life in Greece.

Concerning the life of Pythagoras little is certain. He came from an old Tyrrhean-Phliasian stock, which had migrated to his home, Samos, at the latest in the time of his grandfather. Here he was born, somewhere between the years 580 and 570, as the son of Mnesarchus, a rich merchant. It is not impossible that differences that arose between him and Polycrates, or the antipathy of the aristocrat to this tyrant, drove him out of

---

[1] See Zeller, I⁴. 256 ff., against A. Röth (*Gesch. unserer abendlan. Philos.*, II. b, 261 f., 48 f.). Zeller shows clearly that Pythagoras had no philosophy.

[2] Diog. Laert., VIII. 15, 85.

Samos, where he seems to have entered already upon a career
similar to that of his later life. It is not to be determined
with perfect surety, but may be regarded as by no means improbable, that he made a kind of educative journey to investigate the sanctuaries and cults of Greece. At this time he
came to know Pherecydes. This journey may have extended
also into foreign lands as far as Egypt.[1] About the year 530,
however, he settled in Magna Græcia, the region where (at
a time when Ionia already was struggling with Persia for
existence) were brought together, in the most splendid way,
Greek power and Greek culture. Here was still a more motley
mixture of Hellenic stocks, and here between cities, and in the
cities between parties, the battle for existence was most passion-
ately waged. Pythagoras appeared here and preached, founded
his new sect, and met with the most decided success. He
chose the austere and aristocratic Crotona as the centre of his
operations. It appears that his sect co-operated in the decisive
battle (510 B. C.) in which Crotona destroyed its democratic
rival, the voluptuous Sybaris. But very soon after that event
democracy became predominant in Crotona itself and in other
cities, and the Pythagoreans were cruelly persecuted. These
persecutions were more than once repeated in the first half of
the fifth century, and the sect was entirely dispersed. Whether
Pythagoras in one of these persecutions, perhaps even in the
very first instigated by Cylon in 504, found his end, or whether
in another way, or where, when, and how, is uncertain. His
death is surrounded by myths, but we shall have to place it
at about 500.

Jamblichus, *De vita Pythagorica*, and Porphyry, *De vita
Pythagoræ* (ed. Kissling, Leipzig, 1815–16, etc.), H. Ritter,
Geschichte der pythagorischen Philosophie (Hamburg, 1826); B.
Krische, *De societatis a Pythagora in urbe Crotoniatarum con-
ditæ scopo politico* (Göttingen, 1830); E. Zeller, *Pyth. u. die
Pyth.-saga*, Vortrag u. Abhdl. I. (Leipzig, 1865) 30 ff.; Ed.
Chaignet, *Pythagore et la philosophie pythagoricienne* (Paris,
1873); L. v. Schroeder, *Pyth. u. d. Inder* (Leipzig, 1884); P.
Tannery, *Arch. f. Gesch. d. Ph.*, I. 29 ff.

On the one hand, Pythagoras found his purpose in the
moral clarification and purification of the world of religious

[1] There is scarcely a ground for doubting the testimony of Isocrates
(Busir, 11). The circumstances of the second half of the sixth century
make it appear as in no wise an exceptional case that the son of a patri-
cian of Samos should journey to Egypt.

ideas. He stood in this respect entirely in line with the progress and innovation of the time, and he antagonized, as a point of view antiquated or coming to be so, the religion of the poets, in which he missed a moral earnestness. On the other hand, he was inspired by the same ethical impulse against that weakening of the moral bond to which the new methods of Greek social life threatened to lead, and in fact had already led. He called, therefore, for a return to the old institutions and convictions. Especially in politics, he represented a reaction in favor of the aristocracy as opposed to the growing democratic movement. This opposition determined the peculiar position of the Pythagorean society. The society was, in truth, one of the most important factors in the religious and intellectual advance of the Greek spirit, and at the same time it flung itself against the current of the time as regards ethics and politics.[1] As to the latter, the Ionian Pythagoras preferred the more conservative Dorian character, and the "Italian philosophy" founded by him passed among the ancients as an antithesis to the Ionian.

The emphasis upon the unity of the divine Being and a purely moral conception of the same was carried no farther by Pythagoras and by the Pythagoreans than by the Gnomic poets. Neither was the conception of the purely spiritual here attained, nor a scientific foundation and presentation given to ethical concepts, nor, finally, a sharp contradiction made to the polytheistic popular religion. (Of course we do not include in this statement the doctrines of the neo-Pythagorean and neo-Platonic schools.) On the contrary, Pythagoras had the pedagogic acumen to develop these higher conceptions from those existing in the myths and religious ceremonies. He used in this way the Mysteries, especially the Orphic, and he himself appears to have been connected with the cult of Apollo in particular. He laid particular emphasis upon the doctrine of immortality and its application to a theory of moral religious retribution, and this also took the mythic form of the doctrine

---

[1] Similarly and on a larger scale this is repeated by Plato's work.

of metempsychosis.   But doubtless the Mysteries themselves contained much in harmony with the doctrine of transmigration, especially those Mysteries of the chthonic divinities. But to the ordinary Greeks transmigration was and remained a foreign conception, which in early times they had mocked at,[1] and they were most inclined to lay it at the door of foreign influence.

Whatever of the Pythagorean ethical teaching is certainly proved, may be found in the Gnomic teachings.   But at all events we see there, in the consciousness of duty, in introspection, and in subordination to authority, a greater earnestness and rigor, with at the same time a decided abandonment of sense-pleasure and a powerful tendency to spiritualize life.[2] Many ascetic tendencies doubtless were already connected with 'this.   The pronounced political turn which Pythagoras at the same time gave to his society determined its fate and led it first to victory, then to destruction.   Yet this political tendency is not to be regarded as original, but as the natural consequence of the moral-religious ideal of life.

In order to attain such a goal, Pythagoras founded at first in Crotona his religious society, which soon spread over a greater part of Magna Græcia. But this sect was, to be sure, at first only a kind of Mysteries, and nearest related to it were the Orphics. It is to be distinguished from these only so far as it expressly determined also the political and in part even the private life of its members by its regulations. It sought to evolve also a general education and an all-round method of life out of its moral-religious principle. Its most commendable feature was, that within the society the external goods of life were relatively little prized, and the common activities were directed toward fostering science and art. Thus, the religious in time became a scientific θίασος. To Pythagoras himself may be referred the thorough study of music,

[1] See Xenophanes' witty distich against it : Diog. Laert., VIII. 36.

[2] The so-called "golden poem" wherein the Pythagorean rules of life are laid down was, according to Mullach, collated by Lysis. Zeller is certainly right in saying that it was probably earlier handed down in verse form.

and perhaps in the same connection the beginnings of mathematical investigations which therefore, like medicine, have a point of departure equally independent of that of " general philosophy." [1]

It is no longer certain how much the society directed by Pythagoras himself was in possession of all of the rules by which, according to later accounts, the community life of the members, their initiation, their education even to the particulars of each day's duties, were provided for. The conception taken from later analogies is scarcely credible, that the Pythagoreans were a secret society in which the novitiate first after a long preparation and after the performance of many symbolical formalities could share in the " mysteries." Röth in particular has tried to re-establish this distinction of the esoteric and exoteric. Pythagoreanism was certainly no more and no less a secret society than all the other Mysteries, and there is not the slightest ground for assuming a secret science in it. That the stimulus given by Pythagoras to the spiritual community of life was concerned with music and mathematics, may safely be accepted. All else is doubtful, and probably fabulous. So, too, it is impossible to find out anything certain as to the founder's personal familiarity with these subjects. Even the well-known geometrical proposition is not to be attributed to him in entire confidence. He himself belongs rather to the religious and political life. But the spirit in which he founded his school was of such a nature that scientific interest could and actually did flourish in it.

13. In Greek national life such were the essential conditions for the origin of the philosophy which appeared at the beginning of the sixth century as an independent phenomenon. Its entire course, however, since it was dependent upon the general civilization of the nation, shows a gradual drifting from circumference to centre. The beginnings lie scattered in those circles of Hellenic life where, in friendly as well as in hostile contact with neighboring peoples, it first developed into full independence. Afterwards in the entire Sophistic Enlightenment philosophy centred itself in

[1] See G. Cantor, *Vorlesungen über d. Gesch. d. Math.*, I. 125 f.

the Athens of Pericles ; and there through the great personality of Socrates it became naturalized, it perfected itself,
and established its great schools.

Subjectively viewed, the development of Greek science is
a fully rounded whole. Like all naïve and natural thinking, it began with a recognition of the outer world. Its first
tendency was entirely cosmological, and it passed through
the physical into metaphysical problems. Foundering in
these and at the same time troubled by the dialectic of
public life, the Spirit made itself an object of reflection.
An anthropological period began, in which man appeared
as the most worthy object of consideration, and ultimately
as the *only* object of investigation. Finally, science in its
perfected strength, acquired in the profound study of the
laws of its reason, turned back to the old problems, the
conquest of which came to it now in great systematic
continuity.

See § 2, note. — Hegel, *Gesch. der Philos.*, *Complete Works*,
Vol. XIII. 188. If one strips away the formal from Hegel's
terminology, which served him in his systematization of the
historical processes, then one meets here, as so often in Hegel,
an inspired insight, with which he apprehended the essential
features in the development of historical phenomena.

The origins of scientific reflection are to be sought in the
cities of the seacoast of Ionia, which were in a flourishing
condition about 600 B. C. The happy nature of the Ionian
race was here accompanied by all the necessary material,
social, and intellectual requisitions for science. Its mental alertness, its frequently dangerous curiosity for the novel,
and its creative talent were remarkable. Here, for the
first time, mature minds brought their independent judgment to bear not only upon practical but upon theoretical
questions.[1] The idea of the connection of things was no

---

[1] Plutarch *Sol.*, 3 (concerning Thales) : περαιτέρω τῆς χρείας ἐξικέσθαι
τῇ θεωρίᾳ.

longer formed after the models of mythology, but by personal reflection and meditation. Nevertheless these new endeavors leading to science grew out of the circle of religious ideas, and thereby did science prove itself to be one of the functions which had been differentiated out of the original religious life of human society. At first science treated the same problems that concerned mythological fancy. The difference between the two does not lie in their subject matter, but in the form of their interrogation and the nature of their reply. Science begins where a conceptual problem takes the place of curiosity as to sequences, and where, therefore, fancies and fables are replaced by the investigations of permanent relations.

The common task for the Greek philosopher lay in the necessity to understand the change of things, their origination, destruction, and transmutation into one another. This very change, this process of happening (*Geschehen*) was accepted as a matter of course, and was not required to be explained or reduced to its causes. It had rather to be described, objectified, and conceptually stated. The myth accomplished this in the form of a narrative. To the question, What existed previously? it made answer with a description of the origin of the world, and tells of the battles of Titans and how they finally produced this world. Among men of science this interest in the past gave way to an interest in what is permanent. They no longer asked for the temporal but for the real *prius* of perceived Being. Face to face with the perpetual vicissitudes of individual things, they expressed the thought of a world-unity, by asking what is permanent amid the changes. Consequently they formed as the goal of their research the concept of a world-stuff that changes into all things, and into which all things return when these things vanish from perception. The idea of a temporal origin of things gives place to that of eternal Being, and thus arises the ἀρχή,[1] the first concept of Greek philosophy. The first question of Greek science was, " What is the stuff out of which the world is made, and how is the stuff changed into single things?" Science thus arose from cosmogonies and theogonies.

The transition from the myth to science consists in stripping off the historical, in rejecting chronological narration, and in reflecting upon the Unchangeable. The first science was obviously an investigation of nature.

See S. A. Byk. *Die vorsocratische Philos. d. Gr. in ihrer organischen Gliederung*, 2 parts, Leipzig, 1875 and 1877.

1. THE MILESIAN NATURE PHILOSOPHY

14. The principal centre for these beginnings in science was the chief of the Ionian cities, Miletus. From two generations of scientists in this city, tradition has preserved three names : Thales, Anaximander, and Anaximenes.[2]

---

[1] Arist. *Met.*, I. 3, 983, b. 8. : ἐξ οὗ γὰρ ἔστιν ἅπαντα τὰ ὄντα καὶ ἐξ οὗ γίγνεται πρῶτου καί εἰς ὃ φθείρεται τελευταῖον, τῆς μὲν οἰσίας ὑπομενούσης, τοῖς δὲ πάθεσι μεταβαλλούσης, τοῦτο στιχεῖον καὶ ταύτην ἀρχήν φασιν εἶναι τῶν ὄντων. Omitting the deduction of the Aristotelian categories, οὐσία and πάθος, this definition of ἀρχή, which furnishes an immediate suggestion of the transition from the temporal to the conceptual, may be taken as historical in the sense that it existed among the old Ionians. It is of little importance who introduced the term ἀρχή in this conceptual way. Simpl. *Phys.*, 6 recto, 24, 13 asserts it to be due to Anaximander. The thought was already present in Thales.

[2] It is evident that one need not limit the Milesian philosophy to these three well-known men ; but nothing is traditionally certain. For the allusion of Theophrastus, who (Simpl. *Phys.*, 6) speaks of predecessors of Thales, may also be applied to the cosmogonies ; and the reports of Aristotle, according to which the physicists were those who accepted as ἀρχή the intermediaries between air and water (*De cælo*, III. 5, 303 b, 12) or between air and fire (*Phys.*, I. 4, 187 a, 14) leave open the possibility and probability that he has in mind the later eclectic stragglers. Compare § 25.

R. Ritter, *Gesch. der ionischen Philosophie* (Berlin, 1821) ; R. Seydel, *Der Fortschritt der Metaphysik unter den ältesten ionischen Philosophen* (Leipzig, 1861) ; P. Tannery, *Pour l'histoire de la science hellène*, I. (Paris, 1887).

Thales (about 600 B. C.) answered the question concerning the substantial constitution of the world (*Weltstoff*) by declaring it to be water. This is the only assertion that can be attributed to him with perfect certainty. Even Aristotle,[1] who could give only traditional reports concerning Thales, as early as his time had only conjectures about the grounds of this assertion. When Aristotle states that the moist character of the animal seed and animal nutrition was the occasion for this statement of Thales (and to Aristotle's inference,[2] all later supplementary conjectures appear to refer), we are permitted to attribute this inference to the specific interest in biology, which appealed strongly to the Stagirite, but, for all we know, not at all to Thales. More probable is the conjecture, likewise reported by Aristotle,[3] which brings the teaching of Thales into connection with ancient cosmological ideas. In these the ocean was considered the oldest and most important thing. It would be exceedingly strange if the Ionian thinker, in answer to the question as to the constitution of the world, had not decided in favor of the element so important to his people. The thought of its infinite mobility, its transformation into earth and air, its all-engulfing violence, could not but have held an important place in the minds of seafaring folk. The reported cosmographical[4] ideas of Thales also agree with this, for he is said to have thought that the earth floated in water, and to have given, in connection with this, a Neptunian explanation of earthquakes.

[1] *Met.*, I. 3, 983 b, 22, λαβὼν ἴσως τὴν ὑπόληψιν.
[2] Plut. *Plac. phil.*, I. 3 (*Dox.*, 276). Compare Zeller, I[4]. 175, 2.
[3] See beyond.
[4] Arist. *De cœlo*, II. 13, 294 a, 28.

But it makes no difference whether Thales came to his assertion more through organic than inorganic observations. So much is clear, that the chemical composition of water, the pure H_2O, did not determine his choice of it as the cosmic matter. Rather its fluid state of aggregation and the important rôle that it played in the mobile life of nature determined his decision, so that in the ancient reports ὑγρόν is often substituted for ὕδωρ. The idea of Thales seems to have been to select as the world stuff that form of matter, which promised to make most readily comprehensible, the transformation on the one hand to the solid, on the other to the volatile. More definite data concerning the *modus operandi* of these changes do not appear to have been furnished by Thales. It must remain problematical whether he, like the later philosophers, conceived this process of change as a condensation and rarefaction.

At any rate, Thales represented this fluid cosmic matter as in continuous self-motion. Of a force moving matter and distinguishable from it, he taught nothing.[1] In naïvely considering an event as a thing requiring no further explanation, he advocated, like his followers, the so-called hylozoistic theory, which represents matter as *eo ipso* moving and on that account animated. With this are compatible his πάντα πλήρη θεῶν εἶναι [2] and his ascription of a soul to the magnet.[3] The scientific view of the world had obviously at this stage not yet excluded the imaginative view of nature held by Greek mythology.

---

[1] According to the statements of the later writers (Cicero, *De nat. deor.*, I. 10), Thales placed in antithesis to the cosmic matter the forming divine spirit. Such statements betray, on the one hand, the terminology of the Stoics, and on the other lead us to infer a confounding of Thales with Anaxagoras. The hylozoism of all the ancient physicists, including Thales, is affirmed by Aristotle in *Met.*, I. 3.

[2] Arist. *De anima*, I. 5, 411 a, 8.

[3] *Ibid.*, I. 2, 405 a, 20.

The time in which Thales lived is determined by an eclipse, which he is said to have predicted. In accordance with modern investigations (Zech, *Astronomische Untersuchungen über die wichtigsten Finsternisse*, Leipzig, 1853), this must be placed in the year 585 B. C. His life falls, at all events, in the flourishing period of Miletus under Thrasybulus. The year of his birth cannot be exactly determined; his death may be placed directly after the Persian invasion in the middle of the sixth century (Diels, *Rhein. Mus.*, XXXI. 15 f.). He belonged to the old family of the Thelides, which sprang from the Bœotian Cadmians, who migrated into Asia Minor. Hence the statement that he was of Phœnician derivation (Zeller, I⁴. 169, 1). See § 9 for his practical and political activity; § 10, for his knowledge of mathematics and physics. The Egyptian journeys which later literature reports, are at least doubtful; although, provided that he was engaged in commerce, they are not impossible. None of the writings of Thales are cited by Aristotle, and it is consequently doubtful if he committed anything to writing.

15. If Thales is to be regarded as the first physicist, we meet the first metaphysician in the person of his somewhat younger countryman, Anaximander (611–545 B. C.). For his answer to the question concerning the constitution of the universe is already to be essentially distinguished, in its content as well as in its fundamentals, from that of Thales. Thales had sought to find the cosmic matter in the empirically known, and had seized upon what appears as the most completely mutable. If Anaximander was not content with this theory, it was on account of his pronounced principle [1] that the cosmic matter must be thought as infinite, so that it may not be thought to exhaust itself in its creations. From this it followed immediately that the cosmic matter cannot be found among empirically given forms of matter, all of which are limited. Thus there remained for the definition of the cosmic matter only the quality of its spatial and temporal infinity. Consequently Anaximander said that the ἀρχή is the ἄπειρον.

[1] Arist. *Phys.*, III. 8, 208 a, 8: see Plut. *Plac.*, I. 3 (*Dox.*, 277), ἵνα ἡ γένεσις μὴ ἐπιλείπῃ.

The most important aspect of this dictum is that here for the first time, is the step taken from the concrete to the abstract, from the *anschaulich* to the *begrifflich*. Anaximander explained the sensuously given by the concept. The advance consisted in the fact that the ἄπειρον is distinguished from all perceptible forms of matter. Anaximander thus referred the world of experience to a reality beyond experience, the idea of which arises from a conceptual postulate. He characterized this transcendent reality by all the predicates which his mind conceived as requisite for the cosmic matter. He called it ἀθάνατον καὶ ἀνώλεθρον, ἀγέννητον καὶ ἄφθαρτον; [1] he described it as including all things (περιέχειν) and as determining their motion (κυβερνᾶν); [2] and he designated it in this sense as τὸ θεῖον. But with this first metaphysical concept began then also the difficulty of giving a content to it. That Anaximander conceived the ἄπειρον to be pre-eminently a spatial and temporal infinity, follows from the way in which he arrived at this principle. Concerning his attitude, however, toward the question of the qualitative determination of the ἄπειρον, both antiquity and still more modern investigators have apparently had divided opinions. The simplest and the most natural theory to entertain is the following : that Anaximander did not express himself about the quality of this imperceivable cosmic matter, for the ancient accounts agree that he did not identify it with any one of the known elements. More questionable, certainly, is it whether he, as Herbart (*Complete Works*, I. 196) and his school (Strümpell, I. 29) are inclined to accept, expressly denied the qualitative determination of the cosmic matter, which would have anticipated the Platonic-Aristotelian conception

---

[1] Arist. *Phys.*, III. 4, 203 b, 8. Likewise ἀίδιον and ἀγήρω, see Hippol. *Ref. hær.*, I. 6 (*Dox.*, 559).

[2] Which expression does not mean, as Röth thinks (*Gesch. unserer abendl. Philos.*, II. 142), " a mental guidance." See Zeller, I[4]. 204, 1.

of matter as an undetermined possibility. But, on the other hand, it is certain that Anaximander thought of the ἄπειρον always as corporeal,[1] and only the kind of corporeality can be subject to controversy. The hypothesis, too, expressed repeatedly in later antiquity, is untenable, viz., that he asserted the cosmic matter to be an intermediary state between water and air, or air and fire. On the contrary, the combination of the Anaximandrian principle with the μῖγμα of Empedocles and Anaxagoras[2] which Aristotle gives, led even in antiquity to the conception of the ἄπειρον as a mixture of all the empirical material elements. If now, also, the adherence of Anaximander to hylozoistic monism is — as Aristotle says it is — so very certain that one cannot make him (with Ritter, *op. cit.*) the father of mechanical physics, in opposition to Ionian dynamics,[3] yet, on the other hand, it is incontrovertible that Anaximander in some conjecturable, obscure way must have stated that the ἄπειρον contains in itself all known material elements, and then differentiates these elements in the cosmic process.[4] Doubtless he held an attitude of uncertainty as to the relationship of the ἄπειρον to these particular elements, similar to the mythological primeval idea of Chaos, which idea, to be sure, had already been greatly purified, but not yet thoroughly elaborated and assimilated.

Accordingly Anaximander was doubtless content in merely indicating as ἐκκρίνεσθαι the development of par-

---

[1] Compare Zeller, I⁴. 186, 1, as against Michelis, *De an. infinito* (Braunsberg, 1874).

[2] Arist. *Met.*, XI. 2, 1069 b, 22 : to which add especially *Phys.*, I. 4, 187 a, 20 : οἱ δ᾽ ἐκ τοῦ ἑνὸς ἐνούσας τὰς ἐναντιότητας ἐκκρίνεσθαι, ὥσπερ Ἀναξίμανδρός φησι κτλ. Compare § 22.

[3] Brandis, *Handbuch*, I. 125.

[4] Arist. *Met.*, XI. 2, and Theophrastus (Simpl. *Phys.*, 6) interpret this as a δυνάμει inclusion. The ἄπειρον became to them their ἀόριστος ὕλη.

ticular things from the cosmic matter. Indeed he caused the antithetical Warm and Cold to be differentiated from the ἄπειρον as its first qualitative determinations. Out of the mixture of these two qualities was supposed to be formed then the Fluid, the fundamental material of the finite empirical world. Thus the metaphysical basis to the theory of Thales was complete; for Anaximander taught that the particular parts of the world had been differentiated out of the Fluid. These were the earth, air, and the fire encircling the whole.

The philosopher inserted into this meteorological account of the origin of the world a multitude of single astronomical ideas (§ 10) which, even if they appear childish to us to-day, nevertheless not only show a many-sided interest in nature, but also presuppose independent observations and conclusions. Anaximander reflected upon the facts of organic life also, and there is preserved one observation of his in accord [1] with the modern evolution theory. This is to the effect that animals appeared when the primitive liquid earth dried up, and were originally fish in form. Then some of them, adapting themselves to their new environment, became land animals. This process of development, in its naïve explanation, includes even man.

The single qualitative differentiations are lost again in the perpetual life-process of the cosmic matter, in the same way that they arise out of the ἄπειρον. Anaximander, in the single fragment verbally preserved to us, has described this reabsorption in a poetic [2] manner — reminding us of original Oriental-religious ideas — as a kind of compensation for the injustice of individual existence. ἐξ ὧν δὲ ἡ γένησίς ἐστι τοῖς οὖσι, καὶ τὴν φθορὰν εἰς ταῦτα γίνεσθαι κατὰ τὸ χρεών. διδόναι γὰρ αὐτὰ δίκην καὶ τίσιν [ἀλλήλοις] τῆς ἀδικίας κατὰ

---

[1] Plut. *Plac.*, V. 19 (*Dox.*, 430); Hippol. *Ref. hær.*, I. 6 (*Dox.*, 560). Compare Teichmüller, *Studien*, I. 63 f.

[2] Simpl. *Phys.*, 6ʳ, 24, 13.

τὴν τοῦ χρόνου τάξιν. To this Anaximander united the theory, also similarly Oriental, that the cosmic matter in perpetual transformation creates out of itself world-systems, and again absorbs them.[1] Whether to the view of an endless plurality of successive world-formations was connected also that of a plurality of co-existing worlds, contained in the primitive matter, remains undecided and not probable.[2]

The determination of the dates of the life of Anaximander rests upon the arbitrary statement of Apollodorus, that in the second year of the fifty-eighth Olympiad he was sixty-four years old and directly afterwards died. (Diog. Laert., II. 2.) This is not far from the truth. Further of his biography is not known. His work, to which some one gave the title περὶ φύσεως, was in prose, and appears to have been lost very early. Compare Schleiermacher, *Ueber An.*, *Complete Works*, III. 2, 171 f.; Büsgen, *Ueber das ἄπειρον des A.* (Wiesbaden, 1867); Neuhäuser, *Anax. Milesius*, (Bonn, 1883).

16. We turn back from the metaphysical to the physical point of view when we pass from Anaximander to Anaximenes, for the latter sought the cosmic matter again in the empirically known. Nevertheless the reflections of Anaximander were not ineffectual upon his successor. For when he substituted the air in place of the water of Thales, he had especial reference to the postulate of Anaximander: he explained that the air is the ἄπειρος ἀρχή. He found the claims of the metaphysician to be thus satisfied by the empirical material.[3] At the same time he chose the air on

---

[1] Plut. *Strom.*, fr. 2 (*Dox.*, 579).

[2] See Zeller, I. 212 f.

[3] This is attested expressly by Simplicius, *Phys.*, 6ʳ, 24, 26: see Eus. *Prœp*, I. 8, 3 (*Dox.*, 579) and especially *Schol. in Arist.*, 514 a, 33; ἄπειρον μὲν καὶ αὐτὸς ὑπέθετο τὴν ἀρχήν, οὐ μὴν ἔτι ἀόριστον· κτλ. It is thus impossible to premise with Ritter (*Gesch. der Philos.*, 217) that Anaximenes made a distinction between the air as a metaphysical cosmic matter and the same as an empirical element. Brandis also, who first entertained this view in his handbook, I. 144, has later (*Gesch. d. Entw.*, I. 56, 2) not laid so much stress on it.

account of its easy mutability: οἰόμενος ἀρκεῖν τὸ τοῦ ἀέρος
εὐαλλοίωτον πρὸς μεταβολήν (Schol. in Arist., 514 a, 33). If
we add to this, finally, the single statement which is preserved of his writings: [1] οἷον ἡ ψυχὴ ἡ ἡμετέρα ἀὴρ οὖσα
συγκρατεῖ ἡμᾶς, καὶ ὅλον τὸν κόσμον πνεῦμα καὶ ἀὴρ περιέχει,[2]
we know that his main object was to declare the cosmic
matter to be the most alive and most continuously mobile
of the known elements.   We likewise meet here a very
definite idea of the manner in which the ἀρχή changes into
other kinds of matter: [3] his theory of condensation and rarefaction (μάνωσις or ἀραίωσις — πύκνωσις). Out of the
air through rarefaction originates fire: through condensation, wind, clouds, rain, water, earth, stones, successively
come.   In this enumeration there appears considerable
definiteness in meteorological observations, and at the
same time the physicist's tendency to use the state of
aggregation as a standard for the different changes in
the cosmic matter. Milesian science already knew the
connection of the state of aggregation with the temperature; and Anaximenes taught [4] that rarefaction is identical
with increase of warmth, condensation with increase of
cold.

From these general observations Anaximenes not only
gave a great number of explanations of particular phenomena in which he showed himself to have been a many-
sided and sharp-sighted physicist, but he also gave a theory
of the origin of the world.   To the latter was appended the

[1] Plut. Plac., I. 3 (Dox., 278).

[2] Far from favoring a purely spiritual interpretation of the world
principle, by Anaximenes, as Röth (Gesch. d. abendl. Philos., II. 250 f.)
will have it, this passage shows the naïve materialism of earliest science
as it also appears in the casual remark of Anaximander that the soul is
air. The materiality of the cosmic matter of Anaximenes is proved
beyond a doubt by his theory of condensation and rarefaction.

[3] Hipp. Ref. h., I. 7 (Dox., 560).

[4] Plat. De pr. frig., 7, 3, 947.

safely attested [1] conception of a periodic change of world-
formings and world-destructions, i. e., of a successive
plurality of worlds. It is not certain, however, that he
thought the destruction of the world to be conflagration.

Nothing is known of the life of Anaximenes, and its chronological determination is difficult. See Zeller, I[4]. 219, 1.
Against the conjectures of Diels (*Rhein. Mus.*, XXXI. 27)
there is the probable theory that by the " capture of Sardis,"
with which his death is said to be coincident (Diog., II. 3), we
are to understand the capture by the Ionians in the year 499.
Accordingly his birth would have to be in the 53d Olympiad, as
Hermann has it (*De philos. Jonic. œtatibus*, Göttingen, 1849).
Röth (II. a, 246 f. ; b, 42 f.) makes the date too late by placing
it in the 58th Olympiad. His περὶ φύσεως was written [2] γλώσσῃ
'Ιάδι ἀπλῇ καὶ ἀπερίττω. This is the beginning of a dry practical
prose which shows itself contemporaneously in the historiography of his countryman Hecatæus.

With the destruction of Miletus after the battle of Lade,
494, and the fall of the independence of Ionia, the first
development of Greek science along the lines of natural
philosophy came to an end.[3] When, at least a generation [4]
after Anaximenes, in another Ionian city, Ephesus, the
great scientific theory of Heracleitus appeared, the new
theory did not leave the old theory unused. Heracleitus,
on the other hand, joined to the old theory the religious
and metaphysical problems which had appeared in the
mean time from other directions.

[1] Simpl. *Phys.*, 257?

[2] According to Diog. Laert., II. 2.

[3] The great chronological chasm between Anaximenes and Heracleitus is consistent with the entirely different handling of the problems by
the latter. Therefore the customary way of making Heracleitus a
follower of the Milesians is the less tenable, since the teaching of
Heracleitus absolutely presupposes that of Xenophanes.

[4] If one places the death of Anaximenes at 525 (Diels and Zeller)
and that of Heracleitus, at the earliest, at 475, then the chasm appears
still greater.

2. THE METAPHYSICAL CONFLICT — HERACLEITUS AND THE ELEATICS.

The advance from the speculations in nature-philosophy of the Milesians to the conceptual investigations in Being and Becoming of Heracleitus and his Eleatic opponents was the result of a reaction, which the conception of the world created by Ionian science necessarily exerted upon the religious ideas of the Greeks. The monistic tendency which science showed in seeking the unitary cosmic matter was in implicit opposition to polytheistic mythology, and necessarily became more and more accentuated. It was inevitable, therefore, that Greek science on the one hand should emphasize and reinforce the monistic suggestion which it found in the field of religious ideas, but on the other that it should fall so much the more into sharper opposition to the polytheism of the state religion.

17. The imperturbable champion of this conflict, the man who stands as the religious-philosophical link between the Milesian nature philosophy and the two great metaphysical systems of Heracleitus and Parmenides, and at the same time the man who is the messenger of philosophy from the East to the West, is Xenophanes,[1] the rhapsodist

---

[1] The disposition of the material of the text, whereby Xenophanes, who is generally called the "founder" of the Eleatic school, has been separated from this school, is justified by these two facts: firstly, the theory of Xenophanes in point of time and subject matter precedes that of Heracleitus, and the theory of Heracleitus in the same respects precedes that of Parmenides; secondly, that Xenophanes is neither a genuine Eleatic, nor yet a representative of the Eleatic theory of Being, enunciated first by Parmenides. The importance of Xenophanes lies not within a metaphysical but a religious-philosophical territory, and his strength does not consist in conceptual thought (Arist. *Met.*, I. 5, 986 b, 27, calls him, as opposed to Parmenides, ἀγροικότερον) but in the powerful and grand thought of Oneness. See Brandis, *Handbuch*, I. 359.

of Colophon, who sang in Magna Græcia (570–470). To him antiquity referred as the first champion against the anthropomorphic element in the popular religion. He criticised the representation of gods in human form,[1] and made sport of the poets who attributed to celestials the passions and sins of men.[2] He asserted the singleness of the highest and true God.[3] If we may believe that herein he taught nothing but what was already provided for and hinted at, if not indeed definitely presented, in the Pythagorean doctrine as known to him, and possibly even earlier in the Mysteries, — then that which makes Xenophanes a philosopher is the basis which he developed for monotheism from the philosophy of the Milesian physics. We can condense his teaching into a sentence: the ἀρχή is the Godhead. According to his religious conviction, God is the original ground of all things, and to him are due all attributes which the physicists had ascribed to the cosmic matter. He is unoriginated and imperishable;[4] and, as the cosmic matter was identical with the World-All for the Ionians, so for Xenophanes was God identical to the world-all. He contains all things in himself, and he is at the same time ἕν καὶ πᾶν.[5] This philosophical monotheism,

---

[1] Compare the well-known verse in Clem. Alex. *Strom.*, V. 714 (fr. 5, 6).

[2] Compare Sext. Emp. *Adv. math.*, IX. 193 and I. 289.

[3] "Εἷς θεὸς ἔν τε θεοῖσι καὶ ἀνθρώποισι μέγιστος οὔτε δέμας θνητοῖσιν ὁμοίιος οὔτε νόημα." The metaphysical monotheism in Xenophanes and later in the Greek thinkers — in a certain sense even in Plato — is allied with the recognition also of subordinate deities which are treated as parts of the world. The Stoa was the first to attempt to analyze this relationship in a conceptual way. Side by side with the metaphysical monotheism, there thus continued to exist a mythical polytheism.

[4] According to Arist. *Rhet.*, II. 23, 1399 b, 6, Xenophanes declared it impious to speak of birth and death, of origination and extinction, of a Godhead, ἀμφοτέρως γὰρ συμβαίνειν μὴ εἶναι τοὺς θεούς ποτε.

[5] Compare Simpl. *Phys.*, 6ʳ, 22, 26; ἕν τὸ ὄν καὶ πᾶν . . . Ξενοφάνην . . . ὑποτίθεσθαι.

so energetically defended against the polytheism of the myth, is consequently not theistic but entirely pantheistic, as we use the terms. World and God to Xenophanes are identical, and all the single things of perception lose themselves in that one, unchanging, universal essence.[1] In consequence of his religious predilection, however, Xenophanes emphasized the singleness of the divine cosmic principle more decidedly than the Milesians, to whom this is a self-evident principle, owing to their concept of the ἀρχή. It remains indeed doubtful whether the entire Zeno-like argument for this, founded on the superlatives "mightiest" and "best," can be ascribed to him.[2] To the quality of singleness, however, Xenophanes further ascribed to the cosmic deity that of unity[3] in the sense of qualitative unity and inner homogeneity. Nevertheless, of what this consists he had as little to say as Anaximander concerning the qualitative constitution of the ἄπειρον. In his poetry he attributed to the Godhead in an incidental way all possible functions and powers, spiritual[4] as well as material.[5] Yet out of the mass of his utterances Aristotle could obtain[6] only an indefinite and obscure assertion of the essential homogeneity of all being. It was of greater importance, however, for future philosophical development that Xenophanes followed to its logical conclusion the concept of qualitative unity; and that moreover he extended

---

[1] According to Sext. Emp. *Pyrr. hypot.*, I. 33, the sillograph Timon makes him say; ὅππη γὰρ ἐμὸν νόον εὐρύσαιμι Εἰς ἕν ταὐτό τε Πᾶν ἀνελύετο · πᾶν δ' ἐὸν αἰεὶ Πάντη ἀνελκόμενον μίαν εἰς φύσιν ἔσταθ' ὁμοίαν.

[2] *De Xen. Zen. Gorgias*, 977 a, 23 ; Simpl. *Phys.*, l. c.

[3] In which the ambiguity of the ἕν played a great rôle.

[4] Sext. Emp. *Adv. math.*, IX. 144 : οὖλος ὁρᾷ, οὖλος δὲ νοεῖ, οὖλος δὲ τ' ἀκούει. Simpl. *Phys.*, 6·, 23, 18 : ἀλλ' ἀπάνευθε πόνοιο νόου φρενὶ πάντα κραδαί·ει.

[5] Thus the often mentioned ball-shape of the Godhead or of the World. Compare Hippol. *Ref. h.*, I. 14 (*Dox.*, 565).

[6] *Met.*, I. 5, 986 b, 22. Compare Plat. *Soph.*, 242 d.

it over temporal differentiations in such a way that he
ascribed unchangeability to the Godhead in every respect.[1]
He thereby enters into significant opposition to his predecessors.[2] From the concept of the divine ἀρχή, there vanished the character of mutability which had played so
great a rôle in the Milesian hylozoism.

In the emphasis upon this claim that the ἀρχή is unoriginated and imperishable, and must also be immobile,
excluding therefore κίνησις as well as ἀλλοίωσις, lay the
distinctive innovation of the teaching of Xenophanes.
For just here the concept of the ἀρχή could no longer
serve as an explanation of empirical events.   However,
Xenophanes did not himself appear to have been conscious
of the chasm he left between his metaphysical principle,
and the plurality and changeableness of individual things.[3]
For in an obviously naïve [4] manner he conjoined to his
religious metaphysics a multitude of physical theories.
Nevertheless he does not appear as an independent investigator in physics, but he simply follows the views of
Anaximander, with whose entire doctrine he seems to
have been perfectly familiar,[5] and adds certain more or
less happy observations of his own.   Among the latter

---

[1] Eus. *Præp. ev.*, I. 8, 4 : εἶναι λέγει τὸ πᾶν ἀεὶ ὅμοιον. Hippolyt. *Ref.*,
I. 14 : ὅτε ἐν τὸ πᾶν ἐστιν ἔξω μεταβολῆς. He also denied movement
to the world-all ; compare Simpl. *Phys*, 6ᵣ, 23, 6 : αἰεὶ δ' ἐν τωὐτῷ τε μένειν
κινούμενον οὐδὲν οὐδὲ μετέρχεσθαί μιν ἐπιπρέπει ἄλλοθεν ἄλλη.

[2] This very opposition Aristotle emphasizes in connection with
Met., I. 5.

[3] It is possible, also, that he endeavored to avoid a difficulty here by an
indefinite expression, just as Diogenes, II. 1, reports that Anaximander
(no source of authority given) taught : τὰ μὲν μέρη μεταβάλλειν. τὸ δὲ
πᾶν ἀμετάβλητον εἶναι.

[4] Thus he lets stand the plurality of mythical gods under the metaphysical Godhead.

[5] Theophrastus appears to think him the pupil of Anaximander See
Zeller, I⁴. 508, 1.

belong the very childish ideas about astronomical objects. For instance, the stars were to him clouds of fire, which were quenched when they set and were enkindled when they rose ;[1] he attached great significance[2] to the earth as the fundamental element of the empirical world (with the addition of the water), and he thought it to be endless[3] in its downward direction. His statement was more happy about the petrifactions he had observed in Sicily, as a proof of the original drying of the earth from its muddy condition.[4] Yet Xenophanes apparently held such physical theories concerning the individual and temporary in small esteem compared to his religious metaphysics, which he championed vehemently. To this only can his sceptical remarks in one of his fragments[5] refer.

The differing statements as to when Xenophanes lived can be reconciled most easily by assuming that the time when he, according to his own statement (Diog. Laert., IX. 19), at twenty-five began his wanderings, coincided with the invasion by the Persians under Harpagus (546, in consequence of which so many Ionians left their homes). He himself testifies (loc. cit.) that his wanderings lasted sixty-seven years, at which time he must have attained the age of at least ninety-two. Impoverished during the emigration, if not already poor, which is less probable, he supported himself as a rhapsodist by the public rendering of his own verses. In old age he settled in Elea, the founding of which in 537 by the fugitive Phœnicians he celebrated in two thousand distichs. According to the preserved fragments, his poetic activity was essentially of the Gnomic order (§ 9). He embodied his teaching in a didactic poem in hexameter, of which only a few fragments remain. These have been collated by Mullach ; also by Karsten, *Philosophorum Græcorum operum reliquiæ*, I. 1 (Amsterdam, 1835) ; Reinhold, *De genuina Xenophanis doctrina* (Jena, 1847), and in the different works about Xenophanes by Franz Kern (*Programm,*

---

[1] Stob. *Ecl.*, I. 522 (*Dox.*, 348).

[2] Achilles Tatius in *Isagoge ad Aratum*, 128.

[3] Simpl. *Phys.* 414, 189, 1. Sext. Emp. *Adv. math.*, IX. 361.

[4] Hippol. *Ref.*, I. 14 (*Dox.* 565).

[5] Sextus Emp., VII. 49, 110 ; VIII. 326. Stob. *Ecl.*, I. 224.

Naumburg, 1864; Oldenburg, 1876; Danzig, 1871; Stettin, 1874, 1877); Freudenthal, *Die Theologie des Xenophanes* (Breslau, 1886). Compare *Arch. f. Gesch. d. Philos.*, 1. 322 f.

The pseudo-Aristotelian treatise *De Xenophane, Zenone, Gorgia* (printed in the works of Aristotle, and in Mullach, *Fragm.* I. 271, also under the title *De Melisso, Xenophane et Gorgia*), came from the Peripatetic school. According to the investigations of Brandis, Bergk, Ueberweg, Vermehren, and Zeller, we may believe that the last part of this work doubtless treats of Gorgias, and the first part almost as surely of Melissus. The middle portion presupposes an older presentation about Xenophanes which was referred wrongly by a later commentator to Zeno, and was supplemented with some statements about Zeno's views drawn from other sources. This part of the treatise can be used only with the greatest judgment, and then as illustrative of what on the one hand the fragments, and on the other the reports, of Aristotle give.

The teaching of Xenophanes, immature as it appears, nevertheless discloses the inadequacy of the Milesian concept of the ἀρχή. In or behind the change of single things, he said, should be sought a cosmic principle that creates them all, but yet itself always remains unchanged. But if we seriously conceive of this cosmic principle of Xenophanes as utterly unchangeable, and at the same time regard it as the sole and all-embracing actuality, it is impossible to understand its capacity of being ceaselessly transmuted into individual things. The two thought-motifs that had been fundamental in the concept of the ἀρχή now part company, — on the one hand, the reflection upon the fundamental fact of the cosmic process (*Geschehen*), on the other the fundamental postulate of the permanent, of the unchangeably self-determined, of Being. The more difficult their reconciliation appeared, the more conceivable is it that the young science, at whose command there was as yet no wealth of mediating data, and which on the other hand was developed with naïve unconcern, should fall upon the expedient of thinking out each motif by itself without regard for the other. From this courageous onesidedness,

undaunted as it was at paradoxical consequences, originated the two great metaphysical systems whose opposition
determined later thought. These are the theories of Heracleitus and Parmenides.

18. The doctrine of absolute, ceaseless, and universal
mutability already was even in antiquity regarded as the
kernel of Heracleitanism. Its watchword is πάντα ῥεῖ ; and
when Plato [1] gave the phrase a new turn, ὅτι πάντα χωρεῖ
καὶ οὐδὲν μένει, he gave at the same time the obverse of
the proposition, viz., the denial of the permanent. Here in
this is Heracleitus, "the Dark," essentially distinguished
from the Milesian philosophers, with whom he, under the
name of the "Ionian natural philosophers," is generally
classed (§ 16). Heracleitus found nothing permanent in
the perceptual world, and he gave up search for it. In
the most varied phrase he presented the fundamental
truth of the continuous transmutation of all things into
one another. From every realm of life he seized examples, in order to point out the passage of opposites into
each other. He described in bold figures the ceaselessness
of change, which was to him the essence of the world, and
needed no derivation and explanation. There are no truly
existing things, but all things only *become* and *pass away*
again in the play of perpetual world-movement. The ἀρχή is
not so much immutable matter in independent motion, as
the Milesians had said, but is the motion itself, from which
all forms of matter are later derived as products. This
thought is stated by Heracleitus by no means with conceptual clearness, but in sensuous pictures. Already the
Milesian investigators had noted that all motion and
change are connected with temperature changes (§ 16), and
so Heracleitus thought that the eternal cosmic motion expressed itself by fire. Fire is the ἀρχή, but not as a stuff
identical with itself in all its changes, but rather as the

[1] *Cratyl.*, 402 a.

ever-uniform process itself, in which all things rise and
pass away.   It is the world itself, therefore, in its unorigi-
nating and unperishing mutability.[1]

The exceptional difficulty of this relationship was remarked
by the ancients, and from it, especially, the Ephesian got his
nickname, σκοτεινός.   Herein appeared the amalgamation of
the abstract and the concrete, of the sensuous and the symbolical, which, in general, characterized the entire thought and
habit of expression of Heracleitus.   Neither to oracular pride
nor to the assumption of mysteriousness (Zeller, I[4]. 570 f.) is
this deficiency to be attributed in his writing, but to inability
to find an adequate form for his aspiring abstract thought.
Besides this, a priestly ceremoniousness of tone is unmistakable.   Hence the wrestling with language which appears in
nearly all the fragments; hence the rhetorical vehemence of
expression and a heaping up of metaphors, in which a powerful and sometimes grotesque fancy is displayed.   Concerning
especially his fundamental teaching, his words seem to show in
isolated passages that he had only substituted fire for water or
air.   But more exact search shows that the ἀρχή meant quite a
different thing to him.   He also identified fire and the world-all
and fire and the Godhead; — nay, hylozoic pantheism finds in
the teaching of Heracleitus its own most perfect expression.
Yet he meant that this world principle is only the movement
represented in the fire.   It is the cosmic process itself.

Heracleitus proceeded from the point of view that the
fire-motion is originally in itself the final ground of things,
and accordingly no permanent Being is fundamental in it.
He found fire to be the condition of every change, and
therefore the object of scientific knowledge.   But he did
not only mean this in the sense that " nothing is permanent save change," but also in the higher sense that this
eternal movement completes itself in determined and ever-
recurrent forms.   From this metaphysical thesis he attempted to understand the problem of the ever-permanent
series of repetitions, the rhythm of movement and the law

[1] Fr. 46 (Schust.) κόσμον τόν αὐτὸν ἀπάντων οὔτε τις θεῶν οὔτε ἀνθρώ·
πων ἐποίησεν, ἀλλ᾽ ἦν ἀεὶ καὶ ἔστιν πῦρ ἀείζωον.

of change. *In obscure and undeveloped form originated here the conception of natural law.* It appeared in the vesture of the mythical Εἱμαρμένη, as an all-determining Fate, or an all-powerful Δίκη, menacing every deviation with punishment. Since it is to be regarded as the peculiar object of reason, he called it the Λόγος, — the reason that rules the world.

In the later presentations of this theory, in which its Stoicism appears, it is difficult to get at what is in itself peculiarly Heracleitan (Zeller, I⁴. 606 f.). But the fundamental thought of a world-order of natural phenomena cannot be denied to Heracleitus. Compare M. Heinze, *Die Lehre vom Logos in der griechischen Philosophie* (Leipzig, 1872).

The most universal form of the cosmic process was, therefore, for Heracleitus that of opposition and its elimination. From the notion of the " flow of all things," it followed that every single thing in its continuous change unites in itself perpetually opposing determinations. Everything is only a transition, a point of limit between the vanishing and the about-to-be. The life of nature is a continuous passing into one another of all opposites, and out of their strife come the individual things : πόλεμος πάντων μὲν πατήρ ἐστι, πάντων δὲ βασιλεύς.[1] But as these antitheses ultimately arise only out of the universal and all-embracing, living, fiery, cosmic force, so they find their adjustment and reconciliation in this same fire. Fire is, in this respect, the " unseen harmony." [2] The world-all is consequently the self-divided [3] and the self-reuniting unity.[4] It is at one and the same

[1] Fr. 75.

[2] Compare Fr. 8 : ἁρμονίη γὰρ ἀφανὴς φανερῆς κρείττων. ἐν ᾗ τὰς διαφορὰς καὶ ἑτερότητας ὁ μιγνύων θεὸς ἔκρυψε καὶ κατέδυσεν. Comp. Zeller, I⁴. 604 f. The ἀφανής here obviously characterizes the metaphysical in opposition to the physical.

[3] Plato, *Symp.*, 187 a : τὸ ἐν διαφερόμενον αὐτὸ αὑτῷ. Compare *Soph.*, 242 c ; also Fr. 98.

[4] Heracleitus sought to picture this relationship in the obviously unfor-

time strife and peace; or what seems to mean [1] the same in Heracleitus' terminology, it is at one and the same time want and fulness.[2]

The physical application of these principles afforded a thoroughgoing theory of the elemental changes in the universe. Action and reaction take place in orderly succession, and indeed in such wise that they are constantly balanced in their results. Thus it happens that single things have the appearance of persisting, when two opposing forces temporarily hold each other in equilibrium, as, for instance, the river appears as a permanent thing because just as much water flows to a point as flows from it. Heracleitus designated this rhythm of change as the two " Ways " which are identical, the ὁδὸς κάτω and the ὁδὸς ἄνω.[3] By the first Way the original fire changes itself into water and then into earth through condensation ; by the second the earth changes back through liquefaction to water and then to fire. This double process is true in one respect for the entire world ; for in regularly recurrent periods [4] it develops into individual things from the original fire, and then returns to the initial condition of pure fire. Hence comes the idea of alternating world-formation and world-destruction.[5] On the other hand, this

tunate figure of the bow and the lyre : παλίντονος [-τροπος] γὰρ ἁρμονίη κόσμου ὅκωσπερ τόξου καὶ λύρης. As to the meaning, see Zeller, I⁴. 598 f.

[1] *Ibid*, 641.

[2] Fr. 67. From these determinations apparently come νεῖκος and φιλότης, the different conditions developed by Empedocles (§ 21).

[3] Compare Diog Laert., IX. 8. The designations κάτω and ἄνω are to be understood as first of all spatial, but they appear to have acquired a connotation of value. A thing becomes less valuable, the farther it is from the fiery element.

[4] He has suggested for these the Great Year (18,000 or 10,800 years ?) ; following perhaps the Chaldeans.

[5] The acceptance of successive world-formations and destructions in Heracleitus may be looked upon as assured from the deductions of Zeller, I⁴. 626–640.

orderly change of matter verifies itself in every single
series in nature. How far Heracleitus, however, applied
his view to particular physical objects, we do not know.
In cosmogony, he appears to have been satisfied with bringing the " sea " out of the primitive fire, and then out of the
sea the earth on the one hand, and on the other the warm
air. The only detail authoritatively attested — one that reminds us of Xenophanes — that the sun is a mass of vapor,
taking fire in the morning and becoming extinguished
in the evening, reconciles us to the loss of other theories
of Heracleitus, in case he had any. For Heracleitus was
less a physicist than a metaphysician. He thought out
a single fundamental principle with profound reflection
and vivid imagination. His interest lay in the most
general of principles and in anthropological questions.

It can scarcely be accidental that in the preserved fragments
of Heracleitus there is little peculiarly physical, but much that
is metaphysical and anthropological. If his writing actually
had three λόγοι (Diog. Laert., IX. 5), of which one dealt with
περὶ τοῦ παντός, and both the others were πολιτικός and θεολογικός,
this is proof that we have to do with a philosopher who did
not, as his Milesian predecessors, accord a merely casual
consideration to human life, but made it his prime study.

The conflict of the pure fire and the lower elements into
which everything changes repeats itself in man. The soul
as the living principle is fire, and finds itself a captive in
a body made out of water and earth, which, on account of
its inherent rigidness, is to the soul an abhorrent object.
With this theory Heracleitus united ideas of transmigration, of retribution after death, and the like ; and he, as
Pythagoras, seems to have attached it to certain Mysteries.
In general he took a position in religious matters similar
to that of Pythagoras. Without breaking entirely with
the popular faith, he espoused an interpretation of the
myths that inclined toward monotheism and had an
ethical import.

The vitality of the soul, and consequently its perfection in every respect, depends on its deriving its nourishment from the cosmic fire, the universal reason, the λόγος. The breath is the physical medium of obtaining this nourishment, and cessation of the breath stops activity. A further medium of life, however, is sense perception, which is the absorption of the outer through the inner fire; and this accounts for the depression of soul-activity in sleep. The drier and more fiery, the better and wiser is the soul, and the more does it participate in the universal cosmic reason. Since the cosmic reason is cosmic law, the reasonableness of man consists in his conformity to law, and in his conscious subordination to it. On that account Heracleitus regarded the ethical and political tasks of mankind as expressions of the supremacy of law. His entire aristocratic hate against the democracy, that had attained to power, is revealed in diatribes against the anarchy of the multitudes and their caprice. Only in subordination to order and in the last instance to cosmic law, can man win that serenity which constitutes his happiness. In an apprehension of law, however, and in subordination to the universally valid, Heracleitus found the theoretical goal of mankind. Only the reason and not sense perception guarantees the attainment of this goal, and without the reason eyes and ears are bad witnesses.[1] The great mass

---

[1] The well-known Fragment 11 (Sext. Emp. *Adv. math.*, VII. 126), κακοὶ μάρτυρες ἀνθρώποισιν ὀφθαλμοὶ καὶ ὦτα βαρβάρους ψυχὰς ἐχόντων, is usually interpreted as a disdain of sense knowledge. Schuster (p. 19 f.) has made an attempt (confuted by Zeller, I⁴. 572 f., 656 f.) to stamp Heracleitus as a sensualist on account of his theory of perception. The correct position lies in the mean between these two authorities. Right knowledge indeed arises in sense when the right soul elaborates it. The criterion to which all things are referred is here again conformity to law, which is universally valid and won only through thought. In sleep and through mere individual perception every one has only his own, and therefore a false, world of ideas. The analogy in practical life is

of mankind in this respect are badly off. They do not reflect, but live on as the deluded victims of sense, whose greatest deception consists in its simulation of permanent Being amid the transitoriness of all the phenomena of perception.

Heracleitus of Ephesus, son of Blyson, belonged to the most eminent family of his native city, which traced its origin to Codrus. In this family the dignity of ἄρχων βασιλεύς was inherited, and Heracleitus is said to have surrendered it to his brother. The dates of his birth and death are not exactly known. If he survived the banishment of his friend Hermodorus (compare E. Zeller, *De Herm. Ephesio*, Marburg. 1851), who was forced from the city by the democratic ascendency after the throwing off of Persian domination, his death can scarcely have been before 470. About this time he himself went into retirement to devote himself to science. His birth, since he is said to have lived about sixty years, can be placed between 540–530. With these dates, moreover, the statements of Diogenes Laertius agree, for Diogenes places the ἀκμή of Heracleitus in the sixty-ninth Olympiad. His own writing, in poetically ceremonial prose, supposes that Pythagoras and Xenophanes are already familiar names. It was not probably written until the third decade of the fifth century. His rude partisanship upon the side of the oppressed aristocracy is all that is known of his life, by which is explained his contempt for mankind, his solitariness and bitterness, and his ever emphatic antagonism toward the public and its capricious sentiments.

In the collection and attempt at a systematic ordering of the unfortunately meagre fragments of Heracleitus' book, and in the presentation of his doctrine, the following men have done eminent service: Fr. Schleiermacher (*Her. der Dunkle von Ephesus*, *Ges. Werke III.*, II. 1–146); Jak. Bernays (*Ges. Abh. herausgez. von Usener*, I., 1885, 1–108, and in addition especially the "Letters of Heracleitus," Berlin, 1869); Ferd. Lassalle (*Die Philos. Her. des Dunkeln von Ephesus*, 2 vols., Berlin, 1858); P. Schuster (*Her. v. Ephesus*, Leipzig, 1873, in the *Acta soc. phil.*, Lips. ed., Ritschl, III. 1–394); Teichmüller (*Neue Studien zu Gesch. der Begriffe*, Parts 1 and 2);

shown in Fragment 123, ξυνόν ἐστι πᾶσι τὸ φρονεῖν, ξὺν νόῳ λέγοντας ἰσχυρίζεσθαι χρὴ τῷ ξυνῷ πάντων, ὥσπερ νόμῳ πόλις καὶ πολὺ ἰσχυροτέρως · τρέφονται γὰρ πάντες οἱ ἀνθρώπινοι νόμοι ὑπὸ ἑνὸς τοῦ θείου.

J. Bywater (*Her. reliquiæ*, Oxford), 1877, a collection which includes, to be sure, the counterfeited letters, but those, however, that presumably came from ancient sources; Th. Gomperz (*Zu H.'s Lehre und den Ueberresten seines Werke*, Vienna, 1887); Edm. Pfleiderer, *Die Philos. der Her. v. Eph. im Lichte der Mysterienideen* (Berlin, 1886).

In the theory of Heracleitus, scientific reflection as the sole true method already so far strengthened itself in the abstract development of his concepts that it set itself over against customary opinion and sense appearance with a rugged self-consciousness. To a still higher degree the same attitude appears in the antagonistic theory of the Eleatic School.

19. The scientific founder of the Eleatic school was Parmenides. What had been set forth by Xenophanes in religious assertions about the unity and singleness of the Godhead and its identity with the world, was developed entirely conceptually by Parmenides as a metaphysical theory. That concept, however, which was placed as central and drew all the others entirely into its circle, was Being. The great Eleatic was led up to his theory through reflections of a purely formal logical nature. In a still obscure and undeveloped form the correlation of consciousness and Being hovered before his mind. All thinking is referred to something thought, and therefore has Being for its content. Thinking that refers to Nothing and is therefore contentless, cannot be. Therefore not-Being cannot be thought, and much the less can it be.[1] It is the greatest of all follies to discuss not-Being at all, for we must speak of it as a thought content, that is, as something being, and must contradict ourselves.[2] If all thinking refers, however,

---

[1] Verses 35–40 (Mullach) : οὔτε γὰρ ἂν γνοίης τό γε μὴ ἐόν · οὐ γὰρ ἀνυστόν. οὔτε φράσαις, τὸ γὰρ αὐτὸ νοεῖν ἐστίν τε καὶ εἶναι.

[2] vv. 43–51. Steinhart and Bernays have rightly called attention to the fact that Heracleitus is antagonized here, for he ascribes Being and not-Being alike to the things conceived in the process of Becoming.

to something being, then is Being everywhere the same. For whatsoever also may be thought as in the particular thing, nevertheless the quality of Being (*das Sein*) is in all the same. Being is the last product of an abstraction that has compared the particular thought contents. Being alone remains when all difference has been abstracted from the content determinations of actuality.[1] From this follows the fundamental doctrine of the Eleatics, that only the one abstract Being is.

The philosophy of Parmenides would be complete in this brief sentence ἔστιν εἶναι, if on the one hand there did not follow from this conceptual definition a number of predicates of Being, — predicates primarily negative and susceptible only disjunctively of positive formulation ; and if on the other hand the philosopher did not deviate from the strict logic of his own postulates.

In respect to the first, all time and qualitative distinctions must be denied to Being. Being is unoriginated and imperishable. It was not and will not be, but only is in timeless eternity.[2] For time, wherein perhaps any thing that is, first was and suffered change,[3] is in no wise different from a thing that is. Being is also unchangeable, entirely homogeneous and unitary in quality. It is also not plural, but is the one unique, indivisible,[4] absolute cosmic Being.

Compare Zeller, I[4]. 670. The same dialectic in reference to Being and not-Being is repeated in the dialogue, *The Sophist* (238), in seeking for the possibility of error.

[1] This line of thought is repeated by the Neo-Platonists, by Spinoza *et al.*, and is unavoidable if Being is valid as the criterion of "things being." Compare Kant, *Kr. d. v. Vern.*, Kehrb., 471 f.

[2] v. 59 ff., especially 61 : οὐδέ ποτ᾽ ἦν οὐδ᾽ ἔσται ἐπεὶ νῦν ἐστιν ὁμοῦ πᾶν ἐν ξυνεχές.

[3] v. 96 : οὐδὲ χρόνος ἔστιν ἢ ἔσται ἄλλο παρὲκ τοῦ ἐόντος. This is directed perhaps against the cosmogonies, perhaps against the chronological measure of cosmic development in Heracleitus.

[4] v. 78.

All plurality, all qualitative difference, all origination, all change or destruction are shut out by true Being. In this respect Parmenides has constructed the concept in perfect clearness and sharpness.

But this abstract ontology among the Eleatics nevertheless took another turn through some content definitions obtained from the inner and outer world of experience. This occurred in the two directions resulting from the way in which Parmenides gained the concept of Being from the identity of thinking and the thing thought. That Being, to which thought refers in its naïve conception as if it were its own necessary content, is corporeal actuality. Therefore the Being of Parmenides was identified with the absolutely corporeal. The polemic against the acceptance of not-Being got a new aspect in this way. The ὄν coincides with the πλέον, the μὴ ὄν with the κενόν; and the Eleatics taught that there is no empty space. Therefore Being is indivisible, immovable,[1] and excludes not only qualitative change, but also all change of place. This absolute corporeality is therefore not boundless (ἀτελεύτητον), but is Being[2] that is complete in itself, unchangeably determined, self-bounded, like a perfectly rounded, changeless and homogeneous sphere.[3]

[1] vv. 80, 85; τωὐτόν τ᾽ ἐν τωὐτῷ τε μένον καθ᾽ ἑωυτό τε κεῖται.

[2] v. 88 f. Doubtless Parmenides antagonized the Milesian teaching of the ἄπειρον in all its possible affiliations. But it is utterly unnecessary to think that the opposition of πέρας and ἄπειρον presupposes the number investigations of the Pythagoreans. There is not the slightest trace of this in Parmenides. Inversely it is not impossible that the opposition of the Eleatics against all predecessors made the dual concept so important that the Pythagoreans inserted this among their fundamental antitheses. Doubtless the purely Greek representation influenced Parmenides, in which the measurable and self-determined and never the measureless and undetermined was regarded as perfect. Melissus seems (§ 20) to have neglected this point, and thus to have approached the theory of Anaximander.

[3] v. 102 f.

On the other hand, however, there was again for Parmenides no Being which was not either consciousness or
something thought : ταὐτὸν δ' ἐστὶ νοεῖν τε καὶ οὕνεκέν ἐστι
νόημα (v. 94). As for Xenophanes, so also for Parmenides,
corporeality and thought perfectly coincide in this cosmic
god, this abstract Being : τὸ γὰρ πλέον ἐστὶ νόημα (v. 149).

We can designate, therefore, the Eleatic system neither as
materialistic nor idealistic, because these terms have meaning only when corporeality and thought have been previously
considered as different fundamental forms of actuality. The
Eleatic theory is rather an'ontology which in regard to its content so completely took its stand at the naïve point of view of
the identification of corporeality and thought, as really to exalt
it to the dignity of a principle.

More prominently in the teaching of Parmenides than in
that of Xenophanes does the peculiar result appear : that the
principle, gained by conceptual reflection out of the need
of knowing the real world, proves itself entirely unsuitable
for the purpose. This Eleatic concept of Being could
explain so little of the empirical world that Parmenides
had to deny the existence of that world. All plurality and
diversity, all coming into existence, existing and passing out
of existence, are only illusory appearance, —false names that
mortals have given to true Being.[1] The Eleatic found the
origin of this appearance in sense-perception, of whose illusory [2] character he gave warning. He did not seem, however,
to realize the circle involved in his reasoning. Although
from an entirely opposite principle, he explained in a
sharper epigrammatic way than Heracleitus, how the truth
can be sought only in conceptual thought but never in the

[1] v. 98 f. The conjecture ὄναρ instead of ὄνομ' (v. 98, Gladisch) is
invalidated by, among other things, the circumstance that Sophistry and
Eristic, which were developed from Eleaticism, frequently spoke of the
plurality of names for the one thing that is (§ 28).

[2] v. 54 f.

senses. His ontology is a perfectly conscious rationalism ✓ that shut out all experience and denied all content.

Nevertheless Parmenides believed that he could not do without a physical theory, possibly because he felt the demands of his scientific society in Elea. So the second part [1] of his didactic poem gave a kind of hypothetical and problematical physics which stands out of logical connection with the ontology of the first part. But on the other hand the " Human Opinions " about the many changeable things offered to sensation were not simply reproduced, but were transformed, as they would necessarily have to be, according to his presupposition, if in general plurality motion and change were to be recognized as real. To this belonged first of all the statement that that which is not, is thought [2] as actual side by side that which is; and that out of the reciprocal action of the two are derived multiplicity and the process of individual Becoming. The physical theory of Parmenides was a dualism, a theory of opposites. Although in this respect it reminds us strongly of Heracleitus, the agreement with him is still more apparent in the making whatever really is as the equivalent of the light, and whatever really is not as the equivalent of the darkness.[3] When therefore this pair of opposites was identified with the thin and thick, the light and the heavy, the fire and the earth, the reference was to Anaximander. Yet, on the other hand, there was full recognition of the Heracleitan teaching, which had set fire over against all the other elements as the forming and determining element. If Parmenides did not herein also point out the relation between these two opposites as that of an active

---

[1] v. 18–30; 33–7; 110 f.

[2] On this point later Atomism, which was more logical than even Parmenides himself in physics, regarded not-Being, i. e., empty space, as actual.

[3] v. 122 f.

and a passive principle, nevertheless Aristotle was justified (*Met.*, I. 3, 984 b, 1), inasmuch as for Parmenides the fire, which possesses Being, certainly had the value of an animating, moving principle over against the darkness as a thing not possessing it.

Of the particular theories of Parmenides which have been handed down in a very fragmentary condition, there is not much to remark. With him also the principal stress was laid upon metaphysics. The little information that exists proves that he tried with considerable art to develop the dualism which he derived from his general ontology, and that he even descended to details which he made it his duty [1] to explain in all their bearings. In some particulars he subjoined existing theories to his own without making any actual advance in physics. His astronomical ideas agree so thoroughly with those of the Pythagoreans, with whom he doubtless came in contact, that one must admit the dependence of the Eleatics upon the Pythagoreans in astronomy.[2] As to the origin of man, he held the same view that Anaximander held before him and that Empedocles held after him. Otherwise, excepting some remarks about procreation, etc., only his theory of sensation has come down to us. In this he taught, like Heracleitus, that of the two fundamental elements contained in man, each is susceptible to that which is related to it in the external world. The Warm in a living man senses the fiery connection-in-things (*Lebenszusammenhang*), but even also in the corpse, the cold, stiff body feels what is like it in its surroundings. He expressed the opinion that every man's

---

[1] v. 120 f.

[2] Compare, for details, Zeller, I. 525 f. That Parmenides here showed not the least knowledge of the so-called number-theory, is another proof of the later origin of this philosophical teaching of the Pythagoreans, whose mathematical and astronomical investigations obviously preceded their metaphysical. See § 24.

ideas and intuitions are determined by [1] the mixture of these two elements in him.

There is no ground for doubting the genuineness of the report of Plato [2] that Parmenides in his old age went to Athens, where the young Socrates saw him. The statements of the dialogue *Parmenides*, which presents the fiction [3] of a conversation between Parmenides and Socrates, are not wanting in probability. According to this, Parmenides was born about 515. He came from a distinguished family, and his intercourse with the Pythagoreans is well attested.[4] On the other hand, however, his acquaintance with Xenophanes [5] is also well proved, together with whom he directed the activity of the scientific association in his native city, Elea. Parmenides exercised a decided influence on the political life also of this newly founded city,[6] and is in general represented as a serious, influential, and morally high character.[7] His work was written about 470 or somewhat later. It was in answer to that of Heracleitus, and at the same time it inspired the theories developed somewhat later and almost contemporaneously by Empedocles, Anaxagoras, Leucippus, and Philolaus (Chap. III.). It is in verse, and shows a peculiar amalgamation of abstract thought and plastic poetic fancy. The greater portion of the preserved fragments came from the first and ontological section of the poem, which was perhaps also called περὶ φύσεως. Besides Karsten and Mullach, Am. Peyron (*Parmenidis et Empedoklis fragmenta*, Leipzig, 1810) and Heinr. Stein (*Symb. philologorum Bonnensium in honorem F. Ritschleii*, Leipzig, 1864, p. 763 f.) have collected and discussed the fragments. Compare Vatke, *Parmenidis Veliensis doctrina*, Berlin, 1844 ; A. Bäumker, *Die Einheit des P'schen Seins* (*Jahrb. f. kl. klass. Philol.*, 1886, 541 f.).

20. Whereas Parmenides made a no inconsiderable concession to the customary idea of the plurality and change of things, at least in his construction of an hypothetical

[1] v. 146 f.
[2] *Theœtetus*, 183 e.
[3] *Parmenides*, 127 b ; *Sophist*, 217 c.
[4] Diog. Laert., IX. 25 ; Strabo, 27, 1, 1.
[5] Arist. *Met.*, I. 5, 986 b, 22.
[6] Diog. Laert., IX. 23, according to Speusippus.
[7] Plato, *Theœt*, 183 e: compare *Soph.*, 237 a; *Parm.*, 127 b.

physics his friend and pupil Zeno of Elea proceeded to refute even this customary point of view, and thereby to establish directly the teaching of his master concerning the unity and unchangeableness of Being. The habit of abstract thinking, which was raised to a pre-eminence by Parmenides, manifested itself here in the way in which his pupil turned entirely from the earlier physical tendency of science. Zeno was no longer concerned in apprehending or understanding empirical reality.[1] He was interested only in the conceptual defence of the paradoxes of his teacher. In seeking to discover, therefore, the contradictions which inhere in ordinary opinions regarding the plurality and mutability of things, he employed in a more partisan spirit than Parmenides arguments not based on subject matter or empirical fact, but only those of formal logic.

This appeared primarily in the form of the proof, — first systematically and expertly used, as it seems, by Zeno. By the continuous repetition of contradictory disjunctives, he sought to deny exhaustively all the possibilities of comprehension and defence of the assailed thought, until it was at last brought into obvious contradictions. On account of this keen application of the apparatus of logic, which lets the entire proof seem to be controlled by the law of contradiction, we may suppose that Zeno first had a clear consciousness of formal logical relations. Aristotle even called him the inventor of dialectic.[2]

All the difficulties that Zeno by this method found in the ideas of multiplicity and movement refer to the infinity of space and time, and indeed partly to the infinitely large, partly to the infinitely small. These difficulties simply prove in the last instance the impossibility of thinking exclusively of continuous spatial and temporal quantities

[1] Zeller, II⁴. 538, for unimportant and even trivial notes which seem to controvert this, and for the most part rest upon misconceptions.
[2] Diog. Laert., VIII. 57.

as analyzed into discrete parts, — of thinking of the infinity of the perceptive process. Upon this ground the difficulties of Zeno could find no conclusive solution until the very real and difficult problems resting on them were considered from the point of view of the infinitesimal calculus.

Compare Aristotle, *Physics*, in many places with the comments by Simplicius. Bayle, *Dict. hist. et crit.*, article *Zenon ;* Herbart, *Einleitung in die Philos.*, § 139 ; *Metaph.*, § 284 f. ; Hegel, *Gesch. d. Phil.*, *Complete Works*, Vol. XIII. 312 f. ; Wellmann, *Zenon's Beweise gegen die Bewegung und ihre Widerlegungen*, Frankfort a. O., 1870 ; C. Dunan, *Les arguments de Zénon d'Elée contre le mouvement*, Nantes, 1884.

The proofs advanced by Zeno against the multiplicity of what really is, were two, and they were concerned in part with magnitude, in part with number. As regards magnitude, whatever possesses Being must, if it be many, be on the one hand infinitely small and on the other infinitely great : infinitely small because the aggregation of ever so many parts, of which every one, being indivisible, has no magnitude, can result also in no magnitude ; infinitely great because the juxtaposition of two parts presupposes a boundary between the two, which, as something real, must itself likewise have spatial magnitude, but on this account must again be parted by boundaries from the two minor portions of which the same is true, etc., etc. Again, as regards number, whatever possesses Being must, if it be supposed to be many, be thought as both limited and unlimited. It must be limited because it is just as many as it is, no more nor less. It must be unlimited because two different things possessing Being must be separated by a boundary which as a third must itself be different from these, and must be separated from them both by a fourth and fifth, and so *ad infinitum*." [1]

[1] The second part of the argument is essentially the same in both proofs, and was called by the ancients the argument ἐκ διχοτομίας, in

It is probable, and also chronologically quite possible, that these proofs were even at that time directed against the beginnings of Atomism (§ 23). They are intended to show that the world cannot be thought as an aggregation of atoms. Consistent with this view is the further circumstance that Zeno's polemic was made against the idea of mutability of what possesses Being only in the sense of κίνησις, not in the sense of ἀλλοίωσις (qualitative change). Atomism affirmed κίνησις, and denied qualitative change. There is, in addition, a third argument against the plurality of Being, which Zeno seemed rather to indicate than to develop. This is the so-called Sorites, according to which it is inconceivable how a bushel of corn could make a noise when the single kernels make none. This argument became effective in the polemic against the atomists, who sought to derive qualitative determinations from the joint motion of atoms. Presumably against atomism there was directed another argument of Zeno, which dealt neither with the plurality nor the motion of what possesses Being, but with the reality of empty space, which was the presupposition of movement to the atomists. Zeno showed that if what possesses Being should be thought as in space, this space as an actuality must be thought to be in another space, etc., ad infinitum.

On the other hand, the application which Zeno made of the categories of infinity and finiteness, of the unlimited and limited, appears to suggest a relationship to the Pythagoreans, in whose investigations these ideas played a great rôle. § 19; § 24.

The contradiction involved in the conception of motion Zeno tried to prove in four ways: (1) *By the impossibility of going through a fixed space.* This means that the infinite divisibility of the space to be passed through will not allow the beginning of motion to appear thinkable. (2) *By the impossibility of passing through a space that has movable limits.* This supposes the goal, which is to be reached in any finite time, to be pushed away, though perhaps ever so little. An example of this is Achilles, who cannot catch the tortoise. (3) *By the infinitely small amount of motion at any instant of time,* since the body in motion during any

which dichotomy is used not in the logical but in the original physical sense.

individual instant of time is at some definite point, *i. e.* at rest. He used the resting arrow as an example. (4) *By the relativity of the amount of motion.* A motion of a carriage appears to differ in amount according as it is measured in its process of separation by a stationary carriage or by one in motion in the opposite direction.

Little is known about the life of Zeno. If one holds that the exact chronological reports in the dialogue of Parmenides are fictitious and the statements of the ancients about the ἀκμή are doubtful, nevertheless it is certain Zeno can have been scarcely a generation younger than Parmenides. One will not make a mistake if one places the length of his life at sixty years, between 490 and 430. He was, then, the contemporary of Empedocles, Anaxagoras, Leucippus, and Philolaus, and it is easily possible that he held fast to Parmenides' doctrine of Being in its conceptual abstractness in direct contrast to the remodellings of it by these men. His well-attested ξύγγραμμα was composed in prose, and, to suit his formal schematism, was divided into chapters. In these the single ὑποθέσεις found their *reductio ad absurdum.*[1] If the presentation of these in accordance with their polemic nature had the form of question and answer,[2] then this is probably the beginning of the philosophic dialogue-literature which later developed so richly.[3]

Of lesser significance[4] was Melissus of Samos. Not a native Eleatic, he was also not a complete and consistent supporter of Parmenides's doctrine of Being. He was somewhat the junior of the Eleatic, and lived on into the time of the eclectic tendency in which the opposing theories began to fade out (§ 25). In the main, to be sure, he thoroughly defended the Eleatic fundamental principle, and in a manner obviously antagonistic to Empedocles, Anaxagoras, Leucippus, and in part to the Milesian physics.

---

[1] Plato, *Parm.*, 127 c ff.; Simpl. *Phys.*, 30 v, 139, 5.

[2] Arist. περὶ σοφ. ἐλέγχ., 10, 170 b, 22.

[3] Diog. Laert., III. 48.

[4] Arist. *Met.*, I. 5, 986 b, 27; *Phys.*, I. 3, 186 a, 8. περὶ σοφ. ἐλέγχ. 5, 167 b, 13.

Yet he stood with his doctrine of the infinity of the One in
so striking a contrast to Parmenides, and in such obvious
harmony with Anaximander, that he appears as a real
intermediary between the two.   The form of his arguments
shows the influence of the dialectic schematism of Zeno.
Melissus tried to prove in these that (1) what really is,
is eternal because it can arise out of neither what is nor
what is not; (2) that what really is, is without beginning
and end, temporally and spatially, i. e. infinite (ἄπειρον);
(3) that what really is, is single, since several things that
really are, would limit one another in space and time ; (4)
that what really is, is unchangeable, motionless, and condi-
tionless, because every change involves a kind of origination and ending, and every movement presupposes empty
space which cannot be thought as possessing Being.   It is
thus clear that Aristotle correctly found the conception of
the ἕν in Melissus to be more materialistic than in Parmenides.   What Melissus won by such an approximation to
the Milesian physics, when he still denied every change
to Being, is not clear.   His theory appears, therefore, to be
a compromise without any strong principle.

Melissus, son of Ithagenes, was a navarch, under whom the
Samian fleet conquered the Athenians in 442.   His personal
relation to the Eleatics has not been explained.   His ξύγγραμμα
(περὶ φύσεως or περὶ τοῦ ὄντος, Simplicius and Suidas) was written in prose.   Compare F. Kern, *Zur Würdigung des M.*, (Stettin, 1880) ; A. Pabst, *De M. P. fragmentis* (Bonn, 1889); M.
Offner, *Zur Beurtheilung des M.* (*Arch. f. Gesch. d. Philos.*, IV.
12 f.).

The polemic of Zeno gave clearest expression to the
fundamental principle of the Eleatic philosophy.   He
thought out logically and consistently the conceptually
necessary concept of Being, which in itself alone did not
suffice for the apprehension and explanation of the empirically actual.   The Heracleitan thesis that the essence of

things is to be sought in an orderly process of perpetual change, stood opposed to it. Zeno's argument was purely ontological. It recognized only the one increate and unchangeable Being, and denied the reality of multiplicity and Becoming without also explaining their appearance. The argument of Heracleitus was entirely genetic. It seized upon the process itself and its permanent modes without satisfying the need of connecting this process with an ultimate and continuous actuality. The concept of Being is, however, a necessary postulate of thought, and the process of occurrence is a fact not to be denied. Consequently, from the opposition of these two doctrines, Hellenic philosophy gained a clear view of the task which in an indefinite way underlay the very initial conception of the ἀρχή. This task was from Being to explain the process of phenomenal change.

3. EFFORTS TOWARD RECONCILIATION.

The above problem gave rise to a number of philosophical theories which are best designated as efforts toward reconciliation between the thought *motifs* of the Eleatic and Heracleitan schools. Since all the arguments aim at so modifying the Eleatic idea of Being that from it the orderly process of occurrence in the Heracleitan sense may seem conceivable, they are at once of a metaphysical and physical character.

Two ways were open for the solution of this problem: one led from Parmenides, the other from Heracleitus. The inadequacy of the Eleatic concept of Being to explain empirical plurality and change was due essentially to its qualities of singleness and spatial immobility. If these characteristics, however, were given up, those of non-Becoming, indestructibility, and qualitative permanence could be more strongly maintained in order to explain pro-

cess and change by means of a plurality of objects possessing Being (*Seienden*), with the help of spatial motion.
The theories of Empedocles, Anaxagoras, and the Atomists
moved in this direction. Common to them all was the
pluralism of substances, and the mechanistic method of
explanation, in virtue of which origin, change, and destruction were supposed to be derived merely from the motions
of these substances unchangeable in themselves. These
theories were in extreme antithesis to the hylozoistic
monism of the Milesians in particular. On the other
hand, these three systems were distinguishable from one
another partly as to the number and quality of the substances that each assumed to exist, partly as to the relationships of substances to motion and moving force. The
insufficiency of the Heracleitan theory consisted, however,
not in establishing the concept of the rhythm of the process of occurrence, but in retaining nothing else of what
really is, as entering into these changes. Heracleitus had
recognized no one of the empirical materials, and no
abstract noumenon, and consequently nothing as Being.
If now Parmenides showed that thinking undeniably presupposes something that really is, one would be forced to
try to vindicate the character of Being for the relations
and connections which Heracleitus had retained as the
sole permanence. This the Pythagoreans attempted to do
with their peculiar number theory.

These four efforts toward reconciliation sprang accordingly
simultaneously out of one and the same need. Their representatives were nearly contemporaneous. From this fact are
explained not only a number of the similarities and affinities in
their doctrines, but also the circumstance that they frequently,
particularly in polemics, seem to have referred directly to one
another. This is at the same time a proof of the lively scientific interest and interchange of ideas in the middle of the fifth
century through the entire circle of Greek civilization.

The " efforts toward a reconciliation " used as a basis for
associating these philosophers here is fairly generally recognized

for the first three, although on the one hand Anaxagoras is usually set apart by himself (Hegel, Zeller, Ueberweg), because we have overestimated his doctrine of the νοῦς. On the other hand, Atomism (Schleiermacher, Ritter) has naturally been classified with Sophistry. Compare, respectively, § 22 and § 23. Yet, from the time of the Pythagoreans until now, Strümpell alone has preceded me in this proposed view. Brandis treats indeed the Pythagoreans for the first time before the Sophists, but as a tendency independent of the others.

21. The first and most imperfect of these attempts at reconciliation was that of Empedocles. He proceeded expressly from the thesis of Parmenides that there can be no origination and destruction as such. In his effort to explain apparent origination and destruction, he said that every origination should be regarded as a combination, and every destruction a separation of the original elements.[1] He called the original materials the ῥιζώματα πάντων, and he does not seem to have employed the later customary expression, στοιχεῖα. The predicates of " unoriginated," " imperishable," " unchangeable," belong to the elements. They are eternal Being; and the manifold and change of single things are supposed to be explained by spatial motion, by virtue of which they are mixed in differing relations to one another.

Accordingly, Empedocles should apparently be accredited with the priority of forming *this conception of the element* that has been so powerful in the development of our science of nature. It is the conception of a material, homogeneous in content, qualitatively unchangeable, and liable to changing states of motion and to mechanical division. He got this conception, nevertheless, in the attempt to make the concept of Being of Parmenides useful in the explanation of nature. Much less happy, although historically

---

[1] Plutarch, *Plac.*, I. 30 (*Dox.*, 326) φύσις οὐδενός ἐστιν ἁπάντων θνητῶν οὐδέ τις οὐλομένου θανάτοιο τελευτή, ἀλλὰ μόνον μῖξίς τε διάλλαξίς τε μιγέντων ἐστί, φύσις δ'ἐπὶ τοῖς ὀνομάζεται ἀνθρώποισιν.

quite as effective, was the point of view which Empedocles
formed of the number and essence of these elements.   He
adduced the well-known four: earth, air, fire, and water.

The choice of four fundamental elements was the result
of no systematic conception on the part of Empedocles, in the
way that Aristotle, by whom this theory was established and
made the common property of all literature, later made them a
fundamental part of his system. As it appears, it was the result
of an impartial consideration of the previous philosophic theories
of nature : water, air, fire are to be found as elements among
the Ionians; and earth in the hypothetical physics of the Eleatics.   That Empedocles [1] placed fire over against the three other
elements, and thus returned to the two divisions of Heracleitus
(§ 19), reminds us of this latter.   Nevertheless the number
of elements as four has in it something arbitrary and immature,
as likewise appears from the superficial characterization that
Empedocles gave to each singly.[2]

Empedocles to all appearances was not able to say how
the different qualities of particular things were derived
from their combining.   Quantitative relationships and
states of aggregation might appear to be thus derived,
but not particular qualities.   Consequently Empedocles
seems to have had only the former in mind when he so
described the process of combination and separation, that
therein the protruding parts of one body were supposed to
press into the pores, i. e. into the interstices,[3] of another body.
Empedocles seems to be referring to the former also in
his defining the relationship and the strength of the reciprocal attraction of empirical things by the stereometrical
similarity between the emanations of one substance and
the pores of another.   As to the qualitative difference

---

[1] Arist. *Met.*, I. 4, 985 a, 32 ; *De gen. et corr.*, II. 3, 330 b, 19.

[2] Zeller, I[4]. 690.

[3] That this acceptation presupposed a discontinuity of the original
matter, and hardly was to be thought without the presupposition of empty
space, which he with the Eleatics denied (fr. v. 91, Arist. *De cœlo*, IV.
2, 309 a, 19), appears to have furnished no difficulty to Empedocles.

between individual things, he taught only in very general terms that this difference depends on the different masses in which all or only some of the elements exist in combination.

But the more that Empedocles claimed the character of the Parmenidean Being for his four elements, the less could he find in them an explanation of the motion in which they must exist according to his theory of union and separation. As pure changeless Being, *the elements could not move themselves, but only be moved.* To explain the world, the theory needed further, then, beside the four elements, a cause of motion or a *moving force.* Here, in the statement of this problem, appears first completely Empedocles's opposition to the hylozoism of the Milesians. He was the first in whose theory *force and matter* are differentiated as separate cosmic powers. Under the influence of Parmenides he had accordingly so conceived the world-stuff that the ground of motion could not be found in it itself. So, in order to explain the cosmic process, he had to find a force different from the stuff and moving it. Although Empedocles introduced this dualism into the scientific thought of the Greeks, it appeared not in sharp conceptual, but in mythical-poetic form; for he designated the two cosmic forces which caused the combination and separation of the primitive substances, as Love and Hate.

The personification, which Empedocles moreover, as likewise Parmenides in his didactic poem, extended to the elements, was mythical and poetic; so also the representation inadequate because stated in terms of sense and not developed to conceptual clearness, was of the same character. Indeed, it is not certain from the passages in which his principles (ἀρχαί) were enumerated as six in all, whether or not he thought of the two forces incidentally as bodies (Arist. *De gen. et corr.*, I. 1, 314 a, 16; Simpl. *Phys.* 6 v, 25, 21), which as such were mingled with the other substances. Obviously he formed no sharp idea of the nature of the actuality and the efficiency that belong to Love and Hate. There is the additional

fact that the duality of forces not only was called forth by the
theoretic need of representing the different causes in the opposed
processes of cosmic union and separation; but it was also
occasioned by considerations of worth, in which Love is the
cause of Goodness and Hate of Evil (compare Aristotle, *Met.*, I.
4, 984 b, 32). The view of Aristotle is supported by the predicates which Empedocles (fragment v. 106 f.) attributes to
φιλότης and νεῖκος.

From these presuppositions Empedocles derived an explanation of the cosmic process, not indeed conceiving each
individual occurrence as ever and always arising from a
universal law of combination and separation, but yet satisfying the demands of the Heracleitan philosophy by the
assumption of a perpetual cyclic process of development.
He taught, namely, that the four elements, that he assumed
as alike in their mass, change out of a state of perfect
mingling and equality, separate by the action of the νεῖκος,
and become completely sundered; that then from this state
of separation they pass back through the influence of the
φιλότης to their original absolute intermixture. There results from this a cycle of four continuously dissolving cosmic
states : (1) that of the unlimited supremacy of Love and
of the perfect unification of all the elements, which is called
by Empedocles σφαῖρος and also designated as τὸ ἔν or θεός ;
(2) that of the process of successive separation through
the constantly growing preponderance of νεῖκος; (3) that
of the absolute separation of the four elements through the
sole supremacy of Hate ; (4) that of the process of successive recombination through the increased predominance of
φιλότης.

Compare Arist. *Phys.*, VIII. 1, 250 b, 26.
It is clear that a world of individual things can appear only
in the second and fourth stages of the cosmic process, and that
such a world is characterized every time by the opposition and
conflict between the combining and separating principles.
Here is the place of the Heracleitan fundamental principle in
the Empedoclean conception of the cosmos. On the other

hand, it can be said that the two parts of the Parmenidean
didactic poem appear no longer in the opposition of Being and
Appearance, but in the relationship of changing cosmic states.
The first and third phases are acosmic in the Eleatic sense ; the
second and fourth are, on the contrary, full of the Heracleitan
πόλεμος.

All that we have of the particulars of the theory of Empedocles seems to teach that he regarded the present state of
the world as the fourth phase, in which the elements that
have been separated by Hate are reuniting through Love
into the Sphairos. At least in reference to the formation
of the world he taught that the separated elements have
been brought through Love into the whirling motion that
is in the process of uniting them. Originally the air en-
compassed the whole like a sphere, and by virtue of this
motion fire broke out from below. The air was pressed
below and into the middle, was mixed with the water into
mud, and then formed into the earth. The two hemi-
spheres originated in this way : one was light and fiery ;
the other dark, airy, and interspersed with masses of fire,
which on account of the rushing of the air in rotatory
motion around the earth created day and night.

In particular, Empedocles showed — not without dependence
on the Pythagoreans — highly developed astronomical ideas
concerning the illumination of the moon from the sun, concerning eclipses, the inclination of the ecliptic, etc., and also many
interesting meteorological hypotheses.

Empedocles had an especial interest in the organic
world. He regarded plants as primary organisms and as
having souls like animals. He compared in isolated
remarks the formation of fruit with the procreation of
animals, their leaves with hair, feathers, and scales ; and so
one finds in him the beginnings of a comparative morphology. Also numerous physiological observations of his
are preserved. But especially are there biological reflec-

tions, in which he in some measure in the spirit of the
present theory of adaptation explained, although with fanci-
ful naïveté, the existence of the present vital organisms
by the survival of purposeful forms from things that on
the whole were aimlessly created.[1]

Empedocles did not except man[2] from this purely mechanical origination, and ho constructed a large number of
interesting single hypotheses in respect to his physiological
functions.   The blood plays an important rôle in this
theory.   It was to him the real carrier of life, and in it he
believed he could see the most perfect combination of the
four elements.   It is of especial interest that he conceived
the process of perception and sensation as analogous to his
universal theory of the interaction of elements.   He explained this process as contact of the small parts of the
perceived things with the similar parts of the perceiving
organs, wherein the former were supposed to press upon
the latter, as in hearing; or the latter upon the former, as
in sight.   Since then, in general, such interaction was to
his mind the more close, the more nearly similar were the
emanations and pores, he established the principle, therefore, that all external things are known by that in us
which is similar to them.   Herein was involved to some
degree the idea that man is a microcosm, the finest admix-
ture of all the elements.

Hence it followed for Empedocles that all perceptual
knowledge depends upon the combination of elements in
the body and especially in the blood, and that the spiritual
nature depends on the physical nature.   Just on this

---

[1] Aristotle has brought this thought into abstract expression, and it
contains the whole modern development theory *in nuce*. *Phys.*, II. 8,
198 b, 29; ὅπου μὲν οὖν ἅπαντα συνέβη ὥσπερ κἂν εἰ ἕνεκά του ἐγένετο,
ταῦτα μὲν ἐσώθη, ἀπὸ τοῦ αὐτομάτου συστάντα ἐπιτηδείως, ὅσα δὲ μὴ οὕτως,
ἀπώλετο καὶ ἀπόλλυται καθάπερ Ἐμπεδοκλῆς λέγει, etc.

[2] He appears to have made good use of the tales about the centaurs.

account, moreover he could deplore incidentally, as Xenophanes deplored, the limitation of human knowledge ; and
could assert, on the other hand, with Heracleitus and Parmenides, that true knowledge does not grow out of sense
perception, but only out of reflection ($\nu o \epsilon \hat{\iota} \nu$) and reason
($\nu o \hat{\upsilon} \varsigma$).[1]

Empedocles of Agrigentum, the first Dorian in the history of
philosophy, lived probably from 490–430. He came from a
rich and respectable family which had been partisans for the
democracy in the municipal struggles. Like his father, Meton,
Empedocles distinguished himself as a citizen and statesman,
but later he fell into the disfavor of the other citizens. In his
vocation of physician and priest, and with the paraphernalia of
a magician,[2] he then travelled about through Sicily and Magna
Græcia. Many stories circulated into later time concerning his
death, like that well-known one of his leap into Ætna. In this
religious rôle he taught the doctrine of transmigration and of an
apparently purer intuition of God, like that of the Apollo cult.
These teachings, which were not consistent in content with his
metaphysico-physical theories, show, however, much the greater
similarity to the teaching of Pythagoras (§ 12). Pythagoreanism he certainly knew, and indeed his entire career suggests a
copy of that of Pythagoras. When we consider his political
affiliations, it is improbable that he had any close connection
with the Pythagorean society. Empedocles stood comparatively
isolated, — save his acquaintance with the teachings of Heracleitus and Parmenides, the latter of whom he presumably
knew personally. Nevertheless he seems to have been affiliated with a yet larger body in that he is characterized as one
of the first representatives of rhetoric.[3] He had even connections with the so-called Sicilian school of rhetoric (or oratory), in which are preserved the names of Tisias and Korax as
well as that of Gorgias, whom they antedate.[4] Only $\pi \epsilon \rho \grave{\iota} \ \phi \acute{\upsilon} \sigma \epsilon \omega \varsigma$
and $\kappa \alpha \theta \alpha \rho \mu o \acute{\iota}$ are the writings of Empedocles that can be
authenticated. The preserved small fragments are especially
collated by Sturz (Leipzig, 1805), Karsten (Amsterdam, 1838),
and Stein (Bonn, 1852). Compare Bergk, *De prooemio*, E. Berl.,

---

[1] Fr. v. 24 ; 81.

[2] Thus he pictured himself in the beginning of the Songs of Purification ($\kappa \alpha \theta \alpha \rho \mu o \acute{\iota}$).

[3] Diog. Laert., VIII. 57 ; Sext. Emp. *Adv. math.*, VII. 6.

[4] See below, § 26.

1839 ; Panzerbieter, *Beiträge zur Kritik und Erläuterung des E.*
(Meiningen, 1844) ; Schläger, *E. quatenus Heraclitum secutus
sit* (Eisenach, 1878). — O. Kern, *E. und d. Orphiker* (*Arch. f.
Gesch. d. Ph.,* I. 498 f.).

22. " Older in years, younger in works than Empedocles," [1] Anaxagoras brought the movement of thought,
which had been begun by Empedocles, to an end in one
direction.   He, like Empedocles, was convinced that we do
not use language correctly when we speak of origination
and destruction, since the mass of the world must remain
unchangeably the same.[2]   On this account apparent origination and destruction are better designated as combina-
tion and separation ($\sigma\acute{v}\gamma\kappa\rho\iota\sigma\iota\varsigma$ *sive* $\sigma\acute{v}\mu\mu\iota\xi\iota\varsigma$).   Whatever
enters into combination or whatever suffers separation was
to him, also, a plurality of original substances which he
called $\chi\rho\acute{\eta}\mu\alpha\tau\alpha$ or $\sigma\pi\acute{\epsilon}\rho\mu\alpha\tau\alpha$.   Thus far he agreed with his
predecessor.   But he took decided exception to the arbi-
trary assumption of Empedocles that there are only four
elements, since it is impossible to explain the qualitative distinctions of empirical things by the union of these
four elements.   Since the Parmenidean idea of Being
excludes the new creation and destruction of qualitative
determinations, and demands qualitative unchangeableness for the totality of primitive materials, Anaxago-
ras argued that there are as many qualitative $\chi\rho\acute{\eta}\mu\alpha\tau\alpha$,
different from one another, as there are qualitative deter-
minations in empirical things.   The things of which we
are sensible are composite, and they are named according to
the primitive material that prevails in them at any par-
ticular instant.[3]   Their qualitative change ($\dot{\alpha}\lambda\lambda o\acute{\iota}\omega\sigma\iota\varsigma$)
consists in the fact that other primitive materials enter
into the combination or some are excluded from it.

[1] Arist. *Met.,* I. 3, 984 a, 11.
[2] Fr. 14.
[3] Arist. *Phys.,* I⁴. 187 b.

The χρήματα must, according to this, be thought as divisible ;[1] and in antithesis to the perceived things, which consist of heterogeneous components, we must designate as χρήματα all those substances which fall into homogeneous parts, however far they be divided.   Therefore Aristotle designated the σπέρματα of Anaxagoras as ὁμοιομερῆ, and in later literature they go under the name of homoiomeriai. Consequently, what Anaxagoras had here in mind was nothing other than the chemist's idea of the element. The utter inadequacy of data on which Anaxagoras could depend appears in the development of his theory.   For since observation had as yet not been directed to chemical, but only to mechanical analysis, the constituents of animals, such as bones, flesh, and marrow, as well as metals, were enumerated as elements.   Further, because the philosopher possessed no means of fixing upon a determined number of elements, he declared them to be numberless and differing in form (ἰδέα), color, and taste.

When Aristotle in several places (see Zeller, I[4]. 875 f.) cites only organic substances in Anaxagoras as examples of the elements, he is speaking more out of his preference for this field than of an inclination on the part of Anaxagoras to refer inorganic matter to the organic. There is not the slightest trace to be discovered in Anaxagoras' cosmogony of a qualitative distinction between the organic and the inorganic. In particular, what we may call his teleology is not by any means confined to the organic.

As regards the motion of these substances, Anaxagoras also separated the principle of Being from that of Becoming, but in an entirely different way from what we find in Empedocles. The poetical and mythical form of this thought he stripped off ; but at the same time, instead

[1] In remarkable dependence on Parmenides, Anaxagoras nevertheless makes a polemic, like Empedocles, against the acceptance of empty space (Arist. *Phys.*, IV., 6, 213 a, 22), and at the same time also against the finite divisibility of matter postulated in the concept of atoms.

of reflecting like Heracleitus upon the antagonistic processes of motion, he emphasized again the unity of the cosmic process. Since Anaxagoras, as is the case with all naïve conception, could think of the actual only as material stuff, he had to seek among the numberless χρήματα for one which is the common cause of motion for all the others. This primitive dynamic material or motion-stuff was conceived by him as having life within itself, after the analogy of the Ionian cosmic matter. It moves the others from within itself.[1] Its nature, however, was inferred by Anaxagoras from the character of the world of perception that it brought into being. This world presents itself as an ordered, purposeful whole, and the forming force must also be orderly and purposeful. Therefore after an analogy[2] to the principle actively working in living beings, Anaxagoras called it the νοῦς, the reason, or, as it may best be translated, the *thought-stuff* (*Denkstoff*). Far from being an immaterial principle, the "spirit" is to Anaxagoras corporeal matter, but indeed in a state of exceeding refinement. It is the "lightest," the most mobile, the only matter that moves itself. It represents the λόγος, both in the macrocosm and in the microcosm. As regards the form and movement of the cosmic process, it has all the functions of the Heracleitan fire.

The order (κόσμος) and purposefulness of the empirical world, on which Anaxagoras depended in his assertion of the νοῦς διακοσμῶν τὰ πάντα, was not noted by him so much in single terrestrial things as in the great relationships of the universe, in

---

[1] Aristotle in *Physics*, VIII. 5, 256 b, 24, proved only that Anaxagoras has called the νοῦς the ἀπαθής and ἀμιγής. The predicate ἀκίνητος is only an inference of Aristotle. The mobility of the νοῦς and its implications in single things is clearly set forth in passages like Stob. *Ecl.*, I. 790 (*Dox.*, 392), and Simpl. *Phys.*, 35 *recto*, 164, 23.

[2] Arist. *Met.*, I. 3, 984 b, 15, καθάπερ ἐν τοῖς ζώοις.

the regular revolutions of the heavenly bodies.[1] His monism and the teleological method of his presentation rested on astronomical considerations. Compare W. Dilthey, *Einleitung in d. Geisteswissenschaften*, V. 201 f. He sought in a purely naturalistic way a physical explanation, and was not in the smallest degree concerned with religious matters. If he, as is very doubtful, called [2] the νοῦς God, yet this would only have been a metaphysical expression, as it had been among the Milesians. The doctrine of the νοῦς was taken by Aristotle very much in the sense of an immaterial spirituality, when in the well-known passage (*Met.*, I. 3, 984 b, 17) Aristotle placed the doctrine of Anaxagoras as that of the only sober philosopher among them all. In the Hegelian interpretation, which even to-day is not outgrown, Anaxagoras is placed at the close of the pre-Sophistic development on account of his alleged discovery of the " Spirit." It sounds so fine when in this philosophy of nature the world principle becomes ever more " spiritual " in passing from water through air and fire until finally the " pure Spirit " has been as it were distilled from matter. But this " Spirit " is likewise only living corporeality, i. e., that which moves itself. Anaxagoras with his νοῦς is scarcely a step nearer the immaterial than Anaximenes with air, or Heracleitus with fire. On the other hand, we must not fail to recognize that in this characterization of the moving principle Anaxagoras, in a still more emphatic manner than Empedocles, had taken up the factor of a judgment of value into his theoretic explanation. Admiration of the beauty and harmony of the world dictated to him the acceptance of a thought-stuff arranging the universe according to a principle of order.

This νοῦς, therefore, stands over against the other elements. It alone is in itself pure and unmixed. It is simple, and possesses through its " knowledge " a power over all other material stuff.[3] It plays somehow as a stimulus upon the other substances, which are mixed by it. It participates temporarily to a greater or less degree in the particular things thus originating. For, like all matter, it

---

[1] Simpl. 33 *verso*, 156, 13 ; πάντα διεκόσμησε νόος καὶ τὴν περιχώρησιν ταύτην, ἣν νῦν περιχωρεῖ τά τε ἄστρα, καὶ ὁ ἥλιος καὶ ἡ σελήνη καὶ ὁ ἀὴρ καὶ ὁ αἰθὴρ οἱ ἀποκρινόμενοι.

[2] Cicero, *Acad.* II. 37, 118 ; Sext. Emp. *Adv. math.*, IX. 6.

[3] Fr. 7 and 8.

also is quantitatively divisible and qualitatively unchangeable. Remaining essentially identical with itself, it is distributed in different proportions in single things.[1]

Anaxagoras used this thought-stuff only to explain on the one hand the beginnings of motion, and on the other such single processes which he could not derive from the mechanism of the once for all awakened cosmic motion. What these processes in particular are, we cannot[2] ascertain from the reproaches made against Anaxagoras.[3] So far as our knowledge goes, the application that Anaxagoras has made of his νοῦς theory to explain the cosmic process is limited simply to this, — that he ascribed to the " ordering " thought-stuff the beginning of motion, and that he then conceived the motion to go on mechanically by impact and pressure between the other primitive materials in a manner planned by the νοῦς. Connected with this is the fact that Anaxagoras denied a plurality both of coexisting and successive worlds, and that he aimed to describe only the origin of our present world. Consequently in distinction from his predecessors he spoke therefore of a temporal beginning of the world.

Preceding this beginning is a state of the most perfect mingling of all substances, reminding us of the Sphairos of Empedocles. In this mingling all χρήματα, with the exception of the νοῦς, are so minutely distributed that the whole possesses no particular character.

This idea reminds us on the one hand of Chaos, on the other of the ἄπειρον of Anaximander. In his delineation of this idea, we have the fact that he taught that the mixtures of differing χρήματα let only those qualities come into perception in

[1] How misjudged the meaning is, is clear, for Anaxagoras conceived his νοῦς as a divine being.

[2] It is highly improbable, according to Theoph. *Hist. plant.*, III. 1, 4, that it concerns the genesis of the organism.

[3] Plato, *Phædo*, 97 b; Arist. *Met.*, I. 4, 985 a, 18.

which the components are all harmonized. He also in this way conceived the four elements of Empedocles as such mixtures of primitive matter.[1] Absolute mixture has no quality; ὁμοῦ πάντα χρήματα ἦν is the beginning of the writing of Anaxagoras.

In this Chaos the primitive thought-material first created at one point [2] a rotatory motion of great velocity. This, being extended in broadening circles, led to the formation of the orderly world, and is further being continued on account of the infinity of matter. By this rotation two great masses are first differentiated which were characterized by the opposition of Bright, Warm, Pure-light, and Dry, as against Dark, Cold, Dense-heavy, and Moist, and are designated by Anaxagoras as αἰθήρ and ἀήρ.[3] The latter is pressed into the centre, and condensed into water, earth, and stones. His ideas of the earth show him to have been essentially influenced by the Ionians. He regarded the stars as dissipated fragments of earth and stone that have become glowing in the fiery circle. He saw in the great meteor of Aegospotamoi a confirmation of this theory and at the same time a proof of the substantial homogeneity of the world. Anaxagoras's astronomical view shows highly developed, many-sided ideas and inferences, which rest in part upon his own studies. He explained eclipses correctly ; and while he allowed to the sun and moon altogether too small dimensions, they were nevertheless very great compared to their perceptual size.

Accordingly Anaxagoras was convinced that, as in Chaos, so in all individual things developed from it, the combina-

---

[1] Arist. De gen. et corr , I. 1, 314 a, 24 ; Zeller, I⁴. 876.

[2] Presumably Anaxagoras assumed this point to be the pole star: see H. Martin, Mémoires de l'Institut, 29, 176 f. ; see Dilthey, op. cit.

[3] These antitheses remind us more of the Ionians than of Parmenides. In respect to the manifold of the mixture and the determination of the qualities, they stand in Anaxagoras obviously between the μῖγμα and the Empedoclean elements.

tion of the cosmic elements is so fine and intimate that something at least of each one is everywhere. Thus the organic σπέρματα develop as plants and animals on the separation of the water and earth, which separation was caused by the heavenly fire. But the νοῦς, as the vitalizing principle, stands in intimate relations with these, and its independent power of motion was doubtless introduced here by Anaxagoras as the cause of functions that are not mechanically explicable.[1] He, too, seems to have given especial attention to sense perception, which, however, he derived, in entire opposition to Empedocles, from the reciprocal action of opposites influenced by the feeling of aversion. Accordingly perceptual knowledge acquired in this way is only relative.[2] In contrast to it, the truth is found solely through the λόγος, through the participation of the individual in the world reason.

Anaxagoras originated in Clazomenæ in the circle of Ionian culture, from which apparently he got his rich scientific knowledge and his pronounced positive and physical interest. His birth is (Zeller, I[4]. 865 f., against Hermann) to be placed at about 500. We do not know about his education, particularly how he could have been so powerfully influenced by the Eleatics. He was of wealthy antecedents, and was regarded as an honorable gentleman, who, far away from all practical and political interests, "declared the heaven to be his fatherland, and the study of the heavenly bodies his life's task," — a statement in which, side by side with the presentation of a purely theoretical ideal of life, is to be noted the astronomical tendency which also characterized his philosophy. About the middle of the century Anaxagoras, then the first among philosophers of renown, removed to Athens, where he formed a centre of scientific activity, and appears to have drawn about him the most notable men. He was the friend of Pericles, and became in-

[1] To this the objection of Aristotle applies, that Anaxagoras did not distinguish the principle of thought (νοῦς) from the animating (beseelenden) principle (ψυχή). (De an., I 2, 404 b.) This objection certainly did not arise from immanent criticism.

[2] Arist. Met., IV. 5, 1009 b, 25; Sext. Emp., VII. 91.

volved under the charge of impiety in the political suit brought against Pericles in 434. He was obliged in consequence of this to leave Athens and go to Lampsacus. Here he founded a scientific association, and while high in honor he died a few years later (about 428). The fragments of the only writing preserved of his (as it appears) περὶ φύσεως (in prose) have been collected by Schaubach (Leipzig, 1827) and Schorn (with those of Diogenes of Apollonia, Bonn, 1829); Panzerbieter, *De fragmentorum Anax. ordine* (Meiningen, 1836); Breier, *Die Philosophie des An. nach Aristotles* (Berlin, 1840); Zévort, *Dissert. de la vie et la doctrine d'A.* (Paris, 1843); Alexi, *A. u. seine Philosophie* (Neu-Ruppin, 1867); M. Heinze, *Ueber den* νοῦς *des A.* (*Berichte d. Sächs. Ges. d. W.,* 1890).

Archelaus is called a pupil of Anaxagoras, but appears, nevertheless, to be so much influenced also by other theories that he will be mentioned in a later place. The allegorical interpretation of the Homeric poem, which in part is ascribed to Anaxagoras himself (Diog. Laert., II. 11), in part to his pupil, Metrodorus, has only the slightest relation to his philosophy.

23. The philosopher who desired to abandon the arbitrary theory of the four elements of Empedocles, was obliged, in order to oppose to it a consistent theory, to assert either that the qualitative determinations of things are all primary, or that no one of them is. The first way Anaxagoras chose; the Atomists the second. While in their explanation of empirical occurrence they also postulated a plurality of unchangeable things having Being, they had the boldness to deduce all qualitative distinctions of the phenomenal world from purely quantitative differentiations of the true essence of things. This is their especial significance in the history of European science.

It has been customary in the history of philosophy to treat the theory of the Atomists in inseparable connection with the pre-Sophistic systems. This is explained from the fact that all direct knowledge fails concerning the founder of this theory, Leucippus and his doctrine, and that the teaching of the Atomists lies before us relatively complete only in the form that Democritus developed it. But between Leucippus and Democritus is an interval of certainly forty years, and this lies in that epoch of most strenuous mental labor, — which epoch witnessed in Greece the beginnings of Sophism. Leucippus is the contemporary of Zeno, Empedocles, and Anaxagoras, but Democritus is the contemporary of Socrates, and, in the works of his old age, of Plato. It is also consonant with this difference of years that the fundamental thought of the Atomists in the form of the metaphysical postulate of Leucippus arose from the Heracleitan-Parmenidean problems; but also that the development of that postulate, which Democritus gave to these problems, was for the first time possible upon the Sophistic theories as a basis, especially those of Protagoras (§ 32). To these changed temporal conditions there is the further correspondence in the fact that those theories of the Atomists, which we can refer to Leucippus, remained entirely in the compass of the problems confronting his contemporaries, Empedocles and Anaxagoras. On the other hand, the theory of Democritus gives the impression of being a comprehensive system, like that of Plato. Therefore the reasons from the point of chronology and from that of the subject matter require the beginnings of Atomism in Leucippus to be separated from the system of Democritus, which was conditioned by the subjective turn given to Greek thought. We must make this discrimination, however difficult it may be in details. Accordingly in this place is to be developed only the general metaphysical basis of Atomism, which has grown out of Eleaticism.[1]

It was therefore on the one hand a complete misconception of the primal motives, but on the other a legitimate feeling — although defended entirely falsely in connection with preconceived notions — with which Schleiermacher (*Gesch. d. Philos.*, Complete Works, III. 4 a, 73) and Ritter after him (*Gesch. d. Philos.*, I. 589 f.) sought to classify the Atomists with the Sophists. In Leucippus Atomism arose as an offshoot of Eleaticism. The theory of Democritus, however, far from being itself Sophistic, presupposed the theory of Protagoras. The suggestion of this relation may be found in Dilthey, *Einleitung in die Geisteswissenschaften*, I. 200.

Leucippus, the first representative of this theory, stands in the most marked dependence on the Eleatic teaching. To his mind also, Being excluded not only all origination and destruction, but all qualitative change. Likewise Being coincides with the corporeal, that is, the ὄν with the

---

[1] As to the perfect certainty of ascribing this to Leucippus, see Zeller, I⁴. 843, n. 1.

πλέον. By virtue of this coincidence Parmenides had felt compelled to deny the reality of empty space, and therefore also that of plurality and motion. Should now, however, as the interest of physics demanded, plurality and motion be recognized as real, and a scientific apprehension of the actual again be rendered possible, then the simplest and most logical method was to declare [1] that "Non-Being," the Void (τὸ κένον), did nevertheless exist. The aim of this assumption, however, is simply this: to make possible plurality and mobility for that which really is. Thereby it becomes possible to create a world of experience from the "Void" and the multiform "Full" moving in the "Void," to construct that world from that which has no Being and from a multiplicity of those things that have Being. A categorical physics thus appears in place of the hypothetical physics of Parmenides, and in place of a problematical appears an assertorical and an apodeictic physics.

But while Leucippus departed from the Parmenidean concept of Being only so far as seemed absolutely necessary to explain plurality and motion, he still clung not only to the characteristic of unchangeableness (un-Becoming and indestructibility), but also to the thoroughgoing qualitative homogeneity of what possess Being. In opposition to Empedocles and Anaxagoras, Leucippus therefore taught that all these varieties of what possess Being are homogeneous in quality. He agreed entirely with Parmenides that this quality is abstract corporeality (τὸ πλέον) devoid of all specific qualities. According to the Eleatics, all distinctions are due only to the permeation of that which really is not, by that which really is. So, on the one hand, to Leucippus distinctions between individuals

---

[1] Democritus seems to be the first to have made the pointed remark: μὴ μᾶλλον τὸ δέν ἢ τὸ μηδὲν εἶναι, "*das Ichts sei um nichts mehr real als das Nichts.*" Plut. *Adv. col.* 4, 2 (1109).

that really possess Being exist only in those qualities due
to their limitation through that which really is not; viz.,
empty space.   These are the distinctions of form and
motion.   On the other hand, each of the changeless substances possessing Being must be thought as a corporeality,
homogeneous in itself, a continuum and therefore indivisible.   Being, which is moved in empty space, therefore consists of innumerable, exceedingly small bodies.   Leucippus
called these Atoms (ἄτομοι), every one of which is, like
the Being of Parmenides, unoriginated, indestructible, unchangeable, indivisible, and homogeneous in itself and with
all other Being.   The single cosmic-Being of Parmenides
was broken up into an infinite number of small primitive
elements which, were they not separated by empty space,
would constitute a single element in the sense of Empedocles, and indeed would be the absolute qualitativeless ἕν
of Parmenides.

Of all the transformations of the Eleatic teaching, that of
Leucippus is characterized by a striking simplicity, and by keen
logical limitation to that which is indispensable to a professed
explanation of the phenomenal world.   At the same time it is
clear that the Atomism which became later so important in the
development of scientific theories did not grow out of experience, or observations and the conclusions built upon them, but
directly out of the abstractest metaphysical concepts and
absolutely universal needs for the explanation of actuality.

Up to this point the Atomistic theory has been regarded
as a variant of the Eleatic metaphysic, arising from an
interest in physics.   But, on the other hand, Leucippus is so
far under the influence of Ionian monism that he does
not seek the cause of motion in a force different from
the stuff, but he regards spatial motion itself as a quality,
immanent in the stuff.   The corporeality that is homogeneous in all atoms did not, in his mind, possess the power
to change itself qualitatively, that is to say, ἀλλοίωσις; but
it did possess κίνησις, an original underivable motion that

is *given* in its own essence. In fact, Leucippus seems to have understood by this term not so much that of heaviness, — fall from above downward, — but rather a chaotic primal condition of bodies moving, disorderly, among each other in all directions (§ 32). At all events, the Atomists held this original state of motion as uncaused and self-evident. So we can see in their view the perfect synthesis of the Heracleitan and Eleatic thought: all homogeneous elements of Being are thought as unchangeable, but at the same time as in a state of motion that is self-originated.

This is the extent to which the beginnings of Atomism may with certainty be ascribed to Leucippus. It is an attempt to explain the world by atoms in original motion in empty space. The purely mechanical part of the theory, that the world was formed by collision, lateral and rotatory motion, likewise presented itself to the founder of Atomism in the same form in which Democritus later developed it. It is not so easy to explain, however, how Leucippus solved the more difficult and delicate question regarding the manner in which the various empirical qualities arose from these complexes of atoms; that is to say, the transformation of quantitative into qualitative differences. Of his answer we know nothing. The subjective method which Democritus applied to it was not as yet available to the founder of Atomism, since this method grew out of the investigations of Protagoras. Whether Leucippus [1] was content with setting up this origination

---

[1] To my mind, there is no foundation for the belief that Leucippus in his doctrine of the αἰσθητά employed the antithesis of φύσει — νόμῳ; from its significance and following all tradition, this antithesis is Sophistic. The inference rests upon the obviously late and inaccurate note in Stobæus, *Ecl.*, I. 1104 (*Dox.*, 397 b, 9) from which it might also be adduced that Diogenes of Apollonia was an Atomist. It is certain that Leucippus, as an Eleatic, denied sense qualities as real. For some later

of the qualities out of the quantitative relationships only
as a metaphysical postulate; whether he explained these
qualities, like Parmenides, simply as vain show and illusion; or whether he in an uncertain manner, like Empedocles, derived all other material from the four elements
and their mixtures, so that he too sought to refer empirical
things back to the different form and size of the combining
atoms, — how far, in fact, he in general passed from the
metaphysical principles to the specific development of the
physical theory, — concerning all this it is doubtless too
late to determine.

From the allusions in his theory, and from the very uncertain
reports from the extant literature, it is only safe to say that
probably Leucippus was younger than Parmenides, considerably
older than Democritus and contemporary with Empedocles and
Anaxagoras. It is hardly possible to decide between the different reports, whether his residence was in Miletus, Elea, or
Abdera. Since however his pupil (ἑταῖρος) Democritus doubtless was an Abderite, and came from a scientifically active circle
which we cannot[1] possibly suppose to be that of the Magi,
alleged to have been left behind by Xerxes, we may assume
that a scientific activity was developed in Abdera in the second
half of the sixth century, which city attained its highest glory
under the influence of the colonists from Teos. Leucippus was
its first representative of any significance.[2] Protagoras appears
to have originated in the school of Abdera at a time between
the two great Atomists (§ 26). That Leucippus put his thought
in writing is not entirely certain, but is probable. Nothing of
his work remains, however. In any event, even early in antiquity, there was uncertainty about the authorship of what had
been ascribed to him.[3] Theophrastus ascribed[4] to him the μέγας
διάκοσμος which went under the name of Democritus. It is

reporter this denial is identical with the assertion of their subjectivity
(νόμῳ). Parmenides himself best teaches us how little this equivalence
was possible for a pre-Sophistic thinker.

[1] Zeller, I⁴. 763.

[2] Diels. *Aufsätze Zeller's Jubiläum*, p. 258 f.

[3] *De Xen., Zen., Gorg.*, 6, 980 a, 7; ἐν τοῖς Λευκίππου καλουμένοις
λόγοις.

[4] Diog. Laert., IX. 46.

strange that in the memory of succeeding times and indeed in modern time (Bacon, Alb. Lange), even as in antiquity (Epicurus), he has been entirely overshadowed by Democritus.[1]

24. " Between these and in part already before them," [2] the Pythagoreans sought finally to apply their mathematical studies to the solution of the Heracleitan-Eleatic problem (§ 12).

However in this respect the Pythagoreans form no perfectly homogeneous whole. It appears rather that within the society, corresponding to its geographical extension and its gradual disintegration, the scientific work divided on different lines. Some Pythagoreans clung to the development of mathematics and astronomy; others busied themselves partly with medicine, partly with the investigation of different physical theories (concerning both see § 25); others finally espoused the metaphysical theory, which so far as we know was constructed first by Philolaus and is usually designated as the number theory.

Philolaus, if not the creator, at least the first literary representative of the " Pythagorean philosophy," was an older contemporary of Socrates and Democritus, and cannot, at any rate, be set farther back than Anaxagoras and Empedocles. Indeed he is presumably somewhat younger than the latter two. Of his life we know nearly nothing, and we are even not sure whether he was a native of Tarentum or Crotona. Also that he, like other Pythagoreans about the end of the fifth century, lived for a time in Thebes, is inferred with uncertainty from the passage in Plato, *Phædo*, 61. Nearly as doubtful is his supposed authorship of the fragments that are preserved under his name. They have been collated and discussed first by Böckh (Berlin, 1819). From the investigations of Fr. Preller (article *Philolaos* in *Ersch und Gruber Encykl.*, III. 23, 370 f.), V. Rose (*De Aristotelis librorum ordine et auctoritate*, Berlin, 1854), C. Schaarschmidt (Bonn, 1864), Zeller (*Hermes*, 1875, p. 175 f.), they may be assumed in part to be genuine, but they must be very cautiously introduced into the discussion of the original number theory.

[1] Zeller, I[4]. 761, 843. Compare E. Rhode, *Verhandl. der Trierer Philol.-Versuchungen*, 1879, and *Jahrbücher für Philologie u. Pädagogik*, 1881, 741 f. Diels, *Verhandlungen der Stettiner Philologie Vers.* 1880.

[2] Arist. *Met.*, I. 5 : ἐν δὲ τούτοις καὶ πρὸ τούτων οἱ καλούμενοι Πυθαγόρειοι τῶν μαθημάτων ἀψάμενοι κτλ.

Along with Philolaus are mentioned, in Italy Clinias of Tarentum,[1] in Thebes Lycis the teacher of Epaminondas, and Eurytus
the pupil of Philolaus, a citizen of Crotona or Tarentum. Eurytus in turn had as pupils Xenophilus of Thracian Chalcis, the
Phliasians Phanto, Echecrates, Diocles, Polymastus.[2] From
Cyrene Prorus is mentioned. In Athens Plato brought forward
the two Pythagoreans, Simmias and Cebes, as witnesses of the
death of Socrates. Almost mythical are the Locrian Timæus[3]
and the Lucanian Ocellus. The philosophic teaching of any of
these men is not in any way certainly known. With the dissolution of the Pythagorean League in the fourth century the
school became extinct. The doctrines of the last significant
personality in it, Archytus of Tarentum, merged, so far as our
knowledge goes, into those of the older Academy (§ 38).

A collection of all the Pythagorean fragments is in Mullach ;
Ritter, *Gesch. der pyth. Philos.* (Hamburg, 1826) ; Rothen-
bücher, *Das System der Pythagoreen nach den Angaben des
Aristoteles* (Berlin, 1867) ; Alb. Heinze, *Die meta. Grundlehren
der älteren P.* (Leipzig, 1871), Chaignet, *Pythagore et la philos.
Pythagorienne*, 2 vols. (Paris, 1873) ; Sobczyk, *Das pyth. Sys-
tem* (Leipzig, 1878) ; A Doering, *Wandlungen in der pyth. Lehre*
(*Arch. f. Gesch. d. Philos.*, v. 503 f.).

As to the Pythagorean teaching, only that can be regarded
as genuine which Plato and Aristotle report, together with the
concurrent portions of the fragments transmitted in such questionable shape.

In the Pythagorean society mathematical investigations
were pursued for the first time quite independently, and
were brought to a high degree of perfection. Detailed
views concerning the number system, concerning the series.
of odd and even numbers, of prime numbers, of squares, etc.,
were early instituted. It is not improbable that they,
applying arithmetic to geometry, came to the conception
embodied in the so-called Pythagorean theorem. Herein
must they have had a premonition of the real value of
number-relations in that they represent number as the ruling

[1] Jambl. *De vita Pyth.*, 266.

[2] Diog. Laert., VIII. 46.

[3] The writing bearing this name and concerned with the soul of the
world, usually published in Plato's works, is certainly a later compendium
of Plato's *Timæus.*

principle in space.   Their number theory was strengthened
by the results attained by them in music.   Although later
reports include [1] much that is fabulous and physically
impossible, there can nevertheless be no doubt that the
Pythagorean harmonic shows an exact knowledge of those
simple arithmetical relations (first of all, the string-lengths)
out of which musical melody arises.   To this may be added
that the regular revolution of the stars, — of which they
made especially careful observations, and which are indeed
the standard for all time measurements, — made the world-
order (κόσμος) likewise appear to them to be numerically
determined.   From these premises it can be understood
how some Pythagoreans came therefore to find in numbers
the permanent essence of things, concerning which essence
the battle between philosophic theories had taken place.
On the one hand, numbers might be substituted — since
they were supposed to be self-existent, unchangeable, and
self-unitary — for the abstract Being of the Eleatics as a
principle at least equally available in the explanation of the
phenomenal world.   On the other hand, since Heracleitus
had found that the only permanent in change was in the orderly forms of the nature process, the relationships of number ruling the process of change gave an exacter form to
this idea.   The Pythagorean number-theory attempted to
determine numerically the permanent relations of cosmic
life.   The Pythagoreans said therefore : All is number, and
they meant by this that numbers are the determining essence
of all things.   Since now these same abstract numbers and
number-relationships are found in many different things
and processes, they said also that the numbers are the
original forms which are copied by the things.

    [1] Zeller, I[4]. 317.   The observations of the Pythagoreans in the har-
monic or, as it is called, canonic, were apparently empirically made upon
the heptachord with strings of different length.   That they had no
theory of oscillation, goes without saying.

It is scarcely conceivable that the Pythagoreans came to their predilection for mathematics, music, and astronomy through metaphysics. The inverse is rather true, that they came from such concrete studies, in undertaking to enter upon the solution of universal problems, — as Aristotle (*Met.*, I. 5) also sufficiently indicated by the ἀψάμενοι. For their treatment of geometry and stereometry, and their prevailing arithmetical fondness, see Röth (*Gesch. unserer abendl. Philos.*, II. 2), although he on this territory accredits indeed too much to the old Pythagoreans. Cantor, *Vorles. über d. Gesch. d. Math.*, I. 124.

In order to derive, however, at one and the same time the manifoldness and changeableness of individual things from number relations, the Pythagoreans gave metaphysical meaning to the fundamental opposition which they found in the number theory. They declared that the odd and the even are respectively identical with the limited and the unlimited.[1] As all numbers are composed of the even and the odd, all things also combine in themselves fundamental antitheses, and especially that of the limited and the unlimited. To this Heracleitan fundamental principle there is bound this logical consequence, that everything is the reconciliation of opposites, or a "harmony," — an expression which in the mouth of the Pythagoreans has always the suggestion of musical investigations.

The antithesis, however, acquired among the Pythagoreans in conformity to their later attitude a still more pronounced value than with Heracleitus. The limited was the better, the more valuable to them, as it was to Parmenides. Odd numbers are more nearly perfect than even. In this way the Pythagorean system got a dualistic cast, which is noticeable in all its parts; but this was theoretically overcome by the fact that since the One, the odd-even primitive number, creates both series from itself, so also all the

---

[1] The ground of this identification (Simpl. *Phys.*, 105 r. ; compare Zeller, I⁴. 322) is artificial in that it was obviously made *ad hoc*, and is no natural product of the number theory.

antitheses of the cosmic life are in a grand harmonious unity.

The later Stoic neo-Platonists, i. e. neo-Pythagoreans, tried to find in this antithesis that of force and stuff, spirit and matter, and they deduced the dyads from the divine monads. Nevertheless, not the slightest suggestion of such a conception can be found in the Plato-Aristotelian reports, which would certainly have been particularly observant of this point.

All that we know with any certainty respecting the special doctrine of the Pythagoreans as contrasted with these general principles reveals their effort to construct, in accordance with a scheme of numbers, an harmonic order of things in the various fields. For this there served first the decimal system, in which every one of the first ten numbers is accorded a special significance,[1] derived from arithmetical considerations. The arithmetical mysticism or symbolism of the Pythagoreans seems to have consisted in bringing into relation with numbers the fundamental ideas of various departments of knowledge, and thereby giving expression to the relative rank, value, and significance of these ideas.

There is here the suggestion of the ideal thought of an order of things permanently determined by the number series; but much caprice in oracular symbolizing and parallelizing was obviously developed in details. Beside the number ten of cosmic bodies, the series of elements is about as follows (Jamblichus): (1) point, (2) line, (3) surface, (4) solid, (5) quality, (6) soul, (7) reason, etc.; or, on the other hand, (1) reason as located in the brain, (2) sensation in the heart, (3) germination in the navel, (4) procreation in *genitalibus*, etc. Then the virtues, like justice, were also designated by numbers. At the same time these concepts, which are symbolized by the same number in different series, also suggest and are related to one another. Thus it came about that the soul was called a square or a sphere. Doubtless with this the thought was connected that

[1] In a certain sense the Pythagoreans appear to have regarded the development from the One to the Ten as gradual. Arist. *Met.*, XI. 7, 1072 b. See Zeller, I[4]. 348.

different things should be assigned among a decade of gods. If
one adds that these determinations were given by different
Pythagoreans differently, it is easily understood why this first
scheme of a mathematical order of the world ended in an
unfruitful confusion.

An approximate representation of the division of the
different domains to which the Pythagoreans applied, or
wished to apply, this number theory shows a collection of
pairs of opposites which were arranged in a parallelism,
like the original pair. Even here is the sacred number
ten completed : (1) limited and unlimited ; (2) odd and
even ; (3) one and many ; (4) right and left; (5) male
and female ; (6) rest and motion; (7) straight and
crooked ; (8) light and darkness ; (9) good and evil ;
(10) square and rectangle. This eccentric and in itself
principleless arrangement [1] shows that the Pythagoreans
attempted at least an all-round application of their fundamental principle. Alongside their mathematical, metaphysical, and physical conceptions, the ethical conceptions
theoretically find their place ; [2] but in the development,
nevertheless, the physical interest everywhere outweighs
the others.

While now this completely ontological number system
of concepts satisfied the Eleatic *motif*, yet the physics of
the Pythagoreans was very greatly under the influence of
Heracleitus, as was also the physics of Parmenides. In the
theory of the formation of the world,[3] the Pythagoreans
placed fire in the middle as the original condition of things,

[1] In which always the first-named number is the more nearly perfect.

[2] This beginning of scientific consideration of ethical ideas, of which
intimations are at hand in the special doctrines, likewise bespeaks a
later position for the Pythagorean philosophy.

[3] It must remain uncertain whether they also accepted the theory of
periodic world-formation and destruction. They taught "the great year"
in the sense that, with the return of the original arrangement of the stars,
all individual appearances, persons, and experiences would return.

as the self-determining One, the animating and impelling force. Fire drew around itself, however, the unlimited (i. e., empty) space,[1] and limited (i. e., formed) it in ever-growing dimensions, — a conception which vividly reminds us of the δίνη of Anaxagóras and Leucippus.

The most brilliant achievement of the Pythagoreans was their astronomy, and in this respect they are far in advance of all their contemporaries. They regarded not only the world-all as globular, but also the single stars as luminous globes, which move around the central fire in transparent globular shells, the spheres. Their most important advance here is in the fact that the earth likewise was regarded as a globe, moving around this same central fire. The older Pythagoreans believed that the earth presents always the same side to the central fire, so that mankind on the opposite side never gets sight of the central fire, nor yet of the counter-earth (ἀντίχθων) that is between the earth and the central fire. The counter-earth was conceived, presumably in order to complete the number ten. However, mankind does get sight of the changing aspects of the moon circling outside the earth, as well as of the sun, five planets, and heaven of fixed stars. The distance of the spheres from the central fire was determined by the Pythagoreans according to simple number relationships. Corresponding to this, they assumed that from the revolution of the spheres there resulted a melodious musical sound, the so-called harmony of the spheres. In this way the orderly revolution of the stars became for them the perfect and divine, while the terrestrial world, the world under the moon, was represented as the changing, changeable, and imperfect. Thus the Eleatic static world and the Heracleitan changing world appear to have been apportioned to different regions of the actual world.

[1] The assumption of the κένον is expressly confirmed by Aristotle, *Phys.*, IV. 6, 213 b, 22.

Compare Böckh, *De Platonis systemate cœlestium globorum et de vera indole astronomiœ Philolaicœ* (Berlin, 1810) ; Gruppe, *Die Kosmischen Systeme der Griechen* (Berlin, 1852) ; M. Satorius, *Die Entwickelung der Astronomie bei den Griechen bis Anaxagoras und Empedokles* (Breslau, 1883).

Furthermore, the shape of the elements among the Pythagoreans is worthy of note. Just as they reduced the space forms to number relationships, so they referred the different corporeal elements to space forms, by ascribing simple stereometric forms to the ultimate constituents of matter : the tetrahedron to fire, the cube to earth, the octahedron to air, the icosahedron to water, and, finally, the dodecahedron to the æther, which was added by them to the four Empedoclean elements and conceived as surrounding all the others. If one is able to see in this the result of an interest in crystallography, nevertheless, on the other hand, also here a fantastic caprice is only too apparent.

Although consequently the augury of a mathematical statement of natural law is the permanent service of the Pythagorean philosophy, yet the form of the statement that was advanced by them was little suited to further scientific investigations. Apart from astronomy, this knowledge of the Pythagoreans, to which some value in empirical investigations may be ascribed, stands in no connection with the metaphysical number theory, and has come from such Pythagoreans, who were little, if at all, interested in the number theory (§ 25).

4. The Greek Enlightenment.

THE SOPHISTS AND SOCRATES.

25. After the rapid development in which Greek science at the first onset defined a number of valuable and fundamental concepts concerning nature, a kind of reaction began about the middle of the fifth century. The metaphysical tendency of thought declined. Of hypotheses there were

already many enough, and it seemed more important to test and verify them in application to special kinds of knowledge.

The lively exchange between the different schools led easily to a blending of principles, which thereby lost their harshness, but unfortunately their force as well. The more the circles of scientific activity increased, the more the interest turned to the single problems of science. There began an epoch of *eclecticism* and detailed investigation.

The after-effects of the Milesian researches are met not only among the younger physicists, who regarded the cosmic matter as a compromise between air and water or between fire and air, but also, in a man like *Idæus of Himera*, who agreed with Anaximenes in maintaining that the air was the ἀρχή.[1] A full adaptation, however, of the Milesian teaching to the position of science, in its attempts at compromise, appears in by far the most important of these eclectics, Diogenes of Apollonia.

Nothing is known about his life. It is even doubtful, on account of the Ionian dialect of his writing, περὶ φύσεως (see G. Geil, *Philos. Monatsheften*, XXVI. 257 f.), if the place of his birth was the Apollonia in Crete. Schorn and Panzerbieter have collected the fragments, — Schorn (Bonn, 1829, with those of Anaxagoras) and Panzerbieter (Leipzig, 1830, *Diog. Apollonia*). See Steinhart's article in the *Encyklopädie* of Ersch and Gruber. Schleiermacher, who in his treatise concerning Diogenes (Complete Works, III. 2, 149 ff.) at first placed him very high and chronologically early, came later (*Vorles. über Gesch. der Philos.*, Complete Works, III. 4 a, 77) to view him as a principleless eclectic. Zeller agrees with this last conception (I[4]. 248 f.). D. Weygoldt (*Arch. f. Gesch. d. Philos.*, I. 161 f.) has identified some teachings of Diogenes in some pseudo writings of Hippocrates.

Diogenes anticipated his later point of view in the desire, expressed in the beginning of his writing, for an unambiguous starting-point and a simple and worthy investigation. The hylozoistic monism of the Milesians formed for him

[1] Sext. Emp. *Adv. math.*, IX. 360.

this starting-point, which he defended [1] against pluralistic theories (Anaxagoras and Empedocles) by the subtle conception that the process of Becoming, the change of things into one another and their reciprocal influence, are explicable only by the presupposition of a common fundamental essence, of which all particular things are shifting transformations (ἑτεροιώσεις). The constitutive characteristics, however, of the ἀρχή he regarded on the one hand, like the Ionians, as motion and animation, and on the other, in apparent agreement with Anaxagoras, as reasonableness and purposiveness which are manifested in the proportionate distribution of matter in the universe. So he accepted in the list of predicates of the Air of Anaximenes those also of the Anaxagorean νοῦς, and called [2] this air-spirit a σῶμα μέγα καὶ ἰσχυρὸν καὶ ἀΐδιόν τε καὶ ἀθάνατον καὶ πολλὰ εἰδός. The air, likewise called πνεῦμα, as being the medium of life and of thought, is the uniform and universal reality, both in the microcosm and in the macrocosm. Through condensation and rarefaction, which were respectively (compare § 16) identified with cooling and warming, the cosmic matter changed into individual things. Through the effect of weight, which drove the rarer above and the more condensed below, there were completed the order and motion of the world-all, which was conceived to be in a periodic alternation of origination and destruction. In the organism the air serves as the soul. The soul is denied to plants, and in animals it is found in the blood (after Empedocles). Life depends upon the blood receiving the air, upon the mixing of which the mental condition of the organism depends. With a just presentiment Diogenes pointed out the distinction between the arterial and venous blood. Moreover, his valuable knowledge of the arterial system, his idea of the brain as the seat of thought, his theories of the origin of sense perception, as well as his numerous other physiologi-

[1] Simpl. *Phys.*, 32 *verso*, 151, 30. [2] *Ibid.*, 33 *recto*, 153, 17.

cal and biological observations, show a fine, accurate sense for detailed research in the organic world.

Inversely, there is an approximation to Ionian hylozoism — as it presented itself among the Eleatics to Melissus — in the only pupil of Anaxagoras of whom anything definite is known. This is Archelaus of Athens or Miletus, who identified with the air the original mixture of all the χρήματα of Anaxagoras, and associated the νοῦς essentially with the air (§ 26), similarly to Diogenes, only in a more mechanical way.

In Ephesus, on the other hand, a school continued to exist which actively held to the teaching of Heracleitus. It did not lessen the paradoxes of Heracleitus, but appears to have exaggerated them in so enthusiastic and unmethodical a manner that Plato made sport[1] of them. At least it is reported[2] that Cratylus, the most important of these Heracleitans and a younger contemporary of Socrates, the teacher of Plato, so subtilized the Heracleitan proposition concerning the inability of stepping into the same river twice, as to postulate the impossibility of stepping in even once.

Antiquity[3] associated with Heracleitus a movement developed within the Pythagorean circle, whose leader was Hippasus of Metapontum, approximately a contemporary of Philolaus. He emphasized the Heracleitan moment in the Pythagorean physics so exclusively that fire was for him entirely the ἀρχή in the Ionian sense. The old tradition[4] designated him as the head of the exoteric Acousmatics, who were not initiated into the secrets of the number theory.

On the other hand, Ecphantus, and similarly perhaps

---

[1] *Theæt.*, 179 e. In the same feeling is the entire dialogue of Cratylus written.

[2] Arist. *Met.*, III. 5, 1010 a, 12.

[3] *Ibid.*, I. 3, 984 a, 7.

[4] Jamblichus, *De vit. Pyth.*, 81.

Xuthus,[1] joined the Pythagorean teaching to atomism, to which the transition appears to have been made in the stereometrical construction of the elements as attempted by the Pythagoreans.   Likewise in Ecphantus we find similarities to the νοῦς theory of Anaxagoras.[2]   The atoms, differing in size, form, and force, are so moved by the νοῦς that out of them the unitary spherical shape of the world is perfectly formed and maintained.

While such adjustments and compromises between the metaphysical theories were being attempted, the special interest of this period was in detailed investigation.   This developed vigorously in all domains, and in its progress special departments of science even then were differentiating themselves from general philosophy.   Mathematics [3] was the first to proceed independently ; not only in the Pythagorean school, but among other thinkers (Anaxagoras, and later Plato and Democritus), it found recognition and promotion.   The trisection of an angle, the squaring of the circle, the doubling of the cube, were the pet problems of the time.   A certain Hippocrates of Chios wrote the first manual of mathematics, and introduced the method of designating figures by letters.   There was wanting, it is true, a logical development of the art of demonstration.   However, a considerable amount of knowledge was accumulated, which was obtained in an empirical way, partly experimental and partly tentative.

Brilliant progress in astronomy [4] was made in the fifth and in the beginning of the fourth century, particularly by the Pythagoreans.   Whether it were experience (the circumnavigating of Africa ?) or theoretic reflection upon the

---

[1] Compare Zeller, I⁴. 405, 1.

[2] Details by Zeller, I⁴. 458 f.

[3] Cantor, *Vorles. über d. Gesch. d. Math.*, I. 160 f., 171 f.

[4] Compare O. Gruppe, *Die kosmischen Systeme d. Griechen*, Berlin, 1851.

problems that led to the hypotheses of the central fire and the counter-earth, gradually the theory of the diurnal movement of the earth around the central fire, which alone could explain the apparent rotation of the heavens, was superseded by the theory of the revolution of the earth upon its axis. Hicetas of Syracuse appears to have been the founder of this theory. He was certainly younger than Philolaus, and perhaps a participant in that last phase of Pythagoreanism, as it merged in the Academy [1] (§ 38).

About this time, in other departments of natural science, a richer, more exact treatment of individual facts took the place of ultimate hypotheses. Here appeared a wonderful revolution, when interest in meteorological observations began to give place to interest in the investigation of the organic world, and of man in particular.

Typical in this respect appears Hippo [2] (of Samos?), a naturalist of the time of Pericles, who, inasmuch as he postulated the moist as $\dot{a}\rho\chi\dot{\eta}$,[3] is usually mentioned in connection with Thales; so also Cleidemus,[4] in whose

---

[1] Here, as for the following, we may refer once for all to the *Geschichte der Mathematik, Naturwissenschaft und Medizin in Altertum*, appearing in this same volume of the German edition. This special treatment allows us to make only a brief sketch of these subjects, and to lay the emphasis upon the distinctively philosophical movement.

[2] Compare Schleiermacher, *Ueber den Philosophen Hippon, Complete Works*, Vol. III. p. 408 f.; Uhrig, *De Hippone atheo* (Giessen, 1848).

[3] With special emphasis upon the moist character of animal seed, Arist. *De an.*, I. 2. This explains the one supposition of Aristotle concerning the origin of the teaching of Thales (see § 14). If the charge of Atheism which was made against Hippo refers to the fact that he did not recognize anything as imperishable, and declared that nothing exists except phenomena (schol. in Arist., 534 a, 22), he was, in spite of his moist $\dot{a}\rho\chi\dot{\eta}$, a purely positive anti-metaphysician. This explains Aristotle's prejudice against him ($\phi o\rho\tau\iota\kappa\dot{\omega}\tau\epsilon\rho o\varsigma$, *De an.*, I. 2; $\epsilon\dot{v}\tau\dot{\epsilon}\lambda\epsilon\iota a$ $\tau\tilde{\eta}\varsigma$ $\delta\iota a\nu o\dot{\iota}a\varsigma$, *Met.*, I. 3).

[4] Zeller, I[4]. 927.

researches into the physiology of sensation we find suggestions of Anaxagoras.

Medicine also could not hold itself apart from the influence of the general body of science, and it appeared for a
time as if it would be entirely absorbed into the speculations
of natural philosophy.   The impulse thereto arose from the
Pythagorean circles, and is principally traced back to
Alcmæon,[1] a physician in Crotona, and perhaps a somewhat older contemporary of Philolaus.   He stood aloof
from the number theory, but in common with its adherents held to the doctrine of antitheses.[2]   He also believed
in the fundamental opposition of the terrestrial imperfection and the celestial perfection, which dualism he,
like Philolaus, appears to have developed astronomically.
His medical views depended upon the universal Pythago-
rean-Heracleitan presuppositions, since he defined health
as the harmony of opposing forces.   Specifically, there
were supposed to be fundamental humors whose homogeneous mixing indicated health, while an excess or deficiency of any one of them led to pathological conditions.
Such ætiological theories did not, however, prevent Alcmæon from making careful and valuable investigations.
He is said to be the first to make sections ; he appears
to have been the first to locate thought in the brain, and
to designate the nerves as canals leading thither from
the sense-organs.   Connected with this — for him as well
as later for Democritus and Plato — was the fact that
he in an Eleatic-Heracleitan fashion opposed thought to
perception.

As a type of the temporary amalgamation of medicine
and natural philosophy, we may take[3] the pseudo-Hippo-

---

[1] Unna, *De Alcmœone Crotoniata ejusque fragmentis*, found in Petersen's *Phil. hist. Stud.* 1832 ; R. Hirzel, *Hermes*, 1876, p. 240 f.

[2] Arist. *Met.*, I. 5, 986 a, 27.

[3] Compare Siebeck, *Gesch. der Psychol.*, I. 1, 94 f.

cratic work περὶ διαίτης, which has been proved [1] by Zeller (I. 663 f., against Schuster, *Heraclitus*, 99 f., and Teichmüller, *Neue Studien*, I. 249 f., II. 6 f.) to belong to the time after Empedocles and Anaxagoras and before Plato. This writing pictures in the microcosm of the human body, as well as in the universe, now a constructive and now a destructive battle between fire and water, and it ascribes motion to fire and nourishing power to water. The theory is then carried out in detail, and deviates into a medical psychology which regards the soul as a mixed essence corresponding in miniature to the body.

The merit of Hippocrates (460–377) [2] was that he defended the independence of medicine against such nature-philosophical tendencies, which he contested principally περὶ ἀρχαίης ἰητρικῆς. He separated medicine as a τέχνη from philosophy in a purely Greek fashion as the art of restoring to the body its beauty lost through disease. On the other hand, Hippocrates (περὶ διαίτης ὀξέων) also rejected the purely symptomatic method that was in vogue in the Cnidian school. He urged that the determination of the empirical causes of disease was to be attained by a comprehensive and careful observation of the αἰτίαι ; [3] and in this he found a successor in Diocles of Carystus. He distinguished causes dependent on external events, like climate, seasons, etc., from those subject to the human will, like the diet. Remoter causes are distinguished from the more immediate, but always investigation is limited to experience, and only immanent, not transcendent, ætiolo-

[1] Compare Weygoldt, *Jahrb. f. kl. Philol.*, 1882, 161 f.

[2] The mass of writings passing under the name of Hippocrates are published by Kühn and by Littré, and the latter has made a French translation. Only a small portion of these writings belongs to Hippocrates, and this portion contains several very difficult problems of detail. J. Ilberg, *Studia Pseudippocratea* (Leipzig, 1883).

[3] See C. Göring, *Ueber den Begriff d. Ursache in d. griech. Philos.* (Leipzig, 1874).

gies are sought. As with Alcmæon, the mixture of the four fundamental humors — the blood, phlegm, yellow gall, and black gall — formed likewise the central point of this medical theory. Besides this the school of Hippocrates developed an accurate knowledge of anatomy and physiology. In the former branch the knowledge of the brain and nervous system, and especially, even thus early, of the particular sense nerves, is to be particularly noted; and concerning the latter is the theory of the ἔμφυτον θερμόν, wherein the cause of life was sought. The bearer of life, however, was held to be the πνεῦμα, which is a material wafted like air through the veins.[1] This is an hypothesis which, like similar teachings of Diogenes of Apollonia, seemed to rest upon a presentiment of the importance of oxygen.

Historical research also, like that of natural science, acquired at the end of the fifth century not only greater extent and more manifold form,[2] but also a positive and scientific method. While in Herodotus the naturalistic narrative was still interwoven with myth and saga, and the realistic conception was still permeated with elements of the old faith, the stripping off of the mythical appears to have been perfected in Thucydides, whose mastery of psychological motivation was determined entirely by the spirit of his time, the Attic Enlightenment.

26. But with this internal process of transformation there went on also in the second half of the fifth century a great change in the external relations of Greek science. There was here, too, a powerful influence in the mighty development of the national life which had dawned upon

[1] See H. Siebeck, *Die Entwickelung der Lehre vom Geist* (πνεῦμα) *in der antiken Wissenschaft: Zeitschrift für Vökerspsychologie*, 1881, p. 364 f. Compare with his *Gesch. der Psychologie*, I. 2. p. 730 f.

[2] Logography developed into histories of localities (Xanthus of Sardis and Hippasus of Rhegium, the Lydian and Sicilian histories); then (§ 11), into fuller expositions by Charo of Lampsacus, Hellanicus of Mitylene, Damastes. etc.

Greece during the Persian wars. The glorious struggle for existence which the Greeks made against the Asiatic ascendancy had strained the powers of the people to the utmost, and had brought all their possibilities to their richest unfolding. The most valuable prize of the victory was that impulse for a national unity of mental life, out of which the great creations of Hellenic culture proceeded. Science was involved in this movement. Science was drawn out of the silent circles of the select societies in which it had until then been nurtured. On the one hand, it entered with its discoveries and inventions into the service of practical life ;[1] on the other hand, its doctrines, and particularly its transformation of religious views, were brought through poetry to the apprehension of the common mind.

The view of nature in Æschylus, Sophocles, Pindar, and Simonides appears on the whole in a similar setting as in the Gnomic poets. Direct allusions to philosophy are found first in Euripides (compare especially E. Köhler, *Die Philosophie des Euripides*, I. ; *Anaxagoras und E.*, Bückeburg, 1873), and in Epicharmus, who stood near to the Pythagoreans, but also seems to have been familiar with the other philosophic teachings of his time. (Compare Leop. Schmidt, *Quæstiones Epicharmeæ*, Bonn, 1846 ; Zeller, I⁴. 460 f.) "The divestiture of nature of its gods by science" pressed always further to an ethical allegorizing of the gods (Metrodorus of Lampsacus ; compare § 11). This permitted, on the other hand, the comedy (of Epicharmus, Cratinus, Eupolis) to outdo the anthropomorphism, which had been for good and all outgrown, even to the extent of witty persiflage of their divinities. The weaker faith appeared, the greater seemed the need of supplying its place by knowledge.

Amid such increased intellectual activity there arose in all Greece in the fifth century an impulse for education, aris-

[1] An example may be found in the architecture of Hippodamus of Miletus, whose connection with the Pythagoreans is indeed very doubtful. His magnificent buildings, however, in the Piræus, Thurii, and Rhodes, and the entire development of architecture, presuppose a high degree of development in mechanics and technology. Compare K. F. Hermann, *D. H. Milesio* (Marburg, 1841).

ing out of need, curiosity, and wonder. Everybody desired
to know what the schools had developed through research
and reflection concerning the nature of things. To such
questioning a ready answer was speedily forthcoming.
There were men who engaged to reveal the results of
science to the people. Philosophy stepped out of the
school and forth upon the mart.[1] These public teachers
of science were the Sophists.

That the Sophists converted science into a trade is one of the
chief and heaviest charges which Socrates,[2] Plato,[3] and Aristotle[4] raised against them ; these three thought the dignity of
science as a disinterested research was impaired in this way by
the Sophists. If we cannot agree [5] with this judgment from a
modern point of view, yet the fact is nevertheless to be recognized that when science was taught for pay, it assumed an entirely new social position ; and this is the essential fact in the
whole matter.

This movement showed itself first of all in Athens.
Here, in the middle of the fifth century, the intellectual life
of Greece was concentrated, had attained its highest efflo-
rescence, and had gained its political power and commercial supremacy. Science, like art, crowded into this τῆς
Ἑλλάδος τὸ πρυτανεῖον τῆς σοφίας. Here the need of culture developed most actively among the lesser citizens, here
learning began to have political and social power, and
here the supremacy of culture was personified in Pericles.
Thus in science also Athens absorbed into itself the scattered beginnings of Greek civilization.

Anaxagoras had lived for a long time in Athens. Parmenides and Zeno probably visited Athens, and Heracleitanism
was represented there by Cratylus. All important Sophists

[1] See Windelband, *Praeludien*, p. 56 f.
[2] Xen. *Mem.*, I. 6.
[3] *Gorg.*, 420 c.
[4] *Eth. Nik.*, IX. 1, 1164 a, 24.
[5] See Grote, *Hist. of Gr.*, VIII. 493 f. ; Zeller, I[4]. 971 f.

sought and found here honor and glory. With them began the Attic period of ancient philosophy, its most magnificent period.

The Sophists are, accordingly, first and foremost the bearers of the Greek Enlightenment. The period of their activity is that of the expansion of scientific culture. With less ability in independent creation, the Sophists devoted their energies to revising and popularizing existing theories. Their work was first directed, with an eye to the people's needs, to imparting to the mass of people the results of science. Therein lay, along with their justification, also the danger to which the Sophists succumbed.

Σοφιστής meant originally "a man of science" in general. Then, as Protagoras[1] claimed for himself, it meant "a teacher of science" and of political virtue; later, expressly, a paid teacher of rhetoric (see below). The opprobrium attached to the word Sophist at present is due to the polemics of Socrates, Plato, and Aristotle, which have unfavorably dominated history in its judgment of the Sophists, until Hegel (Complete Works, Vol. XIV. 5 f.) made prominent the legitimate moment of their work. Since then, this has attained a complete recognition (Brandis, Hermann,[2] Zeller, Ueberweg-Heinze), but on the other hand has been exaggeratedly emphasized by Grote (History of Greece, VIII. 474 f.). Compare Jac. Geel, *Historia critica sophistarum* (Utrecht, 1823); M. Schanz, *Die Sophisten* (Göttingen, 1867); A. Chiapelli, *Per la storia della sophistica greca* (*Arch. f. Gesch. d. Ph.*, III.); the fragments in Mullach, II. 130 f.

The difference between the earlier and later Sophists (Ueberweg) is well founded, since in the nature of the case at the beginning the serious and legitimate aspects of the movement were more prominent, while later on appeared the vagaries of the members and the menace of their doctrines to society. This development was so necessary, the consequences were so certainly determined by the precedents, and this distinction is on that account only so relative, that it, particularly for a brief presentation, will not be adopted as a basis of subdivision.

Plato's dialogue *Protagoras* gives in its clear characterization of the principal personages an exceptionally vivid pic-

---

[1] Plato, *Protag.*, 318 d.

[2] Hermann, *Gesch. u. Syst. d. plat. Philos.*, I. 179 f., 296 f.

ture of the entire movement of the Sophists. In spite of the general polemic character of this work, the better aspects of Sophism are not entirely obscured. The most derogatory characterization of the Sophists is given in the dialogue *Sophist* transmitted under Plato's name. The Aristotelian conclusions agree with this dialogue in the main (*Met.*, III. 5; VII. 3). The worst is the definition περὶ σοφ. ἐλέγχ. I. 165 a, 21; ἔστι γὰρ ἡ σοφιστικὴ φαινομένη σοφία οὖσα δ᾽ οὔ· καὶ ὁ σοφιστὴς χρηματιστὴς ἀπὸ φαινομένης σοφίας ἀλλ᾽ οὐκ οὔσης.

The popularizing tendency of Sophistry found an eminent representative in Hippias of Elis. A brilliant polyhistor, he dazzled his contemporaries in all sorts of mathematical, zoölogical, historical, and grammatical learning. At the same time, however, as the dialogue *Hippias Major* shows, he aimed by his somewhat colorless moral teaching to achieve a cheap success with the masses. It was very much the same with Prodicus of Iulis on the island of Ceos, of whose shallow ethics an example is preserved in the well-known Heracles at the Cross Ways.[1] The strength of Prodicus lay in synonymy.

See L. Spengel, Συναγωγὴ τεχνῶν (Stuttgart, 1828); J. Mähly, *Die Sophist Hippias von Elis* (*Rheinisches Museum*, 1860 f.); F. G. Welcker, *Prodikas der Vorgänger des Socrates* (in a smaller work, II. 393 f.). Both were about of an age, and somewhat younger than Protagoras. Nothing further is known concerning their lives. Hippias, who prided himself on his memory and his great learning, was pictured as one of the most conceited Sophists. Prodicus was treated by Plato with playful irony on account of his pedantic pains in word-splitting. For Socrates' relation to him, see § 27.

The instruction that the Sophists were called upon to give had to adapt itself to a specific purpose. Democracy had gained ascendency in Athens and most other cities, and the citizen was brought by duty and inclination into active participation in public affairs. This evinced itself particularly in oratory. With the higher culture of the masses,

[1] Hermann, *Gesch. u. Syst. d. plat. Philos.*, I. 179 f., 296 f.

the greater were the demands upon those who by the
power of the spoken word wished to win influence in the
state. The youth who attended upon the teaching of
the Sophist desired to be trained by him into a cultured
and eloquent citizen of the state. *So the Sophists found
their chief task in scientific and rhetorical instruction for
public life.* The instruction consisted on the one hand in
technical and formal oratory, and on the other in that
learning which appeared especially important for any particular end they had in view. Therein lay not only the
social-historical significance of the Sophists, but also the
tendency of all the independent investigations through
which the Sophists have furthered science. Gorgias of
Leontini and Protagoras of Abdera may be regarded the
most eminent representatives of this phase of Sophism.

For the characterization and criticism of Sophism as a tech-
nique of education in statecraft, one ought to consult especially
Plato's dialogue, *Gorgias.* Concerning the relation of the
Sophists to rhetoric, see Fr. Blass, *Die attische Beredsamkeit
von Gorgias bis Lysias* (Leipzig, 1868). As a typical expression of these attempts of the Sophists which embraced also
legal oratory, may be taken the utterance of Protagoras that
he would pledge himself to [1] τὸν ἥττω λόγον κρείττω ποιεῖν, — an
expression, to be sure, which called forth the crushing criticism
of Aristophanes, who in the *Clouds* imputed it to Socrates.
A more reliable fact about the life of Gorgias is that he was
in Athens in 427 as head of the embassy from his native city
(Thucyd., III. 86). His life has been set by Frei (*Rh. Mus.*,
1850, 1851) in the time from 483 to 375. He made a great
impression in Athens by his eloquence, and exercised a
distinct influence upon the development of rhetorical style.
He spent his protracted old age in Larissa in Thessaly. The
genuineness of both of his preserved declamations (ed. Blass,
Leipzig, 1881) is doubtful. His philosophical treatise bore
the title περὶ φύσεως ἢ περὶ τοῦ μὴ ὄντος (see below). His connection with the Sicilian school of oratory (Corax and Tisias),
and therefore also with Empédocles, is undoubted. His connection with the Eleatics appears equally certain, from the argu-

[1] Arist. *Rhet.*, II. 24; 1402 a, 23.

mentation in his writings. Compare H. E. Foss, *De G. L.* (Halle, 1828); H. Diels, *Gorgias und Empedocles (Berichte der Berliner Akademie).*

Alcidamus of Elea, Polus [1] of Agrigentum, Lycophron, and Protarchus [2] are named as pupils of Gorgias.

Protagoras, doubtless the most important of the Sophists, was born in Abdera in 480 or somewhat earlier. It can be assumed that he was not distant in his views from the school of Atomists in that city. Considerably younger than Leucippus, and about twenty years older than Democritus, he formed the natural connection between the two (see §§ 23, 31). With keen insight into the needs of the time, and much admired as a teacher of wisdom, he was one of the first to make an extended tour of the Grecian cities. He was in Athens many times. In 411, and during the rule of the four hundred, he was there for the last time, and was accused of atheism. He was condemned, and upon his flight to Sicily was drowned. The titles (Diog. Laert., IX. 55) of his numerous writings, only a very few of which are preserved, prove that he dealt with the most varied subjects in the domain of theory and practice. Compare J. Frei, *Quæstiones Protagoreæ* (Bonn, 1845); A. J. Vitringa, *De Prot. vita et philos.* (Gröningen, 1851). Lately Th. Gompertz (*Vienna Session Reports*, 1890) has identified a Sophistic speech with the *Apology of Medicine* in the pseudo-Hippocratic writing, περὶ τέχνης, and has noted its not fully undoubted connection with the teaching of Protagoras.

Antimærus of Mende, Archagoras, Euathlus,[3] Theodorus the mathematician, and in a wider sense Xeniades of Corinth also are to be regarded as pupils of Protagoras. Eminent citizens of Athens, like Critias, probably Callicles, or poets like Evenus of Paros, etc., stood in a less intimate connection with the Sophists.

The practical and political aim of their instruction compelled the Sophists to turn aside from independent nature study and metaphysical speculation, and to content themselves with the presentation, in popular form, of such theories only when they were called for or appeared effective.[4]

---

[1] Plato, *Gorg.*   [2] Plato, *Phileb.*

[3] Plato, *Theætetus.*

[4] Many, like Gorgias, rejected this as perfectly worthless. See Plato, *Meno*, 95 c.

The peculiar task in teaching men how to persuade drove them, on the other hand, to interest themselves more thoroughly in man, especially on his psychological side. Whoever endeavors to influence man by speech must know something of the genesis and development of his ideas and volitions. While earlier science with naïve devotion to the outer world had coined fundamental concepts for its knowledge of nature, Sophistry, so far as it adopted the methods of science, turned to inner experience, and completed the incomplete earlier philosophy by studying the mental life of man. In this essentially anthropological tendency, sophistry turned philosophy on the road to subjectivism.[1]

This new kind of work began first with language. The efforts of Prodicus in synonymy, those of Hippias in grammar, were in this direction. Protagoras was especially fruitful in this respect. Persuaded that theory without practice was as little useful as practice [2] without theory, he connected the practical teaching, to which Gorgias seems to have limited himself, with philological investigations. He concerned himself with the right use of words,[3] in their genders, tenses, modes,[4] etc.

Compare Lersch, *Die Sprachphilos. der alten*, I. 15 f. ; Alberti. *Die Sprachphilos. vor Platon* (Philol., 1856) ; Prantl, *Gesch. der Logik*, I. 14 f.

Similar small beginnings in logic appeared, in addition to those in grammar. That teachers of oratory should

[1] What Cicero (*Tusc.*, V. 4, 10) said of Socrates, that he called philosophy down from heaven into the cities and houses, is equally true for the entire Greek Enlightenment, for the Sophists as well as for him.

[2] Stobæus Florilegium, 29, 80.

[3] Plato, *Phædr.*, 267 c.

[4] Diog. Laert., IX. 53, in which he distinguished εὐχωλή, ἐρώτησις, ἀπόκρησις, and ἐντολή.

reflect how a thing was to be proved and controverted, is obvious. It is also easily credible (Diog. Laert., IX. 51 f.) that Protagoras had his attention drawn to the nature of contradictory propositions, and was the first to teach the method of proof (τὰς πρὸς τὰς θέσεις ἐπιχειρήσεις). Apparently formal logic sprang up here as an art of argumentation, proof, and contradiction. Of how far it was developed in details by the Sophists, we unfortunately know absolutely nothing.[1]

We are better informed concerning their general view of human knowledge. The less the Sophist championed earlier metaphysical and physical learning, and the more he entertained his hearers by his clever opposition to it, and the more vividly again instruction presented tó the consciousness of the rhetorician the possibility of proving different things of the same object, so much the more conceivable is it that these men lost faith in any universally valid truth or in the possibility of any certain knowledge. Their preoccupation with the theory of knowledge led, as things were, by a psychological necessity to skepticism.

This skepticism is the theoretical centre of Sophistry. That this degenerated among the younger Sophists into frivolous argumentation should not lead to the misconception of the scientific seriousness with which the negative epistemology was developed, especially by Protagoras. On the other hand, it was an unhistoric interpretation for those in modern time, following Grote's example, to celebrate Protagoras as the founder of Positivism: E. Laas, *Idealismus und Positivismus*, I. (Berlin, 1880) var. loc. ; W. Halbfass, *Die Berichte des Platon u. Aristoteles über Protagoras* (Strassburg, 1882). Opposed to

[1] That the Aristotelian logic was not without precedents, literary or in the form of practical exercise, may be taken *a priori* as extremely probable. How far these precedents reached cannot be determined from the very few indications from extant literature (see particularly Plato's (?) dialogue *Sophist*). This lack of evidence is one of the most regrettable deficiencies in the history of Greek science. Compare Prantl, *Gesch. d. Log.*, I. 11 f.

this is P. Natorp, *Forschungen zu Gesch. des Erkenntnissproblems*, p. 1 f., 149 f. Compare Fr. Sattig, *Der Protagoreische
Sensualismus* in *Zeitschr. f. Philos.* (1885 f.). The chief
source for the epistemology of Protagoras is Plato's dialogue,
Theœtetus. Yet it is a question how far the presentation
developed in this may be referred to Protagoras himself. The
teaching of Gorgias is in part preserved in the pseudo-Aristotelian *De Melisso, Zenone, Gorgia,* c. 5 and 6 (§ 17); and
in part in Sext. Emp. *Adv. math.*, VII. 65.

In order to establish his skeptical belief about human
knowledge, Protagoras made the eternal flux of Heracleitus his point of departure. But he emphasized still
more than Heracleitus the correlation, in which every
single thing does not so much exist, as momentarily come
into existence, through its relation to other things. From
the disavowal of absolute Being it followed that qualities
of things arise only out of the temporary effect of things on
one another. Quality is the product of motion,[1] and indeed, as Protagoras in a purely Heracleitan manner set
forth, always of two corresponding motions but in opposite
directions. One of these was designated as activity, the
other as passivity.[2] It follows that in general it can never
be said what a thing is, but at most what it becomes in its
changing relation to other things,[3] and the Protagorean cor-
relativeness contained a still greater significance in applying this general theory of motion to the theory of human
perception. Whenever a thing affects one of our senses,

---

[1] It is not clear from the *Theœtetus* whether and how Protagoras
discussed the substratum of the κίνησις. Even if he did not with
Heracleitus deny it, yet he regarded it at any rate as incognizable. It
is conceivable that the Abderite Protagoras developed this theory in
compliance to the demands of Atomism, in which shape Democritus
later received it (§ 32).

[2] *Theœt.*, 156 f.

[3] Similarly the skeptical statements of Xeniades appear to have been
conceived. Compare Zeller, I⁴. 988.

in which the motion proceeding[1] from the object meets a reacting motion of the organ, there then arises in the sense organ the perceptual image,[2] and simultaneously in the thing, the quality corresponding[3] to the image. Therefore every perception teaches only how the thing appears in the moment of perception for the perceiver, and indeed for him alone. Now for Protagoras, sense perception was regarded as the only source of knowledge and of the entire mental life.[4] Therefore there was for him no insight into the Being of things over and above those relations; no idea of what things might be in themselves abstracted from perceptual relations. Rather is everything for each individual[5] just what it appears to him; but it is such only to that individual, and, more exactly, only for his momentary state of perception. The well-known statement[6] has this meaning:

πάντων χρημάτων μέτρον ἄνθρωπος, τῶν μὲν ὄντων ὡς ἔστι, τῶν δὲ μὴ ὄντων ὡς οὐκ ἔστιν.

[1] The ability of the different objects to influence the different sense organs appears already to have led Protagoras to his theory of the different velocities of movements of the objects. See *Theæt.*, 156 c. With this reduction of the qualitative to the quantitative, Protagoras stood entirely in the school of the Atomists (§§ 23 and 32).

[2] Under this term the sensations and also the feelings are classified in the *Theætetus* (156).

[3] That the αἰσθητόν in reality arises with the αἴσθησις, is an addition presumably of those who had extended and applied the theory of the Abderite (according to the *Theætetus*). For such an assertion carries one far beyond the bounds of skepticism. This cannot apply to Democritus.

[4] Whether and how Protagoras has proved and explained this view (μηδὲν εἶναι τὴν ψυχὴν παρὰ τὰς αἰσθήσεις, Diog. Laert., IX. 51) is not known. In the light of the earlier Rationalism (§§ 18–23) this sensationalism seems somewhat unwarranted. It is presaged in the physiological psychology of the later nature philosophy (§ 25).

[5] The explanation of *Theætetus* (152 a) does not permit the ἄνθρωπος in this well-known sentence to refer to the genus. See Arist. *Met.*, X. 6, 1062 b, 13.

[6] *Theætetus*, 152 a; Sext. Emp. *Adv. math.*, VII. 60.

As Protagoras based his philosophy upon that of Heracleitus, so Gorgias founded his upon that of the Eleatics. The former had concluded that to all opinion there is attached a relative, but to none an absolute, truth; the latter sought to demonstrate in general the impossibility of knowledge. While, however, the practical investigations of Protagoras enriched philosophy in the succeeding systems of Plato and Democritus, the argumentation of Gorgias was developed in a captious and sterile dialectic. Gorgias showed: (1) Nothing is. That which is not, cannot be, and even as little can that which is. For that which is, cannot be thought either as unoriginated and imperishable or as originated and perishable; neither can it be thought as one or as many, nor indeed finally as moved, without being involved in obvious contradictions. The arguments of Zeno are everywhere re-employed here (§ 20). Moreover, that which is and that which is not to exist simultaneously, is impossible (against Heracleitus?). (2) Were there something, it would not be knowable; for that which is and that which is thought must be different, — otherwise error would be impossible.[1] (3) If there were knowledge, it could not be communicated, because communication is possible only by means of signs, which are different from the thing itself. There is no warrant that there is a like apprehension of these signs by different individuals.[2]

Howsoever seriously and scientifically the theories of Skepticism were held, even by Protagoras, they nevertheless led to the demoralization of science, and resulted finally in a frivolous diversion in daily life. Gorgias had found

[1] This dialectic is more finely spun out in the dialogue of the *Sophist*.

[2] One is almost inclined to regard these paradoxes of this anti-philosophical rhetorician as a grotesque persiflage of the Eleatic dialectic. At all events, this last is inevitably and fatally involved in its own toils.

that every predication of a subject is doubtful,[1] if indeed there is any difference whatever between subject and predicate. He therefore called in question synthetic judgments. Protagoras himself doubted the reality of mathematical knowledge.[2] Euthydemus, in the spirit of this relativism,[3] said that anything is suitable to everything; one cannot err, for what is spoken exists also as a something thought.[4] One cannot contradict himself; if he appears to, it is only because he is speaking of a different thing, and so on. Since the majority of the Sophists did not take truth seriously from the beginning, their entire art amounted to a dispute with formal adroitness *pro et contra* over anything whatsoever, and to equipping their pupils in this facility. Their principal aim was accordingly to be able to confuse the listener, to drive him into making absurd answers, and to refute one's opponent.

Protagoras also wrote ἀντιλογίαι and καταβάλλοντες;[5] and the practice of the Sophists, especially in later time, in trying to be sensational, consisted simply in that art, which is called Eristic.

Plato's *Euthydemus* describes with many playful witticisms the method of Eristic by the example of the two brothers Euthydemus and Dionysidorus, and Aristotle has taken the pains to arrange systematically these witticisms in the last book of the *Topics* (περὶ σοφιστικῶν ἐλέγχων). The greater number of these witticisms are puns. The ambiguity of the words, of the endings, of the syntactical forms, etc., are in the main the basis of the witticisms (Prantl, *Gesch. d. Log.*, I. 20 f.). The great favor with which these jokes were received in Greece, and espe-

---

[1] *Sophist*, 251 b.

[2] Arist. *Met.*, II. 2, 998 a, 3.

[3] τῶν πρός τι εἶναι τὴν ἀλήθειαν. Sext. Emp. *Adv. math.*, VII. 60.

[4] Here the ambiguity of the copula also plays a part. Lycophron proposed to omit the copula.

[5] The proposition that "man is the measure of all things" is cited as the beginning of this work, and at the same time as the beginning of a work, called ἀλήθεια, which perhaps formed the first part of it.

cially in Athens, is explained by the youthful inclination to quibble, by the southron's fondness for talking, and by the awakening of reflective criticism upon familiar things of daily life.

However, this facetious method was unpromising for the serious progress of science. On the other hand, the convictionless attitude of mind that the Sophists designedly or undesignedly encouraged became a direct menace in its application upon that domain in which, as their entire effort showed, they were alone deeply interested, — the ethico-political. Since the time of the Seven Wise Men (§ 9), the content of moral and civil laws and obedience to them had been a common subject for reflection. But the growing individualism, the inspired activity of the Periclean age, and the anarchy of the Athenian democracy for the first time brought into question through the Sophists the justification of these norms. Since here also the individual man with his temporary desires and needs was declared to be the measure of all things, the binding power of the law became as relatively valid as theoretical truth had been.

See H. Sidgwick, *The Sophists* (Journal of Philology, 1872, 1873) ; A. Harpf, *Die Ethik des Protagoras* (Heidelberg, 1884) ; and the general literature concerning the Sophists and particularly that concerning Socrates. Of the profounder investigations in which the more important Sophists were largely engaged, almost nothing is preserved save individual remarks and striking assertions. At most there is the myth of Protagoras in the dialogue of that name (320 f.). Perhaps the first half of the second book of the *Republic* refers also to something of the same sort. Perhaps the Sophists suffer in this domain, as in theory, from the fact that we are instructed concerning them only from their opponents.[1]

The most important point of view which the Sophists in this respect set up appeared in their contrast of the natural

[1] There is also a fragment found by Fr. Blass (*Univers. Schrift. Kiel.*, 1889) in Jamblichus, *Protrepticæ orationes ad philosophiam*, ch. 20, who attributed it to the Sophist Antiphon.

and social condition of man. From reflection upon the difference and change not only of legal prescriptions but also of social rules,[1] the Sophists concluded that at least a greater part of these had been established by convention through human statute (θέσει sive νόμῳ); and that only such laws were universally binding as were established in all men equally by nature (φύσει). The natural therefore appeared to be of the greater worth, — more nearly permanent and more binding than the social. Natural law seemed higher than historic positive law. The more serious Sophists endeavored then further to strip off from natural morality and natural laws the mass of conventionalities: Protagoras[2] taught that justice and conscience (δίκη and αἰδώς) are the gifts of the gods, and are common to all men; but neither this nor the assertion of Hippias, that "law" violently drives[3] man to many things that are contrary to "nature," sets up any thoroughgoing and necessary opposition between the two legislations. But the more the theory of the Sophists conceived of "nature" as "human nature," and as "human nature" limited to its physical, impulsive, and individual aspect, so much the more did "law" appear a detriment and a limitation of the natural man. Archelaus, the pupil of Anaxagoras, declared that social differences do not arise from "Nature." They are conventional determinations (οὐ φύσει ἀλλὰ νόμῳ).[4] Plato[5] has Callicles develop the theory that all laws are created by the stronger, and these laws, on account of need of protection, the weaker accept. He[6] puts into the mouth

---

[1] Compare Hippias in Xen. *Mem.*, IV. 4, 14 f.

[2] In his myth reproduced by Plato.

[3] Plato, *Prot.*, 337 c.   Similarly, but somewhat more brusquely, Callicles expresses himself in Plato, *Gorgias*, 482 f.

[4] Diog. Laert., II. 16.

[5] *Loc. cit.*

[6] *Republic*, 1, 338 f.

of Thrasymachus of Chalcedon a naturalistic psychology of
legislation, according to which the ruler in a natural body
politic would establish laws for his own advantage. In
this spirit Sophistry contended, in part from the point of
view of " natural right," in part from that of absolute
anarchy, against many existing institutions :[1] not only as
the democratic Lycophron against every privilege of the
nobility, or as Alcidamus against so fundamental a principle of ancient society as was slavery, but finally even
against *all* custom and *all* tradition.[2] The independence
of individual judgment, which the Enlightenment proclaimed, shattered the rule of all authority and dissipated
the content of social consciousness.

In the attacks which already science in its more serious
aspects had directed against religious ideas, it is obvious
that religious authority also would be swept away with the
flood of the Sophistic movement. All shades of religious
freethinking are met with in Sophistic literature : — everything, from the cautious skepticism of Protagoras, who
claimed[3] to know nothing of the gods, to the naturalistic
and anthropological explanations of Critias[4] and Prodicus[5]
as to belief in the gods, and even to the outspoken atheism
of a certain Diagoras[6] of Melos.

27. Against the destructive activity of the Sophists appeared the powerful personality of Socrates, who stood
indeed with his opponents upon the common ground of the
Enlightenment, and like them raised to a principle the inde-

[1] To some extent with positive propositions whose authors, according
to Aristotle (*Pol.*, II. 8 & 7), were Hippodamus and a certain Phaleas.

[2] Compare Arist. *Pol.*, I. 3, 1253 b, 20.

[3] By reason of the vagueness of the object and the brevity of human
life ; compare Diog. Laert., IX. 51.

[4] Compare the verse in Sext. Emp., IX. 54.

[5] Cic. *De natura deorum*, I. 42, 118.

[6] Compare Zeller, I[4]. 864, 1.

pendent reflection concerning everything given by tradition and custom. But at the same time he was unshaken in the conviction that through reflection a universally valid truth could certainly be found.

The reports of Xenophon,[1] Plato, and Aristotle are the chief sources of our knowledge concerning Socrates. The remarkably different light that is cast from such different men upon this great personality makes him stand out in plastic distinctness. Xenophon saw more of the sober, practical, and popular side of the life and character of the man. Plato, on the contrary, beheld the height of his imagination, the depth of his spiritual being, his elevating influence on youthful and highly gifted minds. See S. Ribbing, *Ueber das Verhältniss zwischen d. xenophontischen u. d. platonischen Berichten über d. Persönlichkeit u. d. Lehre d. Sokrates* (Upsala, 1870). Xenophon's representation, so far as the author's knowledge goes, is one of historic fidelity, but it was strongly under the influence of Cynic party prejudice. Plato's writings, however, place in the mouth of Socrates less often Socrates' teachings (only in the *Apology* and the earliest dialogues) than the consequences that Plato has drawn out of them. Aristotle's teaching is everywhere authoritative as regards the teachings of Socrates ; for, following Socrates by somewhat of an interval, and uninfluenced by personal relationship, he was able to set in clear light the essential features of Socrates' scientific work.

H. Köchly, *Sokrates u. sein Volk* (in *Acad. Vortr. u. Red.*, I. 219 f.); E. v. Lasaulx, *Des Sokrates Leben, Lehre und Tod* (München, 1857); M. Carrière, *Sokrates u. seine Stellung in der Gesch. des menschlichen Geistes* (in *Westermann's Monatsheften*, 1864); E. Alberti, *Sokrates, ein Versuch über ihn nach den Quellen* (Göttingen, 1869); E. Chaignet, *Vie de Sokrate* (Paris, 1868); A. Labriola, *La doctrina di Sokrate* (Neapel, 1871); A. Fouillée, *La philos. de Sokrate* (Paris, 1873); A. Krohn, *Sokrate doctrina e Platonis republica illustrata* (Halle, 1875); Windelband, *Sokrates* (in *Praeludien*, p. 54 f.); K. Joël, *Der echte u. der xenophontische Sokrates*, I. (Leipzig, 1892).

[1] The *Memorabilia* are essential for our consideration of this (see A. Krohn, *Soc. u. Xen.*, Halle, 1874). So is the *Symposium*. The question as to the priority of the *Symposium* of Xenophon or the *Symposium* of Plato is not yet fully decided in favor of the former, but is of late accepted. Compare Ch. V. Compare Sander, *Bemerkungen zu Xenophon's Berichten*, etc. (Magdeburg, 1884).

Socrates was born in Athens a little before 469,[1] the son of Sophroniscus, a sculptor, and Phænarete. He learned the trade [2] of his father, and discriminatingly absorbed the various elements of culture of his time, without applying himself to properly erudite studies. Acquaintance with the methods of instruction of the Sophists awoke in him the conviction of the dangerousness of their tendencies. Against them he felt himself called by divine direction [3] to a serious examination [4] of himself and his fellow-citizens, and to unremitting labor in the direction of moral perfection. He was moved by a deep religious spirit and an exalted moral sense in his investigations. He shared with his contemporaries an immediate interest in these investigations; and his own peculiar activity, which began in Athens as early as the commencement of the Peloponnesian war,[5] rests upon these. He belonged to no school, and it was foreign to his purpose to found one. With spontaneous feeling, he sought on the broad public field, which Athenian life offered, intellectual intercourse with every one. His extraordinary exterior,[6] his dry humor, his ready and triumphant repartee brought him into universal notice. His geniality, however, and the fine spiritual nature which lay hidden in his astonishing shell,[7] the unselfishness which he manifested unstintedly toward his friends, exercised an irresistible charm upon all the remarkable personalities of the time, especially upon the better elements of the Athe-

[1] He was at his death (399) over seventy years old.

[2] Concerning a piece, later on pointed out as one upon which the young Socrates was said to have wrought, see P. Schuster, *Ueber die Porträts der griech. Philos.* (Leipzig, 1877).

[3] Plato, *Apol.*, 33 c.

[4] ἐξετάζειν ἐμαυτὸν καὶ τοὺς ἄλλους : *ibid.*, 28 e.

[5] The production of the *Clouds*, 423, attests his popularity.

[6] The humorous characterization of his own Silenus shape is in Xenophon's *Symposium*, 4, 19 f.

[7] Compare the beautiful speech of Alcibiades in Plato, *Symposium*, 215 f.

nian youth. While he in this way obeyed higher duty to the neglect [1] of home cares, in free fellowship a circle of admirers formed itself around him in which especially the aristocratic youth were represented in men like Alcibiades. He held himself as far away from political activity as possible, but the unavoidable duties of the citizen of a state he performed with simple integrity.[2]

At the age of seventy Socrates was accused of " corrupting the youth and introducing new gods." The charges arose originally from low personal motives,[3] but became serious through political complications,[4] in that the aristocratically inclined philosopher, as the most popular and active " Sophist," was to be made answerable for moral degeneration by the democratic reactionary party. Notwithstanding he would have been freed with a small penalty [5] if he himself had not offended [6] the Heliasts by his candid pride in his virtue. The execution of the sentence of death was delayed thirty days by the $\theta\epsilon\omega\rho\iota\alpha$ to Delos, and Socrates disdained in his loyalty [7] to law the flight so easily possible to him. He drank the cup of hemlock in May,[8] 399.

[1] Concerning Xantippe, whose name has become proverbial, see E. Zeller, *Zur Ehrenrettung der Xan.* (in *Vortrag und Abhandlung*, I. p. 51 f).

[2] He made three campaigns, and showed himself, as prytanis, just and fearless against the excited minds of the masses (see Plato. *Apol.*, 32 f.).

[3] The accusers Meletus, Anytus, and Lycon acted out of personal animosity, unless they were men of straw (K. F. Hermann, *De Soc. accusatoribus*, Göttingen, 1854).

[4] See Grote, *History of Greece*, VIII. 551 f.

[5] The verdict of " guilty " was carried only by a majority of three or thirty ; the sentence of death had a much larger majority (more than eighty).

[6] The *Apology* of Plato may be taken as authentic in its essentials.

[7] Compare Plato's dialogue, the *Crito.*

[8] In respect to the external circumstances of the day of his death, Plato's dialogue, the *Phædo*, is certainly historical, although Plato in it

An instructor in philosophy, in the strict sense of the term, Socrates did not have. He called himself (Xen. *Symposium*, 1, 5) αὐτουργός. But apparently he had become familiar with many of the scientific theories, especially with those of Heracleitus and Anaxagoras, not only through the discourses of the Sophists but through his own readings. (Compare K. F. Hermann, *De S. magistris et disciplina juvenili*, Marburg, 1837.) The process of development portrayed in the *Phædo* is scarcely historical, but can be looked upon as a sketch of the Platonic theory of ideas. (Compare Zeller, II⁴. 51.)

Xenophon, as well as Plato, makes Socrates meet persons of every position, calling, and political complexion in his conversations. His relation to young men was an ethically pedagogical and morally spiritual ennoblement of the Grecian love for boys. Among the men who made his popular philosophical method their own are to be named: Xenophon, who stood very near to the Cynics (compare F. Dümmler, *Antisthenica*, Berl., 1882, and *Academica*, Giessen, 1889); also Æschines (not the orator), who wrote dialogues in the same spirit (K. F. Hermann, *De Æsch. Socratici reliquiis* (Göttingen, 1850); and the almost mythical shoemaker Simon (see Böckh, *Simonis Socraticis dialogi*, Heidelberg, 1810, and E. Heitz in O. Müller's *Litteraturgeschichte*, II². 2, 25, note 2).

The legal measures against Socrates are open to the most different constructions. The old view that the philosopher was ruined through intrigues of the Sophists may be regarded as given up, and also the conception originated by Hegel (*Complete Works*, II. 560 f., XIV. 81 f.), according to which, as in a tragedy, Socrates was the champion of the higher Idea, and was ruined by his unavoidable crime of offending the established laws. These great antitheses play no part in the trial. It appears, rather, that through personal and political intrigues Socrates became a sacrifice for the discontent which the democratic reaction fostered against the entire Enlightenment. Although presumably unintentionally, nevertheless Aristophanes did a decided injury to the philosopher in his caricature of him in the *Clouds*,[1] in that he stamped him in the public mind as a type of precisely those Sophistic excesses which Socrates fought most vigorously. (Compare H. Th. Rötscher, *Aristophanes und seine Zeitalter*,

goes far beyond Socrates in his theory of the immortality of the soul (compare *Apol.*, 40 c) not only in his presentation of evidence, but as to his personal conviction.

[1] Compare especially H. Diels, *Verh. d. Stett. Phil. Vers.*, 1880, 106 f.

Berlin, 1817 ; Brandis, in the *Rh. Mus.*, 1828 ; P. W. Forch-hammer, *Die Athener und Soc.*, Berlin, 1837 ; Bendixen, *Ueber den tieferen Schriftsinn*, etc. (Husum, 1838.)

The theory of knowledge of the Sophists had led in all its parts to a relativism of individual opinions. The effort, on the other hand, for a stable and universally valid knowledge formed the central point of the activity of Socrates. The ἐπιστήμη was set in antithesis to the δόξαι by him; yet the ἐπιστήμη is not a complete, erudite possession to be handed down, but an ideal to be striven for in work in common with other men.

Fr. Schleiermacher, *Ueber d. Wert des Sokrates als Philos. in Ges. Werk*, III. 2, 287 ff.

Socrates did not try, therefore, to impart knowledge or to give purely formal instruction, but to engage in a mutual seeking for truth. The basis of this was the conviction that such a norm of truth existed paramount to individual opinion. Therefore his activity found its necessary form in the dialogue, the conversation in which, through the exchange of opinions and through mutual criticism of these, that should be found which is recognizable by all. While the Sophists studied the psychological mechanism by which opinions come to be, Socrates had faith in a law of reason that determines the truth. His whole endeavor was only a continuous invitation to his fellow-citizens to help him in this search. His confession of his ignorance [1] signified this, while he also at the same time herein intimated [2] his failure to attain his ideal of σοφία. Yet he demanded the same measure of self-knowledge [3] also from others. For

---

[1] Plato, *Apol.*, 21 f. ; *Symp.*, 216 d.

[2] Compare Plato, *Symp.*, 203 f. In this connection the term φιλοσοφία wins, as contrasted with the more pretentious σοφία (σοφιστής), its peculiar meaning, "striving for knowledge." See Ueberweg, p. 2.

[3] Compare the oracular γνῶθι σεαυτόν, Xen. *Mem.*. IV. 24 f.; Plato, *Apol.*, 21 f.

nothing more dangerous blocked the way of wisdom than
that conceited affectation of wisdom which the Sophistic
half-education developed in the majority of minds. Therefore his conversation analyzed with exasperating logic the
opinion which at the outset he elicited from others, and in
this superior manipulation of the dialectic consisted the
Socratic irony.[1] But after removing this impediment
Socrates, in leading the conversation, sought to draw out
gradually what was common to the participants. In the
persuasion that serious reflection could find such a common
thought, he " delivered " the slumbering thought from the
mind ; and this art he called his maieutic.[2]

The method of the Socratic investigation corresponded,
in point of content also, to this external schema. He set
the concept as the goal[3] of scientific work over against
the single ideas given by individual perception. When
therefore Socrates in general aimed at definition, he
came into contact with the efforts of the Sophists[4] who had
busied themselves in fixing the meanings of words. But
he on his part went much deeper, in the hope of grasping
the essence of fact and the law governing single cases and
relationships by the application of this universal principle.
In making the answer to the particular question from which
the conversation proceeded depend[5] on the general definition to be sought, he was making man conscious of the law
of logical dependence of the particulars upon the universal,
and exalting that law to the principle of the scientific
method. In the search for universal concepts Socrates still

[1] Plato, *Rep.*, I. 337 a.

[2] With reference to the profession of his mother; Plato, *Theæt.*, 149 f.

[3] Arist. *Met.*, XII. 4, 1078 b, 17 : τὸ ὁρίζεσθαι καθόλου. The technical expression for the concept is, in this connection, λόγος.

[4] Particularly with Prodicus, with whom his relations were uniformly
friendly.

[5] Xen. *Mem.*, IV. 13.

remained strongly fixed in the habits of naïve reflection.
For the inductive procedure, the introduction of which is
accredited to him,[1] consisted in the comparison of arbitrarily collated particular cases, by means of which, however,
a complete induction could not be guaranteed. But, nevertheless, the Socratic method was a distinct advance over the
entirely unmethodical generalizations, which earlier thinkers had drawn from single observations or thought *motifs*.
It began, moreover, to set a methodical treatment in the
place of ingenious fancies.

P. J. Ditges, *Die epagogische Methode des S.* (Cologne,
1864) ; J. J. Guttmann, *Ueber den wissenschaftlichen Stand-
punkt des S.* (Brieg, 1881).   Examples of the Socratic method
are to be found in the *Memorabilia* of Xenophon and in most
of the dialogues of Plato.   Socrates did not advance to a definite formulation of methodical principles, but his entire activity
has given them distinctly the character of an inspired insight.

The realm to which Socrates applied this method of the
inductive definition of concepts included — as in the case
of the Sophists — essentially the problems of human life.
For, as his search for conceptual truth was rooted in the
strength of his moral conviction, science and moral self-
culture were to him in the last instance identical.   The
universally valid truth, which he said was to be found by
means of conversation, is the clearness and certainty of
moral consciousness.

The limitation of philosophy to ethics, and on the other hand
the establishment of scientific ethics, passed even in antiquity
as the essential characteristic of the Socratic teaching. (See
Zeller, II[4]. 132 f.).   Neither the poetic license, with which
Aristophanes (in the *Clouds*) made of him a star-gazer, nor the
passages in the later Platonic dialogues (*Phœdo* and *Philebus*),
in which a teleological nature-philosophy is put into his mouth,
nor, finally, the very homely utilitarian theory, presumably afterward revised [2] by the Stoics, which the *Memorabilia* makes him

---

[1] Arist. *Met.*, l. c.   [2] See A. Krohn, *Xen. u. Soc.* (Halle, 1874).

develop, — none of these can have weight against the very definite expressions of Xenophon (*Mem.*, I. 1, 11) and Aristotle
(*Met.*, I. 6, 987 b, 2). On the other hand, his aversion to
natural science was not in the spirit of Skepticism, but due to
the deficiency of science in ethical value. A universal faith in
the teleological arrangement of the world and in a Providence
over mankind remained side by side with this aversion. See conclusion in Plato's *Apology*, in *Euthyphro*, etc.

In this specific ethical turn, Socrates followed, however,
a psychological principle, which expresses the rationalistic
character of the Enlightenment in its purity. *It is the
formula of the identity of virtue and knowledge.*[1] In the
complicated relationships of civilized life the habitual ob-
servance of national conventions had become insufficient.
In the confusion of public life, where one thing was commended here, another there, every one felt that he needed
knowledge and judgment for making correct decisions.
In the increasing competition in civilization the well-in-
formed[2] man proved himself to be the abler in all departments of life. Socrates expressed himself most clearly as
to this condition, when he, applying the case to morals,
declared that true virtue consists in knowing, and that right
knowing leads always of itself to right acting. Thereby
to know the Good was elevated to the essence of morality
and reflection to the principle of living. Philosophy, as
Socrates understood it, was the independent meditation of
reasoning man upon that law of goodness valid for all
alike. Knowledge is a moral possession, and the common
striving for it he designated as a process of mutual help-
fulness[3] under the name ἔρως. On the other hand, this

[1] See Xen. *Mem.*, III. 9, 4.

[2] *Ibid.*, 9, 10 ff.

[3] This is the Socratic concept of ἔρως, whose extreme importance
appears in the fact that not only Plato and Xenophon, but also other
friends within the Socratic circle, have written about it. Compare
Brandis, *Handbuch*, II. 1, 64.

point of view involved a deterministic and intellectual conception of the will, which makes moral excellence dependent upon intellectual culture, and in general the decision of will exclusively dependent on the clearness and ripeness of the insight.   When he asserted that all evil action proceeds only out of a deficient insight,[1] this is the same as proclaiming entirely in the spirit of the Enlightenment that knowledge is the ethical ideal.   For Socrates all other virtues accord with the fundamental virtue, $\epsilon\pi\iota\sigma\tau\acute{\eta}\mu\eta$,[2] and possessing this all the others are attainable and teachable.   The process begun at the time of the Seven Wise Men was completed in these definitions of Socrates ; and the norms of universal consciousness, after they had for a time been imperilled by individual criticism, during the wild anarchy of opinions were again found by rational reflection and by the recognition of the universal validity therein involved.

The question of the teachableness of virtue is treated in a most engaging dialectic in the dialogue *Protagoras*, while the other dialogues of Plato's earliest period have for their common theme the reduction of the single virtues to the fundamental virtue of knowledge.   These are *Euthyphro, Laches, Charmides*, and *Lysis*.   Compare F. Dittrich, *De S. sententia virtutem esse scientiam* (Braunsberg, 1868) and particularly T. Wildauer, *Die Psychologie des Willens bei Sokrates, Platon und Aristoteles*, Part I. (Innsbruck, 1877).   Besides, the determinism of Socrates stands in a close relation to his eudæmonism (see below).   For the proposition that no one will freely do wrong is founded upon the same basis with that proposition that if one has recognized what is good for him it would be impossible for him to choose the opposite against his own interest.   Compare Xen. *Mem.*, IV. 6, 6 ; Arist. *Magn. Moral.*, I. 9, 1187 a, 17.

In the realm of ethics, moreover, Socrates stopped at this most general suggestion without developing syste-

---

[1] Xen. *Mem*, III. 9.

[2] In Xenophon one still finds the word $\sigma o\phi\acute{\iota}a$ for this ; see *Mem.*, III. 9.

matically that kind of knowing (*Wissen*) in which virtue was said to consist. For the distinctive trait of the
activity of Socrates was that he never lost sight of the
given conditions. Therefore the question, " What then is
the Good ?" always became the question as to what is
the Good in a particular respect and for a particular individual ;[1] and the answer was always found in the suitable,
in that which perfectly satisfies the striving of man and
makes him happy. According to the grosser[2] interpretation of Xenophon, Socrates' ethical theory was utilitarian-
ism, and the value of virtue founded on knowing sank to
the prudential cleverness of acting in every case according
to correct knowledge (*Erkenntnis*) of expediency. The finer
presentation of Plato refers, however, this ὠφέλιμον, which
is assumed as identical with καλόν and ἀγαθόν, to the
health of the soul,[3] to its furtherance toward a true state
of perfection. In both cases, nevertheless, intellectual
virtue is identified with happiness.[4] Right action, toward
which insight guides, makes man happy. The fundamental
conception of ethics in Socrates is thoroughly eudæmonistic, and ancient philosophy did not pass beyond this point.

Compare M. Heinze, *Der Eudämonismus in der griech.
Philos.* (Leipzig, 1883) ; Zeller, II[4]. 149 f. In all particulars
the Socratic morals remained essentially within the compass of
Greek social-consciousness.[5] It sought to find a basis in the

---

[1] *Mem.*, III. 8.

[2] In whose writings, in one passage, it would appear that Socrates
agreed in morals with the relativism of the Sophists: *Mem.*, III. 8,
πάντα ἀγαθὰ καὶ καλά ἐστι πρὸς ἃ ἂν εὖ ἔχῃ, κακὰ δὲ καὶ αἰσχρὰ πρὸς ἃ ἂν
κακῶς.

[3] Particularly note the representation of the *Phœdo*.

[4] Xen. *Mem.*, IV. 1, 2.

[5] To be excepted is only the prohibition of doing evil to an enemy.
If here the contradiction between Plato's and Xenophon's representations is irreconcilable, we are inclined to regard Plato's report as the
true one : for the *Crito*, which treats this prohibition as one already long

reverent recognition of divine law and established usage. Particularly Socrates himself, the model of noble and pure morals, gave high place to civic virtue, to submission to the laws of the state. In the state, however, he would have not the masses, but the good and intelligent, rule (Xen. *Mem.*, III. 9, 10).

Socrates personally supplemented his indifference to metaphysical and physical theories by a deep and religious piety, which led him to believe in the rule of the divine essence in nature and in human life. He likewise supplemented the rationalistic one-sidedness of his ethics by his unswerving faith in obedience to the divine voice, which he believed he heard in himself as δαιμόνιον.

Likewise in the development of this thought, Xenophon, provided the extant form of the *Memorabilia* comes from him, stood at the point of view of commonplace utility, while Plato's *Apology* represents faith in Providence in a high ethical light. In Socrates the rejection of nature knowledge comes about from the fact that such knowledge contains trifles that waste our time.[1] On the other hand, there was the interest of piety, which led [2] him to require a teleological view of the cosmos. It is improbable that he gave an exhaustive development of it, because (*Mem.*, I. 4, and IV. 3) Socrates usually was most prudently reserved on such questions. Even Monotheism he by no means emphasized sharply. He speaks mostly of " the Gods," both in Xenophon and Plato, and no enemy ever once charged him with disavowing " the Gods." [3]   Concerning the δαιμόνιον, compare Ueberweg, I⁴. 107, and Zeller, II⁴. 74.

Regarded on the whole, the activity of Socrates, in that he set up the ideal of reason as against relativism, was an attempt to reform the life morally by means of science. The success of his teaching led among the best friends of

recognized in the Socratic circle, though indeed at variance with popular opinion, clearly belongs to the earliest writings of Plato.

[1] Xen. *Mem.*, I. 1, and IV. 7.

[2] *Ibid.*, I. 4, and IV. 3.

[3] He was reproached with introducing a new divine being, and his enemies appeared to be aiming especially at the δαιμόνιον.

the philosopher to the highest achievements of ancient culture. The principle of reflective introspection, however, which was thus victoriously awakened, and the enthusiasm with which Socrates turned his meditations from the charm of external existence to the value of the intellectual life, were in the Grecian world a new and strange thing. At this point of view the philosophy embodied by him detached itself from its background of culture and took other shape.

28. Under the name "Socratics" a number of schools are usually grouped, which, founded by men of more or less close association with Socrates, stepped forth, directly after his death, with opinions that belonged in their direction and content entirely to the Greek Enlightenment. If we look, nevertheless, more closely, we see that these men and their teaching have a much nearer relationship to the Sophists [1] than to Socrates; and that, especially in the development of these schools, the "Socratic element," which to some degree was still present in Euclid, Antisthenes, and Aristippus, vanishes more and more from sight. These so-called "Socratic schools" should rather be viewed as branches of Sophism which were touched by the Socratic spirit. There were four such schools: the Megarian and the Elean-Eretrian, the Cynic and the Cyrenaic. Among these the Cynics stand nearest to Socrates.

K. F. Hermann, *Die philos. Stellung der älteren Sokratiker u. ihrer Schulen* (in *Ges. Abhandl.*, Göttingen, 1849, p. 227 f.) ; Th. Ziegler, *Gesch. d. Ethik*, I. 145.

The founder of the Megarian school, Euclid, believed in his ability to give content to the Eleatic concept of Being, by identifying it with the Socratic concept of the Good. Yet no victory over the abstract sterility of the Parmenidean principle was won by this method. For even if

[1] Aristotle calls (*Met.*, II. 2, 996 a, 33), for example, Aristippus a Sophist, and with justice.

Euclid defined[1] the Good as the one ever immutable[2] Being, which is given[3] different names by men; even if he characterized the different virtues only as the changing names of the one unchangeable virtue, that is, of knowing, which was thus identified with Being as among the Eleatics; even if he thereby refused[4] reality to all concepts other than to that of the Good; — nevertheless all this led neither to the construction of an ethics nor to an enrichment of theoretical knowledge, but gave evidence of a continuation of unfruitful dialectic in the direction of Eleatic Sophistry. The Megarians, therefore, accomplished nothing in the realm of ethics. The only one of them to whom political teachings are ascribed was Stelpo, the later head of the school, who, however, in this respect had entirely adopted the views of the Cynics. In metaphysics the Megarians were satisfied with the assertion of the unity of that which possesses Being, and with an indirect proof of that assertion resembling the Eleatic argumentations. In this spirit Diodorus Cronus added[5] to the arguments of Zeno new ones which were indeed less significant and far more captious. In these the impossibility of constructing a continuum out of a sum of discrete quantities again played the chief rôle. There was a similar tendency manifested in the investigations of the Megarians concerning the categories of modality. For the assertion that only the actual[6] is possible, and the famous proof ($\kappa\nu\rho\iota\epsilon\dot{\nu}\omega\nu$)[7] of Diodorus Cronus — that the unactual, which has demon-

---

[1] Diog. Laert., VII. 161.

[2] Cicero, *Acad.*, II. 42, 129.

[3] Diog. Laert , II. 106.

[4] *Ibid.*: compare Euseb. *Præp. ev.*, XIV. 17.

[5] Preserved in Sext. Emp. *Adv. math.*, X. 85 f.

[6] Arist. *Met.*, VIII. 3, 1046 b, 29.

[7] Compare Cicero, *De fato*, 6, 12 f.   Later philosophers, particularly Chrysippus, have definitely declared their positions with reference to this argument.

strated itself through its unactuality to be impossible, may not be called possible — point only in a rather abstract way to the refutation of Becoming and change.[1]

Compare F. Deycks, *Die Megaricorum doctrina* (Bonn, 1827) ; Henne, *École de Mégare* (Paris, 1843) ; Mallet, *Histoire de l'école de Mégare et des écoles d'Élis et d'Érétrie* (Paris, 1845).

We can only speak in general of the dates of the life of Euclid of Megara, one of the oldest and truest friends that Socrates had. He was not much younger than Socrates, yet he considerably outlived him, and opened after the death of the master his hospitable house to his friends. About this time a school formed itself around him, and it appears to have remained intact through the fourth century. Of the most of those who are mentioned as adherents of this school, we know only the names. Particulars are reported only of Eubulides of Miletus, the teacher of Demosthenes, of Diodorus Cronus, of Iasus in Caria (d. 307), and especially of Stilpo, who was a native of Megara (Diog. Laert., II. 113 f.). Stilpo lived from 380 to 300, and aroused universal admiration by his lectures. He linked the Megarian dialectics to the Cynic ethics, and decisively influenced thereby his chief pupil, Zeno, the founder of Stoicism. His younger contemporary was Alexinus of Elis.

The most important controversial question arising in reference to the Megarian school concerns the hypothesis set up by Schleiermacher (in his translation of Plato, V. 2, 140 f.) and opposed by Ritter (*Ueber d. Philos. der meg. Schule, Rhein. Mus.*, 1828) and Mallet (loc. cit. XXXIV. f.), accepted by most others, including Brandis and Prantl, and defended by Zeller (I[4]. 215 f.). This hypothesis is to the effect that the representation of the theory of Ideas in the dialogue, the *Sophist* (246 b, 248 f.), refers to the Megarians. If one is convinced that this dialogue is genuinely Platonic, it is difficult to provide for this theory of Ideas. For to presuppose any kind of an otherwise unknown school (Ritter) as the author of so significant a

[1] Since Aristotle cites the proposition as Megarian, that only the actual is the possible, it can scarcely have arisen from the polemic against the Aristotelian categories δύναμις and ἐνέργεια. But possibly the later Megarians, for example Diodorus, developed it in this direction. Compare Hartenstein, *Ueber die Bedeutung der megarischen Schule für die Geschichte der metaphysischen Probleme* (in *Hist. philos. Abhandlungen*, 127 f.).

system as that of the ἀσώματα εἴδη, is forbidden because Aristotle (*Met.*, I. 6 ; *Nic. Eth.*, I. 4) designated Plato distinctly as the inventor of the same. It is certainly very far from having any place in the Socratic schools. But the teaching is even as little consistent with what has been at other times confidently ascribed to the Megarians as with the teaching of any one of the other schools. In no place is there a single indication of it. It stands in so abrupt opposition especially to the abstract theory of Being of the Megarians, that we do not avoid the difficulty by taking for granted a gradual development within the school.[1]

On the other hand, it may be shown that the description [2] which the dialogue, the *Sophist*, gives of this theory of Ideas, agrees completely and even verbally with that phase of the Platonic philosophy expressed in the *Symposium*.[3] There is, accordingly, nothing left but either accept Plato as opposed to an earlier phase of his own teaching and its φίλοι, or to find the author of this criticism of the Platonic philosophy in an Eleatic contemporary of Plato. (For details, see Ch. V.) In neither case can the theory of Ideas treated in the passage in the *Sophist*, nor the developed theory of knowledge connected closely with it and completely Platonic in character, be ascribed to the Megarians. This theory in the *Sophist* amounts to a sensuous knowledge of γένεσις, or a knowledge of the corporeal world plus a conceptual knowledge of οὐσία, which is a knowledge of the non-corporeal Ideas.

The only remaining feature worthy of comment in regard to the Megarian school is its development of the Sophistic art of Eristic. Its abstract theory of unity involved a skepticism regarding all concrete knowledge and a negative trend in its instruction. The prominent fact in re-

---

[1] Zeller seems to believe (II[4]. 261) that the Euclidean theory of Ideas was given up in the course of the development of the school to satisfy the theory of unity. Since the latter theory had been given from the very beginning in the form of Eleaticism there must then be expected conversely a gradual division of the Eleatic One into a plurality of Ideas and this is precisely what Plato accomplished.

[2] See E. Appel, *Arch. f. Gesch. d. Ph.*, V. 55 f.

[3] In this connection there is hardly an allusion to Ideas as causes of the phenomenal world. Zeller, I[4]. 316. The οὐσία as αἰτία is first introduced in the *Phædo*, *Philebus*, and the latter parts of the *Republic*. See Ch. V.

spect to Euclid is that he in polemics followed the method [1]
of neglecting proofs and even premises, and leaped directly
to the conclusion by means of *reductio ad absurdum*. Stilpo
accepted the Sophistic-Cynic assertion, that according to
the law of identity a predicate different from the subject
cannot be ascribed to the subject. The younger members,
Eubulides and Alexinus,[2] got their notoriety by inventing
the so-called " catches." These are questions put in such
a way that no one of the possible disjunctive answers can
be given without involving a contradiction.

See Prantl, *Gesch. der Logik*, I. 33 f.; Diog. Laert., II. 168,
enumerates seven of these " catches," — the Liar, then three
practically identical ones, the Concealed, the Disguised, and
the *Electra*, and further the Horned Man, and finally the Heap
(Sorites) and the Bald-head, which positively and negatively
suggest the *acervus* of Zeno (§ 20).   As was the case with the
Sophistic witticisms, these were in the main reducible to verbal
ambiguities. The lively interest that antiquity had in them was
almost wholly pathological.

Still less significant was the Elean-Eretrian school, which
was founded by Phædo, Socrates' favorite scholar, in his
native city Elis.   Later it was transferred by Menedemus
to his home, Eretria, where it died out about the beginning
of the third century.   It appears to have taken a similar
line of development as the Megarian school and Phædo
agreed with Euclid [3] in all essentials. Menedemus, who
received instruction in the Academy and from Stilpo, co-
operated with Stilpo in turning the school toward Cynic
ethics.   Both schools merged finally, like the Cynic, in the
Stoa.

[1] Diog. Laert., II. 107.
[2] Whose name was facetiously perverted into Ἐλεγξῖνος: Diog.
Laert., II. 109.
[3] Presumably he had received powerful influence from Euclid during his stay in Megara.

Compare Mallet (see above) ; L. Preller, *Phædon's Lebens-schicksale und Schriften* (*Ersch und Gruber*, III. 21, 357 f.) ; v. Wilamowitz-Möllendorf (*Hermes*, 1879).

Phædo, when very young, was taken into captivity by the Athenians, and not long before Socrates' death he was, at the instigation of Socrates, freed from slavery by one of his friends. The genuineness of the dialogues ascribed to him was early very much in doubt. At any rate, as little from the literary activity of this school is preserved as from that of the Megarians. Menedemus, who is said to have died soon after 271 at the age of seventy-four, had (Diog. Laert., II. 125 f.) raised himself from a very low position to one of considerable authority. It is now impossible to determine whether his apparently loose and transitory relation to the Academy was a fact. Only the names of the other members of the school are preserved.

29. Notably more important are the two schools existing immediately after Socrates and not uninfluenced by his ethical doctrine. In these, the Cynic and Cyrenaic, the opposition as to both moral and social conceptions of life took definite form. They had in common an indifference for theoretic science and a desire to concentrate philosophy upon the art of living. Common also was the origin of their philosophy from the Sophistic circle ; and they found partial support in the formulations of Socrates. They were, however, diametrically opposed in their conception of the place of man and his relation to society. This remained a typical opposition for the whole ancient world. Both theories as the result of the cultural and philosophical impulse given by the Sophists reveal the disposition of the Grecian world toward the value which civilization possesses in its control of individual impulses. This common problem put the same limits upon their endeavors in spite of their different conclusions.

The Cynic school was called into life by Antisthenes of Athens, and maintained its popularity on account of the original character, Diogenes of Sinope. Among its more distant followers may be named Crates of Thebes, his wife Hipparchia, and her brother Metrocles.

Antisthenes, born about 440, was not a full-blooded Athenian. He had entered the Sophistic profession of teaching as the pupil of Gorgias, before he came under the influence of Socrates, whose active admirer he became. After the death of Socrates he founded a school in the gymnasium Cynosarges, which he administered for quite a time. Of his numerous writings (Diog. Laert., VI. 15 f.) only a few fragments are preserved, — collected by A. W. Winckelmann (Zurich, 1842). Compare Chappuis, *Antisthène* (Paris, 1854) ; K. Barlen, *Antisthenes u. Platon* (Neuwied, 1891) ; K. Urban, *Ueber die Erwähnungen der Philos. des Antisthenes in den platonischen Schriften* (Königsberg, 1882) ; F. Dümmler, *Antisthenica* (Halle, 1882) and *Akademika* (Giessen, 1889) ; E. Norden, *Beiträge z. Gesch. d. gr. Ph.*, 1–4.

Diogenes, the Σωκράτης μαινόμενος, fled as a counterfeiter from his home to Athens, and ornamented his proletariat and queer existence with the wisdom of Antisthenes. He claimed to put the theory of his teacher consistently into practice. In old age he lived as tutor in the house of Xeniades in Corinth, and died there in 323. Compare K. W. Göttling, *Diogenes der Kyniker oder d. Phil. des gr. Proletariats* (*Geschich. Abhandl.*, I. 251 f.) ; K. Steinhart (*Ersch u. Gruber*, I. 25, 301 f.)

Crates of Thebes, nearly contemporary of Stilpo, is said to have given away his property in order to dedicate himself to the Cynic life. His rich and nobly connected wife followed him into a beggar's existence. Anecdotes only are preserved concerning his brother-in-law, Metrocles. Cynicism continued later as a popular moralizing instruction ; for example in Teles, whom v. Wilamowitz-Möllendorf treats (*Philol. Untersuchungen*, IV. 292 f.), and whose fragments have been published by O. Hense (Freiburg, 1889). Later do we find Cynicism in Bion of Borysthenes, whose sermons greatly influenced later literature (Horace),[1] as upon the other hand the satires of the Phoenician Menippus, which breathe the Cynic spirit, influenced Varro. See Zeller, II³. 246, 3.

As only the Good was Being for the Megarians, for the Cynics virtue appeared to be the only legitimate content and purpose of life. With similar Eleatic one-sidedness they remained averse to all other ideals and disdainful of them. They taught indeed, like Socrates, that virtue consists in knowing, and yet they emphasized the practical

---

[1] Compare R. Heinze, *De Horatio Bionis imitatore* (Bonn, 1889).

side, that is, right action, and especially the consistent
carrying out of moral principles [1] in life. They likewise attributed only so much value, therefore, to scientific investigations as those investigations serve ethical
purposes.

It is to be added that in its epistemology also this school
stood entirely upon the ground of Sophistic skepticism.
It indeed sounds to some degree Socratic for Antisthenes
to demand [2] the explanation of the permanent essence of
things by definition. Yet in his development of this postulate he fell back upon the opinion of Gorgias that of no
subject can an attribute differing in any way from it be
predicated. He made it equivalent to the statement that
only identical judgments are possible.[3]   Accordingly only
the composite are definable ; [4] all simple things, on the other
hand, can be indicated [5] only by their peculiar individual
names, which, however, do not explain the essence of the
fact itself. Thus their theory of knowledge reduced itself
to bare skepticism ; and it also manifested itself in Antisthenes adopting the Sophistic teaching that a contradiction is wholly impossible.[6]

[1] Even in the character of Antisthenes this consistency, this serious
and strict adherence to principles, was the central point. Diogenes
intended assuredly to outdo him in this respect.

[2] To him belongs the definition λόγος ἐστὶν ὁ τὸ τί ἦν ἢ ἔστι δηλῶν.

[3] That the place in the *Sophist*, 251 b, refers to Antisthenes, Aristotle
teaches in *Metaphysics*, IV. 29, 1024 b, 32.

[4] Compare Aristotle, *ibid.*, VIII 3, 1043 b, 24.

[5] The logically central truth of the Cynic teaching appears in the
Platonic statement (*Theæt.*, 201 f.)   This truth is that the ultimate
terms (τὰ πρῶτα) by which all else may be defined are themselves not
definable or reducible to something else. This opinion is closely joined
with that which looks upon these last elements of concepts as the
στοιχεῖα, by which all things are really constituted. This is a view
which in a certain sense sounds like the homoiomeriai of Anaxagoras,
and also like the Platonic theory of Ideas.

[6] Arist. *Met.*, IV. 29, 1024 b, 34.

This purely Sophistic limitation of knowledge to nomenclature had taken on as a most obvious nominalism a distinct polemical tendency against the theory of Ideas. The old tradition placed in the mouths of Antisthenes and Diogenes rough and coarse ridicule of the Platonic theory (τράπεζαν ὁρῶ, τραπεζότητα δ'οὐχ ὁρῶ, Diog. Laert., VI. 53 ; compare *Schol. in Arist.*, 66 b, 45, etc. ; Zeller, II³. 255) ; for these leaders of the Cynics only single things existed *in natura rerum*. The class concepts are only names without content. At the same time it is evident that, since the essence of a thing did not seem to them logically determinable, they claimed that it was producible only in sense perception. Thus they fell into the coarse materialism which regards a thing as actual only as the thing can be held in the hand. Presumably this fact is meant in the *Sophist*, 246 a ; *Theœtetus*, 155 e, *Phœdo*, 79 f. Compare Natorp, *Forschungen*, 198 f.

So much the more was the science of these men limited to their theoretically meagre doctrine of virtue. Virtue, and it alone, is sufficient to satisfy all strivings for happiness. Virtue is not only the highest, but the only good, — the only certain means of being happy. Over against this spiritual and therefore sure possession, which is protected against all the changes of the fateful world, the Cynics despised all that men otherwise held dear. Virtue alone is of worth ; wickedness alone is to be shunned ; all else is indifferent (ἀδιάφορον).[1] From this principle they taught the contempt of riches and luxury, of fame and honor, of sense-pleasure and sense-pain. But with this radical consistency, which ever grew sharper with them, they also despised all the joy and beauty of life, all shame and conventionality, family and country.

The obtrusive moralization of these philosophical beggars appears mainly in their coarse witticisms ; and very many anecdotes relate to Diogenes. There is very little of serious investigation in their moralizing. Antisthenes appears to assert the worthlessness of pleasure, perhaps against Aristippus, and to have sought to demonstrate that man with such a conviction, even if it be not entirely right, would be proof against the

[1] Diog. Laert., VI. 105.

slavery of sense pleasure.[1] In Diogenes this disgust of all
external goods grew to the philosophical grim humor of a prole-
tarian, who has staked his cause on nothing.   Irrespective of
the mental culture to which, so far as it concerns virtue, he
ascribed some worth,[2] he contended against all the devices of
civilization as superfluous, foolish, and dangerous to virtue.
Most dubious in all this was the shamelessness of which the
Cynics were guilty, and their intentional disregard of all the conventions of sexual relations ; similar too was their indifference
to the family life and to the state.[3] For the cosmopolitanism in
which Diogenes took pride[4] had not the positive content of a
universal human ideal, but sought only to free the individual
from every limitation imposed upon him by civilization.   In
particular, the Cynics fought against slavery as unnatural and
unjust, just as already the Sophists had fought.   On the other
hand, it must not remain unnoticed that Antisthenes,[5] in defiance
of the judgment of Greek society, declared that work is a good.
Cynicism finally reckoned also religion among the ἀδιάφορα.   All
mythical ideas and religious ceremonies fall under the class of
the conventionally determined, the unnatural, and are excusable
only because they may be regarded as allegorical expressions of
moral concepts.   Positively the Cynics represented an abstract
monotheism which finds in virtue the true worship of God.

The fundamental purpose of Cynicism in all these determinations is to make man entirely independent.   The wise
man to whom virtue, once gained,[6] is a permanent[7] possession, stands in his complete self-sufficiency[8] over against

[1] See Arist. *Eth. Nic.*, X. 1, 1172 a, 31 ; on the contrary, Plato
(*Phileb.*, 44 b) can hardly be regarded as referring to Antisthenes
(Zeller, II⁴. 308, 1). It is probable that places like the *Republic*, 583 f.,
refer to Democritus. See below, § 33 and § 31.

[2] Diog. Laert., VI. 68, and elsewhere.

[3] From Diogenes on, the Cynics had wives and children in common.
(*Ibid.*, 72.) This is only one of the instances that they manifested of
a levelling radicalism (in distinction from Plato).

[4] *Loc. cit.* 63: see *ibid.*, 11, 38, 72, 98.

[5] *Ibid.*, 2.

[6] It can also be teachable, but more through practice than through
scientific instruction. *Ibid.*, 105 f., 70.

[7] Xen. *Mem.*, 1, 2, 19.

[8] Diog. Laert., VI. 11 f.

the great mass of fools. His reward is the perfect independence in which he is equal[1] to the undesiring gods.
In order to be as independent of external goods as possible,
he reduces his needs to those most external. The less
one needs, the happier[2] one is. The Cynic Wise Man feels
himself free from society also; he sees through its prejudices; he despises[3] its talk; its laws and its conventions
do not bind him. The independent lordship of the virtuous Wise Man does not need civilization and casts it
aside. The Sophistic opposition of $\phi\acute{u}\sigma\iota\varsigma$ and $\nu\acute{o}\mu o\varsigma$ is
constructed into a principle, and all human limitation by
statute is unnatural, superfluous, and in part corrupting.
From the midst of the fulness and beauty of Greek civilization, the Cynic preaches the return to a state of nature
which would avoid all the dangers of civilization indeed, but
would forfeit all its blessings.

30. The joyous wisdom of the life of the Cyrenaics formed
the completest antithesis to the morose seriousness of the
virtue of the Cynics. The leader of this school was
Aristippus of Cyrene, a man of the world, who once
belonged to the Socratic circle, but at other times led a
wandering life as a Sophist. Through his daughter Arete
his conception of life passed down to his grandson, the
younger Aristippus. Soon after this the school branched
out with the special interpretations which men like
Theodorus the atheist, Anniceris, and Hegesias gave to
the Aristippian principle. Among later representatives
Euemerus is to be mentioned.

[1] Diog. Laert., VI. 51.

[2] See the self-description of Antisthenes in Xenophon's *Symposium*,
4, 34 f. In this respect Cynicism showed that Eudæmonism is logically
absence of need. From the eudæmonistic point of view, then, the goal is
the renunciation and suppression of all avoidable desire.

[3] Thus Diogenes accepted the designation of $\kappa\acute{u}\omega\nu$, which was originally a witticism in reference to the seat of the school, the gymnasium,
Cynosargus.

The years of the birth and death of Aristippus cannot be very exactly determined ; his life included from thirty to forty years in the fifth and fourth centuries (435–360). When he was young he was influenced to come to Athens by the fame of Socrates, and often during the course of his life did he return to that city. That he for some time lived in Syracuse in the court of the older and younger Dionysius, that he probably met Plato there, cannot well be doubted. The founding of his school in his native city, the rich and luxurious Cyrene, occurred probably at the end of his life, since all the known adherents to the school were considerably younger than he. Compare H. v. Stein, *De vita Aristippi* (Göttingen, 1855), also his *Geschichte des Platonismus*, II. 60 f.

The technical development of the theory [1] seems to have been completed by the grandson (μητροδίδακτος), of whom nothing further is known. Theodorus was driven out of his home, Cyrene, soon after the death of Alexander the Great. He lived in exile for some time in Athens and at the court of Egypt, but he returned finally to Cyrene. Anniceris and Hegesias (πεισι-θάνατος) were contemporaries of Ptolemæus Lagi. Hegesias wrote a treatise the title of which Cicero mentioned as Ἀποκαρτερῶν (*Tusc.*, I. 34, 84). Euemerus, probably of Messene (about 300), set his views forth in what were well known to antiquity as the ἱερὰ ἀναγραφή. Compare O. Sieroca, *De Euemerus* (Königsberg, 1869).

The smaller fragments are in Mullach, II. 397 f. Compare J. F. Thrige, *Res Cyrenesium* (Copenhagen, 1878) ; A. Wendt, *De philos. Cyrenaica* (Göttingen, 1841) ; Wieland (*Aristip.*, 4 vols., Leipzig, 1800 f.) also gives a graceful and expert exposition.

In his theory of life, Aristippus followed closely the teaching of Protagoras,[2] just as Antisthenes followed the direction of Gorgias. Indeed he developed the relativism of the Protagorean theory of perception to a remarkably valuable psychology of the sense feelings. Sense perception instructs us only as to our own states (πάθη),[3] and is

---

[1] According to Eusebius, *Præp. ev.*, XIV. 18, 31. Compare, besides, Zeller, II⁴ 344.

[2] Which was communicated to him perhaps by his fellow-citizen, the mathematician Theodorus (compare Plato, *Theætetus*).

[3] Sext. Emp. *Adv. math.*, VII. 191 f.

not concerned with the causes of those states (τὰ πεποιη-κότα τὰ πάθη). The causes are not recognizable; our knowledge directs itself only to the changes of our own essence, and these alone concern us. Sensations, since they are a consciousness of our own condition, are always true.[1] In this spirit the Cyrenaics assumed an attitude of skeptical indifference to natural science. They followed Protagoras in the individualistic turn of this theory when they asserted that the individual knows only his own sensations, and common nomenclature is no guarantee of similarity in the content of the thought.

That these epistemological investigations of the school of Aristippus were used for a basis of their ethics but did not evoke their ethics, is proved for the most part by the subordinate position which they received in the later systematizations of the school. According to Sextus Empiricus (*Adv. math.*, VII. 11), the treatment at this time was divided into five parts: concerning good and evil; concerning the states of the soul (πάθη); concerning actions; concerning external causes; and, finally, concerning the criteria of truth (πίστεις).

However, the fundamental problem of the Cyrenaics (as of the Cynics) was that concerning the real happiness of man, and they emphasized simply the included moment of pleasure or displeasure in those states of mind to which knowledge is limited. As, however, Protagoras had referred the theoretic content of perception to differing corporeal motions, the Cyrenaics sought to derive also the affective tone of the same from the different states of motion of him perceiving.[3] Gentle motion (λεία κίνησις) corresponds to pleasure (ἡδονή), violent (τραχεῖα) to dis-

[1] Sext. Emp. *Adv. math.*, VII. 191 f. ; farther, Diog. Laert., II. 92.

[2] Sext. Emp. *op. cit.* 195.

[3] Eusebius, *loc. cit.* ; Diog. Laert , II. 86 f. Likewise the exposition in the *Philebus*, 42 f., which brings this teaching directly into connection with the πάντα ῥεῖ, presumably refers to Aristippus. Compare Zeller, II[4]. 352 f.

pleasure (πόνος), rest from motion to absence of pleasure
and pain (ἀηδονία καὶ ἀπονία). Since now these three
possibilities include the whole range of stimuli, there are
only two, perhaps three πάθη: pleasant (ἡδέα), unpleasant
(ἀλγεινά), and the states of indifference between them (τὰ
μεταξύ).[1] Since, however, among these three possible
states, pleasure alone is worth striving for, ἡδονή is the
only goal of the will (τέλος), and accordingly is happiness
or the Good itself. Whatever gives pleasure is good.
Whatever creates displeasure is bad. All else is indifferent.

The question concerning the content of the concept of
the Good, which was not really answered by Socrates, was
answered by these Hedonists, in that they declared pleasure
to be this content, and indeed all pleasures, whatever their
occasion,[2] to be indistinguishable. By this only the single
momentary state of pleasure is meant. The highest, the
only good, for these Hedonists was the enjoyment of the
moment.[3]

From these presuppositions the Hedonists concluded, with
entire correctness, that the distinction of value between single
feelings of pleasure is determined not by the content or the
cause, but only by the intensity of the feelings. They asserted
that the degree of intensity of the bodily feelings is greater than
that of the spiritual feelings.[4] The later Cyrenaics, particularly
Theodorus,[5] came therefore to the conclusion that the Wise Man
need not regard himself restricted by law, convention, or indeed
religious scruples, but he should so use things as to serve his
pleasure best. Here, again, the Sophistic antithesis between
νόμος and φύσις[6] is repeated, and the natural individual pleasur-
able feeling is taken as the absolute motive of action. Still more
pronounced than in the degenerate phases of Cynicism appeared
here the egoistic, naturalistic, and individualistic trait which is
basal in the common problem of both theories. On the other

---

[1] Sext. Emp. *op. cit.* 199.   [2] Plato, *Philebus*, 12 d.
[3] See A. Lange, *Gesch. des Mater.*, p. 37, 2 ed.
[4] Diog. Laert., II. 90.   [5] *Ibid.*, 99.
[6] See *ibid.*, 93.

hand, Anniceris[1] sought later to temper this radicalism, and to ennoble the desire for pleasure by emphasizing the enjoyment of friendship, of family life, and of social organization as more valuable. At the same time he did not lose sight of the egoistic fundamental principle, but only carefully refined it. With this turn in its course, however, the Cyrenaic philosophy merged into Epicurean hedonism.

Virtue was, accordingly, for Aristippus identical with the ability to enjoy. The utility of science consists in directing men to the proper satisfaction. Right enjoyment is, however, only possible through reasonable self-control ($\phi\rho\acute{o}\nu\eta\sigma\iota\varsigma$).[2] Requisite insight for this frees us from prejudice, and teaches us how to use the goods of life in the most reasonable way. Above all else it gives to the Wise Man that security in himself by which he remains proof against weakly yielding to influences of the outer world. It teaches him, while in enjoyment, to remain master of himself and his surroundings. The problem for both Cynic and Cyrenaic was the attainment of this individual independence of the course of the world. The Cynic school sought independence in renunciation; the Cyrenaic in lordship over enjoyment, and Aristippus was right when he said that the latter was more difficult and more valuable than the former.[3] In opposition to the Cynic ideal of renunciation of the world, the Cyrenaic drew, as his picture of the Wise Man, that of the perfected man of the world. He is susceptible to the enjoyment of life, he knows what animal satisfactions are, and how to prize spiritual joy, riches, and honor. In elevated spirit he scrupulously makes use of men and things, but even then never forgets himself in his enjoyment. He remains lord of his appetites; he never wishes the impossible, and even in the few happy days of his existence he knows how to preserve victoriously the peace and serenity of his soul.

[1] Diog. Laert., II. 96; see Clemens Alex. *Strom.*, II. 417.
[2] Diog. Laert., II. 91.   [3] *Ibid.*, 75.

With these qualifications (reminding us of Socrates), Aristippus went beyond the principle of momentary enjoyment of pleasure when he, for example, explained activity as reprehensible if, on the whole, it yields more unpleasurableness than pleasure. He recommended on this same ground that there be universal subordination to custom and law. Theodorus then went still further, and sought[1] to find the τέλος of mankind, not in individual satisfaction, but in serene disposition (χαρά). This is also already a transition to the Epicurean conception.

If the principle that only educated men know how to enjoy happily verified itself in the temperament and circumstances of Aristippus, his school on the other hand drew another irresistible consequence from the hedonistic principle, viz., pessimism. If pleasure is said to give value to life, the greater part of humanity fails of its purpose, and thus life becomes worthless. It was Hegesias who dissipated the theory of Aristippus with this doctrine. The desire for happiness cannot be satisfied,[2] he taught. No insight, no opulence, protects us from the pain which nature imposes on the body. The highest we can reach and even as τέλος strive for is painlessness, of which death most certainly assures us.[3] The particular ethical teachings of Hegesias appear more nearly like the precepts of the Cynics than like many of the expressions of Aristippus.

Suicide

The isolation of the individual shows itself in the hedonistic philosophers in their indifference to public life. Aristippus rejoiced that in his Sophistic wanderings no interest in politics infringed upon his personal freedom.[4] Theodorus[5] called the world his country, and said that patriotic sacrifice was a folly which the Wise Man is above. These all are sentiments in which the Cynics and Cyrenaics agree almost verbally, and in these the decline of Greek civilization was most characteristically expressed.

Religious beliefs are among the things which the Hedonists shoved one side with sceptical indifference. Freedom from religious prejudices seemed to them (Diog. Laert.., II. 91) to

---

[1] Diog. Laert., II. 98.   [2] *Ibid.*, 94 f.

[3] The lectures of Hegesias πεισιθάνατος are said to have been forbidden in Alexandria because he spoke too much of voluntary death. Cicero, *Tusc.*, I. 34, 83.

[4] Xen. *Mem.*, II. 1, 8 f.   [5] Diog. Laert., II. 98.

be indispensable for the Wise Man.   It is not related, however, that they set up in any way in opposition to positive religion another conception.   Theodorus proclaimed his atheism quite openly.   Euemerus devised for an explanation of the belief in gods the theory to-day called after him, and often accepted in modern anthropology in many forms.   According to this theory, the worship of the gods and heroes is developed from a reverence of rulers and otherwise remarkable men.   (Cicero, *De nat. deor.*, I. 42, 119 ; Sext. Emp. *Adv. math.*, IX. 17.)

5. MATERIALISM AND IDEALISM.

DEMOCRITUS AND PLATO.

The Greek Enlightenment had impeded the progress of natural science by destroying the naïve confidence of the Greek in the validity of human knowledge.   Science was being utilized for practical life, and was in danger of losing its dignity and the independence which it had just achieved. On the other hand, the prevailing interest of the period in psychology had widened the circle of scientific work. Logic and ethics had thus been added to physics, — to use the classification of the ancients.   Conceptions of the psychical aspects of life now stood side by side with those of its physical aspects.   Man had become conscious of his share in the construction of the idea of the world.   The essence of scientific research was found to consist in the examination of concepts and the fundamental proposition of science had its formulation in the law of the domination of the particular by the universal.   At the same time, however, the principle was seen that science could never give satisfaction if it disregarded the connection between human life, as teleologically determined, and the objective world.

The subjective moment had been sundered in its development from the objective, and consequently placed in a

certain opposition to it.   In the mutual interpenetration of
the two, and in the tendency of these principles to coalesce,
did Greek science find the profoundest deepening of its
conceptual life and the greatest broadening of its practical
life.   From the Peloponnesian war until Philip of Macedon, when the political life of Greece was already approach-
ing dissolution, science created its comprehensive systems,
and perfected itself in its ripest undertakings, which are
associated with the three names Democritus, Plato, and
Aristotle.

In the first place, as preparation for the final synthetic
statement of Aristotle, appeared the two metaphysical systems which expressed the greatest opposition possible within
the realm of Greek thought : the materialism of Democritus
and the idealism of Plato.

Both appeared at that culmination point of Greek culture
when the flood of Greek life was passing over to its ebb ;
the Democritan system was about three decades before the
Platonic, and in a remarkable degree independent of it.
Each system developed its doctrine on a broad epistemological basis, and each is related both positively and
negatively to the Greek Enlightenment.   Both were metaphysical systems of outspoken rationalism.   Each in
complete exposition compassed the entire range of the
scientific interest of the time.   Finally, in both became
defined those opposed philosophical views of the world
which have not been reconciled up to the present time.

But there are just as many differences as there are similarities.   Although agreeing with Plato as to the Protagorean theory of perception, Democritus turned back to the
old rationalism of the Eleatics, while Plato created a new
ideal Eleaticism out of the Socratic theory of the concept.
Democritus may therefore appear less progressive and less
original in this respect than Plato, but we must remember
that as to their general metaphysics the principle of phys-

ics dominated the Democritan system, and the principle of ethics the Platonic system. Ethics was incidental in the former system, while in the latter physics was the incident.

In every direction the theory of Democritus shows itself to be an attempt to perfect the philosophy of nature by the aid of the anthropological theories of the Enlightenment, while Platonism was developed as an original recreation out of the same problems. The historical fate of both these philosophies was also determined by this relationship, for the materialism of Democritus was pressed into the background from the beginning, while Plato became the determining genius of future philosophy.

The great significance, which — in this exposition in distinction from all previous ones — is given to Democritus by making him parallel with Plato, is required solely by historical accuracy. A similar view was, for that matter, very common among the writers of antiquity. As a matter of chronology Democritus, who lived between 430 and 360 (§ 31), was about twenty years younger than Protagoras and ten years younger than Socrates. Although he never came under the direct personal influence of the latter, yet it must be taken for granted that a man to whom in all antiquity Aristotle alone was comparable in learning, had not studied the scientific work of the Sophists in vain. To treat him entirely among the pre-Sophistic thinkers, as is customary,[1] would be justified only if no traces of the influence of the Enlightenment are seen in him. We hope to show the contrary in the following exposition of his theory. But, however, this exposition will not support the attempt to stamp the Democritan theory as a kind of Sophistry, as Schleiermacher and Ritter have made it. The strong bias of judgment and vagueness of treatment that has arisen from this interpretation is sufficiently repudiated by Zeller (I⁴. 842 f.). The points of view and theories in Sophistic literature of which Democritus certainly did make use, were arranged by him synthetically in a unified metaphysic, but such a metaphysic lay far outside the horizon of the Sophists. On the other hand, it is to be entirely admitted that even this materialistic metaphysic played a relatively

---

[1] Most unfortunate in this connection is the arrangement of Schwegler-Köstlin, where the Atomists (as also Empedocles and Anaxagoras) were treated before the Eleatics. 3 ed. p. 51 f.

unfruitful part in rejuvenating ancient thought. For ancient thought took a Platonic tendency, and therefore we have been very imperfectly taught concerning the Democritan theory. But the case is entirely different when we consider the *whole* European history of science. Since the time of Galileo, Bacon, and Gassendi, the Democritan teaching has become the fundamental metaphysical assumption of modern natural science, and however sharply we may criticise this theory, we cannot deny its significance (Lange, *Geschichte des Materialismus*, 2 ed., I. 9 f.). Just in this, however, consisted its historical equality with Platonism.

One of the most striking facts of ancient literature is the apparently perfect silence that Plato maintained concerning Democritus.[1] This was discussed many times in antiquity.[2] The neglect is not possibly explained as hate or contempt.[3] Plato was very much interested in men like the Cynics and Cyrenaics whose manner of thought must have been far less in sympathy with his own than that of Democritus, — with men who must have appeared to him far less significant intellectually. That Plato knew nothing of Democritus is chronologically a matter of greatest improbability. If we also admit that Democritus on account of his long journeys entered[4] comparatively late upon his literary activity, yet the amount of his literary work requires that its beginning be set distinctly before Plato's first works, and much the more before Plato's later works : when Plato wrote the *Symposium*, Democritus was seventy-five years old. The more remarkable is it that Plato, who otherwise refers to, or at least mentions, all the other early philosophers, ignores not only Democritus, but also the Atomic teaching.[5] It must therefore

---

[1] The name Democritus occurs nowhere in Plato's writings, and there is nowhere a mention of the Atomic doctrine. When Plato speaks of materialism (compare above), he cannot possibly have Democritus in mind.

[2] Diog. Laert., IX. 40.

[3] As early as Aristoxenus there appears to have been related the foolish story of the designed burning of the Democritan books by Plato. Diog. Laert, *op. cit.*

[4] The time of the composition of his μικρὸς διάκοσμος, Democritus himself (Diog. Laert., IX 41) places at 730 years after the destruction of Troy (see Zeller, I⁴. 762), i. e. about 420.

[5] It is significant that both the *Sophist* and the *Parmenides* — whether they be dialogues written by Plato or originating from the Platonic circle — do not mention Atomism, although there were present

be concluded, at all events, that Atomism — the writing of
Leucippus being doubtful — had found no favor within the circle
of Attic culture. It therefore appears conceivable that the
Athenians were [1] entirely indifferent to the essentially scientific
nature-investigations of Democritus at the time of the Sophists
and Socrates. In Athens one worked at other things, so that
Plato even later also made no mention of the writings of the
great Atomist in developing his own nature-theories. That he
was not really acquainted with them appears to become more
and more doubtful. R. Hirzel has pointed out two places (*Phil.*,
43 f. ; *Rep.*, 583 f.) where references are made to Democritan
ethics (*Untersuchungen zu Cicero's philos. Schriften*, I. 141 f.).
P. Natorp has assented to this (*Forschungen*, 201 f.), but he has
few results in following up " the traces of Democritus in Plato's
writings " (*Arch. f. Gesch. d. Philos.*, I. 515 f.). It would be
more satisfactory to seek negative and positive relations to
Democritus in Plato's later metaphysic (*Philebus*) [2] and in his
philosophy of nature dependent on it (*Timæus*). Compare below the references in the remarks to § 37.

31. Democritus of Abdera, the greatest investigator of
nature in antiquity, was born about 460. He was first
attracted to scientific research in the school of Leucippus,
probably about the time when Protagoras, who was some
twenty years his elder, also belonged to that circle. Having the liveliest sense for individual investigation in natural sciences, he travelled extensively for many years. This
led him through Greece, for a longer time into Egypt, and
over a greater part of the Orient. The exact time of his
return and the beginning of his literary activity, however,
must remain a subject for conjecture, and his death can

important occasions for it in the *Sophist* in the discussion of Being, and
equal occasions in the *Parmenides* in the dialectic over the One and the
Many.

[1] In any case the expression of Democritus (Diog. Laert., X. 36) is
characteristic : ἦλθον εἰς ᾿Αθήνας καὶ οὔτις με ἔγνωκεν. At the time of the
Sophists of the Peloponnesian war, no one, not even Socrates, had the
spirit for serious investigation into the nature studies of Democritus.

[2] H. Usener (*Preussisches Jahrbuch*, LIII. p. 16) has already given
much attention to this (*Philebus*, 28 f.).

only be approximately set at 360. He settled in his home in Abdera. He became highly honored there, and he lived surrounded by those who prosecuted their researches under his direction. He remained distant and apart from the Attic circle of culture, in which little notice was taken of him, but he may have been in occasional intercourse with the physician Hippocrates, who spent his later years in Larissa.

The life of Democritus is fixed by approximately safe data, from his own statement (Diog. Laert., IX. 41) that he was forty years younger than Anaxagoras, and from the statements he made concerning the time of the composition of his μικρὸς διάκοσμος (§ 30). The acquaintance of Democritus with the teaching of both his countrymen, Leucippus and Protagoras, is entirely assured by the testimony of antiquity and the character of his philosophy. He doubtless knew the Eleatics as well, and one possessed of his great erudition could hardly be ignorant of most of the other physicists. Traces here and there in his system show this. He did not accept the number theory of the Pythagoreans. The friendly relationship to the Pythagoreans, attributed to him,[1] can have reference only to his mathematical[2] researches, and perhaps in part to his physiological and ethical undertakings. He also appeared to be very familiar with the theories of the younger physicists. But more important for his development of the Atomic theory were, on the one hand, his own very extensive and painstaking researches, and, on the other, the theory of perception that he obtained from Protagoras. Whether he gave much attention to the theories of the other Sophists, is still doubtful. They were entirely alien to his metaphysical and scientific tendency. But the thoroughness of his anthropology, the significance that he laid on metaphysical and ethical questions, and the single points which he found valid in them, prove, nevertheless, that he was not uninfluenced by the spirit of his time from which he was otherwise somewhat isolated. All these circumstances assign to him the place of one who through the subjective period of Greek science was the banner bearer of the cosmological metaphysic; and in consequence of his partial acceptance of the new elements was

[1] Diog. Laert , IX. 38.
[2] He prided himself particularly on his mathematical knowledge (Clemens Alex. *Strom.*, 304 a).

the finisher of the system. He did not receive the slightest influence from his great contemporary Socrates.

The duration of his travels was at all events considerable, and his stay in Egypt alone is given as about five years.[1] He certainly came to know the greater part of Asia.[2] He got nothing philosophical from his travels, especially since his thought habitually avoided everything mythical. Nevertheless, his gain in breadth of experience and in the results of his collections was only the greater. His return to Abdera after his journeys was the beginning of his teaching, and his literary work may be dated, in view of the extent of these travels, not before 420.[3] Presumably he continued his work into *matura vetustas* (Lucret. *De rer. nat.*, III. 1039). His fellow-citizens honored him with the name σοφία. He seems to have been little interested in public affairs, and he reached the great age [4] of ninety or, according to some, of one hundred and nine years. His intimacy with Hippocrates (§ 39), which is not improbable in itself, has been the occasion for the forgery of letters between the two (printed in the works of Hippocrates).

Geffers, *Quæstiones democriteæ* (Göttingen, 1829); Papencordt, *De atomicorum doctrina* (Berlin, 1732); B. ten Brink, *Verschiedene Abhandlungen* in the *Philologus*, 1851–53, 1870; L. Liard, *De Democrito philosopho* (Paris, 1873); A. Lange, *Geschichte des Materialismus*, I². (Iserl., 1873) p. 9 f.

The literary activity of Democritus was certainly very great. Even if a part of the works which Thrasyllus had arranged in fifteen tetralogies, whose titles are preserved in Diogenes Laertius (IX. 45 f.), — even if this part was wrongfully ascribed to him (for Diogenes mentions there

---

[1] Diodor., I. 98.   [2] Strabo, XV. 1, 38.

[3] It is little probable that Democritus appeared publicly with his theory, especially with his discussion of definitions, before the beginning of the activity of Socrates (about the time of the beginning of the Peloponnesian war). The passage in Aristotle (*De part. anim.*, I. 1, 642 a, 26), is not to be taken to mean with certainty a chronological relationship of the two philosophies, especially when compared with *Metaphysics*, XII. 4, 1078 b, 17. It signifies only that among physicists and metaphysicians Democritus first treated definition, although only approximately; while the direction of the scientific thought of Socrates was turned to ethics.

[4] In reference to the numerous anecdotes about the "laughing philosopher," see Zeller, I⁴. 766.

titles of spurious writings), yet there remains a magnificent number besides. In the genuine works all departments of philosophy, mathematics, medicine, metaphysics, physics, physiology, psychology, epistemology, ethics, æsthetics, and technics are represented. Since the writings themselves do not lie before us, the question of their genuineness must be decided on the score of greatest probability.

The ancients were proud of the works of Democritus, — which by the way were written in Ionian dialect, — not only for the wealth of their contents, out of which Aristotle took so much for his scientific writings, but also on account of their highly perfected form. They placed him in these respects by the side of Plato [1] and other great litterateurs.[2] They admired the clearness of his exposition [3] and the effective power [4] of his buoyant style.

The loss of these writings, which appears to have happened at some time from the third to the fifth century after Christ, was the most lamentable that has happened to the original documents of ancient philosophy. While the work of Plato has been preserved in its complete beauty, there remains of that of his great antipode only a torso that can never be completed.

Compare Fr. Schleiermacher, *Ueber das Verzeichnis der Schriften des Dem. bei Diog. Laert.*, *Complete Works*, Division III., Vol. III. p. 293 f.; Fr. Nietsche, *Beiträge zur Quellenkunde und Kritik des Diog. Laert.*, p. 22.

The Fragments with annotations by Mullach, I. 330 f. (particularly Berlin, 1843) ; W. Burchard, *Democriti philosophiæ de sensibus fragmenta* (Minden, 1830), *Fragmente der Moral des Abderiten Democritus* (Minden, 1834) ; Lortzing, *Ueber d. ethischen Fragmente des Democritus* (Berlin, 1873) ; W. Karl, *Democritus in Cicero's philos. Schriften* (Diedenhofen, 1889).

The insecurity in early time in reference to the writings of the Atomists can be seen in the fact that while Epicurus seems to have called in question the existence of Leucippus (Diog. Laert., X. 13), the school of Theophrastus ascribed the μέγας διάκοσμος

---

[1] Cicero, *Orat.*, 20, 67.   [2] *Ibid.*, *De orat.*, I. 11, 49.

[3] *Ibid.*, *De divin.*, II. 64, 133.   [4] Plutarch, *Quæs. conv.*, V. 7, 6, 2.

to Leucippus (Diog., IX. 46).   Compare E. Rhode and H. Diels, in *Verhand. der Philologischen Versuchungen*, 1879 and 1880, and the former in *Jahrbuch f Philologie*, 1881.   The ethical writings, which V. Rose (*De Arist. libr. ord.*, p. 6 f.) holds as entirely ungenuine, can be taken in part as genuine (Lortzing), especially περὶ εὐθυμίης.   Concerning this last writing and the use Seneca made of it (*De animi tranquillitate*), see Hirzel (in *Hermes*, 1879).

32. The metaphysical principles of the Democritan teaching were given above in the Atomism of Leucippus (§ 23): empty space and numberless self-moving, qualitatively similar atoms.   These atoms differ only in form and size, and in their union and separation all events are to be explained.   Their motions were accepted as self-evident; but the ἀλλοίωσις, the qualitative characteristics of the perceived thing, and the change arising from its motion must remain as inexplicable for Leucippus as for the Eleatics. Here Democritus entered armed with the perception theory of Protagoras.   The perceived qualities of things arise as products of motion.   They belong not to things as such, but are only the manner in which the subject perceiving at the time carries on its representation.   They are, therefore, necessary signs of the course of the world, but they do not belong to the true essence of things.   In contrast to absolute Being, that is, atoms and space, only a relative reality belongs to the sense qualities.   But this relative reality of the images of perception was supposed by Democritus to be derived from absolute reality — the Heracleitan from the Eleatic world.   The realm of the relative and the changing had been known by Protagoras as the subjective, as only the world of representation.   But the objective world, which the Sophist with skeptical indifference had thrust aside, remained still for Democritus the corporeal world in space. When he thus tried to derive the subjective process from atomic motions, Atomism became in his hands outspoken materialism.

The peculiar significance of Democritus in the history of Atomism seems to lie more in this materialism than in his comprehensive detailed investigations. He scarcely changed history in any way in its fundamental cosmological principles ; but the careful development of anthropology, which we cannot after all ascribe to Leucippus, is clearly his chief work.

The unifying principle of Atomism, as it has been developed into a system by Democritus, is the complete development of the concept of *mechanical necessity in nature.* Democritus, as well as Leucippus, designated this as ἀνάγκη, or in the Heracleitan manner as εἱμαρμένη. Every actual event is a mechanics of atoms ; possessing originally a motion peculiar to themselves, they get impact [1] and push by contact with one another. Thus processes of union and separation come about and these appear as the origin and destruction of things. No event is without such a mechanical cause.[2] This is the only ground for explaining all phenomena. Every teleological conception is removed *a limine,* and however much Democritus in his physiology referred to the wonderful teleology in the structure and functions of organisms, nevertheless he apparently saw therein little reason or cause for such teleology in point of fact.

Outspoken antiteleological mechanism is obviously the principal reason for the deep chasm which continued to exist between Democritus and the Attic philosophy, even at those points concerning which Aristotle recognized the value of the investigations of Democritus, — the chasm which divided the teaching of Democritus from that of Aristotle. This was the reason that after the victory of the Attic philosophy, Democritus lapsed into oblivion until modern science declared in favor of his principle and raised him to recognition. A highly significant moment in

---

[1] Since empty space which has no real Being cannot be the bearer of motion, the transit of motion from one atom to another is possible only through contact, and "actio in distans" is excluded. When the latter seems to occur, it is explained by emanations, as in the working of the magnet (as in Empedocles).

[2] Οὐδὲν χρῆμα μάτην γίγνεται, ἀλλὰ πάντα ἐκ λόγου τε καὶ ὑπ' ἀνάγκης.

the human apprehension of the world, and one never to be left out of account, came hereby to clear and distinct consciousness, and ruled all Atomism as a methodical postulate. The charge raised by Aristotle (*Phys.*, II. 4, 196 a, 24) and before him by Plato (*Phileb.*, 28 d) and lately repeated (Ritter), that Democritus made the world one of chance (αὐτόματον, τύχη) rests upon the entirely one-sided teleological use of this expression. Compare Windelband, *Die Lehren vom Zufall*, p. 56 f.

The Atoms are to be primarily distinguished from each other by their form (σχῆμα or ἰδέα),[1] and there are an infinite number of forms. The difference of size[2] is referred in part[3] to their difference of form.[4] Motion dwells within the atoms, as a necessary irreducible function by which each atom, lawless in itself, and each one for itself, is in process of flight in empty space. Where, however, several of them meet, there arises an aggregation. The shock of meeting causes a vortex,[5] which, when once begun, draws more atoms into itself from the space surrounding it. In this whirl Like find Like. The coarse heavy atoms collect in the centre, while the finer and more volatile are pressed to the periphery. The motion of the whole mass has a balanced revolution however. With reference to the individual objects constructed[6] in this way, the order, position,

[1] It is most characteristic that the ἰδέα, the term that appears in Anaxagoras, equally appears in Democritus and Plato for absolute reality. Of course in a different sense Democritus wrote (Sext. Emp. *Adv. math.*, VII. 137) a separate work, περὶ ἰδεῶν.

[2] At all events, the atoms were thought of as so small that they were imperceptible.

[3] Yet in this the different reports do not fully agree, in that occasionally μέγεθος and σχῆμα seem co-ordinated, and atoms of similar forms are assumed to be of different sizes. See Zeller, I[4]. 777. It is, however, not impossible that Democritus had in mind atom-complexes for such cases.

[4] Which, as the only ground of difference, is often quoted. See passages in Zeller, I[4]. 776, 1.

[5] Diog. Laert., IX. 31 f.

[6] Arist. *Met.*, I. 4, 985 b, 13. In this place under τὸ ὄν is to be understood the thing possessing Being constructed out of atoms. For τάξις and

and form of the atoms which constitute them, are the determining factors. The real qualities of a perceived thing
are spatial form, weight, solidity, and hardness. Weight[1]
depends on the mass of matter, with an allowance for
the interstices of empty space. Solidity and hardness depend on the nature of the distribution of matter and empty
space.

These are the primary[2] qualities which belong to the
things in themselves. All others belong to the things only
so far as they affect the perceiving subject. The secondary
qualities are not therefore signs of things, but of subjective
states.[3] Democritus considered color, taste, and temperature
as belonging to the secondary qualities, and he based their
subjectivity on the difference of the impression of the same
object upon different men.[4]

In this theory of the subjectivity of sense qualities (for details, see below) Democritus carried out the suggestions of
Protagoras. His principle of relativity especially shows this.
His polemic against Protagoras was prompted by the fact that he
held, like Plato, side by side with the theory of the relativity of
sense perception, the possibility of a knowledge of absolute reality. On this account, even as Plato, he battled against the Protagorean theory, in which every perception in this relative sense

θέσις could not be marks of distinction between the single atoms, but only
between the complexes. Compare *De generatione et corruptione*, I¹., 314 a,
24, in which things are distinguished by the atoms, and their τάξις and
θέσις. Finally, both of the latter moments (order and position) determine the ἀλλοίωσις, the qualities of particular things.

[1] Heaviness (βάρος) in Atomism very often clearly signifies approximately the same as movableness, i. e. the degree of reaction in pressure
and impact. The direction of the movement in fall is included by the
term in Epicureanism.

[2] The expressions " primary and secondary qualities " have been introduced by Locke. The Democritan distinction had been previously
renewed by Galileo and Descartes. Descartes reckoned solidity among
the secondary qualities, but Locke placed it back among the primary.

[3] πάθη τῆς αἰσθήσεως ἀλλοιουμένης : Theoph. *De sens.*, 63 f.

[4] *Ibid.*

must be called true.   Compare Sext. Emp. *Adv. math.*, VIII.
56, VII. 139 ; Plutarch, *Adv. col.*, 4, 2 (1109).   Democritus
also added to his recognition of the subjectively relative the
assertion of the objectively absolute.   Reality, however, consists of space and geometrical forms of matter, and herein is his
relationship to the Pythagoreans.   Compare V. Brochard, *Protagoras et Démocrit* (*Arch. f. Gesch. der Philos.*, II. 368 f.).

Every place of the meeting of several atoms can therefore become the beginning of a vortex movement that is
ever increasing in its dimensions, and proves to be the point
of the crystallization of a particular world.   On the one
side it is possible that the small worlds thus formed may
be drawn into the vortices of a larger system and become
component parts of it, or on the other hand that they may
shatter and destroy each other in some unfavorable collision.   Thus there is an endless manifold of worlds, and
an eternal living-process in the universe, in which the
single worlds arise and again disappear through purely
mechanical necessity.

As to the form of our own world-system, Atomism taught
that the whole swings in empty space like a ball.   The outermost shell of this ball consists of compactly united atoms,
and the interior is filled with air, while in the middle, like
a disc, rests the earth.   The process of separation of what
is stable and what is flowing, is taking place still in the
earth.   The stars are like the earth, except that they are
much smaller bodies.   Their fires are kindled by the rotation of the whole world, and are nourished by the vapors
of the earth.   Democritus said that the sun and moon are
of large dimensions, and he spoke of the mountains of the
moon.   Both sun and moon were originally independent
atom-complexes.   They have been drawn into the terrestrial system by its revolution, and they were in that way
set on fire.

We cannot here go into the detailed description which the
Atomists made of this division of the elements, as brought about

by the vortex movement; see Zeller, I⁴. 798 f.   Nevertheless, the interpretation still championed by Zeller, I⁵. 874 f., and earlier the universal interpretation, has been shaken by A. Brieger (*Die Urbewegung der Atome*, etc., 1884, Halle; compare *De atomorum Epicurearum motu principali*, M. Hertz, p. 888), and by H. C. Liepmann (*Die Mechanik der Democritischen Atome*, Leipzig, 1885).   This earlier interpretation was that the Atomists regarded the original motion of the atom in the direction of the fall, i. e. downwards as perceived by the senses.   Though the ancient commentators thus brought the motion of the atoms into connection with βάρος (compare above), yet the movement downwards was not expressly mentioned as absolute.   Democritus could easily designate in the vortex system of atoms the opposition between centripetal and centrifugal directions as κάτω and ἄνω.   Accordingly he could have investigated the effect of the "heavy" in the vortex without teaching the conception of the Epicureans that "weight" is the cause of motion.

Atomism has been apparently very much confounded with this in later time.   However in the sources (probably academic) which Cicero (*De fin.*, I. 6, 17) uses, there is the express statement that Democritus taught an original movement of the atoms *in infinito inani, in quo nihil nec summum nec infimum nec medium nec extremum sit.*   Epicurus, on the contrary, degraded this teaching in assuming that the fall-motion is the natural one for bodies.   The *turbulenta atomorum concursio*, on the other hand, here (20) was made a charge against Democritus.   Plato (*Tim.*, 30 a, κινούμενον πλημμελῶς καὶ ἀτάκτως) appears to me to signify this, and doubtless refers here to Atomism.   Compare Aristotle, *De cœlo*, III. 2, 300 b, 16.   In his matured representation of endless space, it is remarkable that Democritus took a point of view in astronomy that was even for his time very antiquated.   He did not think of the shape of the earth as spherical.   He affiliated closely throughout with Anaxagoras, never with the Pythagoreans.   With this exception his single hypotheses, especially his peculiar meteorological and physical hypotheses, make us recognize in him the thoughtful man of research and the penetrating observer.   We find him collecting many kinds of particular observations and explanations even in biology, which Aristotle and others later used.   He agreed with Empedocles as to the origin of organisms (§ 21).

The most important of the elements was thought by Democritus to be fire.   It is the most perfect because it is the most mobile.   It consists of the finest atoms, which are

smooth and round [1] and the smallest of all.   Its importance
consisted in its being the principle of motion in organisms,[2]
and hence it is the soul-stuff.[3]   *For the motion of fire atoms
is psychical activity.*[4]   Upon this principle Democritus built
an elaborately developed materialistic psychology, which in
turn formed the fundamental principle of his epistemology
and ethics.

Fr. Heimsoeth, *Democritus de anima doctrina* (Bonn, 1835) ;
G. Hart, *Zur Seelen- und Erkenntnislehre des Democritus* (Leipzig, 1886).   It is evident that the theory of fire in Democritus
goes back to Heracleitus.   Fire plays, however, in Atomism the
same rôle in many respects as the mind-stuff νοῦς in Anaxagoras.
This is especially true in his explanation of the organic world.
Fire is indeed not the element that is moved by itself alone, but it
is the most movable element, and it imparts its motion to the
more inert material.   It must be understood, from these references and relationships, that Democritus also thought that the
soul and reason were distributed through the entire world, and
that they could be designated as the divine.[5]   Yet it is certainly
a later explanation which attempts to find in his theory a world-
soul like the Heracleitan-Stoic world-soul.   The isolation by the
atomists of the motion of the separate fire-atoms has no reference
to a unitary function.

In physiology Democritus considered the soul atoms to be
disseminated throughout the entire body.   He supposed that
between every two atoms of the material of the human body is
a fire atom.[6]   Thereby he concluded that soul-atoms of different size and motion are associated with different parts of the
body.   He accordingly located the different psychical functions
in different parts of the body, — thought in the brain, perceptions in the different sense organs, the violent emotions (ὀργή)
in the heart, and the appetites in the liver.   The fire atoms were
supposed to be held together in the body by the breath, so that
the diminution of the breath in sleep and death leads to the
diminution or nearly entire destruction of the psychical life.
The spiritual individuality of man is also destroyed at death.

The peculiarity of the Democritan psychology consisted
in the fundamental hypothesis that the life of the soul and

[1] Arist. *De cœlo*, III. 4, 303 a, 14.   [2] *Ibid. De an.*, I. 2, 404 a, 27.
[3] Compare Zeller, I⁴. 814.   [4] Arist. *loc. cit.* 405 a, 8.
[5] Cicero, *De nat. deor.*, I. 43, 120.   [6] Lucret. *De rer. nat.*, III. 370.

its entire qualitatively determined content has its final explanation in the quantitative difference of the motion of atoms. The life of the soul is really also only an atom-motion, although the very finest and most nearly perfect of all motions.[1] This doctrine attempted to elaborate the different kinds of atomic motion which form the true essence of the different psychical functions.

This shows itself in the first place in his theory of perception. Since, for example, the influence of external things upon us, which is manifested in perception, is possible only by contact according to a mechanical principle,[2] sensation can be induced only by emanations of these things pressing upon our organs. The sensitive fire-atoms found in these organs, are thus set in a motion, which precisely is the sensation.[3]   Indeed Democritus, with support from the theory of Empedocles, concludes that in every organ the stimulating motions corresponding to its atomic constitution become perception, when a similar motion meets[4] them from the soul atoms of the organ. Democritus developed these theories for sight and hearing in particular. It is particularly important for his entire theory that he called the influences emanating from objects "small images" ($\epsilon\check{\iota}\delta\omega\lambda a$), in his discussion of sight.

---

[1] That Democritus did not actually deduce the qualitative from the quantitative, but only had assertions and good intentions about it, is quite obvious. It is of course unattainable ; and this shows the impossibility of a logical completion of the materialistic metaphysic. That he, however, sought to work it out systematically, makes him the father of materialism.

[2] Therefore touch is the fundamental sense ; compare Arist. *De sens.*, 4, 442 a, 29. This conception reappears in the "new psychology," — an interesting fact of historical development.

[3] Theoph. *De sens.*, 54 f.

[4] *Ibid.* 56. Developed in respect to the ear.   Here is also the modern conception concerning the specific energy of the sense-organs, as dependent on the peripheral end-organs being suited to the reproduction of different motions. This is approximately the thought of Democritus.

Democritus agreed entirely with Protagoras in his assessment of the epistemological value of these sensations. Since, then, the motion thus called forth is conditioned not only by the transmitting media [1] but also by the independent action of the fire atoms,[2] sensation is no true expression for the nature of perceived things. Therein consists the subjectivity of sense perception and its inability to give true knowledge, and sense does not therefore truly represent the atoms and their connection in empty space. Sense yields only qualitative determinations, like color, taste, and temperature. Democritus associated the formulation of this thought with the Sophistic contrast of the law of nature and the law of man : νόμῳ γλυκὺ καὶ νόμῳ πικρόν, νόμῳ θερμόν, νόμῳ ψυχρόν, νόμῳ χροιή . ἐτεῇ δὲ ἄτομα καὶ κενόν.[3] Thereby to sense experience objective truth is denied.[4] Sense experience yields only an obscure view of what is actual. True knowledge [5] — viz., of the atoms, which are not perceptible to our senses, and of likewise imperceptible empty space — can be attained only by thought.

This rationalism, which in a typical manner stands in contrast to the natural science theory of sense perception, arose out of the metaphysical need of the Protagorean theory of perception, and went beyond it. For a very instructive parallel between

[1] Theoph. De sens., 50.

[2] The Heracleitan-Protagorean moment of this theory lay in this counter-motion particularly.

[3] Sext. Emp., VII. 135.   Compare Theoph. De sens., 63.   He likewise traced the human nomenclature for things back to θέσις.   See Zeller, I⁴. 824, 3.

[4] The occasional strictures about the limitations of human knowledge (Diog. Laert., IX. 72 ; see Zeller, I⁴. 823 f.) are, as also in Empedocles, to be considered only in this relation.   It seems all the more true, since Democritus expressly taught that there might also exist for other things other methods of perception than those of man.   This was consistent with his whole theory.   See Plutarch, Plac., IV. 10 (Dox., 399).   Compare below.

[5] Sext. Emp. Adv. math., VII. 139.

Plato and Democritus, see Sextus Empiricus, *Adv. math.*, VIII.
56.   This rationalism of Democritus corresponds, in fact, entirely
to that of the old metaphysic and the nature philosophy. The
only difference is that here in Democritus it is not only asserted,
but it is also based upon an anthropological doctrine. It is
further to be observed, and it is also of value in drawing a
parallel with Plato (Natorp, *Forschungen*, 207), that Democritus
γνώμη γνησίη refers to space and the mathematical relations possible in space.   It must remain undecided how far connections
with the Pythagoreans are to be supposed. Democritus, at all
events, is as far distant as the Pythagoreans and the Academy
from a really fruitful application of mathematics to physics in
the manner of Galileo.

But, finally, thought itself, which grasps the truth of
things, is nothing else than a motion of atoms, and in so
far is like perception.[1] Furthermore, since thought, as all
kinds of motion, can arise only from mechanical causes,
Democritus saw himself driven to the conclusion that the
νόησις as well as the αἴσθησις presupposes[2] impressions of
εἴδωλα from the outer world upon the body. In view of
the documents that lie before us, it is only supposititious[3]
how Democritus more exactly represented to himself the
process of thought. It is certain[4] that he traced dreams,
visions, and hallucinations to εἴδωλα as their causes.
These are also ideas introduced indeed through bodily impressions, but not by the customary path of perception

----

[1] Although in itself not equivalent on the higher planes. It is likewise dissimilar to all the functions of the fire atoms.

[2] Plutarch, *Plac.*, IV. 8 (*Dox.*, 395).

[3] Zeller (I⁴. 821, 2) thinks that Democritus did not attempt such an investigation concerning the psychological principle in order to establish the
preference of thought to perception. Zeller's view seems improbable, in
the first place, on account of Democritus' elaboration elsewhere of his
epistemological and psychological doctrine; in the second place, on
account of the importance of the matter for his whole system; finally,
because of the traces of such undertakings in his preserved fragments.
Compare G. Hart, *Zur Seelen- und Erkenntnislehre des Dem.*, p. 19 f.

[4] Plutarch, *Quæst. conv.*, VIII. 10, 2; Cic. *De div.*, II. 67, 137 f.

through the organs of sense.[1] Democritus is so far from
holding these images as purely subjective that he ascribes to
them rather a kind of presentient truth.[2] He looks upon the
process distinctly after the analogy of the sense of sight as
the name εἴδωλα shows. εἴδωλα, finer than those influencing
the sense, create a correspondingly finer motion of the
soul atoms, and thus arises our dream knowledge. If now
Democritus regarded thought as the finest motion of the
fire atoms, he must have looked upon the finest εἴδωλα also
as the stimuli of that motion, viz. those εἴδωλα in which
the true atomistic form of things is copied. Thought is
accordingly an immediate knowledge [3] of the most minute
articulation of actuality, — the theory of atoms. These
finest εἴδωλα remain ineffectual to the greater portion of
humanity compared to the gross and violent stimulations
to the sense organs. The Wise Man, however, is alone
sensitive [4] to them, but he must avert his attention from
the senses [5] in order to conceive them.

Compare E. Johnson, *Der Sensualismus des Demokrit*, etc.
(Plauen, 1868) ; Natorp, *Forschungen*, 164 f. To designate Democritus as a sensualist is only justified by the fact that he thought

[1] It does not appear from the preserved passages exactly clear
whether Democritus in his explanation of dreams thought that the
εἴδωλα press in during sleep without the help of the sense organs ; or
that they were those that had pressed in during wakefulness, but on
account of their weakness had first come into activity during a state of
sleep. Perhaps he had both conceptions.

[2] According to Plutarch (*op. cit.*), the dream is able to reveal a
strange life of the soul to the dreamer.

[3] Thought in analogy to sense of sight ; pointed out first by Brandis
(*Handbuch*, I. 333 f.) and abandoned by him (*Gesch. d. Entw.*, I. 145) ;
analogy revived by Johnson. This analogy is to the effect that thought
is an immediate inner perception or the intuitive conception of absolute
reality.

[4] Compare the somewhat dark passage, Plutarch, *Plac.*, IV. 10 :
Δημόκριτος πλείους εἶναι αἰσθήσεις περὶ τὰ ἄλογα ζῷα καὶ περὶ τοὺς σοφοὺς
καὶ περὶ τοὺς θεούς.

[5] See Hart, *op. cit.* p. 19 f.

that the ground of the stimulation and the functioning of thought
is analogous to that of (sight) perception. The distinguishing
characteristic of Democritus is, however, this, that thought
could go on without the help and therefore to the exclusion of
sense-activity. Therefore he is an outspoken rationalist.[1]
These passages in which it is apparently ascribed to Democritus that he drew conclusions from φαινόμενα concerning the
νοητά (Sext. Emp., VII. 140; Arist. *De an.*, I. 2, 404 a, 27),
prove only on the one side that he undertook to explain phenomena from atomic movement: τῷ ἀλλοιοῦσθαι ποιεῖ τὸ αἰσθάνεσθαι
(Theoph. *De sens.*, 49). On the other side these passages show
that he tried to have the theories verify themselves through
their ability to explain phenomena, and to derive appearance
from absolute actuality. λόγοι πρὸς τὴν αἴσθησιν ὁμολογούμενα
λέγοντες (Arist. *De gen. et corr.*, I. 8, 325 a).

33. The Ethics of Democritus, like his epistemology, has
its roots in his psychology. Feeling and desire are κινήσεις,
motions of the fire atoms. As, however, he established in
theory this difference of value, — that only obscure recognition of phenomena takes place in the gross stimulations of the senses, and that insight into the true form of
things is solicited by the gentlest movement of thought, — so
in practice he applied the same distinction. As in metaphysics knowledge is the τέλος,[2] in ethics happiness (εὐδαιμονία) is the τέλος. In the attainment of this happiness
there is also here the fundamental difference between appearance and truth.[3] The joys of sense deceive, and only

---

[1] Just as all pre-Sophistic philosophers (Heracleitus, Parmenides)
are found to have their epistemological rationalism united with a distinctively sensualistic psychology of thought. Compare Windelband, *Gesch.
d. Philos.*, § 6.

[2] Or οὖρος, fr. 8 and 9. With this establishment of a unifying principle for the ethical determination of value, Democritus stood uniquely
by the side of Socrates. Practically he differed from Socrates but
little. Compare Ziegler, *Gesch. der Ethik*, I. 34. Fortunately, *ibid.*
36, there is an allusion indicating that Democritus' pupil, Anaxarchus,
was called Εὐδαιμονικός.

[3] The opposition of νόμος and φύσις prevails also here. Only through
human convention (νόμῳ) desires are of value. The Wise Man lives
here φύσει.

those of the spirit are true. This fundamental thought
shows itself through all the ethical expressions of Democritus as a principle fully parallel to his epistemological
principle. Also here he held the principle as authoritative
that violent and stormy [1] motions disturb the equilibrium of
the soul, i. e. disturb the fire atoms. Such motions bring
with them a state of agitation of the senses. Therefore, in
spite of their apparent momentary pleasure, such motions
lead in reality to lasting dissatisfaction. Fine and gentle
motions of thought have, on the contrary, true pleasure in
themselves.

Compare Lortzing, *Ueber die ethischen Fragmenta Demo-
crit's* (Berlin, 1873) ; R. Hirzel in *Hermes* (1879, p. 354 f.) ; F.
Kern, in *Zeitschr. für Philos. u. philos. Kritik* (1880, supplementary part) ; M. Heinze, *Der Eudämonismus in der griech.
Philos.* (Leipzig, 1873). The attempt to reduce all qualitative
to quantitative relations, which very properly gives a unique
place in ancient philosophy to the Democritan atomism, becomes
the capstone of his ethics. The μικραὶ κινήσεις contain true
happiness in the moral as well as in the intellectual world, and
the μεγάλαι are disturbing and deceptive. For particulars, see
especially G. Hart, *op. cit.*, p. 20 f. If then the value of the
psychical functions is made dependent in both directions upon
the intensity of atomic motion, and indeed in inverse ratio,
then it is difficult not to think of the similar purpose in the
hedonism of Aristippus, who made the same distinction, in a
coarser way to be sure, in estimating the value of the delights
of the senses. It must remain undecided whether Democritus
directly influenced the Cyrenaics, or whether there had been a
common source for the two in the doctrine of Pythagoras.

The pleasures of sense are relative. They have a phenomenal [2] but not an actual value, viz., the value belonging

---

[1] Fr. 20 (Stob. *Ecl.*, I. 40).

[2] Plato, *Rep.* 584 a. The above representation is supported primarily by Plato's *Republic*, 583 f., and *Philebus*, 43 f., whose references o
Democritus appear to Hirzel and Natorp to be certain (see above).
In both instances it is remarkable to see the exposition colored by
medical expressions and examples which probably belong to the writing
of Democritus (περὶ εὐθυμίης).

to φύσις. Sense pleasures differ like the perceptions in different individuals, and depend on circumstances. Every sense pleasure is conditioned [1] only by the cessation of unpleasurable feeling in the desire concerned, and therefore loses its apparently positive character. True happiness consists in peace (ἡσυχία) of the soul, and Democritus generally uses εὐθυμία to designate it. But he also uses many other expressions, as ἀθαμβία, ἀταραξία, ἀθαυμασία, ἁρμονία, ξυμμετρία,[2] especially εὐεστώ. He has for it a very happy simile of a calm of the sea (γαλήνη). By every excess [3] of excitation thought is aroused to ἀλλοφρονεῖν [4] and feeling to stormy unrest. The right condition of gentle harmonious motion of the soul-atoms is possible only through intellectual knowledge. Out of this flows the true happiness of man.

In these definitions the content of the ethics of Democritus is fully on a level with the ethics of Socrates. The ethics of Democritus intimately connected the social worth of man with his intellectual refinement. The ground of evil is lack of cultivation.[5] Happiness therefore consists not in worldly goods,[6] but in knowledge,[7] in the harmonious leading of the life, in a life of temperance and self-limitation.[8] The social worth of a man is to be estimated [9] by his mental calibre and not by his actions; and he who acts unjustly is more unhappy than he who suffers unjustly.[10] Everywhere he regarded the peace of man to be within himself (εὐεστώ). He looked upon the withdrawal from the sense-desires and upon the enjoyment of the intellectual life as true happiness.[11]

[1] Fr. *Mor.* 47.
[2] Both the last terms have a Pythagorean sound.
[3] Fr. 25.
[4] Theoph. *De sens.*, 58.
[5] Fr. 116.
[6] Fr. 1.
[7] Fr. 136.
[8] Fr. 20 ; compare 25.
[9] Fr. 109.
[10] Fr. 224.
[11] It must remain uncertain to what extent Democritus distinguished

The numerous single sentences which have been preserved from Democritus suit entirely the quality of this noble and high view of life. Since they all, however, have been transmitted in a disconnected way, it can no longer be determined whether and how they have a systematic derivation from the developed fundamental principle. In particular is to be emphasized the high worth that Democritus places in friendship,[1] and on the other hand his full understanding of the importance of civil life, from which he seems to have deviated only in reference to the Wise Man [2] with a cosmopolitanism analogous to that of the Sophists. Yet there remains here much that is doubtful.

Democritus maintained an attitude of indifference to religious belief, which was consistent with his philosophy. He explained the mythical forms, in part by means of moral allegories,[3] in part by nature-myth [4] explanations. He accepted, in connection with his theory of perception, essentially higher anthropomorphous beings imperceptible to the senses, but influential in visions and dreams. He called these dæmons εἴδωλα, an expression employed elsewhere in his epistemology for the emanations from things. They are sometimes benevolent, sometimes malevolent.[5]

The school at Abdera disappeared quickly after Democritus died. Even in its special undertaking, it performed,[6] after the leader fell, scarcely anything worth mentioning. Its philosophical tendency, however, became more and more sophistic,[7] and thereby led to Skepticism. Metrodorus of Chios and Anaxarchus of Abdera, the companion of Alexander on his Asiatic campaign, are the notable names. Through the influence of Pyrrho, a pupil of Metrodorus, the Abderite philosophy became Skepticism, and the contemporaneous Nausiphanes formed the connection between it and Epicureanism.

between the perfect happiness of the Wise Man won through the γνησίη γνώμη, and the peace of the ordinary man obtained by temperance and self-control. Compare Th. Ziegler, *op. cit.*, who wishes to put into a similar relationship both of the chief ethical writings, περὶ εὐθυμίης and ὑποθῆκαι.

[1] Fr. 162 f.   [2] Fr. 225.

[3] Clemens, *Cohort.*, 45 f.

[4] Sext. Emp. *Adv. math.*, IX. 24.   [5] *Ibid.*

[6] The astronomical tenets of Metrodorus seem to indicate a relapse into Heracleitan ideas. Compare Zeller, I⁴. 859.

[7] For the theoretical skepticism of Metrodorus, compare Eusebius, *Præp. ev.*, XIV. 19, 5. Whatever is reported of the ethical tendency of Anaxarchus reminds one of Hedonism, and Cynicism as well.

34. Democritus' consummation of the metaphysics of
science by means of materialistic psychology formed in the
total growth of ancient thought only an early dying branch.
The principal tendency of Greek thought perfected itself
nearly contemporaneously in the ethical immaterialism of
Plato at the centre of Attic civilization. The same elements of the earlier science, which were fundamental to
the theory of Democritus, were combined afresh and in an
entirely different manner in the Platonic system under the
influence of the Socratic principle.   Heracleitus, Parmenides, Anaxagoras, Philolaus, and Protagoras furnished the
material for the theory of Plato, but it was worked over in
an entirely original manner from the point of view of conceptual knowledge.

Plato, the son of Aristo and Perictione, was born in
Athens in 427, and came from a distinguished and pros-
perous family. Endowed with every talent physical and
mental, he received a careful education, and he was
familiar at an early age with all the scientific theories that
interested Athens at that time. The political excitement
of the time made the youth desire a political career. The
Peloponnesian war was raging, and during its progress the
internal and external affairs of Athens were becoming
more and more precarious. On the other hand, the rich
artistic development of the time was irresistibly attractive,
and Plato was led to try poetry in many of its forms. Both
Plato's political and poetic longings appear to follow him
in his entire philosophy: on the one side in the lively, although changing interest that his scientific work always
shows in the problems of statecraft, and on the other in
the artistically perfected form of his dialogues. But both
are subordinate to his entire absorption in the personality
and teaching of the character of his great master Socrates,
whose truest and most discriminating pupil he remained
for many years.

Of the general works concerning Plato and his theory there are to be named W. G. Tennemann, *System der plat. Philos.*, 4 vols. (Leipzig, 1792–5) ; Fr. Ast, *Platon's Leben u. Schriften* (Leipzig, 1816) ; K. F. Hermann, *Gesch. u. Syst. der plat. Philos.* (Heidelberg, 1839) ; G. Grote, *Plato and Other Companions of Socrates* (London, 1865) ; H. v. Stein, *Sieben Bücher zur Gesch. des Platonismus* (Göttingen, 1861 f.) ; A. E. Chaignet, *La vie et les écrits de Plato* (Paris, 1871) ; A. Fouillée, *La philosophie de Plato* (4 vols., 2d ed., Paris, 1890).

The nearest pupils of Plato, especially Hermodorus, dealt with his life ; also the Peripatetics, Aristoxenus and others. The expositions of Apuleius and Olympiodorus (published in Cobet's edition of Diogenes Laertius) have been preserved. Besides there is a life of Plato in the *Prolegomena* (printed in Hermann's edition of the Platonic writings). The collection of spurious letters printed with his works is a very untrustworthy source. Only the seventh among them is of any worth. K. Steinhart has published a life of Plato (Leipzig, 1873), which ranks well among the new works.

On his father's side, Plato had the blood of the Codrus family in his veins, and on his mother's he traced his lineage back to Solon.[1] He himself was called after his grandfather, Aristocles, and is said to have been called Plato for the first time by his gymnasium teacher on account of his broad frame. For the determination of the year of his birth, the statements of Hermodorus are decisive (Diog. Laert., III. 6), that when he went to Euclid at Megara in 399, immediately after the death of Socrates, he was twenty-eight years old. That his birthday was celebrated in the Academy on the seventh Thargelion emanates possibly from the Apollo cult, to which many of the early myths about the philosopher seemingly are referable.

That Plato was early remarkable in every physical and musical art is entirely in agreement with every part of the picture of his personality. The particular accounts about his teachers (Zeller, II[4]. 394) throw no light on his own scientific significance. His early acquaintance with the Heracleitan Cratylus is attested by Aristotle.[2] At what points of time in his development the teachings of the other philosophers whose influence is traceable in his works were known to him, cannot be ascertained. Early in his career Heracleitus, the Eleatics, Protagoras and other Sophists, and later[3] Anaxagoras and the Pythagoreans were authorities for him.

[1] It is improbable that his family was poor, as many later writers would have it. His style of life indicates the contrary.

[2] *Met.*, I. 6, 987 a, 32.   [3] Indeed, relatively late : see below.

Plato was hostile to the democracy, as was consistent with the traditions of his family and the political views of his teacher, Socrates. Yet his political inclinations, as he has laid them down in his works, diverge so far from historic aristocracy that his complete abstinence from public life in his native city appears highly conceivable. That he concerned himself in his youth, as was the custom, with epic and dramatic poetry, is not to be doubted, notwithstanding the uncertainty of the particular traditions about it.

Concerning the time when he became acquainted with Socrates, an acquaintance that certainly eclipsed all the early interests of the youth, there is nothing very definite to be said. If he were then, according to Hermodorus,[1] twenty years old, there remained very little room for his poetic attempts, which ceased when he began philosophy. It is probable that Plato had formulated the content of the separate conversations in the earliest dialogues during Socrates' life.[2]

After the death of Socrates, Plato went first, with other pupils of the master, to Euclid at Megara. He soon after began a journey which took him to Cyrene[3] and to Egypt, and he seems to have returned to Athens from this journey about 395. Here he apparently already began, if not his teaching, yet the part of his literary work in which he opposed the different tendencies of the Sophists. About the end of the first decade of the fourth century, he began his first tour to Magna Græcia and Sicily, which not only brought him into personal touch with the Pythagoreans, but also led him to the court of the elder Dionysius of Syracuse. Here he was in close intimacy with Dion, and was thereby drawn into the strife of political parties which ruled the court. Matters became dangerous for him, for the tyrant grew hostile and treated him as a prisoner of war. He delivered Plato over to the Spartan ambassador, and the

---

[1] Diog. Laert., III. 6.

[2] The statement concerning the Lysis, *ibid.* 35, is in itself by no means improbable.

[3] His intimate relations with the mathematician Theodorus, the pupil of Protagoras (see *Theœtetus*), are somehow connected with his stay in Cyrene; possibly also his essentially polemic relation to Aristippus.

latter sent the philosopher to the slave-market of Ægina,
where a man from Cyrene bought his freedom.   About 387
Plato returned to Athens, and founded his scientific society
soon after in the Academy, a gymnasium.   Here, to a continuously increasing band of friends and youths, he imparted
his philosophic theories, sometimes in dialogues, sometimes
in longer discourses.

The only data for this part of his life which are not reported
alike everywhere in the sources have probably been given their
definitive statement by Zeller, II^4. 402.   It is probable that
Plato's *Wanderjahre*, from the death of Socrates until his failure
in Syracuse, were not without interruption, and that he meanwhile had already begun his instruction at Athens, although to
a small circle, and not yet to the closed and organized Academy.
The literary activity of Plato in the interim (395–91) was essentially only a defence of the Socratic doctrine, as Plato conceived
it and had begun to develop it against Sophistry, which was
flourishing more than ever.   Whether or not Plato left his home
a second time for political reasons, during the Corinthian war,
when Athens was again ruled by the democracy,[1] is uncertain.
He probably at that time attempted in Syracuse, perhaps in
collusion with the Pythagoreans, to bring his political principles
into vogue by the exercise of influence upon the tyrant.   For
the treatment which he experienced at the hands of Dionysius,
who seems to have threatened his life, is hardly to be explained
by any mere unpopularity of his ethical parrhesia, but is, on the
contrary, natural enough if Plato entered politics.

At first Plato probably taught in the Socratic manner by conversation, and he sought to construct concepts with the help of
his pupils.   But the more his own opinions became finished, and
the smaller the organization of the Academy grew in numbers,
the more didactic became his work, and the more had it the form
of the lecture.   In the successive dialogues the work of the inter-
locutor becomes fainter and less important.   Later Aristotle and
the other pupils published lectures of Plato.

The philosopher allowed himself only twice to be induced
away from his teaching in the Academy, which teaching

---

[1] That about this time public attention turned again to Socrates, is
shown by the circumstance that even then the rhetorician Polycrates
published an attack upon Socrates.   See Diog. Laert., II. 39.

lasted the entire second half of his life ; and then only through the hope of fulfilling his political ideals. After the death of the elder Dionysius, he sought, with the help of Dion, to influence the younger Dionysius. He had no success in the first attempt in 367, and the third Sicilian journey in 361 brought him into great personal danger again. In this journey his special effort was to reconcile Dion and Dionysius the younger. Only the energetic effort of the Pythagoreans who, with Archytas at their head, representing the power of Tarentum, seems to have saved him.

Plato died in 347, in his eightieth year. He was revered by his contemporaries, and celebrated as a hero by posterity. He was a perfect Greek and a great man, — one who united in himself all the excellences of bodily beauty with intellectual and moral power. He also ennobled the æsthetic life of the Greeks with a depth of spirituality which assured to him an influence for a thousand years.

The political character of the second and third Sicilian journeys is beyond doubt, but that does not preclude the supposition that Plato at that time, in his intercourse with the Pythagoreans, was pursuing his scientific work.   At any rate, the number theory exercised an increasing but scarcely a healthy influence on part of the development of his philosophical thought.   On the other hand, his influence on the Pythagoreans was very fruitful.

The reports of the ancients as to the length of life and the time of death of the philosopher differ only a little. They are easily reconciled in the statement that Plato died in the middle of the year 347. It is also said that he died suddenly in the middle of a marriage feast. The report of Cicero — *scribens est mortuus* — signifies only that Plato was still laboring to perfect his works at the time of his death. The aspersions upon his character in later literature arose from the animosities of the scholastic controversy. They are refuted, however, by the respectful tone with which Aristotle always spoke of Plato, even when he was battling against his theory. It is not entirely impossible that in later time, when Aristotle went his own way and Plato became more Pythagorean in his mysticism, that the relations between the two became less close and somewhat inharmonious.

We can get the most reliable picture of Plato from his own writings. They show in their author the realization of the Socratic ideal: his scientific investigations are carried on with all the seriousness of a moral endeavor seeking its own fulfilment. The serene beauty of his compositions and the perfect purity of his diction reveal the artist who from the heights of the culture of his time gives to the thought of that time a form that transcends the time. With the exception of the *Apology*, they are dialogues in which the conversation and the deciding word, if a decision is reached, fall in by far the majority of cases to Socrates. In reference to their content, only a few of the dialogues have a fixed plan of philosophical research. Rather, almost always threads of thought were spun from the chief problem in any direction and followed to the end. On that account the dialogues are not scientific treatises, but works of art in which scientific " experiences " are reproduced in an idealized form. One remarks this æsthetic character in Plato's use of myths, which appear usually at the beginning or end of an investigation, where Plato cannot or will not develop his thought conceptually. The story form of the argument enhances its poetic power.

By the term " experiences," which are elaborated in Plato's dialogues, we do not mean so much the conferences which the poet philosopher employed or devised as the outer scenery of his works, but the discussions in which he himself led in the circle of his riper friends.[1] Such a dialogue as the *Parmenides* bears even the character of being the æsthetic *résumé* of actually fought out word-battles. The Platonic authorship of these is extremely doubtful, but they must have originated in the Platonic circle. The actually occurring conversation is idealized and universalized in these dialogues, being placed in the mouth of Socrates and other persons, some of whom had already died. Plato shows here his imagination by his selection and

---

[1] This certainly happened later also, when scholastic teaching and practice had place in the Academy, in which teaching the preserved diæreses and definitions may have been used.

adornment of the situations under requirements of fiction, in
which situations these conversations purport to have taken
place ; by the plastic characterizations of the champions of
various theories, in which he uses frequently the effectual means
of persiflage ; and also by the delicate structure of the conversation, which forms itself into a kind of dramatic movement.
Countless allusions, of which only a very few are understood
by us, apply to the historical persons figuring in the dialogue,
and in part perhaps to the companions of Plato.

In the undoubtedly genuine Platonic dialogues, Socrates is
made the speaker of Plato's own views.   The only exceptions are the latest, *Timæus* and *Critias,* and the *Laws.*   In
the first two the reason for this exception is that Plato deals
only with the mythical and not with sure knowledge.   In the
Laws the head of the school has become an authority and
speaks as such.   Usually the dramatic scenery in the first dialogues is much more simple and less ornate ; in the works of
his ἀκμή, the scenic effect is fully developed ; in the *Philebus*,
on the contrary, and in the other later works, it sinks back
again to a schematic investiture.   The conversations are partly
"give and take," partly repetitions whereby sometimes the chief
dialogue is introduced into the discussion of another dialogue.
Although the earlier dialogues follow, on the whole, the second
principle, and the later the first, yet these principles are not safe
criteria for the chronological succession [1] of the dialogues.

The reports of antiquity that Plato divided [2] philosophy into
dialectics, physics, and ethics can refer only to his method in
the Academy.   This division in the dialogues can be made
neither directly nor indirectly.   On the whole, epistemological,
theoretical, metaphysical, ethical, and sometimes physical motives are so interwoven that while here and there the one or the
other interest predominates (in *Theætetus* the epistemological
and theoretical ; in the *Republic* the ethico-political), never does
a conscious sundering of the realms of the problems take place.
This belongs moreover to the poetic rather than the scientific
character of Plato's literary workmanship.

Concerning the myths of Plato, compare especially Deuschle
(Hanau, 1854) and Volquardsen (Schleswig, 1871) ; concerning
the general character of Plato's literary activity, see E. Heitz
(O. Müller's *Literaturgeschichte*, II. 2, 148–235).

---

[1] In *Theætetus* this innovation is made, and reason is given for it
(143 b, c).   The *Phædo* also, which was certainly a late dialogue, and
the probably later *Symposium* returned to the older method.

[2] Cicero, *Acad.,* I. 5, 19.   Compare Sext. Emp. *Adv. math.*, VII. 16.

There is no ground for supposing that any one of the writings of Plato has been lost. On the other hand, the transmitted collection contains many that are undoubtedly questionable and ungenuine. We may take the following as certainly Platonic: the *Apology, Crito, Protagoras, Gorgias, Cratylus, Meno, Theœtetus, Phœdrus, Symposium, Phœdo, Republic, Timæus*, and also probably *Philebus* and the *Laws*. The following are certainly not genuine: *Alcibiades II., Anterastœ, Demodorus, Axiochus, Epinomis, Eryxias, Hipparchus, Clitophon, Minos, Sisyphus, Theages,* and the small studies περὶ δικαίου and περὶ ἀρετῆς. Among the doubtful, *Parmenides, Sophist,* and *Politicus* are of special importance. The criterion of their genuineness is chiefly the testimony of Aristotle, who mentions many of the writings with the name of Plato and title of the book, many only with either name or title, many without certain reference to Plato. To a canon established in this way, there are to be added writings that Plato himself cites, or whose form and content make them Plato's.

Just as important as the question of the genuineness of the writings of Plato, is the question of their order and connection. The chief controversy over the order of the writings is between the Systematic and Historical theories. The Systematic theory, advocated by Schleiermacher and Munk, finds a plan in the whole of Plato's writings, — a consistent system organized at the beginning. Hermann and Grote advocate the Historical theory, which makes each dialogue a stage in the development of Plato's thought. Beside the general reasons for the Historical theory, there are the numerous variations in the establishment, development, and application of the fundamental thesis, - - a thesis which is clearly present although undergoing transformation. In both directions the body of the Platonic writings presents one of the most difficult problems of antiquity, — insolvable in some particulars; yet time has brought about a pretty complete agreement concerning the more important ones.

The works of Plato were arranged and published in antiquity by Aristophanes of Byzantium partially in trilogies, and by Thrasylus in tetralogies. In the Renaissance they were excellently translated into Latin by Marsilius Ficinus, and printed in Greek text at Venice in 1513. Further publications of the works are those by Stephanus (Paris, 1578) which has been cited, the Zweibrücken edition (1781 f.), that of Imman. Bekker (Berlin, 1816 f.), Stallbaum (Leipzig, 1821 f., 1850), Baiter, Orelli, and Winkelmann (Zurich, 1839 f.), K. Fr. Hermann (Leipzig, Teubner, 1851 f.), Schneider and Hirschig (Paris, 1846), M. Schanz (Leipzig, 1875 f.).

Translations with introductions: Schleiermacher (Berlin, 1804 f.), Hieron. Müller and Steinhart (Leipzig, 1850 f.), V. Cousin (Paris, 1825), B. Jowett (Oxford, 1871), R. Bonghi and E. Ferrai (Padua, 1873 ff.).

The most nearly complete and comprehensive picture of the special literature which is not to be reproduced here and also concerning the single dialogues, is given by Ueberweg-Heinze, I[7]. 138 f. The chief writings on the subject are as follows: Jos. Socher (*Ueber Platon's Schriften* (Munich, 1820); Ed. Zeller, *Plat. Studien* (Tübingen, 1839); F. Susemihl, *Prodromus plat. Forschungen* (Göttingen, 1852); *Genetischen Entwickelungen der plat. Philos.* (Leipzig, 1855–60); F. Suckow, *D. wissensch. u. künstlerische Form der plat. Schriften* (Berlin, 1855); E. Munk, *D. natürliche Ordnung der plat. Schriften* (Berlin, 1856); H. Bonitz, *Platonische Studien* (3 ed., Berlin, 1886); Fr. Ueberweg, *Untersuchungen über Echtheit und Zeitfolge plat. Schr.* (1861, Vienna); G. Teichmüller, *D. plat. Frage* (Gotha, 1876); *Ueber die Reihenfolge der plat. Dialoge* (Leipzig, 1879); *Litterar. Fehden im vierten Jahrh. vor Chr. Geb.* (Breslau, 1881 f.); A. Krohn, *Die plat. Frage* (Halle, 1878); W. Dittenberger (in *Hermes*, 1881); H. Siebeck, in *Jahrbuch f. klas. Philologie* (1885); M. Schanz (*Hermes*, 1886); Th. Gomperz, *Zur Zeitfolge plat. Schriften* (Wien, 1887); E. Pfleiderer, *Zur Lösung der plat. Frage* (Freiburg, 1888); Jackson, *Plato's Later Theory of Ideas* (*Jour. of Philol.*, 1881–86); F. Dümmler, *Akademika* (Giessen, 1889); K. Schaarschmidt, *D. Samm. der plat. Schr.* (Bonn, 1866).

With reference to all the different factors, the Platonic writings group themselves somewhat as follows: [1]

[1] To which there have been added lately, but with little success, some philological statistics.

(1) *The Works of Plato's Youth.* These were written under the overpowering influence of Socrates ; in part during Socrates' life, in part in Megara immediately after his death. To this group belong *Lysis* and *Laches*, and, if they be genuine, *Charmides*, *Hippias Minor*, and *Alcibiades I.* ; so, also, the *Apology* and both the apologetic dialogues, *Crito* and *Euthyphro.*

Lysis (concerning friendship) and *Laches* (concerning courage) have purely Socratic content. *Hippias Minor* is also Socratic, and for its genuineness we have Aristotle's authority in *Metaphysics*, IV. 29, 1025 a. This treats the parallel between Achilles and Odysseus from the point of self-conscious virtue. *Charmides* (concerning moderation) and the rather unskilful and incoherent *Alcibiades I.* are doubtful. The *Apology* and *Crito* (concerning Socrates' fidelity to law) are usually placed after the death of Socrates. Included in this class is *Euthyphro* (concerning piety), which also has entirely the character of an apology. *Euthyphro* criticises the charges of impiety made against Socrates by proving that true piety is the Socratic virtue. It is not impossible that the latter three were written about 395, during Plato's residence at Athens, and were an answer to the renewed attacks upon the memory of Socrates.[1]

(2) *The Disputations concerning Sophistical Theories.* In these appear now, besides his criticisms of the Sophists, indications of his own philosophy. These works are supposed to have been written or begun in Athens in the time between the Egyptian and Sicilian journeys. They are the *Protagoras*, *Gorgias*, *Euthydemus*, *Cratylus*, *Meno*, and *Theætetus*. Presumably there belong to this period the first book of the *Republic* and the dialogue concerning justice.

These dialogues, with the exception of the *Meno*, are entirely polemic and without positive result. They form a solid phalanx against Sophism, and show the falsity and insufficiency of its doctrines one after another : the *Protagoras*, by the investigation concerning the teachableness of virtue, which Plato shows

---

[1] Compare above. Further evidence of this is the manner in which several dialogues (*Gorgias, Meno,* and *Theætetus*), which for other reasons are known to belong to that time, contain allusions to the trial of Socrates.

to be presupposed by the Sophists, but incompatible with their fundamental principles ; the *Gorgias*, through a criticism of the Sophistic rhetoric, in contrast with which genuine scientific culture is celebrated as the only foundation for true statecraft ; the *Euthydemus* through the persiflage of eristic ; the *Cratylus* by a criticism of the philologic attempts of the sophistic contemporaries ; the *Theœtetus*, finally, in a criticism of the epistemology of the different schools of Sophists.

Protagoras, dramatically the most animated of Plato's dialogues, heads this series as a masterpiece of fine irony. It is doubtful whether *Gorgias* followed it immediately, for there is a great difference in the fundamental tone of the two. Yet it is entirely natural that the artist, Plato, in the second dialogue, in which he takes a much more positive position, should adopt a more serious tone, and should give a more intensely spiritual expression to his political ideal of life. The *Euthydemus* and *Cratylus*, which perhaps, therefore, are to be placed before the *Gorgias*, follow the *Protagoras*, the irony mounting to the most insolent caricature.

If *Hippias Major* is taken as genuine, it belongs in this class, for it contains Plato's criticism of the sophistic art of Hippias. Yet it is probable, rather, that the *Hippias Major* was the production of a member of the Academy who was fully familiar with the Platonic teachings.

The dialogue concerning justice is a polemic against the Sophists, and, indeed, against their naturalistic theory of the state. This dialogue forms at present the first book of the *Republic*, and was possibly its first edition (Gellius, *Noct. Att.*, XIV. 3, 3). It resembles throughout in tone the writings of this time, which fact does not obtain as to the chief parts of the *Republic*. Also the first half of the second book of the *Republic* (until 367 c) seems to be a copy of a Sophistic speech called *Praise of Injustice.*

In the *Meno* the Platonic epistemology had its first positive expression, even if it is only an exposition developed by suggestions, and stated after the manner of the mathematician. The Pythagorean influences, which are also found in the *Gorgias*, do not oblige us to put the *Meno* in the time after the first Italian journey. It is remarkable that the *Theœtetus*, so soon after the youthful enthusiasm with which the *Gorgias* had proclaimed (174 f.) the vocation of the philosopher to be statesmanship, advocated [1] so pessimistically the retirement of the philosopher

---

[1] The opinion shared by Th. Bergk (*Fünf Abh. z. Gesch. d. gr. Phil. u. Astron.*, Berlin, 1883), that this dialogue should be put as late as the fourth decade of the fourth century, cannot be reconciled with its content.

from public life. Yet the explanation of this may be that Plato
began the *Theœtetus* in Athens, and completed it after or upon
his journey ; for the dialogue refers to a wound that Theæetetus
received in an encounter during the Corinthian war. His clash
with the tyrant and his wily and adroit flatterer (Aristippus?)
is consistent with his experiences at this time. There is perhaps a connection between this and the change of form, which
makes it necessary to place the dialogue at the end of this series.

(3) *The Works of the Most Fruitful Period of Plato's
Activity.* These are the *Phœdrus, Symposium*, and the chief
part of the *Republic*. In the same period were probably
written the *Parmenides, Sophist*, and *Politicus*, which certainly came from the Platonic circle.

The *Phœdrus* may be viewed as Plato's program delivered
upon his entrance (386) into active teaching in the Academy.
Philosophically it contains the fundamental thoughts of this
period in mythical dress: the theory of the two worlds (§ 35)
and the triple division of the soul (§ 36). In the contention
between Lysias and Isocrates he takes the latter's part, but declares thereby (276) that he prefers the living conversation to the
written word. If Plato concentrated from now on his powers in
oral instruction, it is natural that he should appear not to have
published any work in the two following decades.

Not until immediately after the *Phœdrus* did he give the fullest
expression to his entire teaching in the " love speeches " [1] of the
Symposium (385 or 384). The most superb of all his artistic

---

[1] The exposition of these thoughts lies so essentially in the direct
line of the Platonic philosophy that it does not seem necessary to
seek their inspiration in the appearance of a work of Xenophon. Xenophon did not have the slightest occasion to treat the " love-speeches "
by the side of the *Memorabilia* as a separate work, as he manifestly
did treat them. It is rather probable that after Plato idealized the
evening feast (for there is undoubtedly some historical ground for
the description) in his own way, Xenophon felt compelled to give an account of the facts. His additions were especially to the thoroughly practical conception, which Socrates developed, as to the relations of the
sexes. In addition to these practical reasons there are also verbal and
historical grounds for placing Plato's account prior to that of Xenophon's rather than the opposite. Compare A. Hug (*Philol.*, 1852), and
Rettig (*Xen.'s Gastmahl*, Greek and German, Leipzig, 1881).

products, it represents in every respect the acme of his intellectual power.   In the elegance of its rhetoric and in the characterization of single individuals carried out to verbal detail, it is
surpassed by no work.   Upon the background of the cosmology,
suggested in the *Phœdrus* and clearly developed here, it pictures
the ἔρως as the living bond of the Platonic society.

The *Menexenus* has the same general tendencies as the *Symposium* and the *Phœdrus*, but it was probably written not by
Plato, but by one of his pupils.   It boasts somewhat proudly
at the end that Aspasia has many more beautiful speeches like
the given funeral-oration.

During the time of literary silence that immediately followed,
Plato appears to have been going on with his great life work, —
that one, among all his works, which presents the most serious
critical and historical difficulties.   This is the *Republic*.   As it
lies before us, it is wanting in an intellectual and artistic unity in
spite of its subtile, often all too intricate, references and cross-
references.   All attempts to establish such a unity fail.   Following the fruitless dialogue concerning justice, which forms the
first part of the work (first, according to the present divisions,
which were indeed traditional early in antiquity), there comes,
after the insertion of a species of sophistic discourse, the conversation with entirely new persons concerning the ideal state, and
concerning the education necessary for constructing a state by
which the ideal justice may be realized.   Thus there appear two
perfectly unlike parts welded together, but the second and greater
(Books II.–X.) is by no means a decided advance in thought.
In particular, the diatribe taken up again at the beginning of the
tenth book against the poets. stands abruptly in the way between
the proofs that the just man in the Platonic sense is the happiest
man on earth (Book IX., 2d half, 588 f.) as well as after death
(Book X., 2d half, 608 c.)   It is particularly striking that
whereas the teaching about the ideal state and the education
peculiar to it restricts itself entirely to the limits set forth in
the *Phœdrus* and *Symposium*, we find an intervening section
(487–587) which not only expresses the teaching of Ideas as
the highest content of this education in the sense stated in the
Phœdo and developed in the *Philebus*, but also develops in a
more extended way the different metaphysical teachings of the
later period.   These and other single references, which cannot
be followed out in this place, show that there are three strata in
the *Republic:* (1) the dialogue of early origin concerning justice
(Book I., possibly including appendix, 357–67) ;   (2) the outline
of an ideal state as the realization of justice, originating at the
time of his teaching, that followed the *Phœdrus* and *Symposium*

(Books II.-V.), and the entire conclusion from Ch. XII. (Book IX.) ; (3) the theory, dating from the time of the *Phædo* and *Philebus*, of the Idea of the Good, and the critique of the constitutions of the state (487–587). As Plato grew older, he sought to weld these three parts into one another. To accomplish this, he now and then worked over the earlier portions, but he did not succeed in bringing them into a perfect organic union. In accepting a successive genesis of the whole, the simplest explanation is given of the insertions, which appear still further within the different parts in polemic justification. These insertions are attempts to meet objections that had in the mean time been raised orally or in writing.

In the course of the discussion of the theory of Ideas in the Academy, there appeared difficulties in the way of their development. The *Parmenides* and *Sophist* were written especially to express these objections and to discuss them. The *Parmenides* with a dialectic which drew its formal and practical arguments from Eleaticism, tears the theory of Ideas to pieces without reaching a positive result. The contemptuous tone and the boyish immature rôle which is clearly given to the Socrates-Plato, stands in the way of regarding this as Plato's criticism of himself. Probably an older member of the Platonic circle, who was educated in Eleatic sophistry, is the author of this dialogue. The *Parmenides* does not give to Socrates, but to Parmenides, the deciding word, and it bears entirely the Eleatic character of sterile dialectic.[1]

The question about the genuineness of the *Sophist* and the *Politicus* is more difficult. That both have the same author can be inferred from their form. On the one hand, in both, as in *Parmenides*, not Socrates but a friend and guest, who is an Eleatic, leads the conversation ; on the other hand, there is the pedantic and somewhat absurd schematism, with which, by a continuously progressive dichotomy, the concept of the Sophist and statesman is attained. It is therefore impossible to ascribe one dialogue to Plato and the other not to him, as Suckow has attempted. The two stand or fall together. It might be possible to divine an intended caricature of the philosopher in certain externals that are in other respects wholly un-Platonic, but the contents of both forbid this. The criticism of the theory

---

[1] If *Philebus*, 14 c, refers to Parmenides, the notable way in giving up the investigation of ἕν and πολλά is rather a reason for regarding the *Parmenides* as a polemic that had been rejected. This is better than to let both these dialogues stand or fall together, as Ueberweg prefers (I. 151, 7th ed.).

of Ideas which is contained in the *Sophist* (compare § 28) might be conceived, perhaps, as Platonic self-criticism, although weighty reasons are also against it.   But the manner in which it solves the discovered difficulties is not Platonic.[1]   So the *Politicus* contains many points of view which agree with Plato's political convictions.   It is, however, not probable that the philosopher tried to treat the same problem in a book other than the *Republic*, especially since the *Politicus* sets up other teachings which differ on important points.   Convincing reasons are therefore adduced for seeking the authorship of both in a member of the Academy with strong Eleatic sympathies.[2]   It is singular enough that the divergence of both from the Platonic teaching lies exactly in the direction of the metaphysics and politics of Aristotle,[3] who entered the Academy in 367.

About this time the dialogue *Io* may have originated, which indeed makes use of Platonic thoughts in its distinction between poetry and philosophy, but cannot be safely attributed to the head of the school.

(4) *The Chief Works on Teleological Idealism.*   These were written in the time before and after the third Sicilian journey.   They are the *Phædo*, *Philebus*, the corresponding parts of the *Republic* (487 f.), and in connection with these the fragment of *Critias* and the *Timæus*.

The characteristic of this period is the introduction of Anaxagorean and Pythagorean elements into the theory of Ideas. The central concept is the Idea of the Good.   The introduction of these elements finds its full perfection in the *Phædo*, which was written presumably shortly before the third Sicilian journey.

---

[1] In the passage of *Phædo* (101 d), Plato explains the problem of the *Sophist* and also of *Parmenides* as relatively indifferent problems, compared to the importance of the establishment of the theory of ideas.

[2] Who perhaps was prevented by death or other cause from the third proposed dialogue (φιλόσοφος).   That the trilogy seems to be connected as to its external framework (which is moreover very much wanting in fancy) with the conclusion of the *Theætetus*, is not decisive for the Platonic authorship.

[3] The way in which he mentions both dialogues, I cannot recognize as proof of their genuineness, in spite of the conclusions of Zeller (II[4]. 457 f.).

As if conscious of the dangers to be met, Plato gives to this dialogue the tone of a last will and testament to the school. As a delightful counterpart to the *Symposium*, he pictures the dying Wise Man as a teacher of immortality.

After this journey, the philosopher [1] reached the zenith of his metaphysics in his investigations concerning the Idea of the Good, which are embodied in the dialogue *Philebus*. All the thoughts [2] that are expressed there, are to be found again in the less abstract presentation in the middle part of the *Republic*,[3] which was designated above as its third stratum (487–587).[4] Plato has then, as an afterthought, brought into external relationship the incomplete sketches of his philosophy of history (*Critias*), and likewise his mythical theory of nature (*Timæus*) with the scenic setting of the *Republic* (supposably finished at this time).

(5) *The Laws.* This is the work of his old age.

This sketch of a second-best state originated at the time when Plato in his λόγοι ἄγραπτοι entirely went through the theory of Ideas with the Pythagorean theory of numbers in mind. The exposition passes over here into senile formality, although still worthy our admiration. The present form of the work proceeded from Plato even in its details, although the manuscript was said to have been published first by Philip of Opus after the death of Plato. The same scholar had edited the epitome of the *Laws*, which under the title of *Epinomis* was received in the Platonic circle.

35. The epistemological, metaphysical doctrine, known as the theory of Ideas, forms the central point in the

---

[1] The new course that Plato certainly takes, shows itself in the peculiar fact that in the *Philebus* expressions like ἔρως and ἀνάμνησις have lost the specific sense which the earlier dialogues have given them.

[2] Among others, the treatment also of the concept of pleasure which might be claimed to belong to Democritus. (See above.)

[3] In this part a number of pedagogical and political discussions appear to have been sprinkled, which already could have belonged to the earlier sketch of the ideal state and supposably did belong to it. The details cannot be given here.

[4] This interpolated piece begins with a discussion. In this discussion the experiences, which the philosopher underwent with the young tyrant at Syracuse, are made use of detail by detail.

Platonic philosophy. The root of this inspired conception lies in Plato's attempt to transcend the Protagorean doctrine of relativity, whose validity for the world of sense and perception he recognized. By the help of the study of concepts after the Socratic method he tried to attain a safe and a universally valid science of the true essence of things. The final motive of this theory was, however, the ethical need of winning true virtue by true knowledge. The subjective point of departure [1] was, for Plato as for Socrates, the conviction of the inefficiency of customary virtue. The virtue of custom, resting upon convention and prudential considerations, is unconscious of its fundamental principle, and is exposed to the insecurity of change and opinions. Plato showed to Sophistry [2] that it with its pleasure theory took the popular point of view for its own, and he found the reason for this in the fact that Sophistry renounced all real knowledge, and therefore could find no fundamental basis for virtue. In this sense Plato [3] purposely agreed with the Protagorean theory about the value of sense perception and of opinions based on it. He was vigorous in asserting the relativity of such knowledge, and its inability to give us the true essence of things. But precisely for that reason the ethical need drove Plato beyond Sophistry, and led him to fight Protagoras the more energetically with Protagoras' own relativism. If there be virtue of any sort, it must rest on other than relative knowledge, which alone the Sophists considered.

But Socrates had, to the mind of Plato, shown us the way through conceptual science to this other knowledge which is independent of all accident of perception and

[1] Especially *Meno*, 96 f.   Compare *Phædo*, 82 a, and the *Republic* in different places.

[2] Chiefly in the *Gorgias*.

[3] All the points of view of the Sophistic epistemology are discussed thoroughly in the *Theætetus*.

opinion. The methodical development of this postulate was called by Plato the Dialectic.[1] Its object is on the one hand to find individual concepts (συναγωγή), and then to establish the mutual relations of these concepts by division (διαίρεσις, τέμνειν). Plato used the Socratic induction in the main in finding the concepts, and supplemented this by hypothetical discussions in testing and verifying the concepts. These hypothetical discussions draw out all the consequences from the constructed concept, and thus bring it to the touchstone [2] of fact. The dividing of these class concepts is the method which was introduced anew [3] by Plato with the intention of exposing the logical relations between concepts; and therefore connected with this process of dividing there are investigations concerning the compatibility and incompatibility of concepts, i. e., concerning the principle of disjunction.[4]   As the last goal of dialectic, there appeared withal A LOGICAL SYSTEM OF CON-CEPTS,[5] arranged according to their relations of co-ordination and subordination.

Herbart, *De Plat. systematis fundamento*, Vol. XII. 61 f. ; S. Ribbing, *Genetische Darstellung von Platons Ideenlehre* (Leipzig, 1863–64) ; H. Cohen, *Die plat. Ideenlehre* (*Zeitschr. f. Völkerpsych. u. Sprachwissench.* 1866) ; H. v. Stein, *Sieben Bücher zur Geschichte des Plat.* (Gött., 1862–75, 3 vols.) ; A. Peipers, *Untersuchungen über das System Plat.*, Vol. I. (The epistemology of Plato, examined with especial reference

[1] *Phædr* , 265 f. ; *Rep.*, 511 f ; *ibid.*, 533. : *Phileb.*, 16.

[2] *Meno*, 86 ; *Phæd.*, 101 ; *Rep.*, 534. The *Parmenides* similarly (135 f.) ; but applies the Platonic principle in the spirit of the fruitless antinomy of the Eleatic Sophists.

[3] *Phileb.*, 16.

[4] Particularly *Phæd.*, 102 f.

[5] In their method, the *Parmenides*, *Sophist*, and *Politicus* stand entirely on Platonic ground by their happy and logically sharp turns. The application, however, that they make of the method seems a juvenile attempt at independent development rather than an ironical auto-caricature by Plato.

to the *Theætetus*) (Leipzig, 1874) ; *Onotologia platonica* (Leipzig, 1883).

The Protagorean doctrine of relativity is for Plato not only an object of polemic, but, as in the case of Democritus, is an integral part of his system. This will become more evident as we proceed. Skepticism of the senses is the mighty corner-stone of both these systems of rationalism. On the other hand, the ethical point of view of Plato carried with it the attitude — and herein that of Democritus was also one with it — that it could not ascribe to the Sophistic doctrine of pleasure even the worth of a relatively valid moment. This was at least the doctrine in the first draft of the theory of the Ideas, although later, especially in the *Philebus*, Plato's conception was in this somewhat changed (§ 36).

Direct, logical, or methodological investigations were not yet made by Plato, at least not in his writings. On the contrary, one finds numerous isolated statements scattered through his dialogues. In practical treatment the synagogic method outweighs by far the dieretic. Only the *Sophist* and *Politicus* give examples of the dieretic method, and these are indeed very unfortunate examples. Hypothetical discussions of concepts, however, grew to a fruitful principle in the scientific theories of the Older Academy (§ 37).

These concepts include a kind of knowledge that is very different in origin and content from that founded on perception. In perception there comes into consciousness the world of change and appearance. Conception gives us the permanent Essence of things (*οὐσία*). The objective content of conceptual knowledge is the Idea. If true knowledge — thus Plato followed the Socratic ideal — is supposed to be given in the concepts, then this must be a knowledge of what really is.[1] As, therefore, the relative truth of sense perception consists in its translating the changing relations that spring up in the process of Becoming, so the absolute truth of conceptual knowledge (that of Dialectic) consists in the fact that it conceives in the Ideas the true Being, independent of every change. So two different worlds correspond to the two ways of knowing: a

[1] *Theæt.*, 188 ; *Rep.*, 476 f.

world of true reality, the Ideas, the object of conceptual knowledge; and a world of relative actuality, the things that come and go, the objects of sense perception.[1] The predicates of the Eleatic Being belong therefore to the Idea as the object of true knowledge, αὐτὸ καθ' αὐτὸ μεθ' αὑτοῦ μονοειδὲς ἀεὶ ὄν;[2] it is unchangeable, οὐδὲ ποτ' οὐδαμῇ οὐδαμῶς ἀλλοίωσιν οὐδεμίαν ἐνδέχεται.[3] The perceivable individual things, on the contrary, constitute the Heracleitan flux of continuous origination, change, and destruction. The fundamental principle of the metaphysical epistemology of Plato is this: TWO WORLDS must be distinguished,[4] one of which *is* and never *becomes*, the other of which *becomes* and never *is;* one is the object of the reason (νόησις), the other is the object of sense (αἴσθησις). Since, now, the objects are as completely separated (χωρίς) as the methods of knowing are distinct, the Ideas stand as incorporeal forms (ἀσώματα εἴδη) in contrast to material things, which are perceived by the senses. The Ideas, which are never to be found[5] in space or in matter, which indeed exist purely for themselves (εἰλικρινές), which are to be grasped[6] not by the senses but only by thought, form an intelligible world in themselves (τόπος νοητός). *A rational theory of knowledge requires an immaterialistic metaphysics.*

This immaterialism was the peculiarly original creation of Plato. Where in the earlier systems, not excluding that of Anaxagoras, the discussion turned upon the spiritual as the distinctive principle, nevertheless the principle always appeared as a peculiar kind of corporeal actuality. Plato, on the other hand, first discovered a purely spiritual world. The theory of Ideas is, therefore, an entirely new mediation of the Eleatic and the Heracleitan metaphysic, employing the

---

[1] This view is stated most clearly in *Timæus*, 27 f., 57 f. Compare *Rep.*, 509 f., 533. [2] *Symp.*, 211.
[3] *Phædo*, 78. [4] *Tim.*, 27 d.
[5] *Symp.*, 211. [6] *Rep.*, 507; *Tim.*, 28.

opposition between the Protagorean and Socratic theories of knowledge. Precisely for this reason, in the *Theætetus*, Plato brought the Sophistic theory of perception into closer relationship to the πάντα ῥεῖ than the Sophist himself had brought it. On the other hand, the close relationship of the Socratic epistemology to the Eleatic doctrine of Being had already been recognized by the Megarians (§ 28). The positive metaphysic of Plato may be characterized, therefore, as immaterialistic Eleaticism.[1] Therein consists its ontological character (Deuschle). It cognizes Being in Ideas, and relegates Becoming to a lower form of knowing.

The neo-Pythagorean-neo-Platonic conception was an entire misunderstanding of Plato. According to this conception, Ideas possess no independent actuality, but are only thought-forms supposed to exist in the divine mind. Through the neo-Platonism of the Renaissance, and even down to the beginning of this century, this interpretation of Plato obtained. Herbart was of great service in his opposition to it (*Einleit. in d. Philos.*, § 144 f.; Vol. I. 240 f.).

Consistent with the theory of two worlds, as the central point in Platonism, is the manner in which Plato represented our cognition of Ideas in particular.

The primary function of the Ideas is to set forth the logical character of the class concepts, to reveal the common qualities (τὸ κοινόν) of the particulars which the class concepts comprehend. They are, in the Aristotelian phraseology, the ἓν ἐπὶ πολλῶν.[2] But Plato regarded the process of thought, not as analysis, nor as an abstraction by comparison, but as rather a synoptic intuition [3] of reality presented in single examples. The Idea cannot be contained in its perceived phenomenon. It is of another sort, and cannot be found in appearance. In other words, material things do not include the Idea, but are only the

---

[1] The relative pluralistic character of the theory of Ideas is in contrast to original Eleaticism. It did not, as in the earlier attempts at mediation, arise from the need of an explanation of Becoming, but from the circumstance that conceptual knowledge can and must refer to a manifold of independent content-determinations.

[2] *Met.*, I. 9, 990 b, 6.   [3] *Phædr.*, 265; *Rep.*, 537.

copies or shadows[1] of it. Therefore the perceptions cannot include the Ideas as separable integral parts, but are, on the contrary, only the occasions for the apprehension of that Idea that is similar to the perceptions but not identical with them. Since the Idea cannot be created by reflection, it must be regarded as an original possession of the soul which the soul remembers when it sees its copy in the sense world. The recognition of the ideas is ἀνά-μνησις.[2]

In the mythical representation in the *Phædrus*, Plato presupposes that the human soul has gazed upon the Idea with its supersensible faculties, — those related to the world of Ideas, — before its entrance into earthly life, but it remembers them only upon the perception of corresponding phenomena. Thereby out of the painful feeling of astonishment at the contrast between the Idea and its phenomenon is created the philosophic impulse, the longing love for the supersensible Idea. This love is the ἔρως,[3] which conducts it back from the transitoriness of sense to the immortality of the ideal world.[4]

There is an interesting parallel between the intuitive character, which the recognition of Ideas in Plato possesses, and the γνώμη γνησίη of Democritus. In Plato also analogies to optical impressions predominate. Both Democritus and Plato have in mind immediate knowledge of the pure forms (ἰδέαι), the absolutely actual [5] which is attained wholly apart from sense percep-

---

[1] *Rep.*, 514 f.; *Phædo*, 73.

[2] *Meno*, 80 f.; *Phædr.*, 249 f.; *Phædo*, 72 f.

[3] *Phædr.*, 250 f., and especially *Symp*, 200 f.

[4] The theory of the ἔρως takes on thereby in the *Symposium* a more universal aspect of beholding the living principle of all Becoming (γένεσις) in the desire for the Idea (οὐσία), and so prepares the way for the teleological interpretation of Ideas.

[5] One has the same right to speak of " sensualism " in Plato as in Democritus. Both explain true knowledge of the ὄντως ὄν as the reception of the ἰδέαι by the soul, not as an act of sense perception, although as illustrated by the analogy to optical perception.

tion.   The exposition of this teaching appears in Plato (*Phœdrus* and *Symposium*) in mythical form.   For since it is a question of the time-process of the knowledge of the eternal, of the genesis of the intuition of the Absolute, a dialectic presentation is not possible.

Since the Ideas are hypostasized class-concepts, in their first draft there are for Plato as many Ideas as there are class concepts or general names for different perceptual things.   There are, therefore, Ideas of all that is in any wise thinkable,[1] — Ideas of things, qualities and relations, of products of art and nature, of the good and of the bad, of the high and of the low.[2]   The later dialogues (*Symposium*, *Phœdo*, *Timæus*) speak only of such Ideas as have an inherent value, such as the good and the beautiful ; of such as correspond to nature products, like fire, snow, etc. ; and, finally, of mathematical relations, like great and small, unity and duality.   Aristotle reports that Plato in later time did no longer recognize Ideas of artifacts, negations, and relations, and that he held, in place of these, essentially nature class-concepts.[3]   An exacter determination of the circle within which the philosopher, especially in different periods of his development, extended or wished to extend his theory of Ideas, cannot be made.

In general the chronological order of the dialogues indicates that Plato originally constructed a world of Ideas according to his logical and epistemological view of class concepts.   In the course of time, however, he came more and more to seek in this supersensible world the highest values and the fundamental ontological forms, according to which the sense world of Becoming is modelled.   From the world of Ideas there thus arose an

---

[1] *Rep.*, 596.

[2] For particular proofs, consult Zeller, II³. 585 f.   The dialogue *Parmenides* proves with fine irony to the " young Socrates " that he must accept also the Ideas of hair, mud, etc. (130 f.).   In as late a writing as the middle part of the *Republic*, Plato used the Ideas of bed, etc , to illustrate his theory.

[3] *Met.*, XI. 3, 1070 a, 18.

ideal world. The norms of value thus took the place of class
concepts. The ethical motive became more and more influential in his philosophy, as appears also in what follows.

The more thoroughly the theory of Ideas in their first
draft distinguished the two worlds from each other, the
more difficult it became to determine the relation of the
things of sense to their respective Ideas. The characteristic
of this relation most frequently given in the dialogues *Meno*,
Theœtetus, *Phœdrus*, and *Symposium*, and likewise in the
Phœdo, is similarity. This is consistent with the thought
which the philosopher developed in those same dialogues
concerning the origin of concepts; for similarity forms the
psychological ground through which,[1] stimulated by perception, the recollection of the Idea is said to come. Similarity,[2] however, is not equivalence. The Idea never appears
fully in the things,[3] and accordingly Plato designated the
relationship of the two as $\mu\acute{\iota}\mu\eta\sigma\iota\varsigma$[4]. The Idea is thus
regarded[5] as the original (*Urbild*) ($\pi\alpha\rho\acute{\alpha}\delta\epsilon\iota\gamma\mu\alpha$), the sensed
object as the copy (*Abbild*) ($\epsilon\acute{\iota}\delta\omega\lambda o\nu$). Exactly herein
consists the small amount of reality which the corporeal

[1] Now one would say: according to the law of the association of
ideas, which moreover Plato enunciated expressly in this respect in the
Phœdo, 73 f.

[2] In view of the same the *Parmenides* raises the dialectic plea
(131 f.), that it presupposes a *tertium comparationis* for the Idea and the
phænomenon and forms an infinite regress. It is the objection of the
$\tau\rho\acute{\iota}\tau o\varsigma$ $\acute{\alpha}\nu\theta\rho\omega\pi o\varsigma$. Compare Aristotle, *Met.*, VI. 113, 1039 a, 2.

[3] Plato was probably prompted to emphasize this by the incongruity
of actual life with the ethical norm; primarily, however, from the theoretical point of view by the fact that the mathematical concepts are
factors in the consideration, and that these are never the result of perception. See *Phœdo*, 73 a; *Meno*, 85 e. The hypothetical discussion of
concepts stands furthermore in most exact connection with this.

[4] Whether he thus early adopted this expression from the Pythagorean number theory need not be discussed.

[5] See the freely accommodative and relatively early presentation in
the *Republic*, 595 f.

world possesses in contrast to the ὄντως ὄν. On the other hand, viewed from its logical side, the Idea is the unitary, the permanent,[1] in which the things of sense in their origination, change, and destruction have only temporary and occasional part (μετέχειν).[2] This relationship is, again, ontologically so viewed that the change of qualities of sensible things is reduced ultimately to a coming and going of Ideas. On account of this change the Idea at one time participates in the particular thing (παρουσία),[3] and at another leaves it.[4]

The later phase (*Phædo*) of the theory of Ideas has a thought that seems to have been absent from the original statement, viz., that in the Ideas the causes may be somehow found for the things of sense appearing as they do appear. The purpose of Plato was originally only to recognize permanent true Being. The theory of Ideas in the *Meno*, *Theœtetus*, *Phædrus*, and *Symposium* does not attempt to be an explanation of the world of phenomena. The significance of the *Sophist* is that it proposes this problem. Confronting the theory of Ideas with other metaphysical theories, the *Sophist* asks how this lower world of sense-appearance and its Becoming can be conceived as deduced from supersensible forms which are removed from all motion

---

[1] The *Parmenides* (130 f.) makes also at this point some dialectic objections of the Eleatic sort. Plato (*Philebus*, 14 f.) very curtly deals with these.

[2] *Symp.*, 211 b.   [3] *Phœd.*, 100 d.

[4] The way in which the *Phædo* develops this (102 f.) shows a remarkable analogy to the teaching of Anaxagoras, which teaching is also significant in other respects in this dialogue (see below.) As in Anaxagoras, the individuals are said to owe the change of their qualities to the entrance or exit of the qualitatively unchangeable χρήματα (§ 22), so here the Idea is added as giving a quality and as augmenting the thing (προσγίγνεσθαι). Or it disappears again when, of mutually exclusive Ideas, the one already inherent in the thing shuts out the other. This explanation is essentially that of the Herbartian conception of Ideas as *absolute Qualitäten*.

and change.   It shows that immaterial Eleaticism is as un-
able as early Eleaticism to explain this problem.   For in
order to explain the motion of the sense-world, Ideas must
themselves be endowed with motion, life, soul, and reason.
But the εἰδῶν φίλοι deny [1] to the Ideas all these qualities,
especially the most important quality of motion.

The Platonic philosophy reaches its zenith in the solution
of this problem.   The *Phœdo* declares that in the Ideas
alone is the cause (αἰτία) of the phenomenal world to be
found, and however this relationship is to be conceived, the
sense object is indebted to the Idea alone for its qualities.[2]
This is the strongest of Plato's convictions, and to prove
it is the greatest problem of the dialectic.   There are introduced in the same dialogue, however, the two elements,
Anaxagoreanism and Pythagoreanism,[3] through which this
new phase of the theory of Ideas took shape in his mind.

---

[1] *Soph.*, 248 f.   The author of the *Sophist* founds this criticism
(247 d) upon the definition that the ὄντως ὄν must be thought as δύναμις,
and whatever possesses Being must be thought as power in order to
explain Becoming (*das Geschehen*).   Although this expression is not
to be explained in the spirit of the Aristotelian terminology (Zeller, II³.
575, 3), still this view lies nowise in the direction in which Plato later
solved the problem.   δύναμις is active power (see *Republic*, 477, where
δύναμις is used in the sense of a faculty of the soul).   Ideas are, however, final causes, and not such "faculties" as are definable only
through their effects (*Rep.*, loc. cit.).

[2] *Phœdo*, 100 d, where reference seems to be made to the dialogue
Sophist.

[3] About the time of this change Aristotle entered the Academy;
hence his exposition of the genesis of the theory of Ideas (*Met.*, I. 6).
The great significance which is ascribed in the *Metaphysics* to the Pythagorean theory in its bearing on Plato is not consistent with the content
of any of the foundation dialogues, *Theœtetus*, *Phœdrus*, and *Symposium*.   Practically it begins first with the *Philebus*.   But even the
Phœdo shows, in its choice of persons and also in its discussion of the
problems, that account is taken of the Pythagorean philosophy.   Nevertheless (*Met.*, XII. 4, 1078 b, 9) Aristotle himself elsewhere remarks

If the Ideas cannot themselves move and suffer change, they can be the causes of phenomena only in the sense that they are the purposes which are realized in phenomena. The only conception which therefore, from the point of view of the theory of Ideas, appears to be possible as an explanation of phenomena, is the teleological.[1]

The true relation between the Idea (οὐσία) and the phenomenon (γένεσις) is that of purpose. Plato found in the νοῦς-theory of Anaxagoras an attempt to make this point of view valid. But while he subjected the insufficient development of this theory to a sharp criticism,[2] he maintained in addition that the establishment as well as the development of a teleological view of the world is possible only to a theory of Ideas.[3]

The same theory is further developed in the *Philebus* and in the corresponding part of the *Republic*. If the *Sophist*[4] from a formal and logical point of view called attention to the fact that a similar κοινωνία, a relationship of co-ordination and subordination, exists between Ideas as well as between phenomena and Ideas, so the *Republic*[5] and the *Philebus*[6] emphasized also the systematic unity of the οὐσία, and found it in the Idea of the Good, as including all other Ideas within itself. Thus the pyramid of concepts reached its apex, not by means of a formally logical process of abstraction, but, as it happens in the entire Platonic dialectic, by means of an ontological intuition, expressing here its final and highest ὑπόθεσις.[7] For since all

that the original conception of the theory of Ideas was independent of the number theory.

[1] *Phileb.*, 54 c. : ξύμπασαν γένεσιν οὐσίας ἕνεκα γίγνεσθαι ξυμπάσης.

[2] *Phædo*, 97 f.

[3] *Ibid.*, 99 f. He called this the δεύτερος πλοῦς of philosophy, and the development of philosophy as a theoretical explanation of phenomena he sketched in 95 c, ff.

[4] *Soph.*, 251 f.

[5] *Rep.*, 511 b.

[6] *Phileb.*, 16 f.

[7] *Phædo*, 101 b; *Rep.*, *loc. cit.*

that is, is for some good, the Idea of the Good or of the absolute purpose is that to which all other Ideas are subordinated, this subordination being teleological rather than logical. The Idea of the Good stands, therefore, even above Being and Knowing, which are the two highest disjunctives.[1] It is the sun [2] in the realm of Ideas from which everything else gets its value as well as its actuality. It is the World Reason. To it belong the name of νοῦς and that of Godhead.

This immaterialistic perfecting of the Anaxagorean thought is set by Plato in the *Philebus* (28 f.) and stands opposed to the system of irrational necessity of Democritus. In this connection, as a matter of fact, the νοῦς and the Godhead and the Idea of the Good, so far as it included all the others under it, were identified with the total world of Ideas (αἰτία; compare Zeller, II³. 577 ff., 593 f.). Neither is there here any suggestion of a personal divine spirit. Compare G. F. Rettig, Αἰτία *im Philebus* (Bern. 1866); K. Stumpf. *Verhältnis des plat. Gottes zur Idee des Guten* (Halle, 1869).

The teleological cosmology of Plato consisted in his regarding Being or the world of Ideas as both purpose and cause[3] of phenomena or the world of matter, and besides these teleological causes he recognized no other causes in the strict meaning of the term. Likewise in the particular relations of phenomena those things which present themselves to sense perception as acting and having effect are valid for him only as secondary[4] causes (ξυναίτια). The true cause is purpose.

However, the Idea never realizes itself fully in corporeal

---

[1] *Rep.*, 508 f.   [2] *Ibid.*; compare 517 b.

[3] In *Philebus*, 26 e, the search for the fourth principle is opened with the expressed explanation that ἡ τοῦ ποιοῦντος φύσις (the essence of activity) may be distinguished only in name from the cause (αἰτία). If this αἰτία in the purpose is found in the Idea of the Good, then is the concept of the teleological cause attained.

[4] *Phædo*, 99 b, where the cause is distinguished from the οὗ ἄνευ τὸ αἴτιον οὐκ ἂν ποτ' εἴη αἴτιον.

things.   This thought was peculiar to the first draft of the theory of Ideas, and it got new support and significance in Plato's tendency toward Pythagoreanism which set the perfect and imperfect worlds in opposition to each other.   The more, however, the world of Ideas became the ideal world, the perfect Being or the kingdom of Worth, the less could it be viewed as the cause of imperfection in the world of sense.   The world of imperfection could rather only be sought in the thing that has no Being.   For the sense world as eternally " becoming" has part not only in that which has Being (the Ideas), but also in that which has no Being ($\mu\grave{\eta}$ ὄν).[1] Empty space[2] was regarded as having no Being by Plato as by the Eleatics. Plato moreover regarded empty space, like the Pythagoreans, as in itself formless and unfashioned, and precisely for that reason as pure[3] negation (στέρησις) of Being. But the formless is capable of all possible forms, and retains them by virtue of mathematical determinations.   In this sense the *Philebus*[4] makes the Pythagorean fundamental opposition a part of his teleological metaphysic, in that he defined as the two first principles of the world of experience the ἄπειρον (endless formless space) and the πέρας (the mathematical limitation and formation of that space). Out of the union of the two the world of the individual things of sense appears, and the fourth and highest principle forms the basis of this "mixing."   This principle is the αἰτία, the Idea of the Good, or the cosmic reason, the νοῦς.

[1] *Rep.*, 477 a.

[2] That the $\mu\grave{\eta}$ ὄν which is designated in the *Philebus* as the ἄπειρον and in the *Timæus* (§ 37) as δεξαμένη, ἐκμαγεῖον, etc., is space, Zeller has proved (III³. 605 f.; see also H. Siebeck, *Untersuchungen*, 49 f.). On this account the word "matter" has been avoided, lest it imply its unavoidable subordinate meaning, "unformed stuff."   "Unformed stuff," the ὕλη of Aristotle, had not yet had its meaning determined by Plato.

[3] Compare Arist. *Phys.*, I. 9, 192 a, 6.   [4] *Phileb.*, 23 f.

Mathematics, whose importance for the dialectic has been emphasized above, had an ontological importance also in Plato's system. Mathematical forms are the link by means of which the Idea shapes space teleologically into the sense world.[1] Here for the first time is explained the position which the philosopher assigns this science in connection with his epistemology. Mathematics is a knowledge not of the phenomenal world but of the permanent world. For that reason in the earlier dialogues it seems to have been used only for dialectic [2] purposes. Its objects, however, especially geometrical objects, have still something of sense in them, which distinguishes them from the Ideas in the later evaluation of the Ideas. Therefore mathematics belongs, according to the schema of the *Republic* (509 f., 523 f.) not to the δόξα (the knowledge of γένεσις), but to νόησις (the knowledge of οὐσία). Within οὐσία it is to be distinguished as διάνοια from the peculiar ἐπιστήμη, the knowledge of the Idea of the Good. Mathematics appears, then, in the education of the ideal state as the highest preparation for philosophy, but only as preparation.

Concerning Plato as a mathematician, his introduction of definitions and the analytic method, see Cantor, *Geschichte der Mathematik*, I. 183 f.

In his latter days Plato borrowed from the Pythagorean number theory the principle by which he hoped for a systematic presentation and articulation of the world of Ideas. Logical investigations [3] toward this end were given up as soon as from the teleological principle the Idea of the Good had been placed at the head. The Pythagorean method of developing concepts according to the number series commended itself to him. In adopting this method, Plato

---

[1] A good parallel exists also here between Plato and Democritus, although in the latter's theory in the place of the teleological αἰτία of the *Philebus* stood the ἀνάγκη (ἡ τοῦ ἀλόγου καὶ εἰκῇ δύναμις καὶ τὰ ὅπῃ ἔτυχεν, *Phileb.*, 28 d), and although the κένον and the σχήματα (the ἰδέαι of Plato) produce the sense world. In view of this, one can see in the exposition in the *Philebus*, 23–26, a reference to Democritus, whose teaching this dialogue appears to have used in other places (§ 33).

[2] The *Meno* shows how we can know Ideas by geometrical examples (Pythagorean doctrine).

[3] *Sophist*, especially 254 f.

also symbolized single Ideas by ideal numbers. The elements of the Ideas are the ἄπειρον and the πέρας in analogy
to the principles laid down for the sense world in the *Philebus*. The ἄπειρον has here the significance of " intelligible
space." [1] Out of the ἕν which he identified [2] with the Idea
of the Good, he derived all other Ideas, as a graded series
of conditioning and conditioned (πρότερον καὶ ὕστερον).

Traces of this senile attempt are to be found in the *Philebus*
and the *Laws*. In other respects we are instructed only by
Aristotle concerning these ἄγραπτα δόγματα : *Met.*, I. 6, XII.
4 f. ; compare A. Trendelenburg, *Plat. de ideis et numeris doctrina ex Arist. illustrata* (Leipzig, 1826), and Zeller, II³. 567 f.

36. Measured by its first motive, Plato's theory of Ideas
is an outspoken ethical metaphysic. Consequently Ethics
was the philosophical science which he chiefly and most
fruitfully built upon. Among the Ideas that the dialectic
undertook to develop, social norms had a prominent place.
The immaterialism of the double-world theory necessarily
involved an ascetic morality that was very uncharacteristic
of Greek thought. The *Theœtetus*,[3] for example, sets up
an ideal of retirement from the world for the philosopher
who, since earthly life is full of evil, finds refuge as quickly
as possible in the divine presence. The *Phœdo* [4] further
develops this negative ethics in all its details. It pictures
the whole life of the philosopher as already a dying, a purification of the soul from the dross of sense existence. The
soul in the body is, as it were, in prison, and it can free
itself only by knowledge and virtue.

This view, which is particularly like that of the Pythagoreans among the ancient moral theories, took in the
metaphysical theory of Ideas a special form, by virtue
of which the psychological basis was created also for

[1] Compare H Siebeck, *Untersuchungen*, 97 f.
[2] Aristox. *Elem. harm.*, II. 30.
[3] 172, 176 f.   [4] 64 f.

the positive ethics of Plato. In the theory of the two worlds the soul must take a peculiar intermediary position, — a theory that could be developed not without difficulties and contradictions. On account of its ideal character the soul must be capable of conceiving the Ideas, and on this account must be related to them.[1] The soul belongs to the supersensible world, and should have all the qualities of that world, — non-origination, indestructibility, unity, and changelessness. But since it is the carrier of the Idea of life,[2] and as cause of motion is itself eternally movable, it is not identical to the Ideas, but very similar to them.[3] Therefore for Plato it had pre-existence and lasted beyond the earthly body. Yet in that changeless timelessness of Being which belongs to the Ideas it has likewise only a share, since it also belongs to γένεσις but it is not identical with the Ideas. On the other hand, the Socratic principle required that the soul's goodness and badness must not be attributed to external fate, but to the soul itself.[4] Since its essence, related as it is to the world of Ideas, cannot be answerable for a bad decision, its *higher nature* must be considered as deformed by the temporary inclinations of the senses.[5] Hence the theory of the three " parts "[6] of the soul. This theory, although represented mythically in the *Phædrus* (consistent with its subject matter), became in the *Republic* an entirely dogmatic basis of ethics. There is the part that is related to the Ideas, the directing, reasoning part (ἡγεμονικόν, λογιστικόν). Then there are the two passionate (*affektvolle*) parts. One is the nobler: it is the strong activity of will (θυμός, θυμο-ειδές). The other, less noble, consists of sensuous appetites (ἐπιθυμητικόν, φιλοχρήματον). These three parts appear in the *Phædrus* and the *Republic* as the Forms (εἴδη) of

[1] *Phædo*, 78 f.   [2] *Ibid.*, 105 d.
[3] ὁμοιότατον; *ibid.*, 80 b.   [4] *Rep.*, 617 f.
[5] *Ibid.*, 611 f.   [6] *Phædrus*, 246 f.

activity of the soul in its unity. Hence in the *Phædrus*,
also, the soul that is described there as a unity, unites in
itself in the next life all the functions that in the dialogues
are ascribed to its three parts.[1] The myths of the *Timæus*
for the first time expressly speak of the μέρη, of which the
soul is composed, and treat the parts as separable, in
such a way that one part, the νοῦς,[2] is immortal, the others
mortal.

Jas. Steger, *Plat. Studien*, III. ; *Die plat. Psychologie*
(Innsbruck, 1872) ; P. Wildauer, *Die Psy. des Willens*, II.
(Innsbruck, 1879) ; H. Siebeck, *Gesch. der Psy.*, I. 1, 187 f. ;
Schulthess, *Plat. Forschungen* (Bonn, 1875).

Plato's psychology was by no means only a result of his
theory of nature, but was a metaphysical presupposition for it,
resting upon ethical and epistemological motives. This is
shown in the beginning of the myth in the *Timæus*. Pre-
existence is supposed to explain our knowledge about Ideas
(by ἀνάμνησις), and on the other hand to explain our guilt, on
account of which the supersensible soul is bound in an earthly
body (see myth in *Phædrus*). The post-existence of the soul,
on the other hand, makes possible not only the striving of the
soul to reach beyond earthly life after a completer identification
with the world of Ideas, but above all it makes possible moral
recompense. Thereupon Plato illuminated this teaching everywhere by mythical representations of judgment at death, of
wanderings of souls, etc. (see *Gorgias*, *Republic*, *Phædo*). Consequently, however weak the proofs may be which Plato had
adduced for individual immortality, yet his absolute belief in it
is one of the chief points of his teaching. Of the arguments
on which he founded this belief, the most valuable is that
wherein he (*Phædo*, 86 f.) contended against the Pythagorean
definition of the soul as the harmony of the body by the proof
of the soul's substantial independence through its control over
the body.[3] His weakest argument is that in which the *Phædo*

[1] In the *Phædrus* that previous determination of the soul is ascribed
to the sense appetites, which explains the errors of earthly life. In the
Phædo, the fortunes of the soul after death are made dependent on the
adherence of its sensuality. Pre-existence and post-existence are ascribed
in both cases to the whole soul.   [2] *Tim.*, 69 f.

[3] The Mendelssohn copy of the *Phædo* (Berl. 1764) especially raises
this point in the spirit of the philosophy of the Enlightenment.

sums up and crowns all the other arguments: a dialectic sub-
reption from the double meaning of the word ἀθάνατος, in which
the soul is explained as immortal because it can exist in no
other way than as a living thing (*Phædo*, 105 f.). Compare
K. F. Hermann, *De immortalitatis notione in Plat. Phædone*
(Marburg, 1835); *id. de partibus animæ immortalibus* (Gött.,
1850); K. Ph. Fischer, *Plat. de immortalitate animæ doctrina*
(Erlangen, 1845); P. Zimmermann, *Die Unsterblichkeit der
Seele in Plat. Phæd.* (Leipzig, 1869); G. Teichmüller, *Studien*,
I. 107 f.

The relationship of the three parts to the essence of the soul
is very difficult, and is not made perfectly clear. Plato maintains clearly, on the whole, the unity of the soul, but only in a
few places particularly emphasizes it. On the one hand, the
Phædrus makes all the three parts belong to the essence of
the individual, in order to make conceivable the fall of the soul
in its pre-existence. On the other hand, it appears as if both
the lower parts originated in the union of soul and body, and on
that account again were stripped off entirely from the true essence
of the soul (νοῦς) after a virtuous life (*Rep.*, 611; *Phædo*,
83). The abrupt and direct opposition of the two worlds made
this troublesome point in his system (*Rep.*, 435 f.). So also
the specific psychological meaning of the three parts, whose
origin is made clear by ethical evaluation, is undetermined.
In spite of some similarities, this division is in no wise identical
with the present-day psychology and its customary triple division
into ideas, sensations, and desires. For the αἰσθήσεις did not,
according to Plato, belong to the λογιστικόν, but must, although
he has not expressly stated it, be ascribed to both the other
parts. On the other hand, there belong to the νοῦς not only the
knowledge of Ideas, but also the virtuous determination of the
will, which, according to Socrates, corresponds to that knowledge.
We come nearest to the Platonic thought when we think of the
life of the soul as ordered into three different degrees of worth.
Each degree has its own theoretic and practical functions in
such a way that the lower functions may exist without the
higher, but the higher appear — at least in this life — in connection with the lower. So plants have ἐπιθυμητικόν (*Tim.*, 77;
Rep., 441); animals have θυμοειδές in addition to ἐπιθυμητικόν;
and men have, besides these two functions, the λογιστικόν. The
νοῦς is localized in the brain, θυμός in the heart, and ἐπιθυμία in
the liver.[1]

In the application of this to ethnography, he claimed for the

[1] Agreeing with Democritus.

Greeks the excellence of λογιστικόν (*Republic*, 435 e), allowed to the warlike barbarians of the north the predominance of θυμός, and to the weak barbarians of the south that of ἐπιθυμία.

Upon the basis of this psychological theory, Plato went beyond not only the abstract simplicity of the Socratic theory of virtue, but also the ascetic one-sidedness of his own first negative statements. That moral conduct alone makes man truly blessed [1] in this or the other life,[2] is his fundamental conviction. But even if he was inclined to find this true happiness only in the most complete perfection of the soul, in which happiness the soul is a sharer in the divine world of Ideas; and even if therefore he refused [3] as unworthy of the soul every utilitarian principle of conventional ethics, yet he recognized other kinds of happiness as justifiable moments of the HIGHEST GOOD. These kinds of happiness are all which, in the entire sweep of the soul's activities, appear as true and noble joys. The *Philebus* [4] develops such a graded series of goods. Plato contended also, in this dialogue, against the theory that would find the τέλος [5] only in sense pleasure. But against the view of those who explain all pleasure as only illusory, he held fast to the reality of a pure and painless sense-pleasure,[6] and he contended against the one-sided view that sought true happiness only in insight.[7] But while he on the other hand recognized the legitimacy of intellectual pleasure, he laid claim to it not only for rational knowledge (νοῦς), but also for correct ideas in every science and art.[8] Above all this, however, he set the participation in ideal evaluations and

---

[1] *Rep.*, 353 f.

[2] Compare entire conclusion of *Rep.*, Books IX., X.

[3] *Rep.*, 362 ; *Theœt.*, 176 ; *Phœdo*, 68 f.

[4] See *Laws*, 717 f., 728 f.   [5] As already seen in *Gorgias*.

[6] Supposably Democritus.

[7] These statements could be aimed just as well against Antisthenes, Euclid, or Democritus (*Phileb.*, 21, 60).

[8] *Phileb.*, 62 f.

their actualization in individual activity.[1] All the beauty
and vitality of Greece was amalgamated here in the tran-
scendental ideal of the philosopher, and a similar union
of the two sides of reality was already suggested in the
series of objects which the *Symposium* [2] develops as the
working of the ἔρως.

A. Trendelenburg, *De Plat. Philebus consilio* (Berlin, 1837) ;
Fr. Susemihl, *Ueber die Gütertafel im Philebus* (Philol. 1863) ;
R. Hirzel, *De bonis in fine Philebi enumeratis* (Leipzig, 1868).

However, Plato founded the development of his theory
of virtue in a still more systematic way upon his triple
divisions of the soul.   While his first dialogues took pains
to reduce the single virtues to the Socratic εἶδος of knowledge, the later dialogues proceeded upon the theory of the
distinct independence and the respective limitations of the
particular virtues.   In so far as the one or the other part
of the soul preponderates in different men according to
their dispositions,[3] are they suited to developing one or
another virtue.   For every part of the soul has its own
perfection, which is called its virtue and is grounded in its
essence.[4]   Accordingly Plato constructed a group of four
cardinal virtues which at that time were beginning to be
frequently mentioned in literature.   There is the virtue
of wisdom (σοφία) corresponding to the ἡγεμονικόν ; that of
will-power (ἀνδρία), corresponding to the θυμοειδές ; that of
self-control (σωφροσύνη), corresponding to the ἐπιθυμητικόν.
Finally, since the perfection of the whole soul consists [5] in
the right relations of the single parts, in the fulfilment of
the soul's particular task through every one of these parts
(τὰ ἑαυτοῦ πράττειν), and in the regulative control of

[1] *Phileb.*, 66 f.   [2] *Symp.*, 208 f.
[3] *Rep.*, 410 f.   [4] *Rep.*, 441 f.
[5] In the entire *Republic* the ascetic thought of stripping off the lower
parts of the soul is entirely put aside.

reason over the two other parts,[1] so we have as a fourth virtue that of an equable arrangement of the whole. This last is called by Plato δικαιοσύνη.[2]

The last term, which is scarcely understandable from the point of view of individual ethics, arises from the peculiar derivation which Plato has given to these virtues in the *Republic*. Loyal to the motive of the theory of Ideas, the Platonic ethics sketched not so much the ideal of the individual as that of the species; it pictured less the perfect man than the perfect society. The Platonic ethics is primarily social ethics. It does not treat of the happiness of the individuals, but that of the whole,[3] and this happiness can be reached only in the perfect state. The ethics of Plato perfected itself in his teaching of the ideal state.

K. F. Hermann, *Die historischen Elemente des platonischen Idealstaates* (*Gesch. Abhandl.*, 132 f.); Ed. Zeller, *Der plat. Staat in seiner Bedeutung für die Folgezeit* (*Vorträge und Abhandl.*, I. 62 f.); C. Nohle, *Die Staatslehre Plat.'s in ihrer geschichtlichen Entwickelung* (Jena, 1880).

Whatever[4] may be the natural and historical origin of the state, its task is the same everywhere, according to Plato: viz., so to direct the common life of man that all may be happy through virtue. The task can be accom-

[1] Since already σωφροσύνη is possible only through the right rule of the appetites, σωφροσύνη and δικαιοσύνη are not mutually exclusive. Compare Zeller, II³. 749 f.

[2] The most usual verbal translation, *justice*, concerns only the political, not the moral spirit of the case. *Righteousness* does not fully state the Platonic meaning.

[3] Precisely on that account the philosopher must share in public life, even if he would find his happiness only in his turning from the earthly and in his devotion to the divine. See above; also *Rep.*, 519 f.

[4] The first book of the *Republic* develops critically the views of the Sophists on this point. How far in the representation of the genesis of the state, given in the second book (369 f.), positive and negative analogies appear, cannot be discussed here.

plished only by ordering all the relations of society according to the principles of man's moral nature. The perfect state is divided into three distinct parts, like the soul of man. There are the producers, the warriors, and the administrators. The great mass of citizens ($\delta\hat{\eta}\mu\rho\varsigma$; $\gamma\epsilon\omega\rho\gamma\rho\grave{\iota}$ $\kappa\alpha\grave{\iota}$ $\delta\eta\mu\iota\rho\nu\rho\gamma\rho\acute{\iota}$), corresponding to the $\grave{\epsilon}\pi\iota\theta\nu\mu\eta\tau\iota\kappa\acute{o}\nu$ or $\phi\iota\lambda\rho$-$\chi\rho\acute{\eta}\mu\alpha\tau\rho\nu$, are entrusted with providing for the material foundation of the life of the state by caring for its daily needs ; and they are prompted to make this provision by their own sensuous appetites. The warriors and officials ($\grave{\epsilon}\pi\acute{\iota}\kappa\rho\nu\rho\rho\iota$), corresponding to the $\theta\nu\mu\rho\epsilon\iota\delta\acute{\epsilon}\varsigma$ in the unselfish fulfilment of duty, have to guard the state externally by repelling invasion, internally by executing the laws. The rulers, finally ($\check{\alpha}\rho\chi\rho\nu\tau\epsilon\varsigma$), corresponding to $\lambda\rho\gamma\iota\sigma\tau\iota\kappa\acute{o}\nu$ or $\acute{\eta}\gamma\epsilon\mu\rho\nu\iota\kappa\acute{o}\nu$, determine, according to their insight, the legislation and the principles of administration. The perfection however of the entire state — its " virtue " — is justice ($\delta\iota\kappa\alpha\iota\rho\sigma\acute{\nu}\nu\eta$),[1] that every one may get his right. Justice consists in these three classes having their proper distribution of power, while at the same time every one fulfils his own peculiar task. Therefore the rulers must have the highest culture and wisdom ($\sigma\rho\phi\acute{\iota}\alpha$), the warriors an undaunted devotion to duty ($\grave{\alpha}\nu\delta\rho\acute{\iota}\alpha$), and the people an obedience which curbs the appetites ($\sigma\omega\phi\rho\rho\sigma\acute{\nu}\nu\eta$).

The constitution of the ideal state for Plato is an aristocracy in the strictest sense of the word. It is a rule of the best, — the wise and virtuous. It places all legislation and the entire direction of society in the hand of the class of the scientifically cultured ($\phi\iota\lambda\acute{o}\sigma\rho\phi\rho\iota$).[2] The task of the

---

[1] Therefore the corresponding virtue of the individual, the ethical equilibrium of the parts of his soul, is designated by the same name.

[2] Thus must the celebrated sentence (*Rep.*, 473 d) be understood. There will be no end to the sorrow of man until the philosophers (the scientifically cultured) rule or the rulers are philosophers (are scientifically cultured).

second class is to execute practically the orders of the highest class, and to maintain the state and preserve its interests both internally and externally. The mass of mankind have to work and obey.

Since, however, the object of the state does not consist in the securing of any merely outward benefit, but in the virtue of all its citizens, Plato demanded that the individual should merge himself entirely in the state, and that the state should embrace and determine the entire life of its citizens. Plato thus went beyond the political principle of the Greeks. The development which this idea found in the social organization of the πολιτεία was restricted, nevertheless, to the two higher classes, which were taken together under the name of " guardians " (φύλακες). For the mass of the δῆμος there is accessible no virtue founded on knowledge, but only the conventional virtue of society, which is enforced by the strict execution of the laws and attained through utilitarian considerations. The Platonic politics leaves therefore the third class to itself. In its desire for acquisition, this class is moved by a fundamentally sensuous motive ; and it performs its duty when by its labor it furnishes the material foundation for the life of the state, and yields to the guidance of the " guardians." But the prenatal and present life of the " guardians " are to be controlled by the state. Impressed by the importance of the propagation of the species, Plato would not leave marriage to the voluntary action of the individual, but decided that the rulers of the state should provide for the right constitution of the following generation by a fitting choice of parents.[1] Education of the youth in all departments belongs to the state, and gives equal attention to bodily and spiritual development. In the latter it progresses from folk-lore and myths through elementary instruction to poetry and music, and thence through math-

[1] *Rep.*, 416 b.

ematical training to interest in philosophy, and, finally, to the knowledge of the Idea of the Good. In the different steps of this education, which is the same for all the children of the two higher classes, those children are pruned out by the state officials that no longer seem to show fitness of disposition and development for the higher tasks. Different grades of officials and warriors are thus formed from these. This sifting process leaves ultimately the élite, who succeed to the position of archons and dedicate their lives partly to the furthering of science and partly to the administration of the state. Herein are the two upper classes a great family ; every form of private possession is renounced,[1] and their external wants are cared for by the state support, which is furnished by the third class.

The Platonic state was accordingly to be an institution for the education of society. Its highest aim was to prepare man by the sensible for the supersensible world, by the earthly for the divine life. The social-religious ideal is that which floats before the philosopher in his methodical delineation of the " best " state. As all the higher interests of man will be included by this social community of life, so the philosopher believed that the state should have exclusive control not only of education and science but also of art and religion. Only that art shall be allowed whose imitative[2] activity is directed upon the Ideas, especially the Idea of the Good.[3] The Greek καλοκἀγαθία consisted in *nobleness* the evaluation of everything beautiful as good. Plato reversed the order of this thought by establishing only the good as the really beautiful. In the same way the ideal state accepts in the main the myths and the culture of the Greek state religion as educational material for the third class of society, and partly also for the second class, especially in childhood.[4] But the state expunges from the

---

[1] *Rep.*, 416 b. [2] *Ibid.*, 313.
[3] *Ibid.*, 376 f. [4] *Ibid.*, 369 f.

myths all things immoral and ambiguous, and permits their
use only as the symbolical representations of ethical truths.
The religion of the philosophers, however, consists in science and virtue, of which the highest goal is the attainment
of likeness to the Idea of the Good, — the Godhead.

Plato did not conceive his city as an imaginary Utopia, but in
all earnestness as a practicable ideal.   He employed therefore
in many particulars, especially in social arrangements, numerous
features of the then existing Greek states, and he preferred, naturally enough, the stricter and more aristocratic ordinances of the
Doric race.   Though he was convinced that out of the existing
circumstances his ideal could be realized only through force,[1]
yet he had none the less faith that if his proposal were tried, he
would bestow upon his citizens lasting content, and would make
them strong and victorious against all foreign attack.   In the
incomplete dialogue, *Critias*, the philosopher tried to develop
this thought, — that the state founded on culture should show
itself superior to the Atlantis, the state founded on mere external power.   An idealizing of the Persian wars probably floats
before him.   The description is broken off at the very beginning,
and there is wonderful similarity in the picture of the Atlantis
to the institutions of former American civilizations.
    As to details, we should make a comparison of the *Republic*
with all of Plato's other writings.   The *Politicus* offers many
similar thoughts, but with the interweaving of much that is
foreign, and it has predilection for monarchical forms of government.   It deviates from the *Republic*, especially in its theory of
the different kinds of constitutions, contrasting three worse
forms with three better.[2]   The kingdom is contrasted to the
tyranny, the aristocracy to the oligarchy, the constitutional to
the lawless democracy.   Inexact sketches are drawn of the
seventh, or best, state in contrast to these.   In the *Republic*,[3]
Plato used his psychology to show how the worse constitutions
come from the deterioration of the ideal states.   These are the
timocracy in which the ambitious rule, the predominance of the
θυμοειδές; the oligarchy in which the avaricious rule, the predominance of the ἐπιθυμητικόν; the democracy or realm of universal license; and, finally, the tyranny or the unfettering of
the most disgraceful arbitrary power.
    The aristocratic characteristics of the Platonic state corre-
spond not only to the personal convictions of Plato and his

---

[1] *Rep.*, 540 d.   [2] *Polit.*, 302 f.   [3] *Rep.*, 545 f.

great teacher, but are developed necessarily from the thought that scientific culture can be obtained only by the very few. In scientific culture is the highest virtue of man, and his only title to political administration (*Gorgias*). Likewise, the exclusion of all non-intellectual labor from the two directing classes is consistent with the universal Greek prejudice against the proletariat. However, it is justified by Plato in the reflection that all true labor presupposes love for its task, or brings love with it; and accordingly, that all manual work necessarily lowers the soul to the sensuous, and makes distant its supersensible goal. From the same motive came the exclusion of family life and private possessions. It is misleading to speak here of a communism. The community of wives, children, and goods is expressly delimited to the two higher classes. This was not to satisfy a claim for universal equality, as was the case in the naturalistic investigations of radical Cynicism, but, on the contrary, to prevent private interest from interfering in any way with the devotion of the warrior and ruler to the welfare of the state. It is, in a word, a sacrifice made to the Idea of the Good.

The peculiar character of the ethics of Plato, and at the same time its tendency to go beyond actual Greek life, consisted in the complete subordination of the individual life to the purpose of the political whole. In contrast to the degenerating Hellenic culture the philosopher held an ideal picture of political society, which could first actually be when the Platonic thought predominated: that all earthly life has value and meaning only as an education for a higher supersensible existence. To a certain extent the hierarchy of the Middle Ages realized the Platonic state but with the priests in place of the philosophers. Other moments of the Platonic ideal — for example, the control of science by the state — have been realized also to some extent in the public measures of some modern nations.

Concerning Plato's theory of education see Alex. Kapp (Minden, 1833); E. Snethlage (Berlin, 1834); Volquardsen (Berlin, 1860); K. Benrath (Jena. 1871); concerning his attitude toward art, K. Justi, *Die æsth. Elemente in der plat. Philos.* (Marburg, 1860); concerning his attitude toward religion, F. Ch. Bauer, *Das Christliche des Platonismus* (Tübingen, 1873). Compare, also, S. A. Byk, *Hellenismus und Platonismus* (Leipzig, 1870).

Similarly Plato's ethics also experienced as disadvantageous a later transformation in the *Laws* as his theoretic philosophy in the lectures of his old age. In pessimistic [1] despair [2] as to the realization of his political ideal, the philosopher attempted to sketch a morally ordered community without the controlling influence of the theory of Ideas and its devotees. In the place of philosophy, on the one hand religion presented itself in a form much nearer to the national mode of thought, and on the other mathematics with its Pythagorean tendencies to music and astronomy. Philosophical culture was replaced by practical prudence [3] (φρόνησις), and precise conformity to law and the Socratic virtue by a moderate dependence on ancient worthy customs. Thus the state in the *Republic* changed, when it appeared in the later writings, into a mixture of monarchico-oligarchic and democratic elements, — the ideal power into a compromise with historical conditions. Moreover, all this is set before us in a long-winded, unconcentrated presentation, which seems to be wanting the last finishing touches and the final redaction.[4]

Just because the *Laws* give details of contemporaneous life, they are of high antiquarian, even if of very little philosophical value. They represent so great a deterioration, not only from the theory of Ideas, but from Plato's entire idealistic thought, that the doubts which have been wisely put aside again as to their genuineness are yet entirely conceivable. Compare Th. Oncken, *Staatslehre des Arist.*, 197 f.; E. Zeller, II[3]. 809 f.; the five essays by Th. Bergk, concerning the History of Greek Philosophy and Astronomy (Leipzig, 1883); E. Prætorius, *De legibus Plat.* (Bonn, 1884).

37. The epistemological dualism of the theory of Ideas allowed and demanded a dogmatic statement concerning ethical norms of human life, but no equivalent recognition

---

[1] *Laws*, 644. The conviction as to the badness of the world grew up here to the extent of a belief in an evil world-soul, which works against the divine soul. Compare § 37. See *Laws*, 896 f.

[2] *Ibid.*, 739 f.

[3] *Ibid.*, 712, in exact antithesis to *Rep.*, 473.

[4] *Ibid.*, 746 f.

of nature phenomena. For although Plato had fully determined that the tasks of metaphysics lay in regarding the
Ideas and especially the Idea of the Good as the cause of
the sense-world, that world nevertheless remained to him
as before a realm of Becoming and Destruction. According
to the premises of his philosophy, this realm could never
be the object of dialectic or true knowledge. The point of
view of the theory of Ideas presupposes a teleological view
of nature, but it offers no knowledge of nature.

In his latter days, complying with the needs of his
school, Plato drew natural science also within the realm of
his research and theory, — which science he in the spirit
of Socrates had earlier entirely avoided. He, nevertheless,
remained always true to his earlier conviction, and emphasized it with great clearness and sharpness at the beginning
of the *Timæus*, in which the result of these investigations
was set down.[1] This was to the effect that there can be no
ἐπιστήμη of the Becoming and destruction of things, but
only πίστις: no science, but only a probable conclusion.
He claimed therefore for his theory of nature, not the value
of truth, but only of probability. The presentations in the
Timæus are only εἰκότες μῦθοι, and, however closely related
to his theory of Ideas, they nevertheless form no integral
part of its metaphysics.

Aug. Böckh, *De Platonica corporis mundani fabrica* (Heidelberg, 1809) ; *Untersuchungen über das kosmische System des Plat.*
(Berlin, 1852) ; H. Martin, *Études sur le Timée* (2 vols., Paris,
1841).

Plato's philosophy of nature stands, then, not in the same, but
in a very similar relationship to the metaphysic of his theory of
Ideas, as the hypothetical physics of Parmenides to his theory of
Being. In both cases it seems to have been a regard for the needs

---

[1] *Tim.*, 28 f; which discussion, 27 d, begins with the recapitulation of
the theory of the two worlds. The relation of the philosophy of nature
to the theory of Ideas is characterized most exactly by sentence 29 c;
ὅτι περ πρὸς γένεσιν οὐσία, τοῦτο πρὸς πίστιν ἀλήθεια.

and wishes of the pupils that occasioned their descending from interest in permanent Being to an experimental interest in the changeable.   Plato designated expressly this play with the εἰκότες μῦθοι as the only permissible diversion from his dialectic, which was his life-work (*Tim.*, 59 c.).   Although a critical and often, indeed, polemical consideration of existing opinions appeared here, the formal moment of which Diels (*Aufs. z. Zeller-Jub.*, 254 f.) made of great importance in Parmenides, Plato took account of the fact that a school that had a school-membership of the organization and range of the Academy could not hold itself indefinitely aloof from natural science, and that such a school would be obliged finally to come to some terms or other.[1] While, however, upon the basis of the theory of Ideas a perfect knowledge of the comparative worth of the individual, society, and history could be obtained, yet the determination of the reality of nature through the Idea of the Good was not to be developed with equal certainty as to details.   Suppose, then, physics and ethics to be the two wings of the Platonic edifice, the ethical wing is like the main portion of the edifice in style and material ; the physics is, however, a lighter, temporary structure, and is merely an imitation of the forms of the other.

That which pressed upon the philosopher and was treated by him with careful reserve was, remarkably enough, made of the greatest importance by his disciples in later centuries.   The teleological physics of Plato was regarded through Hellenistic time and the entire Middle Ages as his most important achievement, while the theory of Ideas was pressed more or less into the background.   Relationships to religious conceptions are chiefly accountable for this, but still more the natural circumstance that the school had an especial fondness for the more tangible and useful part of his teaching.   This explains why already Aristotle (*De an.*, I. 2, 404 b, 16) contended against the myths of the *Timæus* as though they were serious statements of doctrine.

The basis for the myths of the *Timæus* is the metaphysics of the *Philebus.*   The sense world consists of infinite space, and the particular mathematical forms which that space had taken on in order to represent the Ideas.   But conceptual knowledge cannot be given of the efficacy of these highest purposes.   Consequently the *Timæus* begins

---

[1] Concerning the influence of Eudoxus, see H. Usener, *Preuss. Jahrb.,* LIII. 15 f.

by personifying this efficacy mythologically as the world-forming God, the δημιουργός. It is purposeful force; it is good, and because of its good-will has made the world.[1] In the act of creation it had in view the Ideas, those pure unitary forms of which the world is a copy.[2] The world is therefore the most perfect, best, and most beautiful,[3] and since it is the product of divine reason and goodness, it is the only world.

The perfectness of the *one* world which is reasserted with especial solemnity at the end of the *Timæus*, is a necessary requisite of the teleological basis of thought. The denial of the opposite proposition, that there are numberless worlds (*Tim.*, 31 a), appears as a polemic against Democritus, especially in connection with what immediately precedes (30 a). According to Democritus' mechanical principle, the vortices arise here and there in the midst of chaotic motion, and out of these the worlds arise. According to Plato, the ordering God forms only one world, and that the most perfect.

That, however, this world corresponds not perfectly with the Ideas,[4] but only as closely as possible, is due to the second principle of the sense world, to space into which God has built the world. Space is known neither by thought[5] nor sense. It is neither a concept nor percept, Idea nor sense object. It is the μὴ ὄν or what possesses no Being, without which the ὄντως ὄν could not appear, nor the Ideas[6] be copied in sense things. It[7] is the ξυναίτιον in comparison to the true αἴτιον; and so also the things formed in it in the individual processes of the world are ξυναίτια.[8] They form a natural necessity (ἀνάγκη)[9] beside

[1] *Tim.*, 29 c.   [2] *Ibid.*, 30 c.

[3] The teleological motive of the teaching of Anaxagoras, which was accepted already in the *Phædo*, forms one of the fundamental teachings of the *Timæus*.

[4] *Tim.*, 30 a, 46 c.   [5] *Ibid.*, 52.

[6] Which are midway between Being and not-Being. *Rep.*, 477 f.

[7] *Tim.*, 68 e, meaning a second kind of αἰτία.

[8] *Ibid.*, 46 c; *Phædo*, 96 f.

[9] *Tim.*, 48 a, another term used completely in Democritan sense.

the divine reason, which necessity under certain circumstances stands in the way of the teleological activity of the
divine reason. Space [1] ($\chi\acute{\omega}\rho a$, $\tau\acute{o}\pi os$) is that wherein the
cosmic process comes to pass ($\grave{\epsilon}\kappa\epsilon\hat{\iota}\nu o$ $\grave{\epsilon}\nu$ $\hat{\phi}$ $\gamma\acute{\iota}\gamma\nu\epsilon\tau a\iota$) which
takes on all bodily forms ($\phi\acute{\upsilon}\sigma\iota s$ $\tau\grave{a}$ $\pi\acute{a}\nu\tau a$ $\sigma\acute{\omega}\mu a\tau a$ $\delta\epsilon\chi o\mu\acute{\epsilon}\nu\eta$,
also the $\acute{\eta}$ $\delta\epsilon\xi a\mu\epsilon\nu\acute{\eta}$ or $\grave{\upsilon}\pi o\delta o\chi\grave{\eta}$ $\tau\hat{\eta}s$ $\gamma\epsilon\nu\acute{\epsilon}\sigma\epsilon\omega s$), and is indeterminate plasticity ($\check{a}\mu o\rho\phi o\nu$ $\grave{\epsilon}\kappa\mu a\gamma\epsilon\hat{\iota}o\nu$). Out of this
Nothingness [2] God creates the world.

The identity of Platonic "matter" of the $\tau\rho\acute{\iota}\tau o\nu$ $\gamma\acute{\epsilon}\nu os$ (*Tim.*,
48 f.) with empty space is most certainly proved by his con-
struction of the elements out of triangles (see below), in which
connection the philosopher identified the mathematical body
immediately with the physical body. See also J. P. Wohlstein,
Materie und Weltseele im platonischen System (Marburg, 1863).

The cosmos must also, as the most perfectly perceivable
thing, possess reason and soul. The first task of the demiurge in the creation of a world is the creation of a world-
soul.[3] As the life-principle of the All, the world-soul must
unite in itself its Form-determining capacity, its motion and
its consciousness. The world-soul is the mean between the
unitary (the Idea) and the divisible (Space), and possesses
the opposite qualities of sameness ($\tau a\upsilon\tau\acute{o}\nu$) and change
($\theta\acute{a}\tau\epsilon\rho o\nu$). It holds in itself all numbers and dimensions.
It is itself the mathematical form of the cosmos, is distrib-
uted by the demiurge into harmonious relations, in which
distribution an inner circle of changing motions and an
outer circle of uniformity (the place of the fixed stars and
planets) is to be distinguished. The latter is again divided
proportionately within itself. By means of these circles,
each moved according to its own nature, the world-soul is
supposed to have set the entire cosmos into motion. By
means of this motion, permeating the whole and returning [4]
to itself, the world-soul created in itself and in individual

---

[1] *Tim* , 49 f.   [2] Compare the claims of Democritus.
[3] *Tim.*, 35 f.   [4] *Ibid.*, 37.

things consciousness, perception, and thought. The most perfect kind of knowledge, however, is the circular movement of the stars, which continually returns to itself.

The particulars of this extremely imaginative description of the *Timæus* are obscure, and have been subject to controversy (see Zeller, II³. 646 ff.). The tendency toward the number theory of the Pythagoreans as well as toward their astronomy and harmonics is unmistakable. In the division of the world-soul, with which the divisions of the astronomical world are identical, harmonic proportion and arithmetical means play the chief rôle. The important thought is that with this general division of the mass and motions of the cosmos, a perpetual definiteness of form (πέρας) belongs to space, which is a companion principle of the ἄπειρον in the *Philebus* (§ 35). The mathematical was therefore not for Plato entirely identical with the world-soul; but it was in the most intimate connection with it, and was in a similar intermediary position between the Ideas and the sense world.

The characteristic of the Platonic theory of motion is that it referred all motions of individual objects to the teleologically determined motion of the whole. It thus was in antipodal opposition to Atomism, which considered motion to be an independent function of single atoms. It is remarkable that the *Timæus* emphasizes many times (Zeller, II³. 663, 3) the connection, nay the identity, between motions and intellections. The "right idea" is referred, for example, to the θάτερον, to irregular motions; rational knowledge, on the other hand, is referred to ταὐτόν, the uniform, circular motions (*Tim.*, 37).[1] It is also here characteristic that all particular acts are referred to the universal functioning power of the world-soul. Thus to the world-soul is lacking the characteristic of personality.

The further mathematical formation (πέρας) of empty space is accomplished in the individual things, which have been introduced by the demiurge into the harmonious system of the world-soul; and, firstly, in the formation of the elements (στοχεῖα). Besides an artificial deduction of their fourfold number,[2] which introduced air and water as the two

[1] If in these theories any use is made of Democritus — which I regard by no means improbable — his teachings have, at any rate, received an independent treatment.

[2] *Tim.*, 31 f.

means between fire and earth, Plato [1] gave a stereometrical development from these four elements, which development, as among the Pythagoreans, presents the four regular bodies as the fundamental forms of the elements. The tetrahedron is the fundamental form of fire; the octahedron, of the air; the icosahedron, of the water; the cube, of the earth. He conceived, however, these fundamental bodies as constructed out of planes, and indeed of right-angle triangles which are sometimes isosceles, and sometimes of such a nature that the catheti stand in the ratio of one to two.[2] With this construction the transformation of space into corporeal matter seemed to be conceived. From the different magnitudes and numbers of these indivisible plane-triangles [3] were next derived with clever fancifulness the physical and chemical qualities of individual stuffs, their distribution in space, their mingling, and the continuous motion in which they exist.

Plato also believed that the individual elements and stuffs are in a determined part of space according to the predominating mass, to which the scattered parts then strive to return. It is not entirely clear how he introduced the relationships of weight into this thought. At any rate, he had been sensible of the fact that the direction from above downward cannot be regarded as absolute; but that in the world-sphere only the two directions, to the centre and to the periphery, exist.

Plato's astronomical views differ from those of the Pythagoreans essentially in his acceptance of the stationariness of the earth. According to his theory, the earth rested like a sphere in the middle of a spherical-shaped world-all. Around the " diamond " axle of this world with daily revolution from east to west swings in the outermost periph-

[1] *Tim.*, 53 f.

[2] The square is constructed out of the former; the equilateral triangle, of the latter.

[3] Which accordingly take the place of the ἄτομα and σχήματα of Democritus.

ery the heaven of the fixed stars, in which the single
stars are conceived as " visible gods "[1] in continuous perfect movement upon their own axes.   That revolution is
communicated to the seven spheres, viz., the five planets,
the sun and the moon.   These intersect the first circle (of
the fixed stars) in the direction of the zodiac.   The planets,
sun and moon, have, however, within their orbits their own
reverse movements of differing velocity.

The last proposition as an astronomical explanation of the
apparent irregularity of the movements of the planets, remained
for a long time authoritative. The methodical principle
lying at its basis has been strikingly formulated by Plato or
his followers in the question : τίνων ὑποτεθεισῶν ὁμαλῶν καὶ τεταγ-
μένων κινήσεων διασωθῇ τὰ περὶ τὰς κινήσεις τῶν πλανωμένων φαινόμενα (comp. Simplicius with Aristotle, De cœlo, 119).

The theory of motion in the Timæus concludes with a
detailed account of the psycho-physical process of perception.[2] It is concerned with establishing those conditions
of motion of external objects and of the body which call
forth the motions of the soul, its sensations and feelings.[3]
With great pains in this connection the investigations of
the physiologists, just as the theory of Protagoras,[4] were
adjusted to the teleological theory of motion.   Since the
subjective moment is, moreover, separated from the objective in αἴσθησις, the nature philosophy confirms the epistemological point of departure which the Theœtetus had illuminated.

Finally, by way of appendix, the Timæus gives a sketch
of a theory of diseases and their cures, and thus yields to
the encyclopædic demands of the Platonic school.

[1] Tim., 40 a.

[2] Ibid., 61 f.   For details, see H. Siebeck, Gesch. der Psych., I., 1,
201 f.

[3] In this respect the exposition of the Timæus is supplemented by
that of the Republic and the Philebus, while it develops empirically the
theoretical principles of the Theœtetus.

[4] And perhaps much also which belongs to Democritus.

6. ARISTOTLE.

A career of nearly forty years in teaching gathered a large number of superior men around Plato, and gave to the operations of his school, in its treatment of ethico-historical and scientific medical studies, that comprehensiveness of which indications appeared in his later dialogues.[1] To the stately number of men that belonged to the school more or less closely, empirical research owed much valuable enrichment in the immediately succeeding time, but philosophy gained at their hands scarcely anything worthy of mention. Only the one man, Plato's greatest pupil, who it is true did not remain in the ranks of the Academy, but founded a school of his own, was called to bring to completion the history of Greek philosophy with his wonderful system of thought. This man was Aristotle.

The history of the Academy is generally divided into three and perhaps five periods: the Older Academy, which lasted about a century after the death of Plato; the Middle Academy, which filled out the second century, in which period we distinguish two successive schools, that of Archesilaus and that of Carneades; the New Academy, which extended to neo-Platonism, and in which the dogmatic movement advocated by Philo of Larissa is to be distinguished from a later eclecticism of Antiochus of Ascalon. The two later phases belong to the syncretic skepticism of Greek philosophy. For general comparisons, see H. Stein, *Sieben Bücher zur Gesch. d. Platonismus* (3 vols., Göttingen, 1862-75).

38. The so-called Older Academy stood entirely under the influence of that less healthy tendency which the Platonic philosophy in later time had shown theoretically toward the Pythagorean number theory and practically toward a popular and religious system of morals. Speusippus (d. 339), the nephew of Plato, took charge of the

---

[1] See H. Usener, *Ueber d. Organisation d. wissenschafilichen Arbeit im Alterthum (Preuss. Jahrb.* 53, 1 ff.); E. Heitz, *D. Philos. schulen Athens (Deutsche Revue,* 1884).

school after Plato, and Xenocrates of Chalcedon followed
Speusippus. To the same generation belonged Heracleides
of Pontic Heraclea and Philip of Opus. The astronomer
Eudoxus of Cnidus and Archytas of Tarentum, head of the
Pythagoreans of that time, stood in a loose relation to the
Platonic school. The following generation of the school
yielded to the spirit of the time, and turned essentially to
ethical investigations. Polemo of Athens was then head
of the school, from 314 to 270, and since his gifted pupil,
Crantor, died before him, Crates of Athens became his
successor.

An exact description of all the Academicians of this time is
in Zeller, II³. 836 f. ; F. Bücheler, *Acad. philos. index Hercula-
nensis* (Greifswald, 1869). Our knowledge concerning the different tendencies within the Academy arises from the fact that
after Plato's death, as Speusippus had been designated by Plato
to succeed him as scholarch, Xenocrates and Aristotle left
Athens. The former was afterward chosen to lead the school ;
the latter somewhat later founded a school of his own.

Judging by what has come down to us about Speusippus, he
was a vague and diffuse writer. Diogenes Laertius (IV. 4 f.)
gives a list of his writings, and these touch upon all parts of
science. The most appear to have been ὑπομνήματα in reference
to his career as a teacher. It was these that Aristotle had in
mind in his frequent and mostly polemical references to Speusippus. A writing is particularly mentioned which was concerned
with the Pythagorean number, and so also the Ὅμοια, which is
an encyclopedic collection of the facts of natural history arranged
by name. Compare Ravaisson, *Speus. de primis rerum principiis placita* (Paris, 1838) ; M. A. Fischer, *De Speus. vita*
(Rastadt, 1845). Xenocrates, Plato's companion upon his third
Sicilian journey, who was distinguished for his strong, serious
personality, was hardly more significant as a philosopher than
Speusippus. Diogenes Laertius (IV. 11 f.) mentions the long list
of his writings. R. Heinze, X. (Leipzig, 1892), gives a comprehensive exposition of his theory with the fragments appended.
Heracleides came from the Pontic Heraclea, was won over to
the Academy by Speusippus, and had especially as an astronomer independent importance. Plato passed over to him, during his last journey to Sicily, the leadership of the Academy.
When after Speusippus' death Xenocrates was chosen scholarch,

Heracleides went to his home and founded there his own school, which he administered until after 330. He was a many-sided, æsthetically inclined, and productive writer, and he was familiar not only with the Platonic and Pythagorean teaching, but also with Aristotelianism. Compare Diog. Laert., V. 86 f. ; Rouler, *De vita et scriptis Her. Pon.* (Loewen, 1828) ; E. Deswert, *De Her. Pon.* (Loewen, 1830) ; L. Cohn (in *Comment. phil. in hon. Reifferscheid*, Breslau, 1884). Philip of Opus probably edited the *Laws* of Plato, and was besides the author of the *Epinomis*. The renowned astronomer Eudoxus (406–353) joined the Academy for some time according to the many different testimonies of the ancients (Zeller, II³. 845 f.), and he developed its astronomical theories. But on other questions, especially ethical ones, he deviated widely from the Academy. A. Böckh, *Ueber die Vierjahrigen Sonnenkreise der Alten, besonders den eudoxischen* (Berlin, 1863).

Among the later Pythagoreans, Archytas was pre-eminent. In the first half of the fourth century he played a great rôle in his native city, Tarentum, as scholar, statesman, and general. Whatever has been transmitted with any assurance concerning him and others, shows us that just as the Pythagoreans influenced Plato in various ways, so also Plato on his side influenced to such a degree the Pythagoreans, that the theory of numbers in its last phase fused perfectly with the theory of Ideas, which was nominally its rival. The significance of Archytas lay in the realm of mechanics and astronomy. His philosophy agreed throughout with that of the Older Academy. On account of the close personal relationship in which he stood to Plato, the genuineness of those fragments may well be possible in which he gave a Platonic turn to Pythagoreanism. These fragments are collected by Conr. Orelli (Leipzig, 1827) ; see Mullach, II. 16 f. ; G. Hartenstein, *De Arch. Tar. frag. philos.* (Leipzig, 1833) ; Petersen (*Zeitschr. f. Altertumswissenschaft*, 1836) ; O. Gruppe, *Die Frag. des Arch.* (Berlin, 1840) ; Fr. Beckmann, *De Pythagoreorum reliquiis* (Berlin, 1844) ; Zeller, V³. 103 f. ; Eggers, *De Arch. Tar.* etc. (Paris, 1833).

Polemo and Crates owe the leadership of the Academy more to their Athenian birth and their own moral worthiness than to their philosophical significance. Crantor originated in Soli in Cilicia, and was known particularly through his writing, περὶ πένθους. H. E. Meier, *Ueber die Schrift,* περὶ πένθους (Halle, 1840) ; F. Kayser, *De Crantore Academico* (Heidelberg, 1841).

The Older Academy took in general the *Laws* of Plato as its point of view. It pushed the theory of Ideas aside to make way for the number theory. Thus Speusippus on his side ascribed to numbers a reality that is supersensible and separated from the objects of sense, — the same which Plato had given to the Ideas. Similarly Philip of Opus in the *Epinomis* declared that the highest knowledge upon which the state in the *Laws* must be built is mathematics and astronomy. For these sciences teach men eternal proportions, according to which God has ordered the world and by which he is leading it to a true piety. Besides this mathematical theology Speusippus, accommodating himself to the spirit of his school, recognized to a greater degree than Plato the worth of empirical science. He dilated upon an αἴσθησις ἐπιστημονική, which participates in conceptual truth.[1] But he had no explanatory theory of this, rather only a collection of facts arranged logically as he presented them in his compendium (ὅμοια ὀνόματα) which was manifestly intended for the use of the school. Xenocrates divided philosophy into dialectics, ethics and physics as a basis for instruction.[2] He held firmly to the theory of Ideas, but recognized that mathematical determinations had, in contrast to the sense world, an independent reality similar to that of the Ideas. He distinguished, accordingly, three [3] realms of that which can be known: the supersensible, the mathematically determined forms of the world-all, and the sense objects. To these objects there corresponds, first, the ἐπιστήμη, including dialectics and pure mathematics; secondly, the δόξα, which as an astronomical theory is given both an empirical and a mathematical basis; thirdly, the αἴσθησις, which is not false, but exposed to all sorts of delusions.

The Platonists seem to have thought that the chief task of their metaphysics was the teleological construction of a graded series of mediatory principles between the

---

[1] Sext. Emp., VII. 145.   [2] *Ibid.*, 16.   [3] *Ibid.*, 147.

supersensible and the sensible. In the solution of this
task, however, two opposing tendencies made themselves
felt, which are connected with the names of Speusippus
and Xenocrates. If the former abandoned the theory of
Ideas, it was essentially because he could regard the Perfect and the Good,[1] not as the αἰτία of the more Imperfect, the Sensible, but rather as its highest teleological
result. He therefore postulated numbers as the ἀρχή,
and unity and plurality as their elements and next in order
geometrical magnitudes and stereometrical forms, to whose
fourfold number he added the Pythagorean ether.[2] Besides this, he found the principle of motion in the world-
soul (νοῦς), which he seems to have identified with the
central fire of the Pythagoreans. The goal of motion is
the Good, which as the most perfect belongs at the end.
Xenocrates contrasted with this evolution theory the theory
of emanation, in that he derived numbers and Ideas from
unity and indeterminate duality (ἀόριστος δυάς). Numbers
are to him identical with the Ideas, according to the
schema of Plato's ἄγραπτα δόγματα. He also further
defined the soul as self-moving number.[3] Thus there is
a descent from the unity of the Good down to the Sensible; and between the world-soul and corporeal things
exists a completely graduated kingdom of good and bad
dæmons. In this very contrast Plato's pupils showed
that they were engaged upon the unsolved problems of
Plato's later metaphysics, in that they desired to develop
further his teaching on its religious side. The opposition
between αἰτία and συναίτιον, between Idea and space,
between the perfect and the imperfect, grew entirely to[4]
a religious antithesis of the Good and the Bad. They —
especially Xenocrates — surrendered the monistic motive

[1] Arist., Met., XI. 7, 1072 b, 31.   [2] See § 24.
[3] Plato, Procr. an., I. 5 (1012); see Arist., Anal. past., II[4]. 91 a, 38.
[4] See R. Heinze, Xenocr., p. 15 f.

in the teaching of their master to fantastic speculations which turned particularly upon the cause of evil[1] in the world.

More interesting than the fantastic Pythagorizing by the leaders of the school is, on the other hand, the high development of mathematics which arose in the Pythagorean-Platonic circles at this time, even to the solving of the more difficult problems. There was the diorism of Neocleides, the theory of the proportion in Archytas and Eudoxus, the golden section, the spiral line, the doubling of the cube by the application of parabolas and hyperbolas (see Cantor, *Gesch. der Math.*, I. 202 f.). Then there was the astronomy taught by Hicetas, Ecphantus, and Heracleides, concerned with the stationariness of the fixed heaven of stars and the turning of the axis of the earth. Herakleides thought of Mercury and Venus as satellites of the sun. See Ideler, *Abhandl. d. Berl. Akad. d. Wiss.*, 1828 and 1830. On the other hand, however, there is the fact that those men, who were only indirectly related to the school, developed the relationship of certain motives of Platonism with other teachings. Thus Heracleides still held to the Platonic construction of the elements when he advocated the synthesis that Ecphantes sought between Atomism and Pythagoreanism (§ 25). Eudoxus likewise conceived the ἰδέαι entirely in the sense of the homoiomerii of Anaxagoras.[2]

With such a mathematical corruption of the theory of Ideas there was conjoined the lapse into popular moralizing on the part of the older Academicians. Only in some measure, however, did the energy of their religious spirit compensate for this deterioration. As concerns morals, the school can hardly be made answerable for the hedonism of Eudoxus,[3] especially since Heracleides appears[4] to have openly antagonized it. The theory of goods, however, found in the *Philebus*[5] was cultivated much more in an accommodative sense: for Speusippus sought happiness in the

---

[1] See Arist., especially *Met.*, XIII. 4, 1091 b, 22.

[2] *Ibid.*, I. 9, 991 a, 16, with the commentary of Alexander Aphr. (*Schol. in Arist.*, 572 b, 15).

[3] Arist. *Eth. Nic.*, I. 12, 1101 b, 27.

[4] Athen., XII. 512 a.   [5] Compare above, § 36.

perfect development of natural gifts;[1] Xenocrates, though recognizing fully the value of virtue, nevertheless recognized external goods as also necessary to the attainment of the highest good. He set for the majority of mankind[2] the practical φρόνησις in place of the ἐπιστήμη which falls to the lot of the few, and finally, in opposition to the Stoics, described[3] virtue, health, pleasure, and wealth as the various goods, evaluating them in that order.

It is especially noteworthy that according to all that we know the social-ethical character and the political tendency of the Platonic morals were not further fostered among his pupils. Rather in the Academy the quest after correct rules of living for the individual came more and more into the foreground. Nature philosophy still engaged the attention of theorists, as can be seen in Crantor's commentary to the *Timæus*. Ethical researches, however, took on the individualistic aspect of the period. Polemo taught that virtue, which is the essential condition of happiness, completely gives satisfactory happiness (αὐτάρκη πρὸς εὐδαιμονίαν) only in connection with the goods of the body and life. Virtue cannot be practised in scientific research, but in action.[4] Scarcely a step was necessary from such views to those of the Stoa.

39. Beneath these different efforts of the Older Academy would obviously lie a fundamental tendency to adjust Plato's idealism to the practical interests of Greek society and of the empirical sciences. But dependence upon Pythagoreanism on the one hand and on the other a general lack of philosophical originality always stunted all these undertakings. In the mean time the problem was solved by him who had brought with him into the Platonic theory

---

[1] Clemens, *Strom.*, II. 21 (500). Compare concerning Polemo, Cicero, *Acad.*, II. 42, 131.

[2] Clemens, *Strom.*, II. 5 (441).

[3] Sext. Emp. *Adv. math.*, XI. 51 f.   [4] Diog. Laert., IV. 18.

an inborn predilection for medicine and the science of nature. This perfecter of Greek philosophy was Aristotle (384–322).

Fr. Biese, *Die Philos. des Aristoteles* (2 vols., Berlin, 1835–42) ; A. Rosmini-Serbati, *Aristote esposto ed esaminato* (Torino, 1858) ; G. H. Lewes, *Aristotle, A Chapter from the History of the Science* (Lond. 1864 ; German, Leipzig, 1865) ; G. Grote, *Aristotle* (incomplete, but published by Bain and Robertson, 2 vols., London, 1872) ; E. Wallace, *Outlines of the Philosophy of Aristotle* (Oxford, 1883).

The home of Aristotle was Stagira,[1] a city in the neighborhood of Athos, on that Thracian peninsula which had been colonized [2] chiefly from 'Chalcis. He came from an old family of physicians. His father, Nicomachus, was body-physician and a close personal friend of the king, Amyntas, of Macedon. Detailed reports about the youth and education of the philosopher are wanting. His education was in the charge of his guardian, Proxenus of Atarneus, after the death of both his parents. He was only eighteen years old when he entered the Academy in 367, and his connection with it was uninterrupted until Plato's death, so far as we know. He won a prominent place in it very quickly, grew early from the position of a pupil to that of a teacher in the band, was the champion literary spirit of the school through his brilliant writings which at once made him famous, and in public lectures concerning the art of speaking, antagonized Isocrates, to whose anti-scientific rhetoric the Platonic school had never been reconciled.[3]

Concerning the life of Aristotle, see J. C. Buhle, *Vita Arist. per annos digesta*, in the Bipontine edition of the works, I. 80 f. ;

[1] Also Stageiros.

[2] Aristotle disposed in his will (Diog. Laert., V. 14) of a piece of property in Chalcis, which he perhaps inherited from his mother, Phæstias.

[3] In spite of the advances Plato showed to him in the *Phædrus* as always preferable to Lysias.

A. Stahr, *Aristotelia*, Part I., on the life of Aristotle (Halle, 1830). Of the ancient biographies of the philosopher, the more valuable, those of the older Peripatetics, are lost, and only a few of the later remain.

It is uncertain whether Aristotle grew up in Stagira or in Pella, the residence of the Macedonian kings. It is as little determinable when his father died, and where he himself lived under the tutelage of Proxenus, — in Stagira or Atarneus.[1] We are also entirely restricted to the following suppositions as to his educational training : it is scarcely to be doubted that, according to the family tradition, as the son of the Macedonian court physician, he was destined by his family for medicine and received a training for it ; in the intimate relationship existing between scientific medicine, in which Hippocrates was the leading spirit, and the Democritan studies of nature, it may be supposed that these were the first elements in the early education of our philosopher. At any rate, he grew up in this atmosphere of the science of medicine in northern Greece, and he owed to it his respect for the results of experience, his keen perception of fact, and his carefulness as to details in investigation, which contrast him with the Attic philosophers. On the other hand, it must be said that one must not magnify too much the reach of knowledge that his seventeen years in the Academy brought to him. It was certainly later that Aristotle got his immense scientific erudition, — in part, to be sure, during his attachment to the Academy, but chiefly during his stay in Atarneus, Mitylene, and Stagira before he began to teach. It is possible that Aristotle remained true to this scientific inclination while he was in the Academy, and that he was in part responsible for gradually causing more attention to be paid to those matters (§ 37). At first, however, the spirit of the Platonic school must have turned him in other directions, and what we know of his activity in the twenty years of his study, of the form and contents of his writings of that time, the rhetorical lectures, etc., do not allow us to suppose that such inclinations predominated in him.

The malicious school gossip which was circulated in later time about the relations between Aristotle and his great teacher should be passed over with a deserved silence. See particulars in Zeller, III³. 8 f. If one holds himself to that which is safely testified to, especially in the writings of Aristotle, one finds a simple human relationship. The pupil looked upon his teacher

---

[1] The later references to Atarneus can be explained by the fact that Hermeias was for a long time an auditor of Plato.

with great reverence.[1] But the more mature he became, the more independently did he pass judgment upon Plato's philosophical positions. He recognized with accurate glance their essential defects, and he did not conceal his doubts, if his aged master directed his theory upon unfortunate lines. Nevertheless he remained a member of the fraternity with his own independent circle of activity, and he separated from the school only at the moment when after his master's death perversity was exalted to principle in the choice of an insignificant head of the school. Nothing makes against the conclusion that in these difficult relations Aristotle avoided both extremes, with that worthy tact that always characterized his actions.

See below concerning the writings of this period. That his relation to Isocrates was somewhat strained, we see on the one hand from Cicero's reports (*De orat.*, III. 35, 141; *Orat.*, 19, 62; compare *Quint.*, III. 114), and on the other from the shameful pamphlet which a pupil of the orator published against the philosopher. Aristotle showed here also his noble self-control, when he later in the *Rhetoric* did not hesitate to give examples from Isocrates.

After Plato's death Aristotle in company with Xenocrates betook himself to Hermeias, the ruler of Atarneus and Assus, and a true friend to Aristotle. Aristotle married his relative, Pythias, later after the tyrant had met an unhappy end, the victim of Persian treachery. Previously he seems to have migrated for a time to Mytilene, and perhaps also for a short time to Athens.[2] In 343 he obeyed the summons of Philip of Macedon to undertake the education of the then thirteen-year-old Alexander. Although we are entirely without information concerning what kind of education this was, yet the entire later life of Alexander bore the best witness of its effect. Also later the philosopher remained in the best of relations with his great pupil, although the treatment of the nephew of Aristotle, Callisthenes, by the king may have brought a temporary estrangement.

[1] Compare the simple beautiful verses of Aristotle from the elegy to Eudemus: *Olympiod. in Gorg.*, 166.

[2] See Th. Bergk, *Rhein. Mus.*, XXXVII. 359 f.

The regular instruction of the young prince ceased, at all events, when he was entrusted by his father, after 340, with administrative and military duties. The relation of the philosopher was therefore more independent of the Macedonian court, and the next years he was engaged for the most part in scientific work in his native city, in intimate companionship with his somewhat younger friend, Theophrastus, who became a real support to him in the following time. For when Alexander entered upon his campaign in Asia and Aristotle saw himself entirely free of immediate further obligation to him, he went with his friend to Athens and founded his own school there. This school, in the universality of its scientific interest, in the orderliness of its methods of study, and in its systematic arrangements for joint inquiry, very soon rose above the Academy, and became the pattern of all the later societies of scholars of antiquity. Its place was the Lyceum, a gymnasium consecrated to the Lycian Apollo, from whose shady walks [1] the school got the name of Peripatetic.

Twelve years (335–323) Aristotle administered this school in ceaseless activity. When, however, after the death of Alexander, the Athenians began to rise up against the Macedonian rule in Greece, the position of the philosopher became dangerous, standing as he did in such close connections with the royal house. He betook himself to Chalcis, and in the following year a disease of the stomach cut short his active and honorable career.

Concerning Hermeias [2] of Atarneus, see A. Böckh, *Kleine Schrift*, VI. 185 ff. ; P. C. Engelbrecht, *Ueber die Beziehungen zu Alexander* (Eisleben, 1845) ; Rob. Geier (Halle, 1848 and 1856) ; M. Carrière (*Westermann, Monatsh.*, 1865). Aristotle owed to

[1] Probably from the custom of lecturing part of the time *ambulando*. See Zeller, III³. 29 f.

[2] In memory of this friend, Aristotle dedicated his hymn upon virtue: Diog. Laert., V. 7.

his relations with different courts and to his own easy circumstances the abundance of the scientific expedients which among other things made his extensive collections possible. The reports of the ancients concerning the greatness of the sums placed at his disposal are obviously somewhat overestimated. One cannot doubt, on the whole, from his court relationships, the support which he found for his work.

Concerning the relations of the philosopher and his great pupil, gossip has circulated widely, just because there has been wanting any trustworthy information about it. If the friendship in later years was actually somewhat cooler (as Plutarch also reports, *Alexander*, 8), yet it was entire foolishness and slander on the part of later opponents to charge Aristotle with a share in the supposed poisoning of the king (see Zeller, III³. 36 f.). The favorable relations of the philosopher to the Macedonian court were most clearly confirmed by the events after the death of the king. Doubtful as the single statements here again may be, it is certain that the philosopher left his circle of activity at Athens in order to avoid a political danger. How great it had become can no longer be determined; for the reports concerning the charges of impiety,[1] concerning his defence and the excuse for his escape in the expression that he wished to spare the Athenians a second crime against philosophy, — all this smacks, especially in its details,[2] strongly of an attempt to make Aristotle's end as nearly as possible like that of Socrates.

To every depreciation that the character of Aristotle has suffered, his system of science stands as the best contradiction. It is a creation of such magnificent proportions and of such construction that it can have been only the work of a life filled with the pure love of truth, and even then it is almost beyond our comprehension. For the Aristotelian philosophy includes the entire range of knowledge of that time in such a way that it comprehends all the lines of earlier development at the same time that it considerably elaborates the most of these lines. It turns upon all territories an equal interest and an equal intellectual appreciation.

[1] See E. Heitz in O. Müller, *Lit. Gesch.*, II². 253 f.

[2] Compare E. Zeller in *Hermes*, 1876 ; H. Usener, *Die Organisation der wissenschaftlichen Arbeit bei den Alten: Preuss. Jahrb.*, LIII. 1 f. (1884).

Aristotle met the demands of the history of science more completely than Plato.   Even in his *Ethics* the purely theoretic and not the practical interest is fundamental.   He is the scientific spirit κατ᾽ ἐξοχήν.   In him the process of the independence of the spirit of learning completes itself.   He is, in the wonderful many-sidedness of his activity, the embodiment of Greek science, and he has for that reason remained "the philosopher" for two thousand years.

Furthermore he became " the philosopher," not as an isolated thinker, but as the head of his school.   The most striking characteristic of his intellectual personality is the administrative ability with which he divided his material, separated and formulated his problems, ordered and co-ordinated the entire scientific work.   This methodizing of scientific activity is his greatest performance.   To this end the beginnings already made in the earlier schools, especially in that of Democritus, might well have been of service.   But the universal sketch of a system of science in the exact statement of methods such as Aristotle gave, first brings these earlier attempts to their complete fruition.   His conduct of the Lyceum can be looked upon not only as a carefully arranged and methodically progressive instruction, but also, above all, it must especially be viewed as an impulsion to independent scientific research and organized work.[1]

The great number of facts and their orderly arrangement are only to be explained through the combined efforts of many forces guided and schooled by a common principle.   All this appeared and was developed in the Aristotelian writings.   The activity of the school, which is itself a work of the master, forms an integral constituent of his great life-work and his works.

The collections of writings transmitted under the name of Aristotle do not give even an approximately complete picture of the immense literary activity of the man.   They apparently include, however, with relatively few exceptions, just that part of his work upon which his philosophical significance rests, viz., *his scientific writings.*

[1] Compare E. Zeller in *Hermes*, 1876; H. Usener, *Die Organisation der wissenschaftlichen Arbeit bei den Alten*: *Preuss. Jahrb.*, LIII. 1 f. (1884).

The preserved remainder of the Aristotelian writings forms still a stately pile, even after the genuine have been separated from the doubtful and spurious. But in extent it is manifestly only a smaller part of that which came forth from the literary workshop of the philosopher. From the two lists of his writings that antiquity has preserved (published in the Berlin edition, V. 1463 f.) the one of Diogenes Laertius (V. 22 f.), which was changed by the anonymous Megarian, probably by Hesychius, is supposably based upon a report of the Peripatetic Hermippus (about 200 B. C.), concerning the Aristotelian collection in the Alexandrian library. The other list originated with the Peripatetic, Ptolemæus, in the second century A. D., and was preserved partly by Arabic writers (Zeller, III³. 54).

The traditional collection appears essentially to have come from the published Aristotelian writings, which somewhere in the middle of the first century B. C. were prepared by Andronicus of Rhodes with the co-operation of the grammarian Tyrannion. In modern time it was printed first in a Latin translation in 1489, together with the commentaries of Averroës, and in a Greek translation in Venice in 1495 ff. Of the later editions may be mentioned the Bipontine, by Biehle (5 vols., incomplete, *Biponti et Argentorati*, 1791 f.) ; that of the Berlin Academy (text recension by Imm. Becker, annotations by Brandis, fragments by V. Rose, index by Bonitz 5 vols., Berlin, 1831–70) ; the *Didot* edition by Dübner, Büssemaker, and Heitz (5 vols., Paris, 1848–74) ; stereotype edition of Tauchnitz (Leipzig, 1843). Concerning a special edition of his single works, see Ueberweg, I⁷. 186 f. German translations are in different collections, particularly in J. v. Kirchmann's *Philos. Bibliothek*.

These preserved writings offer problems for solution which differ from those in the Platonic writings, but are no less difficult. Indeed, there is but little agreement among the authorities as to the questions involved. The discussion has been only a little concerned with the chronology of single works ; it has had more concern with the very doubtful genuineness of many of them ; it has found its greatest concern with the literary character, the origin and purpose of the single writings and of the collection.

J. G. Bühle, *De librorum Aristotelis distributione in exotericos et acroamaticos* (Bipontine ed., I. 105 f.) ; Titze, *De Arist. operum serie et distinctione* (Leipzig, 1826) ; Ch. Brandis (*Rhein. Mus.*, 1827) ; A. Stahr, *Aristotelia*, Part II., *Die Schicksale der Arist. Schriften* (Leipzig, 1832); L. Spengel, *Abhandl. der bair. Akad. der Wiss.*, 1837 f. ; V. Rose, *De Arist.*

librorum ordine et auctoritate (Berlin, 1854) ; H. Bonitz, *Arist. Studien* (Vienna, 1862 f.) ; Jac. Bernays, *Die Dialoge des Arist.* (Berlin, 1863) ; E. Heitz, *Die verlorenen Schriften des Arist.* (Leipzig, 1865) ; the same in O. Müller's *Litteratur Geschich.*, II². 256 f. ; F. Vahlen, *Arist. Aufsätze* (Vienna, 1870 f.) ; R. Shute (Oxford, 1888).

The writings [1] of Aristotle are divided with reference to their literary character into three classes : —

(1) *The Works published by Aristotle himself, and intended for a wider circle of readers.*

Of these no single work is complete, and only fragments are extant. They originated in the main during Aristotle's attendance at the Academy, and showed strongly the influence, even in their titles, of the Platonic philosophy. They were, on the whole, dialogues, and if they did not also possess the artistic fancy with which Plato managed this form, they are striking, nevertheless, in their fresh intuitions, happy inventions, florid diction, as well as in the richness of their thought.

These ἐκδεδομένοι λόγοι were counted by Aristotle, in his occasional mention of them in his didactic writings, as belonging to the general class of ἐξωτερικοὶ λόγοι. By this class he seems to have understood the more popular treatment of scientific questions in antithesis to the methodical and scholastic cultivation of science. The latter, which centres in the lectures of the head of the school, appeared later as the acroamatic writings. The opposition of the exoteric and the acroamatic teaching does not, then, necessarily signify in itself a difference in content of doctrine, but only a difference in form of presentation. There is no word about a secret teaching. It may, however, be accepted as true that the exoteric writings originated when he was in the Academy, and the acroamatic, when he was an independent teacher ; and from this fact even essential differences are easily explained. See Zeller, III³. 112 f.; H. Diels, *Sitzungsber. der Berl. Akad.*, 1883 ; H. Susemihl, *Jahrbuch f. Philol.*, 1884.

Aristotle owed his literary fame in antiquity to his published

---

[1] Excepting the personal writings like the verses, the testament (Diog. Laert., V. 13 f.), and the letters, of which scarcely anything genuine is preserved.

writings, and certainly in all justice if we may judge from the few preserved specimens.[1] For if, on account of the "golden flow" of his words, he is classed with Democritus and Plato as a model,[2] nevertheless this praise cannot be applied to the writings that have been preserved. The "golden flow" is so seldom in these writings that it is more supposable that they are excerpts from his dialogues that were made either by Aristotle himself or by some of his pupils.[3]

The composition of the Aristotelian dialogues is said to have been distinguished from the Platonic by a less vivid treatment of the dramatic setting, and also by the circumstance that the Stagirite himself gave the leading word. In content they were affiliated in part closely to the Platonic dialogues. Thus, the *Eudemus* especially appears to have been a detailed copy of the *Phœdo*. Other titles like περὶ δικαιοσύνης, Γρύλλος ἢ περὶ ῥητορικῆς, σοφιστής, πολιτικός, ἐρωτικός, συμπόσιον, Μενέξενος remind us immediately of the works of Plato and his school. Others refer directly to popular philosophical discussions, like the three books περὶ ποιητῶν, περὶ πλούτου, περὶ εὐχῆς, περὶ εὐγενείας, περὶ ἡδονῆς, περὶ παιδείας, περὶ βασιλείας.[4] The genuineness of all of these has not been established, nor is it certain that all were in the form of the dialogue. It is very improbable that the Προτρεπτικός was in this form (R. Hirzel, in *Hermes*, X. 61 f.). The most significant, and, as it appears, those most independent of the Platonic influence among these exoteric writings, are the three books of the dialogue περὶ φιλοσοφίας. (See Bywater, in *Jour. of Philol.*, 1877, 64 f.)

(2) *The Compilations;* partly critical excerpts from scientific works (ὑπομνήματα), partly collections of zoological, literary-historical, and antiquarian data which Aristotle, probably with the help of his pupils, used as material for scientific research and theory.

These also have unfortunately been lost except a very few fragments, although it appears that at least a portion of them had been published either by Aristotle himself or by his pupils.

[1] See Cicero, *De nat. deor.*, II. 37, 95.

[2] See place in Zeller, III[3]. 111, 1.

[3] See Fr. Blass, *Att. Beredtsamkeit*, 427 note; also *Rhein. Mus.* 1875.

[4] Dedicated to Alexander, as also περὶ ἀποικιῶν.

To these last belong the notes of the philosopher concerning the later lectures of Plato : περὶ τἀγαθοῦ and περὶ τῶν εἰδῶν. Compare Ch. Brandis, *De perditis Aristotelis de bono et ideis libris* (Bonn, 1823). There are also reports of some extracts from the *Laws*, the *Republic*, and the *Timœus*, the critical notes about Alcmæon, the Pythagoreans, — especially about Archytas, — Speusippus, and Xenocrates. Also the writings *De Melisso Xenophone Gorgia* arose from a like need in the Peripatetic school. The fruits of this comprehensive study of the history of philosophy appear in the numerous historical relations which the Aristotelian didactic writings generally set up in entering upon the treatment of problems. The προβλήματα serve similar purposes of instruction and of research, although their present form is a later conception of the school. Compare C. Prantl, *Abhand. der Münchn. Akad.*, VI. 341 f. The same holds good for all the definitions and diæreses which antiquity then possessed.

In the magnificent collections which Aristotle planned in the Lyceum must first be mentioned the ἀνατομαί, the descriptive basis for zoölogy, furnished, it seems, with illustrations. Then there is the collection of the rhetorical theories under the title τεχνῶν συναγωγή, and of the rhetorical models ἐνθυμήματα ῥητορικά ; besides the collection relating to the history of tragedies and comedies, and the questions raised about the different poets, Homer, Hesiod, Archilochus, Euripides, and others ; finally, the historical miscellanies: the πολιτεῖαι, reports concerning one hundred fifty-eight Greek state constitutions, νόμιμα βαρβαρικά, δικαιώματα τῶν πόλεων, and besides Ὀλυμπιονῖκαι, ᾽πυθιονῖκαι, περὶ εὑρημάτων, περὶ θαυμασίων ἀκουσμάτων, παροιμίαι, etc.

Concerning the character of these scientific materials, which until the present time were apparently entirely lost, some years ago a very surprising disclosure was made, partly by the fortunate discovery of a most important piece, the Πολιτεία τῶν᾽ Ἀθηναίων (published by G. Kaibel and U. v. Wilamowitz-Möllendorf, Berlin, 1892 ; translated into German by G. Kaibel and A. Kiessling, Strassburg, 1891); the literature on it, especially on its genuineness, has, as may be expected, quickly appeared ; a complete review can be found in the English edition of J. E. Sandys (Lond., 1893, p. lxvii). To be sure, the beginning and end are wanting, but by far the greatest part is preserved in nearly a complete continuity. It appears not as a dry collection of facts, but as a ripe historical work clearly and perfectly developed. The greatness of conception, the practical simplicity of representation, the accuracy of judgment make it appear a worthy writing of the master in whose last years its composition must have occurred. Should this history of the Athenian constitution be the work of one of his pupils, then would it indeed be a new honor for the Lyceum.

Although many of those collections that are attributed to Aristotle may have come from his pupils, or perhaps even later, and although by no means can all those titles refer to writings of the philosopher himself, they nevertheless give proof of the versatility and cyclopedic character of the scientific work of the school. Upon all territories, both historical and scientific, he gave the fruitful impulse to seek out the entire existing material and to place it in order, and thus to make it available for scientific treatment. The Lyceum, in its storing of the treasures of erudition, was, to a higher degree than the Academy, the centre of culture of Greece.

(3) *The Didactic Writings originating in the school and intended for its use.* It is these only that have been preserved, and they together make what is known as the collection of Aristotle's works. They are not complete, however, and in many cases probably not in the original form. They nevertheless exhibit in the highest degree some peculiar characteristics. A sharply impressed, delicately worked out, and consistently developed terminology is common to them. On the other hand, complete absence of grace and of æsthetic motive of presentation is to be noted. The scheme of investigation is, on the whole, the same: the precise formulation of the problem, the criticism of opinions which are submitted concerning the problem, the careful discussion of the single points of view as they appear, the comprehensive marshalling of the facts, and the striving for a clear and conclusive result. In all these respects the Aristotelian writings make a complete antithesis to the Platonic; the difference being that between science and æsthetics. The Aristotelian writings afford different and therefore less attractive enjoyment. It must not be forgotten that the excellences of the Aristotelian works are qualified in many striking ways. The unequal development, wherein many parts give the impression of

being masterly and final and others of being hasty and sketchy; the disorder which predominates in the principal writings of the transmitted series of books; the — in part verbal — repetitions of even lengthy sections; the unfulfilled promises, — all these facts forbid the belief that the writings in their present form were intended by Aristotle for publication; while, on the other hand, in point of form and content the interconnection of the works is evident, and is emphasized by numerous cross references that are often reciprocal.

All these characteristics are only explicable and are also fully conceivable upon the hypothesis that Aristotle entertained the purpose of developing into text-books the written notes that he had made the basis of his lectures. These text-books would have been manuals of instruction for the Lyceum, and would have been given into the hands of his pupils. In addition it is supposable that Aristotle undertook this work in direct connection with his lectures, and about the same time with reference to the sciences treated by him. He probably pursued this work during the twelve years of his leadership. Before, however, this giant work came to an end, death had seized him. Excepting the smaller works, which perhaps were waiting to be included in his larger works, only parts of the *Logic* — the *Topics* in particular — appear to have been completed. It may also be accepted that the gaps which thus remained were filled in part by the most intimate pupils, probably on the basis of their notes of the Aristotelian lectures. These interpolations were made by different pupils differently. Thus in the school many redactions of the text-books were handed on, and among such redactions many later productions of the school slipped in. This went on until Andronicus of Rhodes published the first edition (60–50 B. C.), which lies at the basis of the present documents.

The close relationship between the preserved writings of Aristotle and his actual teaching is evident, even if we take no account of such direct evidence as his address to his auditors at the conclusion of the *Topics*. The question is only as to a clearer determination of the relationship, and it would appear as if all the opinions expressed about the relationship may be justified to a certain extent. Undoubtedly the notes of the philosopher form the body of the discourses ; — not only such sketches as he might use for his lectures, but on the other hand also such as he had made ready for the text-book.[1] The latter set forth in a wonderful manner the clearness and ripeness of the Aristotelian spirit. Other facts, especially the different redactions of the same book, hardly allow another interpretation than that of Scaliger, that interpolations from the writings of the auditors have taken place. In accordance with this theory the presence of such parts or of entire writings which cannot in form or content be ascribed to Aristotle, is most simply explained.

A very venturesome but in itself a not incredible theory was spread in antiquity concerning the fate of the Aristotelian manuscripts.[2] They were supposed to have fallen with the property of Theophrastus to his pupil, Neleus of Scepsis in Troas, and to have been hidden in a cellar by his descendants out of fear of the mania for collecting of the kings of Pergamus. Afterwards they were found and purchased in a much damaged state by the Peripatetic Apellicon of Teos and removed to Athens. When Sulla conquered that city, the writings fell into his hands and were published at Rome by the grammarian Tyrannion, and finally by Andronicus of Rhodes. This story does not explain, of course, the remarkable condition of the transmitted documents. It is indubitably proved in the case of single writings — as is obvious — that the Peripatetic school possessed the scientifically most important writings of its founder from the beginning. On the other hand, it is nevertheless not improbable that the rediscovery of the original manuscripts afforded

---

[1] In this fact and in the smaller importance of the copies by his auditors consists the chief difference between the character of the *corpus Aristotelicum* and the somewhat analogous form in which a series of Hegel's lectures is presented to us. Hegel had not begun a remodelling of his *Hefte* for text-books, while, on the other hand, we owe the most valuable of the preserved works of Aristotle to the fact that he had begun such a remodelling.

[2] Plutarch, *Sulla*, 26 ; *Strab.*, XIII. 1, 54 ; compare E. Essen, *Der Keller zu Skepsis* (Stargard, 1886).

Andronicus not only the occasion but also, as far as the manuscripts reached, the distinct ground for his standard edition in contrast to the school tradition.

Since the didactic writings form internally a perfectly consistent whole, the question about the order of their origination is comparatively unimportant. The question is, moreover, entirely purposeless, since it may be accepted that work upon the writings was continuously and simultaneously carried on in connection with the lectures repeatedly given during the twelve years of his activity as a teacher. It nevertheless appears that the *Logic* was the first to be conceived, and relatively to the others was brought more nearly to completion.

Compare with the following Zeller, III[3]. 67–109.

The preserved didactic writings are most simply arranged in the following groups : —

(a) *The Treatises on Logic and Rhetoric* — the *Categories*, the very doubtful treatise *On the Proposition*, the *Analytics*, and the *Topics*, including the last and comparatively independent book *Concerning the Fallacies ;* and the *Rhetoric*.

The grouping of the logical works, in the customary series, under the name ὄργανον, occurred first in the Byzantine period. A special edition is published by Th. Waitz (2 vols., Leip., 1844–46). The genuineness of the καταγορίαι is doubted, especially by Prantl (*Gesch. d. Log.*, I. 207 f.). The conclusion of these writings, i. e., concerning post-predicaments, can at all events not be ascribed to Aristotle, and the remainder of the book appears to be based upon his sketch only in essentials. Περὶ ἑρμηνείας is subject to stronger suspicions to which even as early a writer as Andronicus gave expression. The *Analytics* is a masterly logical groundwork, which develops the theory of the conclusion and of proof in two parts (ἀναλυτικὰ πρότερα and ὕστερα), each consisting of two books, — the second part being not so completely rounded out as the first. Joined to it, as the most complete of all the works, is the *Topics*, which treats of the method of probability. In connection with it, as its ninth book (Waitz), there is περὶ σοφιστικῶν ἐλέγχων. There are preserved besides a great number of titles of logical-epistemological theoretical discussions, of which the Aristotelian authorship is more or less doubtful : περὶ εἰδῶν καὶ γενῶν, περὶ τῶν ἀντικειμένων, περὶ καταφάσεως, συλλογισμοί, ὁριστικὰ, περὶ τοῦ πρός τι, περὶ δόξης, περὶ ἐπιστήμης, etc.

The first two books of the *Rhetoric* may be regarded as genuine in spite of some difficulties (Spengel in *Abh. der Münch.
Akad.*, VI.). The third is doubtful. The so-called *Rhetoric
to Alexander* is, on the contrary, generally regarded as spurious, but it probably belongs to the Peripatetic school. The
Rhetoric of Theodectes is also mentioned, which was published
during the life of Aristotle. This work embodied the teachings
of the philosopher, and was probably based upon his lectures.

(*b*) *The Writings on Theoretic Philosophy* — the *Metaphysics*, which in Aristotelian terminology was called " first
philosophy " or " theology ; " besides, the book on mathematics being lost, the *Physics*, the *History of Animals*, the
Psychology, and the three minor treatises belonging to
these three.

The *Metaphysics* (special edition by Brandis, Berlin, 1823 ;
Schwegler, with translation and commentary, Tübingen, 1847–
48 ; Bonitz, Bonn, 1848–49 ; translated into German, Berlin,
1890 ; Greek edition by W. Christ, Leipzig, 1886) has preserved its traditional name for the philosophic science of principles, because of its *place* in the ancient collection (μετὰ τὰ
φυσικά).
From the fourteen preserved books the second (a ἔλαττον) is
certainly to be set apart as a school compilation of many parts
welded together. Among the other thirteen books the first,
second, third, fifth, sixth, seventh, and eighth books (numbered
according to the Berlin edition) form a connected but not a completed, and also not a finally edited investigation, to which after
a break the ninth book also belongs. The fourth book, which
was cited by Aristotle himself, under the title περὶ τοῦ ποσαχῶς,
is a school manual containing a discussion of terminology.
The first eight chapters of the tenth and the first half of the
eleventh book are either an Aristotelian sketch or a school-
extract from the chief investigation. The second half of the
eleventh book is an outline of the teaching of the Godhead.
The conclusion of the tenth book is a compilation from the
Physics, obviously not by Aristotle. Books twelve and thirteen
appear to be an older form of the criticism of the Platonic
Ideas. The preserved collection is so much the more unique,
since it is the more probable that it was taken in hand soon
after the death of Aristotle, perhaps by Eudemus.
From the series of mathematical writings only the discussion

περὶ ἀτόμων γραμμῶν is extant, and its transmitted form is probably spurious.

Of the eight books of lectures on the science of nature, φυσικὴ ἀκρόασις, — the modern name would be " philosophy of nature," — books five, six, and eight treat περὶ κινήσεως. The earlier books are concerned with universal principles in the explanation of nature (περὶ ἀρχῶν); the seventh book gives one the impression of being a preliminary sketch. Astronomy and physics proper are included as developments : περὶ οὐρανοῦ, περὶ γενέσεως καὶ φθορᾶς μετεωρολογικά. A number of separate treatises are lost, the μηχανικά is spurious, and also the περὶ κόσμου. See below, § 49.

The parallel work to the περὶ τὰ ζῷα ἱστορία, of which book ten is presumably not genuine, is the περὶ φυτῶν, which is lost. On the other hand, some restorations of the former are preserved : περὶ ζῴων μορίων, περὶ ζῴων γενέσεως, περὶ ζῴων πορείας.

Among the most mature works belong the three books περὶ ψυχῆς (published by Barthélemy St. Hilaire, Paris, 1846 ; A. Torstrick, Berlin, 1862 ; A. Trendelenburg, 2d ed., Berlin, 1877 ; E. Wallace, Cambridge, 1882). With these are collected a number of treatises on physiological psychology : περὶ αἰσθήσεως καὶ αἰσθητῶν ; περὶ μνήμης καὶ ἀναμνήσεως ; περὶ ὕπνου καὶ ἐγρηγόρσεως ; περὶ ἐνυπνίων and περὶ τῆς καθ' ὕπνον μαντικῆς ; περὶ μακροβιότητος καὶ βραχυβιότητος ; περὶ ζωῆς καὶ θανάτου ; περὶ ἀναπνοῆς. The writing περὶ πνεύματος owes its origin to the Aristotelian school.

(c) *The Writings on Practical and Poetic Philosophy :* the *Ethics* (in the Nicomachean and Eudemean versions), the *Politics*, and the *Poetics*.

Among the preserved forms of the Ethics, the so-called Ἠθικὰ Μεγάλα is essentially only an extract from both the others, of which, moreover, the ten books of the Ἠθικὰ Νικομάχεια appear to be nearest to Aristotle's design. The seven books of the Ἠθικὰ Εὐδήμεια appear to be based on the notes of Eudemus. The identity of the Nicomachean *Ethics* V.–VII. and the Eudemian IV.–VI. allows room for various interpretations of a mutual supplementation of the two redactions. Of smaller ethical treatises nothing is preserved. The essay περὶ ἀρετῶν καὶ κακιῶν is spurious.

The eight books of the likewise incomplete *Politics* (published by Susemihl, Leipzig, 1870) are problematic as to their preserved order. See literature in Zeller, III³. 672 f. Books seven and eight should undoubtedly come directly after book three. The

transposition of books five and six is still in dispute. The
Economics is not genuine.

The fragment περὶ ποιητικῆς is preserved, but only in a very
fragmentary and altered condition (published by Susemihl,
Leipzig, 1865, and Vahlen, Berlin, 1867; G. Teichmüller,
Aristotelische Forschungen, Halle, 1860 and 1869).

40. The effort to transform the Socratic-Platonic conceptual philosophy into a theory that will explain the
phenomenal world was the centre of the Aristotelian
philosophy. The conviction that the tasks of science can
be solved only by the Socratic method — the method of
conceptual knowledge — was taken for granted by Aristotle, and was his reason for reckoning himself in later time
still within the Platonic circle. The advance, however,
which he made upon Platonism was based on his insight
into the insufficiency of the theory of Ideas to explain
empirical facts. It is true that Plato had in the end very
emphatically asserted that the Ideas, which at first for
him meant only permanent Being, were also the αἰτία of
the world of sense. However, as Aristotle later showed,
Plato had not been able to harmonize this thought with his
first conception of the world of Ideas. Aristotle justly found
the ultimate ground for this inharmony in Plato's fundamental ascription of a self-substantial separate reality to the
world of Ideas. This transcendence of the Ideas, which essentially is only a duplication of the empirical world, must
be annulled. The Ideas must not be conceived as different
from the objects of experience and as existing separate
from them. They must be known as the peculiar essence
of existence, as its determining content. Plato's weakness
as well as his greatness lay in his theory of two worlds.
The fundamental thought of Aristotle was that the supersensible world of Ideas and the world of sense are identical.

The polemic of Aristotle against the theory of Ideas, especially in the first, sixth, and twelfth book of the *Metaphysics*,
concealed the fact to the earlier criticism that his antagonism

was far outweighed by the importance of the rôle assigned in his
own philosophy to the theory of Ideas; for his dependence on
that theory was an accepted fact by him and the circle of his
pupils, although Aristotle only incidentally alluded to it. The
polemic was directed solely against the χωρισμός, the hypostasizing of Ideas into a second and higher world. He pointed out
the difficulties involved therein: that the Ideas make neither
motion nor knowledge conceivable, and that their relation to
the world of sense has not been satisfactorily and consistently
defined. In other respects the Stagirite shared throughout the
fundamental conceptions of the Attic philosophy: he defined
the problem of philosophy to be the knowledge of what really
is,[1] and he asserted that this knowledge is not acquired by perception,[2] precisely because the things of sense change and are
destroyed.[3] He likewise characterized the universal, the concepts, as the content of true knowledge, and accordingly also of
the truly actual.[4] However, from the beginning Aristotle united
a genetic theory with his ontology, and he demanded that
science explain the origin of phenomena from what really is.[5]
He insisted, therefore, that the Ideas be so understood that
they, as the true essence of sense objects, make these objects
conceivable. If Aristotle did not solve his problem perfectly,
it was due entirely to his continuous dependence on fundamental
definitions of the Platonic philosophy.

See Ch. Weisse, *De Platonis et Aristotelis in constituendis
summis philosophiæ principiis differentia* (Leipzig, 1828);
M. Carrière, *De Aristotele Platonis amico ejusque doctrinæ justo
censore* (Göttingen, 1837); Th. Waitz, *Platon u. Aristoteles*
(Cassel, 1843); Fr. Michelis, *De Aristotele Platonis in idearum
doctrina adversario* (Braunsberg, 1864); W. Rosenkrantz, *Die
platonische Ideenlehre und ihre Bekämpfung durch Aristoteles*
(Mainz, 1869); G. Teichmüller, *Studien* (1874), p. 226 f.

Since the essence of things is known by means of class
concepts, the fundamental problem of Aristotelianism is
the relationship of the universal to the particular. When
Aristotle made this fundamental principle of scientific
thought — recognized by Socrates in inspired intuition —
an object of separate preliminary investigation, he created

---

[1] *Anal. post.*, II. 19, 100 a, 9.　　　[2] *Ibid.*, I. 31, 87 b, 28.

[3] *Met.*, VI. 15, 1039 b, 27.

[4] *Ibid.*, II. 4, 999 a, 28; II. 6, 1003 a, 13.

[5] *De an.*, I. 1, 402 b, 16.

the *science of logic*. He introduced this science as a universal theory of scientific method[1] preliminary to single
practical investigations. In this self-knowledge of science
the historical process of emancipation of the intellectual
life perfects itself into full consciousness. As the " Father
of Logic," Aristotle represented the maturity of Greek
scientific development.

Although Aristotle certainly separated the single branches of
science and fixed upon their relationship of rank, yet the preserved documents offer no generally complete division. On the
one hand, he treated the branches pedagogically, proceeding
from the facts up to their causes, and on the other he inversely
proceeded from the principles down to the consequences. The
division in the Academy at one time was into logical, physical,
and ethical researches,[2] at another time into theoretic, practical,
and poetic science,[3] while in the Peripatetic school[4] the division
into theoretic and practical science was customary. So much
appears to be certain, viz., that Aristotle introduced the *Logic*
(*Analytics* and *Topics*) as a universal and formal preparation
or methodology for all other branches, since he himself does
not mention it under " theoretic " sciences.[5]

A. Trendelenburg, *Elementa logices Aristoteleæ* (3d Ad.,
Berlin, 1876) ; Th. Gumposch, *Ueber die Logik u. d. logischen
Schriften des Arist.* (Leipzig, 1839) ; H. Hettner, *De logices
Aristotelicæ speculativo principio* (Halle, 1843) ; C. Heyder,
Die Methodologie der arist. Philos. (Erlangen, 1845) ; C.
Prantl, *Gesch. d. Logik*, I. 87 f. (see *Abhandl. der bayer. Akad.*,
1853) ; F. Kampe, *Die Erkenntnisstheorie des Arist.* (Leipzig,
1870) ; R. Eucken, *D. Methode der arist. Forschung* (1872,
Berlin) ; R. Biese, *D. Erkenntnisslehre des Arist. u. Kant's*
(Berlin, 1877).

The principle of the Aristotelian logic is the thought
that just as in *natura rerum* the universal or conceptually
defined essence is the cause or ground of definition of the
particular, so also the ultimate task of an explanatory

[1] *Met.*, III. 3, 1005 a, 33.　　[2] *Top.*, I. 14, 105 b. 20.
[3] *Met.*, I. 1025 b, 18.
[4] See *Eth. Eud.*, I. 1, 1214 a, 10 ; *Met.*, I. 993 b, 20.
[5] *Met.*, V. 1, 1026 a, 18, counts as such only physics, mathematics,
and theology (metaphysics).

250 HISTORY OF ANCIENT PHILOSOPHY

science consists in deriving (ἀπόδειξις) the single from the universal, and thereby in attaining the conceptual necessity of the empirically actual.[1] Scientific explanation consists in understanding the perceptually known from its causes. It is the reproduction by the process of knowledge — in the relationship of ground and consequent — of the real relation of the universal cause to its particular result.

However, all knowledge consists [2] only in the union of concepts (λόγος as συμπλοκή of ὄνομα and ῥῆμα), that is, in the premise (πρότασις) or in the judgment (ἀπόφανσις), since either as an affirmative judgment (κατάφασις) it expresses [3] real union or as a negative judgment (ἀπόφασις) real separation of the determinations of content that are thought in the subject and predicate. So the last task of all scientific explanation (ἐπιστήμη) is the derivation (ἀπόδειξις) of particular judgments from the universal. On this account the *theory of the conclusion and proof*, which he himself called the Analytics, formed the centre of the Aristotelian logic.

The Aristotelian Analytic acquired the appearance of an abstract formal logic through misunderstandings and through the misapplied development of it by the School in later times. In truth, it was conceived by Aristotle methodologically in the most vital relationship to the practical tasks of science ; and therefore in the Peripatetic school the logical treatises are rightly called "organic." But just for this reason are they ruled throughout by a number of epistemological presuppositions concerning that which really is and the relationship of thought to Being. The highest presupposition, even if not expressly formulated by Aristotle, is the identity of the forms of apprehending thought with the forms of relationship belonging to actuality.[4] Thus the first systematic sketch of logic includes in close union the three points of view under which this science was later treated. These are the formal, methodological, and epistemological.

---

[1] *Anal. post.*, I. 2 f.   [2] *De cat.*, 4, 2 a, 6.
[3] *Met.*, III. 7, 1012 a, 4.
[4] See *Met.*, IV. 7, 1017 a, 23 ; ὁσαχῶς λέγεται, τοσαχῶς τὸ εἶναι σημαίνει.

One can determine the formal difference between Plato and
Aristotle by noting that the point of departure of Plato is the
concept, of Aristotle the judgment. Aristotle sought truth and
error only in the union of concepts [1] in so far as such a union
is asserted or denied. If this emphasizes principally the quality
of the judgment, yet the syllogistic, as the theory of the establishment of the judgment, demands a treatment of quantity and
thus a distinction between general and particular judgments
(καθόλου — ἐν μέρει).[2] The consideration of judgment from the
points of view of relation and modality was still distant from
Aristotle. When he pointed out that the content of judgment
is the knowledge either of actuality or necessity or possibility,[3]
this assertion rests upon that principal point of view in his
Metaphysics (§ 41), and has nothing to do with modality in its
modern sense (Kant, *Critique d. r. Vernunft*, § 9, Kehrb. 92 f.).
But, finally, all researches which Aristotle instituted for distinguishing judgments are decided by reference to the theory of
the conclusion, that is, by the question what significance they
can have in the conclusion. As mediating between the two, he
treated in a thoroughgoing way the theories of reasoning:
Anal. prior., I. 2 f.

The Aristotelian syllogistic is the search for that which
can [4] be derived with perfect certainty from given propositions. It finds the fundamental form of inference in the
establishing of the particular proposition through the universal, and the subsumption thereunder (inference by subalter-
nation). To this so-called first figure of the syllogism he
referred its other two forms (σχήματα), which are characterized [5] by the different logical place of the middle term
(μέσον) in both premises (τεθέντα), and thus mediate in the
conclusion (συμπέρασμα) the differing relations of the two
chief concepts (ἄκρα). So Aristotle conceived that the
result of the syllogism is always an answer to the question,
whether at all and to what extent one of these concepts
is subsumed under the other; that is, how far the universal
determination of the latter concept holds for the former.

---

[1] *De an.*, III. 6, 430 a, 27. Compare *De interpr.*, I. 16 a, 12.
This thought was hinted at in the dialogue of the *Sophist*, 259 f.

[2] *Anal. prior.*, I. 1, 24 a, 17. [3] *Ibid.*, 2, 25 a, 1.

[4] *Ibid.*, 1, 24 b, 19. [5] *Ibid.*, 4–6.

The syllogistic includes accordingly a system of rules, by which, provided universal propositions are established, particulars can be derived from them. According to the purpose of the philosopher, it would therefore be established how in *the perfected science* all particular knowledge may be derived from universal principles and its subject matter be explained. For practice a universal schematism of proof was accordingly given, in which the tentative efforts of the Sophists for an art of proof[1] were carried out to their scientific conclusion. For the Aristotelian *Analytics* with a perfectly conclusive certainty solved this definitely circumscribed problem, viz., according to what rules propositions follow from given propositions. It is therefore conceivable, on the one hand, that this system during the entire Middle Ages, when science was directed not to research but to proof, passed as the highest philosophical norm, and on the other hand that this system in the Renaissance, which was filled with a need for new knowledge and sought an *ars inveniendi*, was set aside in every part as insufficient. Indeed the limitations of the system of Aristotle, like its greatness, consisted in its attention to the entire process of inference from the point of view of the subsumptive relations between concepts. It analyzed these relations, moreover, with absolute completeness. See Ueberweg, *System der Logik*, § 100 f.

Proof and inference, which make up the form of the completed science, presuppose ultimate premises, which are not derived from more universal propositions but are immediately certain (ἄμεσα).[2] These (ἀρχαὶ ἀποδείξεως) are,[3] in part the axioms that rule all knowledge, among which are the law of contradiction and that of the excluded middle; in part special propositions, applying to the separate branches and those arrived at only from the exact knowledge of the objects[4] themselves.

The highest principles of explanatory theory cannot be accordingly demonstrated, but only strengthened as to their validity for all particulars. They must be sought out by

---

[1] His investigation also concerning contradiction, indirect proof, and false conclusions answers this end.

[2] *Anal. post.*, I. 3, 72 b, 18.   [3] *Ibid.*, 7, 75 a, 39.

[4] *Anal. prior.*, I. 30, 46 a, 17.

science in its development (investigation in distinction from ἀπόδειξις). The process of induction (ἐπαγωγή), as opposed to deduction, promotes this attempt. Induction ascends from the facts of experience (ἐμπειρία) and the opinions (ἔνδοξα) about experience to the universal conceptual definitions by which the former are explained. This task of investigation, directed to the establishment of principles, is called Dialectic[1] by Aristotle. The *Topics* develop its method. Its results are not logically certain in themselves, but only probable. They have, however, the character of knowledge in so far as they explain phenomena; while on the other hand this dialectic, operating as it does with probable proof (ἐπιχειρήματα) forms, where it is used in the practical service of politics, the scientific foundation of rhetoric.

Immediate certainty formed an extremely difficult, but also the most important, tenet of the Aristotelian theory of knowledge. In contrast to Plato, the Stagirite here distinguished the logical from the psychological point of view in a very suggestive way. The ultimate and fundamental propositions, from which all inference proceeds, are logically undemonstrable, but they are neither psychologically innate, nor are they gained in early life. They must rather be won from experience, through which they cannot be demonstrated but only presented. What the nature of these highest principles is, Aristotle did not explain. From the logical laws valid for all sciences, he mentioned only the above, — especially the principle of contradiction as the most unconditional and most universal fundamental principle.[2] He emphasized very rightly that particular principles belong to the individual sciences, but he did not develop these in detail.

What Aristotle understood by induction is to be carefully discriminated from the present meaning of the word. He, for instance, did not mean by induction a kind of proof that is different from the syllogism, but, on the contrary, a method of research and discovery. From this very fact he was satisfied in its application with a relatively universal (ἐπὶ τὸ πολύ) everywhere, where human knowledge does not lead to the absolutely universal. The syllogistic explanation of all particulars from uni-

[1] *Met.*, III. 2, 1004 b, 25; *Top.*, I. 2, 101 b, 2.
[2] *Met.*, III. 3, 1005 b, 17.

versal principles floated before him as the ultimate ideal of all science. But, as a matter of fact, the material of experience reaches in many ways (and everywhere in the special sciences) only to an approximate comprehensiveness, which satisfies the needs of explanation within empirical limits. At this point Aristotle caused the investigator of nature to assume the rôle that the philosopher is obliged to relinquish.

Another practical point of view, the political, supplements scientific exactness in the science of rhetoric by means of instructive persuasiveness (ἐνθύμημα), which is supported upon what is in general true. Accordingly rhetoric in the scientific form that Aristotle first gave to it, is in respect to its purpose, an auxiliary science of politics. But in its content and the technism developed from it, it is a branch of Dialectic and the *Topics*. For if a speech be parliamentary, juridical, or æsthetic (συμβουλευτικόν, δικανικόν, ἐπιδεικτικὸν γένος— *Rhetoric*, 1, 3), it must always begin with popular ideas in order to lead the auditors to the speaker's goal. We can refer here only in a general way to the accuracy of the applied psychology with which Aristotle gave his directions in the *Rhetoric*.

When Aristotle thus regarded the derivation of the particular from the universal as the ultimate problem of science, but maintained that the insight into the highest principles, though not indeed proved, is sought for and clarified by the epagogic investigation based upon facts, this apparent circle of reasoning explains itself from the conception which he held of the human thinking process and its relation to the essence of things. He held this, moreover, in intimate connection with his general view of the world. For he meant that the historical and psychological development of human knowledge corresponds inversely to the metaphysical and logical connection of things, in that the thinking process, bound as it is to sense perception and developing from it, is recipient of the phenomena ; and that then from the phenomena it advances by induction to a conception of the true essence of things. Out of this as their fundamental ground the perceivable things arose, and are therefore to be entirely explained by the perfected science through the process of deduction.

The inverted parallelism in which the method of deduction (*Analytics*) and that of investigation (*Topics*) exist in Aristotle's teaching, is explained by his distinction between psychological and logical relations. That, for instance, which is the πρότερον πρὸς ἡμᾶς, i. e., the phenomena, is the ὕστερον τῇ φύσει; conversely, that which is the πρότερον τῇ φύσει, i. e., the essence of the thing, appears in the development of our ideas as the ὕστερον πρὸς ἡμᾶς.[1] While the relationship between cause and effect is identical with that between ground and consequent for the ideal of a perfect explanatory science, this relation in the genesis of knowledge is inverted. In investigation the (sensible and particular) result is the basis of our knowledge of (conceptual and universal) cause. As soon as we, in accordance with the philosopher's explanations, discriminate between the ideal problems of explanatory science and the actual process of investigations leading to it, all apparent differences and difficulties of some of his single expressions vanish. Aristotle made use of his universal metaphysical concepts of possibility and actuality (§ 41, and Zeller, III³. 198 f.) for conceiving the psychogenetic development of perception in his explanatory theory, in that he assumed that the concept of Essence that has not come actually into consciousness is latent as an undeveloped possibility in sense representation.

The most important point is that, accordingly, human knowledge can obtain a conception of the essential and the permanent only through exact and careful scrutiny of the facts. In these teachings Aristotle theoretically adjusted Platonism to empirical science. Aristotle was not at all the nominalist or empiricist that he has been represented here and there; but he showed that the problem which Plato set for himself, and which he made his own, was to be solved only through the widest elaboration of the facts.

The fundamental philosophical question about the conceptual essence of that which really is, could be solved, according to Aristotle, only in systematic connection with the explanation of the facts. The logical form of these solutions for which all science accordingly strives, is Definition [2] (ὁρισμός) in which the permanent essence (οὐσία, τὸ τί ἦν εἶναι) is established as the ground of the changing conditions and manifestations (τὰ συμβεβηκότα) for every

[1] *Anal. post.*, I. 2, 71 b, 34.
[2] See especially the sixth book of the *Topics*.

single phenomenon ; but at the same time the conceptual
dependence upon the more universal is expressed. The
logical form is therefore the judgment of determination in
which the subject is defined by its superordinated class-concept and by its own specific characteristic. These determinations of concepts are based partly upon deduction and
partly upon induction, but they in turn presuppose ultimately underivable and only illustrable definitions of the
highest class-concepts (γένη).

Concepts appear thus here as content of immediate knowledge,
and their unfolding (the analytical judgments of Kant) gives
the highest axioms of the deductive theories. See Zeller, III³.
190 f. Here appears a wider development of the Socratic-
Platonic principle for the explanation of reality. M. Rassow,
Arist. de notionis definitione doctrina (Berlin, 1843) ; C. Kühn,
De notionis definitione qualem Arist. constituerit (Halle, 1844).

The Aristotelian system of concepts has no point of unification like the Platonic Idea of the Good. As a scientifically inclined thinker, he remained entirely conscious of
the many possible independent points of departure for
scientific theory, and he demanded only that every branch
of knowledge should grow from his peculiar principle. He,
however, made no attempt to collect and systematically to
arrange the indemonstrable principles (θέσεις ἀναπόδεικτοι),
and just as little the resulting immediate premises (προτά-
σεις ἄμεσοι).

The possible kinds of predicates, the Categories, are the
highest class-concepts for logical investigation, and are
irreducible. They represent the different points of view
under which the different concepts can be made elements
of a proposition or judgment by virtue of the factual relations of their contents. Aristotle gave ten [1] categories :
οὐσία, ποσόν, ποιόν, πρός τι, ποῦ, ποτέ, ποιεῖν, πάσχειν,
κεῖσθαι, ἔχειν. He sometimes, however, omits the last two.[2]

[1] *Top.*, I. 9, 103 b, 21 ; *De cat.*, 4, 1 b, 25.
[2] *Anal. post.*, I. 22, 83 b, 16; *Phys.*, V. 1, 225 b, 5; *Met.*, IV. 7,
1017 a, 24.

A. Trendelenburg, *Gesch. der Kategorienlehre* (Berlin, 1846) ; H. Bonitz, *Arist. Studien,* Part VI. ; Fr. Brentano, *Von der mannigfachen Bedeutung des Seienden nach Arist.* (Freiburg in Breisgau, 1862) ; W. Schuppe, *Die arist. Kategorien* (Gleiwitz, 1866) ; Fr. Zelle, *Der Unterschied in der Auffassung der Logik bei Arist. u. Kant* (Berlin, 1870) ; G. Bauch, *Aristotelische Studien* (Dobberan, 1884) ; W. Luthe, *Die arist. Kategorien* (Ruhrort, 1874) ; A. Gercke, *Ursprung der arist. Kategorien (Arch. f. Gesch. d. Ph.,* IV. 424 f.).

Metaphysical motives enter into Aristotle's theory of the categories no more than into his whole system of logic, which has, as its most general presupposition, the identity of the Form of thought with that of Being. The principle of this theory is manifestly concerned with the office the elements of judgment (τὰ κατὰ μηδεμίαν συμπλοκὴν λεγόμενα, — cat. 4) are fitted to assume in the judgment itself. They are either that whereof affirmation is made, and which can only be subject, i. e., the οὐσία, the τί ἐστι ; or that which is predicated of the substance, and is to be thought as actual only in connection with it. Aristotle made this contrast of the οὐσία to all the other categories (*Anal. post.,* I. 22, 83 b, 24). Under the συμβεβηκότα he distinguished (*Met.,* XIII. 2, 1089 a, 10) only modes and relations (πάθη, πρός τι). In the minute enumeration of possible predicates, the advance is unmistakable from quantitative and qualitative determinations to spatial and temporal relations and thence to causal relations and dependence. Also the grammatical distinctions of substantive, adjective, adverb, and verb, appear to play parts in the ten or eight categories. The medial categories, κεῖσθαι and ἔχειν, were held by the philosopher occasionally as unnecessary, compared to the active and passive.

41. Aristotle's attempt to reconcile the theory of Ideas with his empirical conception of the world is developed in his *Metaphysics,* chiefly in his theory concerning that which really is (οὐσία). The conviction that only a conceptual universal can be the object of true knowledge, i. e., absolute actuality, forbids us thinking the content of temporary, particular perceptions as οὐσία. On the other hand, the conviction that the universal does not have a higher actuality, separated from sense objects, forbids the hypostasizing of class concepts in the Platonic manner.

True actuality is the individual which is thought of con-ceptually in contrast to changing states and conditions (συμβεβηκότα). Accordingly in it, and only in it, does the general determination (εἶδος) become actual. The ulti-mate object of scientific knowledge is neither the particular form perceived nor the schemata of abstraction, but the thing which maintains its conceptual essence in the change of its sensible phenomenal aspects.

In the concept of the οὐσία, both antithetical tendencies of Aristotelian thought come together in such a way that his defini-tion thereof is as difficult as it is important. Here is a task which, as it happens, is not facilitated by the technical use of the word οὐσία in the preserved writings. Plato gave form to this concept in antithesis to γένεσις, and constructed the same opposition between λόγος and αἴσθησις, and Aristotle remained everywhere loyal to the same use of the terms. But he gave objectively to οὐσία and accordingly subjectively to λόγος an entirely different content. He asserted most positively that complete metaphysical reality belongs only to the individuals [1] as over against a dualism (χωρισμός). The class concepts (εἶδη and γένη, species and genera) are always only qualities, which are common to several things, can be actual only in things, and predicated [2] of things. They subsist not παρὰ τὰ πολλά but κατὰ πολλῶν. [3] This factor in the teaching of Aristotle makes him later appear as the opponent of scholastic realism, i. e., as the opponent of the recognition of the metaphysical priority of the class concepts, and it makes him also appear as a nominalist by the same sign. This tendency is expressed so strongly in the preserved form of the writing περὶ κατηγοριῶν [4] that there the individual things are designated as πρῶται οὐσίαι, beside which the γένη can be called only by way of derivation δεύτεραι οὐσίαι. On the other hand, Aristotle distinguished with exactitude every present perception of phenomenal things from the conceptually recognizable substances (ἡ κατὰ τὸν λόγον οὐσία). [5] He asserted that these, permanent in contrast to phenomena, are determined by the εἶδος. The εἶδος is true Being: τὸ τί ἦν εἶναι ἑκάστῳ καὶ

[1] *Met.*, II. 6, 1003 a, 5.
[2] *Ibid.*, VI. 13, 1038 b, 8; *Anal. post.*, I. 4, 73 b, 26.
[3] *Anal. post.*, I. 11, 77 a, 5.
[4] *De cat.*, 5, 2 a, 11. See *Met.*, IV. 8, 1017 b, 10.
[5] *Met.*, V. 1, 1025 a, 27.

τὴν πρώτην οὐσίαν.[1] This οὐσία is, then, the essence which is
determined and recognizable by its universal, permanent
qualities. It is an essence which is the basis of the perceptual
phenomenal forms. Therefore οὐσία can sometimes mean essence, sometimes species, sometimes Form, sometimes stuff.
Met., VI. 3, 1028 b, 33 ; Zeller, III³. 344 f.

Metaphysical reality is, then, to be found between the
class-forms and the perceptual forms : viz., in the conceptually determined individual thing. Aristotle attempted to
obviate the difficulty of this manner of representation by
the universal relationship which governs his entire undertaking : *the relationship of matter to Form, of possibility
to its actuality.* This mediation between the universal,
conceptual essence of things and its particular, perceptual phenomenon, he found in the *Principle of Development.* His conception of the nature process (γένεσις)
was : that therein the permanent, original essence (οὐσία)
of things passed over from mere possibility (δύναμις), into
actuality (ἐνέργεια) ; that this process completes itself
when matter (ὕλη), which contains all possibilities in itself,
yields to the Form (εἶδος, μορφή) that is latent in it. Aristotle took analogies in part from human technical activity,
and in part from the life of organic bodies, for grounding
this theory, and they became to him the fundamental
ideas of his conception of the world.

These fundamental ideas were for Aristotle the universal form
of apperception, under which he regarded all things and sought
to solve all problems, — sometimes too in a very schematic way.
When we speak of a formalism of the Aristotelian method, the
formalism lies in the predominance of these concepts of relation,

---

[1] *Met.*, VI. 1032 b, 1. The apparent terminological contradiction
between this passage and *De cat.* 5, does not necessarily mean that the
categories are spurious. The contradiction is explained away by the
fact that on the one hand οὐσία means sometimes the perceived thing
(*Met.*, II. 4, 999 b, 14, οὐσία αἰσθητή, *ibid.*, VII. 2, 1028 b, 24) sometimes essence, while Εἶδος, on the other hand, means sometimes species-
concept, sometimes Form.

which are not always in point of content the same for the
philosopher. This is shown very plainly in their application to
the problematic relation of the particular with the universal. On
the one hand, that is to say, the class forms the undetermined
possibility (ὑποκείμενον, ἀόριστον) which is not actual for itself
alone: viz., the material which is formed and accordingly actualized in the οὐσία by a specific difference (τελευταία διαφορά).[1]
On the other hand, these universal determinations are also
the Forms through which and on account of which all actualization of the possible is explicable.[2]   There is no doubt that
Aristotle's acceptation of the double meaning (Form and Class-
concept) of the εἶδος is an important factor in the unsolved
difficulties of the situation.

The examples that Aristotle used [3] for elucidating this fundamental relationship, viz., house, statue, growth of plants, prove
on the one hand that the principal motive of this most important doctrine was the need of explaining process and change ;
on the other hand, that the philosopher had in mind sometimes
the work of the artisan upon the plastic material and sometimes
the organic process of development. The ratification therein
found of the teleological presupposition developed to a universal
principle of explanation.   Aristotle is throughout governed by
Plato in this formation of his fundamental principle, and the
ascendency of his philosophy wholly obscured the mechanical
conception of the world of Democritus.

In this connection Aristotle perfected in these concepts of
relation the ripest synthesis of the Heracleitan and Eleatic principles that inspired ancient philosophy. Those who had tried
to recognize the permanent had, Plato not excepted, not been
able to explain Becoming. Those to whom change was patent
had been able to give to it either no substrate, or no meaning
comprehensible in view of the essence of that which really is.
Aristotle established the concept of that which possesses Being
as the substance that realizes itself and is conceived in the process from possibility to its actualization. He believed, accordingly, that this definition satisfied both the ontological and the
genetic interest of science. The earlier systems, he taught,[4]

---

[1] Arist. *Met.*, VII. 6, 1045 a, 23.

[2] Precisely for this reason Aristotle has used οὐσία and εἶδος many
times as equivalents, while in the stricter meaning the οὐσία is a σύνο-
λον ἐξ ὕλης καὶ εἴδους.

[3] *Met.*, VI. 8, 1033 a, 27; VII. 2, 1043 a, 14 ; VIII. 6, 1048 a, 32 ;
Phys., I. 7, 190 a, 3, etc.

[4] *Phys.*, I. 6 ff. ; especially I. 8, 191 a, 34.

have furnished the proof that Becoming is to be explained as derived neither out of that which is nor out of that which is not, nor out of the union of the two. So it remained to conceive of that which is as something which in its inmost essence is in the process of development. It remained also to formulate the concept of Becoming so that it formed the transition from a condition of a substratum, that no longer is, to one that not yet is, for which the transition is essential.

Compare J. C. Glaser, *Die Metaphysik des Arist.* (Berlin, 1841) ; F. Ravaisson, *Essai sur la Métaphysique d'Arist.* (Paris, 1837–46) ; J. Barthélemy St. Hilaire, *De la Métaphysique* (Paris, 1879) ; G. v. Hertling, *Materie und Form bei Arist.* (Bonn, 1871).

The fundamental relation between matter and Form is applied on the one hand to individual things, and on the other to relations between things in such a way that insight into the essence of Becoming (*das Geschehen*) is made to result from it. In every individual thing Form and matter are in such correlation that there can be no such thing as formless matter or matterless Form. But precisely on this account they are not to be regarded as distinct pre-existing potencies which have found their union in the individual ;[1] but the same unitary essence of the individual, in so far as it is a potentiality and in so far as it is viewed only as a possibility, is matter; and in so far as it presents a complete actuality it is Form. There exist neither pure potentialities nor perfectly actualized Forms. The οὐσία is not merely δυνάμει, nor purely ἐνεργείᾳ. It is rather a potentiality, in the continuous process of actualization. The temporal change in its conditions is determined by the changing measure of this actualization. Aristotle called the potentiality which belongs to the essence of the individual[2] and comes to reality in the individual, the ἐσχάτη ὕλη.

---

[1] The potential tree and the complete tree do not exist independent of and before the growing tree. They are only different conceptions of the thing that is forming itself in the tree.

[2] *Met.*, VII. 6, 1045 b, 18 ; VI. 10, 1035 b, 30. The expression is used in the logical sense. In the descending process from the most universal,

On the other hand, this relationship becomes entirely different whenever it obtains between different individual things.   In this case, where one is the receptive matter and the other is the moulding Form, the two stand also in a relation of necessary reciprocity.   Yet they exist also independent of each other, and only in their union create the new thing in that now the one is the matter and the other is the Form.[1]   In all these cases the relation of Form and matter is only a relative one, because the same thing can be conceived in one aspect as Form and in another aspect as matter for a higher Form.

There is, therefore, a scale of things in which every individual is the Form in respect to what is beneath it and the matter in respect to what is higher.   This system of development must, however, have a limit, both below and above : below in a matter which is no longer Form ; above in a Form which is no longer matter.   The former is stuff-material ($\pi\rho\dot{\omega}\tau\eta$ $\ddot{\upsilon}\lambda\eta$) ; the latter is pure Form or Godhood ($\tau\grave{o}$ $\tau\acute{\iota}$ $\mathring{\eta}\nu$ $\epsilon\mathring{\iota}\nu\alpha\iota$ $\tau\grave{o}$ $\pi\rho\mathring{\omega}\tau o\nu$).   Since, however, matter is pure possibility, it does not exist for itself, but ever in formed states.   It is, nevertheless, the foundation for the realization of all particular Forms.   On the other hand, the concept of pure Form, as absolute reality, excludes all matter, all pure possibility, and signifies accordingly perfect Being.

Aristotle did not expressly formulate the two different uses of the schemata of possibility and actuality, matter and Form (*potentia* and *actus*), but he thoroughly applied them in practice.   One

undetermined possibility ($\pi\rho\dot{\omega}\tau\eta$ $\ddot{\upsilon}\lambda\eta$) to ever narrower definition of essence and logical determination, the specific difference, by which the individual is distinguished in its *genus proximum* from other individuals, is " the last."   This difference coincides with the form of the individual. Yet sometimes this is entirely turned about and designated as $\pi\rho\dot{\omega}\tau\eta$ $\ddot{\upsilon}\lambda\eta$ of the individual.   See *Met.*, IV. 4, 1014 b, 32.

[1] Thus the timber exists, and the thought of the house in the head of the builder exists, each by itself.   The house is the result of the co-operating influence of the Form of the latter with the material.

use of these terms is suited to organic development, the other to technical activity. In this difference alone can be explained the fact that this difficult subject is sometimes so presented as if δύναμις and ἐνέργεια were identical in essence, and only different ways of conception or phases of development of the same οὐσία uniting εἶδος and ὕλη in itself. At other times Form and matter are represented as separate realities, which influence each other. There is a kind of reconciliation between both methods of representing the case; for also in the first method the two factors, which are separated only *in abstracto* are yet so treated as if one influenced the other;[1] the automatic or self-developing process is so presented as if it divided itself into a moving Form and a moved Stuff.[2]

In presenting matter[3] thus on the one hand as the not-yet actual, on the other, nevertheless, as the unoriginated and indestructible[4] basis (ὑποκείμενον) of all Becoming, in conceiving the system of the latter as an unbroken progress from possibility to actuality, finally in defining the Godhead as an absolutely pure exclusion of all possibility from himself, the Aristotelian philosophy, like the Platonic, established differing grades and kinds of metaphysical reality. The lowest is matter whose positive character is recognized by Aristotle in his rejection of the Democritan-Platonic term μὴ ὄν and in his desire to call it στέρησις in so far as it is thought *in abstracto* as deprived of all Form. The highest is the Form complete in itself and entirely changeless, corresponding to the Idea, or αἰτία of Plato. Between these two extremes there is the whole realm of graded things, in which and between which, movement passes from the lower to the higher grades of actuality. Different grades of knowledge correspond in Aristotle to the different grades of Being. Matter as the ἄμορφον, ἄπειρον, and ἀόριστον, is also the ἀειδές and the ἄγνωστον.[5] Since all systematic knowledge is directed toward the εἶδος and the οὐσία, and God is pure form and primary essence, the object of the highest and most perfect knowledge is the Godhead. The things of Becoming must, however, be conceived in that their εἶδος is developed out of their ὕλη.

---

[1] As shown especially in the activity of the soul; § 42.

[2] *Phys.*, III. 2, 202 a, 9.

[3] See Jas. Scherler, *Darstellung und Würdigung des Begriffs der Materie bei Arist.* (Potsdam, 1873).

[4] *Met.*, VII. 1, 1042 a, 32; 3, 1043 b, 14.

[5] *Phys.*, III. 6, 207 a, 25; *Met.*, VI. 10, 1036 a, 8; *De cœlo*, III. 8, 306 b, 17.

Motion, Becoming, and Change is a transition from the condition of possibility to that of actuality, and is based in part upon the essence of the individuals themselves, in part upon their relations to one another. Development belongs accordingly to the nature of things, and is eternal, without beginning or end.[1] Every motion (κίνησις) presupposes on the one hand moved material, which is the primal state of possibility, and on the other hand the moving Form, which is the final state of actuality. Form is then the cause of the motion which is to be found[2] in that which really is. In so far as the ἐνέργεια creates this process of actualization, it is also called by Aristotle ἐντελέχεια. On the other hand, motion, precisely as transition, is determined not only by that which is about to become and which exercises the impelling force; but also by that out of which it is to become, — by the matter to be changed and bearing in itself the possibility of change. Matter stands, however, in an essential relation to its Form, and has therefore the tendency to realize[3] the Form. In this, matter reciprocates the influence of Form. As possibility, it is also possibility for something else, and in so far it conditions movement to the extent of preventing perfect realization of the Form, and of bringing about incidental results which do not directly follow from the Form. In this sense *matter is the cause of the imperfect and the accidental in nature.*

Thus, according to Aristotle, two kinds[4] of causes are to be distinguished in the explanation of motion : the formal causes and the material causes. The former are teleological (οὗ ἕνεκα); the latter are mechanical (ἐξ ἀνάγκης). Purpose and nature-necessity are of equal importance as principles of the cosmic process. The Platonic and Democritan explanations of nature are reconciled in the relation of Form and matter.

---

[1] *Phys.*, VIII. 1, 252 b, 5.　　[2] *Met.*, VIII. 8, 1049 b, 24.

[3] *Phys.*, I. 9, 192 b, 16.　　[4] *De part. an.*, I. 1, 639 b, 11.

Aristotle incidentally [1] distinguished four principles ($\dot{a}\rho\chi\alpha\dot{\iota}$) in explaining movement: $\dot{\upsilon}\lambda\eta$, $\epsilon\dot{\iota}\delta$os, $\dot{\upsilon}\phi$' ο$\dot{\upsilon}$, $\tau\dot{\epsilon}\lambda$os. But the three last are together always contrasted with the first. If the three are sometimes separated in the realm of particular processes, they form nevertheless more frequently only *one* principle (especially in the organic development of the individual) in that the essence of the fact ($\epsilon\dot{\iota}\delta$os), as the thing to be realized ($\tau\dot{\epsilon}\lambda$os), is the moving force ($\kappa\iota\nu o\hat{\upsilon}\nu$).

In this sense as teleological cause the substance or essence is entelechy. The expressions $\dot{\epsilon}\nu\dot{\epsilon}\rho\gamma\epsilon\iota\alpha$ and $\dot{\epsilon}\nu\tau\epsilon\lambda\dot{\epsilon}\chi\epsilon\iota\alpha$ are generally indifferently used in Aristotle, and an exact difference is hardly attempted, certainly not developed, between the two words. See Zeller, III[3]. 350 f. The etymology of the word $\tau\dot{\epsilon}\lambda$os is obscure: see R. Hirzel, $\dot{\epsilon}\nu\tau\epsilon\lambda\dot{\epsilon}\chi\epsilon\iota\alpha$ *und* $\dot{\epsilon}\nu\delta\epsilon\lambda\dot{\epsilon}\chi\epsilon\iota\alpha$ (*Rhein. Museum*, 1884).

The reality, which Aristotle ascribed to matter, appears most significantly in the reciprocal actions that he gave to it in its relation to final cause. It is due to the indeterminateness of $\dot{\upsilon}\lambda\eta$,[2] that the Forms are imperfectly realized. In this respect matter is a principle of obstruction. Hence it follows that for Aristotle nature's laws, which originate in the conceptual forms of things, are not without exceptions, but are valid only $\dot{\epsilon}\pi\dot{\iota}$ $\tau\dot{o}$ $\pi o\lambda\dot{\upsilon}$.[3] In this way he explained unusual phenomena, $\tau\dot{\epsilon}\rho\alpha\tau\alpha$, — abortions, monstrosities, and the like. But furthermore the positive character of matter appears in that it leads to accidental results [4] in motion on account of its indeterminate possibilities, and these accidents are not immediately involved in the essence or purpose.[5] Aristotle named these $\sigma\upsilon\mu\beta\epsilon\beta\eta\kappa\acute{o}\tau\alpha$, accidental; their appearance he called chance, $\alpha\dot{\upsilon}\tau\acute{o}\mu\alpha\tau o\nu$; [6] and, within the region of purposed events, $\tau\acute{\upsilon}\chi\eta$.[7] Aristotle's conception of accident, therefore, is entirely teleological. It is also logical so far as the purpose is identical with the concept. See W. Windelband, *Die Lehren vom Zufall* (Berlin, 1870) p. 58 f., 69 ff.

The application of the name $\dot{a}\nu\acute{a}\gamma\kappa\eta$ to the efficiency of the stuff makes us at once see Aristotle's intention of recognizing

[1] *Met.*, I. 3, 983 a, 26 ; IV. chap. 2; *Phys.*, II. 3, 194 b, 23.

[2] *De gen. an.*, IV. 10, 778 a, 6.

[3] *De part. an.*, III. 2, 663 b, 28 ; *De gen. an.*, IV. 4, 770 b, 9.

[4] *Phys.*, II. 4 ff.

[5] These happen $\pi\alpha\rho\dot{a}$ $\phi\acute{\upsilon}\sigma\iota\nu$ (*Phys.*, II. 6, 197 b, 34), in which $\phi\acute{\upsilon}\sigma\iota$s = ο$\dot{\upsilon}\sigma\acute{\iota}\alpha$ = $\epsilon\dot{\iota}\delta$os. Compare the expression $\pi\alpha\rho\alpha\phi\upsilon\acute{a}$s, *Eth. Nic.*, I. 4, 1096 a, 21.

[6] *Phys.*, II. 6, 197 b, 18.   [7] *Ibid.*, 5, 196 b, 23.

the Democritan principle of mechanism, while at the same time the teleological activity of the Form is manifestly only a development of the Platonic concept of the αἰτία. Democritus thought that an event is determined only through what preceded it; Plato thought an event determined by what shall issue from it. Aristotle sought to reconcile this antagonism, and so he attributed to matter one kind of determination and to form the other kind. His teaching is therefore the last word of Greek philosophy on the problem of Becoming (§ 13).

But, however much the philosopher takes account of the Democritan motive, yet in this solution the Platonic thought obviously preponderates. For not only the higher actuality belongs to the final cause in contrast to that of the material cause, but also in their operations they are so distinguished that all results of value come from the final cause, while all that is less important comes from the material cause. Matter is the ground of all imperfection, change, and destruction. To its positive capacity for obstruction and deflection Aristotle ascribed, with a far better right, all those consequences with which Plato overloaded the μὴ ὄν. This preference of the Stagirite for his teacher shows itself also in his introduction of mechanical causes under the names συναίτιον and οὗ οὐκ ἄνευ, which are taken from the *Phædo* and the *Timæus*.[1] In this way mechanical causes are characterized directly as causes of the second class, or accidental causes. Matter alone could not move, but if it is moved by the Form, it nevertheless is a determining factor in the movement. Matter is, then, in every respect a secondary cause.

With this active antagonism the Aristotelian teaching manifests, in spite of its effort at harmony, an expressly dualistic character which ancient thought could not overcome. For the independence of existence and activity, attributed to matter in the explanation of nature, permeates the entire system along with his fundamental monistic principle, that matter and Form are essentially identical, and matter is only a striving toward the realization of Form. All the oppositions meet finally in Aristotle's conception of God.

Every motion in the world has a (relative) ἀρχή, which is the Form that causes it. Since, however, on account of its connection with matter, this Form is also itself moved, the series of causes would have no end[2] unless there

---

[1] *Phys.*, II. 9, 200 a, 5 ; *Met.*, IV. 5, 10 15 a, 20.

[2] *Met.*, XI. 6, 1071 b, 6.

exists, as an absolute ἀρχή of all motion, the pure Form, the sharer of no mere possibility and therefore of no motion, — the Godhead. Itself unmoved, it is the cause of all motion, the πρῶτον κινοῦν.[1] Eternal even as motion [2] itself, unitary and single even as the band of the entire system [3] of the universe, and unchangeable,[4] it calls all the motions of the world forth, but not by its own activity. That would be a motion in which the Godhead, as without matter, cannot share.[5] But it calls forth all the motion of the world through the desire of all things for it, and through the endeavor of all things to actualize κατὰ τὸ δύνατον the Form that is eternally realized in the Godhead. As the object of desire, it is the cause of all motion: κινεῖ ὡς ἐρώμενον.[6]

The essence of the Godhead is immateriality,[7] perfect incorporeality, pure spirituality, νοῦς. It is thought, which has no other content than itself (νόησις νοήσεως),[8] and this self-contemplation (θεωρία) is its eternal blessed life.[9] God wishes nothing, God does nothing.[10] He is absolute self-consciousness.

In the conception of the Godhead as the absolute Spirit who, himself unmoved, moves the universe, Aristotle's theory of nature culminated in such a way that he designated his science of principles as a theology. The scientific establishment of monotheism, which, since Xenophanes, formed a leading theme of Greek philosophy, appeared here completed as its ripest fruit. In its form it is like the so-called cosmological proof; in its content, through its concept of the Godhead as a pure spirit, it is far superior to all the earlier attempts. The fundamental principles of Plato are just at this point, however,

---

[1] *Met.*, III. 8, 1012 b, 31.   [2] *Phys.*, VIII. 6, 258 b, 10.
[3] *Met.*, XI. 8, 1074 a, 36.
[4] ἀναλλοίωτος and ἀπαθός : *Met.*, XI. 7, 1073 a, 11.
[5] *Ibid.*, 1072 b, 7.   [6] *Ibid.*, 1072 a, 26.
[7] *Ibid.*, 1073 a, 4 : κεχωρισμένη τῶν αἰσθητῶν.
[8] *Ibid.*, 1074 b, 34   [9] *Ibid.*, 1072 b, 24.
[10] *Eth. Nic.*, X. 8, 1178 b, 8 ; *De cœlo*, II. 12, 292 b, 4.

decisive for Aristotle. For the Aristotelian doctrine centres [1] in God all attributes which Plato had ascribed to the Ideas, and the way in which the Stagirite determined the relation of God to the world is only the exact and sharp definition of the teleological principle, which Plato had indicated by the αἰτία. On this account the Aristotelian Godhead shares with the Platonic Idea the characteristic of transcendence. In his theology, Aristotle is the perfecter of Platonic immaterialism. Thought conceived itself and hypostasized its self-consciousness as the essence of the Godhead.

The self-sufficiency of the God of Aristotle, to whose absolute perfection there can be no want,[2] whose activity, directed upon himself and upon naught else, can be no activity nor creation in our sense of the word, did not satisfy the later religious need. This idea is, however, the true corner-stone of his system, and at the same time eloquent testimony for the theoretic character of the Aristotelian philosophy.

Jul. Simon, *De deo Aristotelis* (Paris, 1839) ; A. L. Kym, *Die Gotteslehre des Aristoteles und das Christentum* (Zürich, 1862) ; L. F. Goetz, *Der aristotelische Gottesbegriff, mit Bezug auf die christliche Gottesidee* (Leipzig, 1871).

42. Aristotle looked upon nature as the organic bond of all individuals, which actualize their Form in their motions, and in their totality are determined by pure Form as their highest purpose. There is, therefore, only this one[3] world, and this world is permeated[4] in its activity with a purpose both in the motions and relationships of the individual things. The actualizing of the purposes of things, however, occurs always through the motion of matter (κίνησις or μεταβολή). This motion[5] is either change of place (κατὰ τὸ ποῦ — φορά), or change of

----

[1] Therefore, in contrast to Speusippus, the Homeric citation is given in the spirit of monism : οὐκ ἀγαθὸν πολυκοιρανίη · εἰς κοίρανος ἔστω. *Met.*, XI. 10, 1076 a, 4.

[2] He is αὐτάρχης. *Ibid.*, XIII. 4, 1091 b, 16.

[3] *De cœlo*, I. 8, 276 a, 18 ; *Met.*, XI. 8, 1074 a, 31.

[4] *Phys.*, II. 2 and 8 ; *De cœlo*, I. 4, 271 a, 33 : ὁ θεὸς καὶ ἡ φύσις οὐδὲν μάτην ποιοῦσιν. *Polit.*, I. 8, 1256 b, 20.

[5] *Phys.*, V. 2, 225 b, 18 ; II. 1, 192 b, 14.

quality (κατὰ τὸ ποιόν — ἀλλοίωσις), or change in quantity (κατὰ τὸ ποσόν — αὔξησις καὶ φθίσις).

Ch. Lévêque, *La physique d'Aristote et la science contemporaine* (Paris, 1863).

φύσις was, in truth, in Aristotle not a substance, nor an individual, but a unitary somewhat, the total teleological life of the corporeal world. In this sense he spoke of the activities, purposes, etc., of nature. In connection with his theory of nature belongs therefore also that of the soul, because, although not corporeal itself, the soul as Form of the body is its principle of motion. On the contrary, all those bodies are excluded from his definition of nature which get their form and motion from human activity, and not from their own essence.[1]

Teleology in Aristotelianism was not only a postulate, but also a developed theory. It was not at all a mythical imagining, but an essential doctrinal principle. The Platonic principle in this theory did not displace the Democritan, but the Democritan is accepted as a factor, since the mechanical motion having its basis in the material appears as a means toward the actualization of the Form.

The teleological fundamental principle, that there is a relationship of rank and value among phenomena, governs Aristotle's conception of the three kinds of motion. Change of place is the lowest, yet it is indispensable to the higher processes. For qualitative changes perfect themselves always by spatial dislocations, like condensation and rarefaction.[2] On the other hand, growth is always conditioned [3] by the qualitative processes of assimilation and the consequently necessary spatial changes. Thus this division makes the gradation into *mechanical, chemical*, and *organic* processes, in which the higher always involves the lower.

Under the class concept of μεταβολή, which is, to be sure, often made equivalent to κίνησις, Aristotle contrasted origination (γένεσις) and destruction (φθορά) to κίνησις in the narrower sense. This kind of change concerns, however, only the compounded individual things, since there is no absolute origination and destruction :[4] further, one of the three kinds of motion is always present in this change.

In his investigation into the fundamental principles of mechanics, Aristotle came to look upon the world as limited

[1] *Phys.*, II. 1, 193 a, 31. [2] *Ibid.*, VIII. 7, 260 b, 4.
[3] *Ibid.*, 260 a, 29; *De gen. et corr.*, I. 5, 320 a, 15.
[4] *Ibid.*, 3, 317 a, 32.

in space, but on the other hand as moving in time without beginning or end. He disallowed reality to empty space, and denied *actio in distans*. Motion is possible only through contact.[1]

The form of the limited world-all is the most perfect, i. e., it is a sphere. Within the world there are two fundamental kinds of motion, — in a circle and in a straight line. Of these two, the former, as self-limiting and unitary, is the more nearly perfect, while the latter involves the opposition of the centripetal and centrifugal directions. These primitive spatial motions are distributed among different kinds of matter. The natural medium of the circular motion is the æther, out of which the heavenly bodies are formed. Motions in straight lines belong to the elements (στοιχεῖα) of the terrestrial world.

Thus Aristotle separated his world-all into two essentially different systems: the heaven with the regular, circular motions of the æther, and the earth with the changing, antagonistic, and straight-line motions of the elements. The heaven is the place of perfectness, regularity, and changelessness. The earth is the theatre of imperfection and of the eternally changing manifold. While earthly things come and go, while their qualities are received and lost, while on earth there is increase and diminution, yet the stars do not become nor pass away. Like the blessed gods, they suffer no change, and in unchangeable revolutions they move in orbits eternally the same.

In the definition of space (τόπος) as " the boundary of an enclosing body on the side of the enclosed "[2] Aristotle went beyond the relative space relationships of particular bodies, but did not, therefore, reach an intuition of space. In contesting the notion of the void, he had Democritus[3] particularly in mind.

[1] *Phys.*, III. 2, 202 a, 6.
[2] *Ibid.*, IV. 4, 211 b, 14 ; *De cœlo*, IV. 3, 310 b, 7.
[3] *Phys.*, IV., 4–6.

In the dispute as to the reality of space, he contended against Plato's position, to whose construction of the elements he opposed [1] the distinction between mathematical and physical bodies. Against the notion of the endlessness of the corporeal world (ἄπειρον) he maintained [2] that the world can be thought only as complete and perfected, as a fully formed thing. Time, on the contrary, as the "measure of motion" [3] and as not actual in itself, but used only for computing,[4] is beginningless and endless, like the motion that belongs necessarily to Being. Therefore the Aristotelian philosophy offered in opposition to all earlier philosophy no picture of a creation of the world, and contended against in this respect the presentation in the Platonic *Timæus*.

On the other hand, his philosophy in its essentials was greatly influenced by the *Timæus*. For the antagonism, formulated by Aristotle in an authoritative way for many hundred years, — the antagonism between the heavenly and the terrestrial world, — was based entirely upon that which Plato had developed in his divisions of the world (see Plato), and also upon those dualistic reflections that had been peculiar to the Pythagoreans in early times. Aristotle developed these notions in a theoretic way. He gave the theory greater forcefulness conceptually than had been the case with Plato's mathematical development of it; these notions became transformed at once into qualifications of value.

Such a theory obtained also in the contrast drawn between the æther and the four elements. Also in this the Eleatic invariability, unoriginatedness, etc., was attributed to the Godhead [5] in that he explained the stars as living things moved by reasoning spirits of a higher and superhuman order [6] (θεῖα σώματα).[7] Therefore there must be for these a better matter, the æther, corresponding to their higher form.

Aristotle's particular conceptions concerning mechanical motion have no peculiarities. His very anthropomorphic division into drawing, pushing, carrying, and turning he did not further develop, and he did not reach the point of formulating laws of mechanics.

O. Ule, *Die Raumtheorien des Arist. und Kant's* (Halle, 1850); A. Torstrick, *Ueber des Arist. Abhandlung von der Zeit* (*Philol.* 1868); H. Siebeck, *Die Lehre des Arist. von der*

[1] *De cœlo*, III. 1, 299 a, 12.
[2] *Phys.*, III. 5 f.
[3] *Ibid.*, IV. 11, 220 a, 3.
[4] *Ibid.*, 14, 223 a, 21.
[5] *Meteor.*, I. 3, 339 b, 25.
[6] *Eth. Nic.*, VI. 7, 1141 a, 1.
[7] *Met.*, XI. 8, 1074 a, 30.

Ewigkeit der Welt (Unters. z. Ph. d. G., 1873); Th. Poselger, *Arist. mechanische Probleme* (Hannover, 1881).

The astronomical theory of the Stagirite was, that around the stationary sphere of the earth the hollow spheres revolve concentrically, in which spheres the moon, sun, five planets, and the fixed stars are placed. Aristotle conceived that these last, by virtue of their relatively unchanging position, have only a common sphere. This heaven of fixed stars in the outermost circle of the world is set in motion by the Godhead,[1] while the other spheres find the principle of their movements in their own spirits. Aristotle followed here Eudoxus and Callippus, the pupil of Eudoxus, when in his explanation of aberrations he ascribed to the planets a plurality of spheres dependent on one another in their movements. The star concerned was supposed to have its seat in the lowest of these spheres. He conceived in his development of this theory fifty-five spheres in all. The motions of the planets influence the motions of the elements, and in this way the planets in general influence terrestrial life.

The theory of the spheres in the form established under the name of Aristotle pushed aside the riper conceptions of the Pythagoreans and Platonists. It itself had to yield later to the hypothesis of the epicycles. J. L. Ideler, *Ueber Eudoxus* (*Abhandl. d. Berl. Acad.*, 1830).

Aristotle provided for a later demonology in his theory of the subordinate gods of the spheres of the planets, as on the other hand his theory of the dependence of earthly existence on the stars gave occasion for astrological superstition. To the changing positions of the sun, moon, and planets in relation to the earth, he attributed the character of eternal change, which in earthly life is to be contrasted with the eternal regularity of the "first heaven." [2]

Aristotle developed the differences between the earthly elements from their tendencies to move in straight lines in

---

[1] κινεῖ ὡς ἐρώμενον, as above mentioned.
[2] *De gen. et corr.*, II. 10, 336 b, 11.

opposite directions. Fire is the centrifugal, earth the centripetal element. Between the two there is the air, which is relatively light, and the water, which is relatively heavy. Therefore the earth has its natural place in the middle point of the world-all; and successively toward the periphery of the heaven, stand water, air, and fire.

But the elements have qualitative differences as well as mechanical, and these are not originally and in particular derived from mathematical differences. In their development [1] Aristotle used the same pairs of opposites which had played a great rôle already in the most ancient nature-philosophy and afterward in the younger physiology. These opposites were warm and cold, dry and moist. Of these four fundamental kinds of sensation, he called the two first active and the two last passive, and constructed accordingly out of the four possible combinations the qualities of the four elements, each one of which must include [2] an active and passive quality. Fire is warm and dry; air is warm and moist; earth is cold and dry; water is cold and moist. No element appears unmixed in any individual thing; on the contrary, there is a mixture of all elements in each thing.

Aristotle explained the common elemental meteorological phenomena by means partly of the mechanical, partly of the chemical qualities of the elements, using the earlier theories in a most comprehensive way. Moreover he made a special study of the distinctly chemical processes, and distinguished between bodies of equal and of unequal parts, and investigated the origin of new qualities arising from the combination of simple bodies.

Concerning the predecessors of Aristotle as to the doctrine of the elements, see Zeller, III[3]. 441, 2. For Aristotle to have assumed the four elements of Empedocles is consistent with the traces elsewhere found of the influence of that philosopher. The

[1] *De gen. et corr.*, II. 2 and 3.   [2] *Meteor.*, IV. 1, 378 b, 12.

assertion as to the primariness of qualities was aimed expressly
against Plato and Democritus, and therewith Aristotle turned
away from mathematical science to an anthropocentric view of
nature. For, inasmuch as the first qualities of the elements
were deduced from tactile sensations, so the wider chemical
investigations were chiefly derived from mixtures of other sense-
qualities, especially from those of taste and smell, but also as
well from those of hearing and sight. In this way the investigations of physiological psychology (*De an.*, II., and in smaller
treatises) complete the specific chemical treatments which form
Meteorologia, IV.

The contrast of active and passive qualities involved, on the
one hand, the thought of the internal vitality of all bodies. On
the other hand, it led in the whole of the system to the application which the different kinds of matter receive in the organisms.
Yet the present division into organic and inorganic chemistry is
not to be read into his division of οἱμοιομερῆ and ἀνομοιόμερῆ,
even if the latter were also designated as more completely representing organic purposiveness.

That, finally, this beginning of chemical science at first had at
its disposal very sporadic and inexact knowledge, and in Aristotle was still limited [1] to clumsy methods of experimentation,
like boiling, roasting, etc., cannot be wondered at. Neither does
it detract from the value of the first special treatment of chemical
problems. See Ideler, *Meteorologia veterum* (Berlin, 1832).

The series of grades of living creatures is determined by
differences of soul, which as the entelechy of the body [2] in
all things is the Form that moves, changes, and fashions
matter. Souls also have a relative ranking.[3] The lower
can exist without the higher, but the higher only in connection with the lower. The lowest kind of soul is the
vegetative (τὸ θρεπτικόν), which is limited in its functions
to assimilation and propagation, and belongs to plants.
The animal possesses in addition to this the sensitive soul
(τὸ αἰσθητικόν), which at the same time is appetitive (ὀρε-
κτικόν), and has also to some degree the power of locomotion
(κινητικὸν κατὰ τόπον). Man possesses, besides both these
other souls, reason (τὸ διανοητικόν τε καὶ νοῦς).

[1] *Meteor.*, IV². f.   [2] *De an.*, II. 1, 412 a, 27.
[3] *Ibid.*, 3, 414 b, 29.

The purposiveness of the organism is explicable from the activity of the soul. The soul builds [1] for itself out of matter the body as an organ, or as a system of organs. It finds its limitations only in conflict with matter, whose nature-necessity leads to Forms, that are from the circumstances purposeless or purpose-thwarting.

The significance of Aristotle as an investigator of nature lies in his development of organology. Under his principal teleological treatment came the questions of systematology, of morphology, of anatomy and physiology, and of biology, in a way that was for his time exhaustive and for many centuries authoritative. His philosophical principle was that nature strives upward from the very first signs of life, which signs can be seen even in inorganic processes, and that the striving is expressed in an unbroken series from the lowest kinds of spontaneous creations to the highest form of terrestrial life which is manifested in man.

When Aristotle conceived the soul as a principle of independent motion of the individual, he attributed to it a number of functions (especially all the vegetative) which pass in the present-day science as purely physiological. The soul was thought by Aristotle to be incorporeal but nevertheless bound to matter which is the possibility of its activity and does not therefore exist for itself alone. It has its seat in a particular organic matter, — in the θερμόν or the πνεῦμα, — which is related to the æther and is supposed to be found in animals in the blood chiefly. In this doctrine Aristotle allowed himself to be misled back into the popular view, which was opposed to the insight of Alcmæon, Democritus, and Plato, that the heart is the principal organ of the soul; and the brain plays the secondary rôle of a cooling apparatus for the blood boiled in the heart. The *spiritus animales* of later times were developed theoretically from Aristotle's physiological psychology.

The three grades of life of the soul correspond in general, although only very vaguely, to Plato's three divisions of the soul. Yet this doctrine is conceived and developed with much more

[1] See classical development of the human form: *De part. an.*, IV. 10, 686 a, 25.

conceptual sharpness and clearness in Aristotle than in his predecessor.

Aristotle's predilection for teleology in the realm of the organic sciences, in which his thoroughgoing treatment of the facts most brilliantly appears, in no way hindered the care of his observations and comparisons. It rather sharpened to a high degree his insight into the anatomical structure of the organs, their morphological relations, their physiological functions, and their biological significance. Some mistaken analogies and unfortunate generalizations, which have been correctly enough charged against him by modern investigators, cannot injure the fame which is due him in this field. They are only the excrescences and imperfections of his great and comprehensive conception. In details he utilized chiefly the previous works of Democritus, whose mechanical theory, it must be said, had not stood in the way of his conception and admiration of the purposefulness of organisms.

See J. B. Meyer, *Aristoteles' Tierkunde* (Berlin, 1855); Th. Watzel, *Die Zoölogie des Aristoteles* (in three parts, Reichenberg, 1878–80).

The psychology of Aristotle has two parts, which, although running over into each other, still reveal the predominance of two distinct scientific points of view: (1) the general theory of animal souls, a doctrine of the psychical processes which are possessed in common by animals and men, although developed in man more richly and more nearly perfectly; (2) the doctrine of the *νοῦς* as the distinctive possession of man. We can designate these two views as the empirical and speculative sides of Aristotle's psychology. The former he treated essentially as an investigator by carefully recording, ordering, and explaining the facts. The latter view, on the contrary, was governed partly by his general metaphysics, partly by his interests in epistemology and ethics.[1]

K. Ph. Fischer, *De principiis Aristotelicæ de anima doctrinæ* (Erlangen, 1845); W. Volkmann, *Die Grundzüge der aristo-*

---

[1] Aristotle himself distinguished between the physical and philosophical treatment of the soul: *De an.*, I. 403 b, 9; *De part. an.*, I. 1, 641 a, 17.

telischen Psychologie (Prague, 1858); A. E. Chaignet, *Essai sur la psychologie d'Aristote* (Paris, 1883); H. Siebeck, *Geschichte der Psychologie*, I. 2, pp. 1–127 (Gotha, 1884).

Aristotle found predecessors in empirical psychology, — which is partly physiological psychology, as we to-day designate it, but is not entirely embraced by it, — partly in the physicians and later nature-philosophers, partly in Democritus, and also perhaps in Plato in the *Timœus*. But he also betrayed in his theory of the νοῦς the inclination which had led all early philosophers to adjust their conceptions of psychology to their epistemological and ethical views.

The animal soul is differentiated from the vegetable soul essentially by its concentration and unity (μεσότης),[1] which is wanting in plants. Sensation is the fundamental form of activity (αἴσθησις), which he explained[2] by the concert of action between the active, Form-giving perceived thing and the passive, impressionable perceiving thing, — an action mediated in different senses through different media. The most primary sense and common to all animals is the sense of touch, with which Aristotle likewise classified taste. In value, however, hearing is first.

However, the activity of the special senses is restricted to receiving those qualities of the external world which are peculiar to the senses themselves, — senses which are in the similarity of their material adapted to such reception. The combination of the psychic elements, nevertheless, into complete perceptions and the conception of the conditions of things, which are common to the different senses — the conception of their number, their spatial and temporal connections, their conditions of motion — takes place through the central sense organ, the " common-sense " (αἰσθητήριον κοινόν), which has its seat in the heart. In this central organ arises our knowledge of our own activities.[3] In it the ideas remain[4] as φαντασίαι after the external stimulus has ceased. Imagination becomes memory (μνήμη) as soon as

[1] *De an.*, II. 11, 424 a, 4.   [2] *Ibid.*, 5, 417 a, 6.
[3] *Ibid.*, III. 2, 425 b, 17.   [4] *Ibid*, 3, 427 b, 14.

it becomes recognized as the copy of an earlier perception.
The entrance of remembered ideas is conditioned upon the
series in which they are bound together. Upon the basis
of this association of ideas voluntary recollection is possible
in man (ἀνάμνησις).[1]

H. Beck, *Arist. de sensuum actione* (Berlin, 1860) ; A. Crata-
cap, *Arist. de sensibus doctrina* (Montpellier, 1866) ; Cl. Bäumker,
Des Arist. Lehre von dem äusseren und inneren Sinnesvermögen
(Leipzig, 1877) ; J. Neuhäuser, *Arist. Lehre von dem sinnlichen
Erkenntnisvermögen und seinen Organen* (Leipzig, 1878) ; J.
Freudenthal, *Ueber den Begriff des Wortes φαντασία bei Aristo-
teles* (Göttingen, 1867) ; Fr. Scheiboldt, *De imaginatione dis-
quisitio ex Arist. libris repetita* (Leipzig, 1882) ; J. Ziaja, *Die
aristotelische Lehre vom Gedächtnis und von der Association der
Vorstellungen* (Leobschütz, 1882).

Aristotle's idea of single processes of perception is conditioned by the general principles of his philosophy of natural
science, and is in many ways distinguished from that of his predecessors. The most important point in the theoretic part of
his animal psychology is his insight into the synthetic character
of perception, which is expressed in the hypothesis of the
common-sense. Aristotle did not follow further the valuable
thought that consciousness of activities, i. e., the inner perception as distinguished from the objects of those activities, is
rooted in this synthesis. In the doctrine of the association of
ideas and in the distinction between voluntary and involuntary
memory he scarcely advances beyond Plato.

Next to the different grades of ideas, desire (ὄρεξις) is
the second fundamental form of the activity of the animal
soul. It originates in the feeling of pleasure or displeasure
(ἡδύ and λυπηρόν), which is derived from the ideas so far
as the content of these promises to fulfil a purpose or not.
Therefore affirmation or negation results, which express
the essence of the practical life of the soul in pursuit or
in aversion (διώκειν — φεύγειν).[2] In all cases, then, the idea
of the agreeable is the cause of pleasure and desire, and *vice
versa*. Desire, however, calls [3] forth teleological move-

---

[1] See the writing περὶ μνήμης καὶ ἀναμνήσεως.
[2] *De an.*, III. 7, 431 a, 15.   [3] *De mot. an.*, 7, 701 b, 7.

ments of the organs through their warming or their cooling
which follow physiologically from the intensity of the
feelings of pleasure and displeasure.

In the fundamental division into theoretical and practical [1]
activities of souls, Aristotle associated feeling with the desire as
a constant accompanying phenomenon. Yet he taught, on the
other hand, entirely in the spirit of the Socratic psychology, that
every desire presupposes the idea of its object as something of
value. He represented indeed the genesis of desire as a conclusion wherein the momentary content of the idea is subsumed
under a more universal teleological thought.[2] The result is,
then, affirmative or negative, as in a conclusion. It is, moreover, interesting that Aristotle identified the act of agreement
or disagreement in the practical functions of feeling and desire
exactly with the logical terms of affirmative and negative judgments (κατάφασις and ἀπόφασις). This showed in him, not only
in his psychology but in his entire teaching, the characteristic
tendency to subordinate the practical under the prevailing
determinations of the theoretical.

All these activities of animal souls constitute in man the
material for the development of the Form peculiar to him,
i. e., the reason (νοῦς). No longer a Form of the body, but
rather of the soul, it is purely immaterial, is not to be confused with the body as a potentiality, and as mere Form it
is simple, unchangeable, and incapable of suffering.[3] The
νοῦς does not originate with the body, as the animal functions of the soul originate. It enters from without [4] as
a higher, godlike activity, and it therefore alone remains
after the body has passed away.[5]

The fundamental activity of the soul is thought (διανοεῖσ-
θαι),[6] and its object is those highest principles, in which
the ultimate ground of all Being and knowing is immediately
(ἄμεσα) conceived. Only in so far as the reasoning insight

[1] This he also calls θυμός; *Pol.*, VII. 7, 1327 b, 40: see P. Meyer,
ὁ θυμός apud Aristotelem Platonemque, Bonn, 1877.

[2] *De mot. an.*, 7, 701 a, 8; *Eth. Nic.*, VII. 5, 1147 a, 26.

[3] *De an.*, III⁴. 429 a, 15.   [4] *De gen an.*, II. 3, 736 b, 27.

[5] *De an.*, III. 5, 430 a, 23.   [6] *Ibid.*, III. 4, 429 a, 23.

can become the cause of desire, is the reason also practical.[1] This higher kind of ὄρεξις is designated as βούλησις.

In the human individual, however, the reason is not pure Form but self-developing Form. Therefore we must again distinguish also in human reason between its potentiality and its actuality, between its passive material and its active Form. Therefore, although Aristotle designated[2] the νοῦς itself as ποιοῦν, he contrasted it with its potentiality which is capable of being actualized, as the νοῦς παθητικός. This potentiality exists, however, in the theoretic functioning of animal souls, yet only so far as these functions can become in the human organism the occasion for reflection upon those highest and immediately certain principles.[3] Historical development of the reason in men is therefore this, — that through the persistence of sense impressions (μονή)[4] general notions arise (τὸ πρῶτον ἐν τῇ ψυχῇ καθόλου), and these then form the entire occasion in the epagogic process for the knowledge of the actual reason appearing upon the original *tabula rasa*[5] of the νοῦς παθητικός. The actualizing of the reason is dependent upon the physiological process of representation, and it remains so because the sensuous pictures are always associated also with the supersensible product of the thinking process.[6]

Jul. Wolf, *De intellectu agente et patiente doctrina* (Berlin, 1844) ; W. Biehl, *Ueber den Begriff des νοῦς bei Aristoteles* (Linz, 1864) ; F. Brentano, *Die Psychologie des Aristoteles insbesondere seine Lehre vom νοῦς ποιητικός* (Mainz, 1867) ; A. Bullinger, *Aristoteles Nus-Lehre* (Dillingen, 1884) ; E. Zeller,

---

[1] *De an.*, III. 10, 433 a, 14.   [2] *Ibid* , 5, 430 a, 12, 19.

[3] These functions man shares with the beast ; but among animals they are not instruments of the reason because the active principle of reason is wanting. This relation does away with the doubt raised by Zeller, III³. 576 f.

[4] *Anal. post.*, II. 19, 99 b, 36.   [5] *De an.*, III. 4, 429 b, 31.

[6] *Ibid.*, 7, 431 a, 16.

Ueber die Lehre des Aristoteles von der Ewigkeit des Geistes (*Sitzungs-Berichte der Berl. Ak.*, 1882).

The difficulties of Aristotle's theory of the νοῦς lie first in the fact that the reason in our usual terminology is defined and treated as the peculiarity of the human soul, but it is thereby so restricted that it can fall no longer under the class concept of the soul as " the entelechy of the body." With Aristotle the true relationship is rather this : that the νοῦς bears the relation to the human ψυχή (and in so far this is true of animal souls) as the animal ψυχή bears to the body.[1] In some respect the distinction is the same in the German between *Geist* and *Seele*, and in the Middle Ages a similar distinction was made between *spiritus* or *spiraculum* and *anima*. Therefore the reason in itself is thought to be pure actuality, and to have no relation to the body, to come from without into the body and to live after the body. Aristotle's " possibility " is, on the contrary, the animal ψυχή ; and therefore the νοῦς παθητικός [2] is also mortal (φθαρτός). On the other hand, the animal ψυχή does not become the νοῦς παθητικός until by the influence of the νοῦς ποιητικός upon it. In itself it is empty so far as reasoning knowledge goes, and only offers the occasion for the reasoning knowledge to actualize itself.

On account of this the Aristotelian didactic writings leave in a very uncertain state the question of individual immortality, concerning which the commentators were in lively dispute even until the Renaissance.[3] For doubtless, according to the Aristotelian definition of a concept, all those psychical contents which compose the essence of the individual belong to the νοῦς παθητικός, which is destroyed with the body. Pure, universal rational knowledge of the νοῦς ποιητικός has remaining in it so little that is individual, that according to the characteristics that are ascribed to it — pure actuality, unchangeableness, and eternalness — a difference between it and the divine spirit cannot be made out. We cannot decide whether or by what method Aristotle tried to solve this problem.

But, at any rate, his speculative psychology shows a strong dependence upon the Platonic, and particularly upon the form of Platonism in the *Timæus*. In both cases, to the distinction between a reasoning and an unreasoning part [4] of the soul there

[1] So the νοῦς in Aristotle is called a higher kind of soul: *De an.*, II. 2, 413 b, 26.

[2] *Ibid.*, III. 5, 430 a, 24.

[3] See Windelband, *Gesch. der neueren Phil.*, I. (Leipzig, 1878), p. 15 f.

[4] *Eth. Nic.*, I. 13, 1102 a, 27. There is also in Aristotle a νοῦς χωριστός : *De an.*, III. 5, 430 a, 22.

is added the postulate that the former is immortal and the latter is mortal with the body.

The psycho-epistemological conception which Aristotle developed concerning the temporal actualizing of the νοῦς in man, resembles, also, the Platonic conception. For if the epagogic processes of μνήμη and ἐμπειρία lead to the highest principles, whose certainty rests upon the immediate intuition of the νοῦς, if indeed the natural way from the πρότερον πρὸς ἡμᾶς to the πρότερον τῇ φύσει does not include the grounding of the highest premises, but ultimately only the occasion for immediate intuition of the same to enter, — then this theory is only the development and refinement of the Platonic doctrine of ἀνάμνησις.

The διάνοια, the knowledge which the reason possesses, has a theoretical and practical use (ἐπιστημονικόν and λογιστικόν).[1] The former as θεωρία leads to ἐπιστήμη, the latter as φρόνησις to τέχνη. But it is also true that the practical reason in itself is only a theoretic activity, an insight into the right principles of action. Whether the individual shall follow that knowledge or not depends upon his free choice.

L. Schneider, *Die Unsterblichkeitslehre des Aristoteles* (Passau, 1867) ; K. Schlottmann, *Das Vergängliche und Unvergängliche in der menschlichen Seele nach Aristoteles* (Halle, 1873) ; W. Schrader, *Aristotle de voluntate doctrina* (Brandenburg, 1847) ; J. Walter, *Die Lehre von der praktischen Vernunft in der griechischen Philosophie* (Jena, 1874).

43. Furthermore, the practical philosophy of Aristotle was built up on these universal theoretic principles. The goal of every human action is a Good, to be realized by activity (πρακτὸν ἀγαθόν). Yet this goal is only a means to the highest goal, Happiness, on account of which all else is desired. To perfect εὐδαιμονία belongs also the possession of the goods of the body, of the outer world, and of success ; but since these are only accessories, their lack will only give a certain limitation [2] to the amount of happiness. The essential condition of happiness, on the contrary, is activity, and indeed, the activity peculiar to man ; that is, it is that of reason.[3]

Now the state (ἕξις) [4] which renders possible to man the

---

[1] *Eth. Nic.*, VI. 2, 1139 a, 11.　　[2] *Ibid.*, VII. 14, 1153 b, 17.

[3] *Ibid* , I. 6, 1097 b, 24.　　[4] *Ibid.*, II. 4, 1106 b, 11.

perfect use of his peculiar activity is virtue. Virtue has in certain bodily qualities its natural aptitude, out of which it is developed [1] only by use of the reason. From the exercise of virtue, pleasure [2] follows as a necessary result of perfect activity.

The problem of the reason is twofold : first, it is concerned with knowledge ; secondly, with the direction of desire and action through knowledge. In this way, Aristotle distinguished between the dianoëtic and ethical virtues.[3] The former are higher. They unfold the pure formal activity of the νοῦς, and give the most noble and perfect pleasure. The human being finds in them his possible participation in the divine blessedness.

K. L. Michelet, *Die Ethik des Aristoteles* (Berlin, 1827) ; G. Hartenstein, *Ueber den wissenschaftlichen Wert der aristotelischen Ethik* (in *Hist.-philos. Abhandl.*, Leipzig, 1870); R. Eucken, *Ueber die Methode und die Grundlagen der aristotelischen Ethik* (Frankfort a. M., 1870) ; P. Paul, *An Analysis of Aristotle's Ethics* (London, 1874) ; A. Ollé-laprune, *De Aristoteleæ ethices fundamento* (Paris, 1880). Concerning the Highest Good, G. Teichmüller, *Die Einheit der aristotelischen Eudämonie* (in *Bulletin de la classe des sciences hist.*, etc., *de l'académie de St. Pétersbourg*, XVI. 305 ff.). Concerning dianoëtic virtues, see C. Prantl (München, 1852, *Glückw.-schr. an Thiersch*) and A. Kühn (Berlin, 1860).

The sense for what is actual, the thoroughgoing investigation of facts, and the inclination to bring qualitative distinctions to the same touchstone, are shown in the practical philosophy of Aristotle perhaps more than in his theoretical philosophy. The Nicomachæan ethics definitely refused to take its point of departure from the abstract Idea of the Good, adopting in its stead the Good so far as it is an object of human activity (I. 1, 1094 a, 19). In the determination of the concept of happiness, also, which to him was obviously the highest good, he included the possession of material wealth and good fortune, although always subordinated to the exercise of the reason, if the reason is to reach complete and untrammelled development. Only this potential value justifies the consideration of earthly good in ethics.

[1] *Eth. Nic.*, VI. 13, 1144 b, 4. [2] *Ibid.*, X. 4, 1174 b, 31.
[3] *Ibid.*, I. 13, 1103 a, 2.

The dialectic that had been developed by Socrates upon the question of the relation of pleasure and virtue was completed with exalted simplicity by Aristotle ; for he taught, in antagonism to the one-sided doctrines, that pleasure is never the motive, but always the result of virtue. Therefore, also, the activity of the reason unfolding itself in virtue is always the measure of the worth of the different pleasures (*Eth. Nic.*, X. 3. ff.).

In respect to the psychological characterization of virtue, Aristotle laid weight upon its conception as a continuous condition and not as a single state. On the other hand, he found a δύναμις for it in bodily qualities, such as the characteristics of the natural disposition, temperament, inclination, and feelings. These are also in children and animals, but they are not there under the rule of the reason.

The dianoëtic virtues are related to theoretical as well as to practical insight. The latter is either τέχνη as the knowledge of the right, requisite for artistic creation, or φρόνησις as the recognition of justice, which recognition is necessary for activity in public or private life (*Eth. Nic.*, VI. 5 ff.). The φρόνησις is also split into (1) σύνεσις, the understanding of objects and relations which are the cause of its activity, and (2) εὐβολία, the knowledge of teleological processes. The σοφία is of more value, for it is the knowledge having no ulterior purpose, but sought on account of itself. Its content is highest actuality and first principles. Its application to single sciences and departments is ἐπιστήμη ; its knowledge of itself is διάνοια, or the νοῦς as pure Form. It is that θεωρία, in which the highest happiness consists (*Met.*, XI. 7, 1072 b. 24 ; see *Eth. Nic.*, X. 7, 1177 a, 13), and this makes the perfectness of God : ἡ θεωρία τὸ ἥδιστον καὶ ἄριστον. This is ethically, as well as metaphysically, the fundamental principle of the philosophy of Aristotle. It is rooted in his personality : and is the expression of that pure joy in knowledge that forms the basis of all science and is the absolute condition of the independence of science. In the logic of Aristotle Greek science recognized and formulated its essence, and in his ethics its practicability.

As the dianoëtic virtues have their seat in the intellect, the ethical virtues have theirs in the will. Rational insight, as experience teaches us, is not alone sufficient for right action, but there must be added to it the strength of the will (ἐγκράτεια),[1] in order to give the insight validity

---

[1] Not reckoned among the virtues : *Eth. Nic.*, IV. 15, 1128 b, 33.

in contrast to the affections and desires.[1] This is only possible by the will choosing freely what it knows to be good.

Ethical virtue is, then, that continuing state of the will by means of which practical reason rules the desires. Besides disposition and insight, virtue also needs for its development exercise,[2] because the direction of the will must be established through habit. The ἦθος is developed out of the ἔθος.

The control of the desires by the reason consists in the right mean being chosen[3] between the extremes, toward which uncurbed desires press. It is the task of practical insight to recognize this right mean in individual relations by using our knowledge of objects and of human nature; and it is the business of virtue to act according to this insight (ὀρθὸς λόγος).

Out of this principle Aristotle developed from his accurate knowledge of the world and human kind the single ethical virtues in a rising series, which seem[4] not to have been systematically grounded, articulated, or delineated. The purely Greek fundamental principle in it is that of the value of moderation.

A. Trendelenburg, *Das Ebenmass, ein Band der Verwandtschaft zwischen griechischen Archäologie und griechischen Philosophie* (Berlin, 1865).

Although Aristotle regarded right insight as the *conditio sine qua non* of right action, yet he was still conscious that it is, after all, the province of the will to follow right insight, and that the will has the power of doing the wrong thing contrary to right insight. It is for us to say (ἐφ᾿ ἡμῖν) whether we wish to act well or ill. The investigation concerning freedom that Aristotle made (*Eth. Nic.*, III. 1–8) directs itself indeed against the Socratic intellectualism, and views the question essentially from

---

[1] See the polemic against the Socratic doctrine, *Eth. Nic.*, VII. 3 ff.

[2] *Ibid.*, II. 1, 1103 a, 24. [3] *Ibid.*, 5, 1106 a, 28.

[4] See, nevertheless, F. Häcker, *Das Einteilungs- und Anordnungsprinzip der moralischen Tugendreihe in der nikomachischen Ethik* (Berlin, 1863); Th. Ziegler, *Gesch. der Ethik*, I. 116.

the point of responsibility.¹ The question is, how far a human being can be regarded as the ἀρχή of his own activity.² This freedom is annulled through ignorance of the facts and through external force. The προαίρεσις is essential to it, which is the decision through choice between contemplated possibilities.

The dogmatic completeness which characterized the Platonic ethics was not reached by Aristotle's system. Aristotle made amends for it by his deep rational insight into the manifold relations of life. The virtues treated by him are: courage (ἀνδρεία), as the mean between fear and daring; temperance (σωφροσύνη), between intemperance and insensibleness; liberality (ἐλευθεριότης), and in larger relationships magnificence (μεγαλοπρέπεια), between stinginess and prodigality; high-mindedness (μεγαλοψυχία), and in affairs of less importance ambition, between vaingloriousness and self-abasement; mildness (πραότης), between irascibility and indifference; friendliness (also called φιλία), between obsequiousness and brusqueness; candor (ἀλήθεια), between boastfulness and dissembling; urbanity (εὐτραπέλεια), between trifling and moroseness;³ finally, justice (δικαιοσύνη), which consists in recognizing the rights of men neither too much nor too little. The philosopher gives an exhaustive treatment of justice (*Eth. Nic.*, V.), on the one hand because in a certain sense it comprehends⁴ in itself all the virtues in respect to our fellows, on the other because it is the foundation of the political life of society. Its fundamental principle is equality,⁵ — either the proportional equality of merit or the absolute equality of legal rights. Therefore Aristotle distinguished distributive justice (τὸ ἐν ταῖς διανομαῖς or τὸ διανεμητικὸν δίκαιον), and commutative justice (τὸ ἐν τοῖς συναλλάγμασι or τὸ διορθωτικὸν δίκαιον).⁶ Both investigations led to interesting details of political economy and political law.

---

¹ With express reference indeed to criminal law, *Eth. Nic.*, III. 1, 1109 b, 34. Metaphysical aporia from freedom of the will are not yet considered in this connection; and only once in connection with the law of the excluded third term: *De interpr.*, 9, 18 b, 31.

² *Eth. Nic.*, III. 5, 1112 b, 31; 3, 1111 a, 73.

³ Also shame (αἰδώς) and sympathy are mentioned by Aristotle in this series, but they indicate excellences of temperament (*Eth. Nic.*, II. 7, 1108 a, 32); in other words, φυσικαὶ ἀρεταί.

⁴ *Ibid.*, V. 3, 1129 b, 17.   ⁵ *Ibid.*, 5, 1130 b, 9.

⁶ Wherever the latter legally carried out would not satisfy the ethical need, and where the former takes its place, there reigns the virtue of fair-mindedness (τὸ ἐπιεικές).

A principle in this series of virtues is to be found only in its content, since the formal mean (μεσότης) is everywhere the same. The principle consists in the gradual advance from the individual relations toward the social relations and among the latter, from the external to the more spiritual relations of life. At the beginning stands courage, the virtue of self-preservation of the individual; at the end justice, the ethical basis of the state.

Finally, the beautiful representation of friendship, whose ideal the philosopher found in the common striving for the beautiful and good (φιλία)[1] forms a transition to the treatment of social life. He applied this standard to some similar relations of friendship, to conventional and unconventional social relations, raising the latter from their utilitarian origin to means for ethical ennoblement. The same obtains also in regard to the state. See R. Eucken, *Aristoteles' Anschauung von Freundschaft und Lebensgütern* (Berlin, 1884); also *Aristoteles' Urteil über die Menschen* (*Arch. f. Gesch. d. Ph.*, III. 541 ff.).

Man, however, who is designed by nature (ζῷον πολιτικόν)[2] as an essentially social being, can perfect his activity only in communal life. The natural and fundamental form of society is the family (οἰκία); the most perfect, however, is the state. Since the ethical virtues of man can develop perfectly[3] only in the life of the state, so also, although the state arose[4] out of the needs of utility, the state is essentially and theoretically the actualization of the highest good of the active man (τἀνθρώπινον ἀγαθόν).

This idea seemed so important to Aristotle that in the beginning of his *Ethics* he designated the whole of practical philosophy as πολιτική,[5] which is divided into the theory of the conduct of the individual (*Ethics*) and the theory of the conduct of the whole (*Politics*). The relationship is not to be so conceived as if ethics set up an ideal of perfect individuality, and as if politics then showed how this ideal was developed by society. But as the whole is more valuable and essentially

---

[1] *Eth. Nic.*, VIII. f. [2] *Pol.*, I. 2, 1253 a, 3.

[3] In the treatment of friendship, Aristotle used frequently the expression συζῆν. See *Eth. Nic.*, IX. 12, 1171 b, 32.

[4] See conclusion of *Ethics* and beginning of *Politics*.

[5] Which he also called philosophical anthropology (ἡ περὶ τὰ ἀνθρώπινα φιλοσοφία) in *Eth. Nic*, X. 10, 1181 b, 15.

earlier than the parts, so also a man as an active being attains
in social life a more perfect actuality than in isolation (*Eth.
Nic.*, I. 1, 1094 b, 7).

Aristotle agreed with Plato and the author of the dialogue,
Politicus, in the ethico-teleological conception of the life of
the state. But he was thinking here, as in general, not of
the transcendent, but the immanent teleology. His state is
no form of government of superhuman beings, but the perfection
of the earthly life, the full actualization of the natural disposition of man. On the other hand, Aristotle was far from
letting man be swallowed up in the state, as was the case with
Plato. The individual's participation in the divine holiness of
the θεωρία remains his independent enjoyment, even if he must
be guided by social education to dianoëtic and ethical virtue.
While subordinating the citizen to the community, Aristotle
nevertheless gave to him in private life[1] a very much greater
circle of independent activity, since he expressly contended
against the Platonic conception[2] of a community of wives,
children, and property. So his theory of the state held the
happy mean between the socialism of Plato and the individualism of other schools, and it became thereby the ideal expression
of Greek life.

Aristotle gave the same relative independence also to the
family, the natural community, upon which the state is built.
The family is the prototype of the political forms in its relationships of man to wife, parents to children, and to slaves.[3] The
conception of marriage reached a height in Aristotle which
antiquity did not surpass. He saw in it an ethical relationship between peers in which only from natural disposition
the man is the determining, the wife the determined element.
Slavery, which he desired to treat in all humaneness, is an indispensable groundwork for family and political life. He justified it — feeling its practical importance for Greece — because
only through it the good of leisure (σχολή)[4] is made possible for
the citizen, and this leisure is a condition necessary to the exercise of virtue. He also was of the opinion that natural disposition has predetermined one man as slave, another as free
citizen.

See W. Oncken, *Die Staatslehre des Aristoteles* (Leipzig,

[1] He said emphatically that the state consists in individuals that are
in some respects like and in others unlike. *Politics*, IV. 11, 1295 a, 25.

[2] *Ibid.*, II. 2 ff

[3] *Eth. Nic.*, VIII. 12, 1160 b, 22.

[4] Concerning the word "leisure," see *Ibid.*, X. 7, 1177 b, 4.

1870) ; C. Bradley, *The Politics of Aristotle ;* P. Janet, *Histoire de la science politique* (Paris, 1887), I. 165 ff.

The living and perfected virtue of all its citizens is the final purpose of the state. For the realization [1] of this purpose we must take the material at hand ; viz., a natural, historical and concrete society in a particular environment. Although it is impossible to fix upon a valid norm for the constitution of all states, nevertheless under all circumstances the actual constitution must be measured by the general purpose of the state, and its worth will be assessed according to its sufficiency (ὀρθή) and deficiency (ἡμαρτημένη). The political constitution is an arrangement in which the rule is in the hands of a justly ordained power. Therefore the worth of a state depends on the ruling power keeping the purpose of the state (τὸ κοινὸν συμφέρον) in view. Since the rule may be in the hands of the one or the few or the many, there are [2] six possible forms of political constitutions, — three good and three that are deficient. The former three are monarchy (βασιλεία), aristocracy, and " polity " (πολιτεία) ;[3] the latter three are despotism (τυραννίς), oligarchy, and democracy (δημοκρατία).[4] With the fine analysis of an observing statesman, Aristotle investigated the essential principles of these different forms, their conditions, their rise, their fall, and their legitimate transmutation one into another. With the firm hand of a philosopher he drew his estimate of these various forms after the " concept " of a state.

[1] *Pol.*, VII. 4, 1325 b, 35.

[2] Aristotle changed the somewhat external principle of division of the number of rulers (*Ibid.*, III. 17, 1287 b, 37) by considerations about the character of the different peoples.

[3] *Ibid.*, 7, 1279 a, 25.

[4] What Aristotle here calls πολιτεία in the narrower sense was later known as democracy (δημοκρατία). Polybius has a better name for the Aristotelian democracy, which is ὀχλοκρατία.

Among the good constitutions, monarchy and aristocracy are the most perfect, since they are the rule of the best man or men, ethically speaking. Of these, monarchy would be preferred if we could hope that it would ever correspond entirely to its concept; that is, to the rule of one man who surpasses all others in virtue.[1] In reality the aristocracy offers greater guarantees. Among the degenerate kinds of constitutions, the rule of the masses is always less unendurable, that of tyranny the most abominable.

Under the presupposition of fulfilling all conditions which were demanded for realizing the political ideal, the idea of the best state was delineated, whose development Aristotle began but did not complete.[2] The best state must have the fundamental form of " polity " at least, but the administration of public affairs must, as in the aristocracy, be in the hands [3] of the virtuous. It would be a state of peace and not of war,[4] and its chief task would be the correct education of all its citizens. The citizens would not only be efficient in practical affairs, but they would [5] also be sensible to beauty and finally capable of the highest enjoyment, that is, of that which attends knowledge.

The incompleteness of the Aristotelian writings is perhaps nowhere so much to be regretted as in the *Politics*. The torso of this work shows a wonderful thoroughness, a philosophical penetration of all the political conditions of Hellenic history, the clearest understanding of the limitations and the developments of political life. These excellences make all the more keen our regret that the ideal picture of the state, based on what he has given, was only proposed and not developed. In

---

[1] *Pol.*, V. 10, 1310 b, 31.   [2] *Ibid.*, VII. 4 ff.

[3] Aristotle distinguished — in a manner not entirely consistent to the new theory of the three kinds of power, but yet with an approximate suitability — τὸ βουλευόμενον περὶ τῶν κοινῶν, τὸ περὶ τὰς ἀρχὰς, τὸ δικάζον (*Ibid.*, IV. 14, 1297 b, 41).

[4] *Ibid.*, VII. 14 f.   [5] *Ibid.*, VIII. 2 f.

the same way the theory of eduction of Aristotle comes to an
abrupt end after a sketch of the elementary principles of education, suggesting many valuable points of view. It put forth in a
clear way that all æsthetical training is to bring about the
ethical and theoretical unfolding of what is essentially human.

With Aristotle's practical philosophy is connected the
Poetics, the science of the creative activity of man. But
in the preserved writings, this science is developed only on
the side of beauty in fine art, and particularly in reference
to poetry in the *Poetics*.

J. Bernays, *Zwei Abhandlungen über die aristotelische Theorie
des Dramas* (Berlin, 1880) ; A. Döring, *Die Kunstlehre des
Aristoteles* (Jena, 1876) ; the details of a rich bibliography are
found in Döring, p. 263 ff. ; Ueberweg-Heinze, I[7]. 225.

All art is imitation, and the different arts are to be distinguished partly by their media, partly by the objects to be
imitated.[1] The *media* of poetry are words, rhythm, and harmony.[2] The objects of poetry are men and their conduct,
good or bad.[3] Tragedy, to whose analysis the preserved
fragment on poetry is essentially limited, presents directly
to the spectator in beautiful language a significant and
complete action through its different characters.[4]

The purpose of art, however, is to arouse the emotions of
man in such a way that he may be freed and purified (κάθαρσις) from their power — precisely through their arousal
and intensification. This is possible only when art presents,
not the empirically actual, but that which could be in itself
possible, — so presenting it that it raises the object into
universality.

[1] *Poet.*, 1 f.   [2] *Ibid.*, 7, 1447 a, 22.   [3] *Ibid*, 2 f.

[4] The celebrated and much discussed definition of tragedy is (*Ibid.*,
6, 1449 b, 24): ἔστιν οὖν τραγῳδία μίμησις πράξεως σπουδαίας καὶ τελείας,
μέγεθος ἐχούσης, ἡδυσμένῳ λόγῳ, χωρὶς ἑκάστου τῶν εἰδῶν ἐν τοῖς μορίοις,
δρώντων καὶ οὐ δι᾽ ἀπαγγελίας, δι᾽ ἐλέου καὶ φόβου περαίνουσα τὴν τῶν
τοιούτων παθημάτων κάθαρσιν.

The ethical result of tragedy, the purification of the passions, whether the κάθαρσις is used in religious, medical, or· other analogy, goes accordingly hand in hand with its intellectual significance. Art, like philosophy, presents the actual in its ideal purity (*Poetics*, 9, 1451 b, 5), and is more than the mere facsimile of individual facts, as the ἰστορία presents them. This conception of the universal significance annuls the emotions of fear and sympathy through which tragedy has to operate.

The long strife over the meaning of the Aristotelian definition of tragedy has gradually resolved itself into the belief that the healthiness which this κάθαρσις brings with it rests upon this idealizing of the æsthetic result, — upon an exaltation to immediate knowledge of the universal.

Thus Aristotle fulfilled upon this territory, in contrast to the greatest poetic performances of his nation, the task of its philosophy, which is no other than the attainment of *the self-consciousness of Hellenic culture*.

B. HELLENIC-ROMAN PHILOSOPHY

44. If in the philosophy of Aristotle the essence of Greek civilization was reduced to conceptual expression, yet it appeared when the sun of Greece was setting. The philosophy of Aristotle was the legacy of dying Greece to the following generations· of man.

The spiritual decay of the Grecian civilization at the time of its Enlightenment had advanced in ever-widening circles, and from then on led to its external destruction. Already, since the conclusion of the Peloponnesian war, which destroyed forever the vitality of Athens, the centre of Greek culture, the influence of the Persian power in the politics of Greece had been dominant. Moreover, out of this lamentable situation Greece got freedom only through subjection to the Macedonian kingdom. Likewise in the succeeding time Greece in intermittent and inconsequential movements could only occasionally stagger to an independence amid the vicissitudes of the Hellenic kingdoms, especially of Macedonia. Finally, however, it entirely lost its political independence by its being incorporated into the Roman Empire, in order to save here and there a wretched respectability.

But precisely through its political decadence Greece fulfilled in a higher sense the problems of its civilization. The kingly pupil of the ripest Greek philosopher had borne the victorious Greek spirit into the far East with his conquering arms. In the enormous mingling of the peoples, which was begun by his campaign of conquest and furthered by the varying battles of his successors, did Greek culture become the common possession of the ancient world, and finally the commanding spirit of the Roman Empire, and the eternal possession of humanity.

After the creative period of Greek philosophy there followed, therefore, centuries of criticism, appropriation, readjustment, and remodelling. This second section of the history of ancient thought is incomparably much poorer in content, although covering a longer period of time. Every conceptual principle for comprehending and judging reality had been presented by Greek science in its youthful inspiration. There only remained for the epigones to see their way clearly in their variously animated world, to employ the previously discovered points of view in every possible way, to combine the inherited thought, and to make this combination fruitful for the purposes of the new situations of life.

The very little originality which the Hellenic-Roman philosophy shows in contrast to Greek philosophy is true even of neo-Platonism, its most significant intellectual phenomenon. In all the independence which its religious principle seemed to give to it, neo-Platonism remained inextricably bound to the thought of Plato and Aristotle.

From the *critical point of view*, which is the authority for the divisions of this survey, Hellenic-Roman philosophy appears to be only a gleaning of Greek philosophy. It is only the " after-effects " (Brandis) of Greek philosophy in the Hellenic and Roman realms. Among these after-effects the great systems of Stoicism and Epicureanism are to be reckoned, not only because they took root and blossomed in those times when the divisions between Greek and barbarian began to break down, but especially also for these two reasons : (1) because they, though with great refinement in details, represented in general only a new distortion of the old principles which the original development of Greek thought, until Aristotle, had gained ; (2) because they made this distortion in a typical manner from the new points of view of *individual practical wisdom*.

On the whole, the second section of this history is less important to philosophy than to the history of civilization and literature. This is a natural result of the fact that in this period the literary sources, although very far from pure, are nevertheless very much richer. Therefore on this account this period is extraordinarily rich in interesting, difficult, and various problems still unsolved, although its product of philosophical principles and fundamental concepts is relatively small.

With this relative deficiency in originality we note the appearance in the post-Aristotelian philosophy of the great school-associations, with their wholesale scientific productions, rather than of single personalities. It is true, detailed research also here betrays individual shadings in the construction of single theories, although often indeed seen with difficulty and not with full certainty ; yet such variations stand in value and significance far behind the great and general antagonisms of the school systems. Moreover, such antagonisms are much less those of scientific theory than those of the conception of life and its conduct.

The post-Aristotelian philosophy showed, therefore, the peculiar phenomenon of the practical convictions of different schools existing in sharp conflict, while the peculiar scientific differences became gradually obliterated. Scientific activity was turned to special researches, and found neutral ground partly in nature studies, partly in history, especially the history of literature. Upon this neutral ground, although with a certain agreement in fundamental conceptions and methods, the representatives of the different schools were in active rivalry. This ardent cultivation of the special sciences had the most universal results of Greek philosophy for its obviously valid fundamental principles, and interest in metaphysical problems passed more and more into the background. Erudition pressed out the spirit of speculation. The special sciences became independent.

The beginning of this specialization in science already existed in the Abderite, the Platonic, and particularly the Aristotelian schools. In the Hellenic period specialization was, however, the more remarkable because the period was wanting in great determining personalities and organizing fundamental principles. This popular impulse for specialization was limited neither to Athens nor to Greece. Rhodes, Alexandria, Pergamus, Antioch, Tarsus, etc., became scientific centres, in which scholarly work by means of great libraries and collections was being systematically carried on. Later Rome, and finally also Byzantium, entered into the competition.

That now, however, the conflict between the schools was no longer waged over theoretical but practical philosophy, was due not only to the fact that Aristotle had given the final word to the speculative movement, but also to the changing character of the times and the changing philosophical demands. The more the Greek national life and spirit faded through the universal mixing of nations and their destinies, so much the more the individual retired within himself and away from the changing external world. From the great maelstrom of things he sought to save as much as possible of inward peace of mind and sure happiness, and to secure them within the quiet of his individual life. This, then, in Hellenic time is what was expected from philosophy : it should be the director of life ; it should teach the individual how to be free from the world and to stand independent by himself. The determining, fundamental point of view of philosophy became that of *practical wisdom.*

The Greek Enlightenment showed tendencies in this direction in the teachings of Socrates, especially, however, in the teachings of the Cynics and Cyrenaics, which expressed through their atomistic principles the dismemberment of Greek society (see § 29 f.). Opposed to this the great systems of Greek science, especially Platonism and Aristotelianism, had maintained the higher thought with the essential political tendency of their ethics. The post-Aristotelian philosophy even in the schools of both masters turned to the ethics of the individual. The antagonisms that developed between them concerned fundamentally only their subtleties and the enriched developments of the simple types which Greek life in its bloom had brought forth.

While then the essence of Greek philosophy was exclusively directed to a unified conceptual knowledge of the world, the science of the succeeding centuries divided (1) into specialization into single branches, for which methodical bases had been established ; and (2) into a philosophy which made all knowledge an ancillary maiden to the art of living, and was concerned entirely in setting up an ideal of a perfect, free, and happy man. This art of living still retained the name of philosophy, and it is only this side of the scientific life of antiquity which is to be followed out further in this place.[1]

Individualistic ethics, which the post-Aristotelian schools made the burden of their philosophy, was virtually called to restore to the cultured world of antiquity the religion lost in the Greek Renaissance. Its fundamental problem [2] was on this account the release of man from the power of the outer world and the vicissitudes of life. But virtue, as the Stoics and Epicureans taught it, did not prove adequate to be the solution of this problem; thus philosophy also became drawn into the great religious movement which had possessed the races of the Roman Empire. In that movement the terrified mind seized upon all kinds of religious forms and cults, and eagerly pressed on to a saving conviction. The more this tendency became predominant in philosophy, and the more philosophical interest passed from ethics to religion, so much the more did Platonism, the specific religious form of philosophy, come into the foreground. Its transcendent metaphysics, its separation of the material and immaterial worlds, its teleological principle, which regarded the life of nature and man with reference to a divine cosmic purpose, made it seem called to give scientific form to the amalgamation of religions. Its concept of the world was equal to absorbing the religious forms of the Orient. It gave the philosophic material with which Christianity, the new religion, constituted itself into a didactic system. Out of it the Hellenic world tried, finally, to create its own religion as the daughter of science.

[1] For the development of the special sciences since Aristotle one should consult the respective parts of this manual.

[2] See K. Fischer. *Gesch. der neueren Philos.*, I. (2 ed., Mannheim, 1865), p. 33 f.

This gradual transmutation of ethics into religion divided the Hellenic-Roman philosophy into two parts (see above, Introduction); in the former of which the ethical interest predominated; in the latter, the religious interest; Syncretic Platonism made the transition. The controversies between the schools and their adjustment in Skepticism and Eclecticism, preceded the transition period. Patristics on the one hand, and neo-Platonism on the other came after this transition.

1. The Controversies of the Schools.

45. The development of the Peripatetic school took a similar course to that of the Academy (§ 38). It had in fact, at first, its significant centre in the person of the old friend and coadjutor of its founder; to wit, in Theophrastus. Theophrastus knew how to direct the activities of the school, how to inspire the development of the sciences in the true spirit of the master, and how to give to the Lyceum an eminent position in the intellectual life of Athens through the brilliancy of his lectures. Yet for him in his recasting and supplementation of the Aristotelian doctrine, and also for the majority of his associates, the empirical outweighed the philosophical interest, and so more and more the school tended to the specialization of scientific work. Thus Theophrastus developed the science of botany especially; Aristoxenus, the theory of music; Dicæarchus, historical sciences. History seems to have taken the most space in the scientific work of the school. Literary-historical and scientific-historical work were especially carried on in this and the succeeding generations of the Peripatetic school, and to such a degree that this school is designated as the unique centre of the above very learned but little creative spirit.

The ethical questions, also, were treated by all these men, and especially by Eudemus, more particularly upon their empirical side and with reference to popular morality. On the other hand, however, the ethical questions were subordinated to a theological interest, in which metaphysical demands seem to have been centred. Influenced doubtless by Platonic and Pythagorean doctrines, Eudemus inclined to emphasize the transcendence of the divine Being, and in a similar manner to maintain the speculative psychology of Aristotle with the transcendence ($\chi\omega\rho\iota\sigma\mu\acute{o}\varsigma$) of the reason. There was another tendency, which, beginning with Theophrastus, ran counter to the above, and developed the principle of immanence, both metaphysically and psychologically. This tendency grew to a thoroughgoing pantheism and naturalism in the person of Strato, who from 287 to 269 followed Theophrastus as head of the school.

When Strato explained the concept of pure Form metaphysically and psychologically as unnecessary and equally as impossible as that of pure matter, he practically identified God and the world on the one hand, and on the other thought and perception. The whole world-system and all particular events therein are only explainable by the qualities and forces in things under the law of mechanical necessity. Warmth is the most important force among these, both in the macrocosm and in the microcosm. The soul is the unifying reasoning power ($\mathring{\eta}\gamma\epsilon\mu o\nu\iota\kappa\acute{o}\nu$), and it has the senses as its organs. Thus the activity of sensation is never complete without thought. Thought, however, on its side is limited to the given perceptual content.

The theory of Strato seems to be, on the whole, a victory for the Democritan element that was in the Aristotelian doctrine, although in particular assertions Strato approaches very near the Stoic philosophy.

W. Lyngg, *Die peripatetische Schule* (in *Philosophische Studien*, Christiania, 1878) ; H. Siebeck, *Die Umbildung der peripatetischen Naturphilosophie in die der Stoiker* (*Unters. z. Philos. d. Gr.*, 2 ed., 181–252).

Theophrastus, from Eresus in Lesbos, was about twelve years younger than Aristotle. He probably got acquainted [1] with Aristotle in the Academy, and he remained a lifelong friend to the Stagirite. He shared the residence of Aristotle after the latter bade adieu to the Macedonian court, and was his right-hand man in the administration of the Lyceum. Theophrastus afterwards assumed the conduct of the Lyceum himself, and directed it with the greatest success. An attempt to drive the philosophical schools out of Athens (306 B.C.) seems to have failed solely by reason of the respect in which he was held (F. A. Hoffmann, *De lege contra philosophos imprimis Theophrastum auctore Sophocle Athenis lata*, Carlsruhe, 1842). There have been preserved of his numerous works (list in Diog. Laert., V. 42 ff.) the two botanical works, περὶ φυτῶν ἱστορίας and περὶ φυτῶν αἰτιῶν, — of the greatest importance, since the corresponding works of Aristotle are lost, — certain fragments of his metaphysics, of the history of physics, besides some minor treatises. The ἠθικοὶ χαρακτῆρες, a description of moral failings based on many observations, are a selection from the ethical work of this philosopher. These are published by J. G. Schneider (Leipzig, 1818); Fr. Wimmer (Breslau, 1842–62); a portion of the metaphysics in Chr. Brandis' *Separat-ausgabe der aristotelischen* (Berlin, 1823), p. 308 ff. ; also newly published by H. Usener (Bonn, 1890); *Characters*, Dübner (Paris, 1842) and E. Petersen (Leip., 1859); Philippson, ὕλη ἀνθρωπίνη (Berlin, 1831); H. Usener, *Analecta Theophrastea* (Bonn, 1858); the same in XVI. volume of *Rhein. Mus.;* Jac. Bernays, *Th.'s Schrift über die Frömmigkeit* (Berlin, 1866); H. Diels, *Dox. Gr.*, p. 475 ff. ; E. Meyer, *Gesch. der Botanik*, p. 164 ff. ; Th. Gomperz, *Ueber die Charactere Th.'s* (*Wiener Sitz.-Ber.*, Berlin, 1888).

The naturalism of Theophrastus seems to be expressed in his subsumption of thought under that of motion (κίνησις), although he did not materialize the concept in the Democritan manner. The dubious consequences, that followed for the Aristotelian concept of God, seem to have been expressly deduced first by Strato.

The significance of Theophrastus lies in the realm of science, and it is to be regretted that only few fragments of his history of natural science have been preserved (φυσικὴ ἱστορία). On the whole he contented himself with the perfecting of the Aristotelian system, and he probably remained its most complete representative. The results in logic also, which he reached

---

[1] Diog. Laert., V. 36.

with the aid of Eudemus, concerning the modality of the judgment and the theory of the hypothetical syllogism, are only of minor importance.

Eudemus of Rhodes seems to have been a man of less significance, although he also possessed encyclopedic knowledge and wrote extensive works, later widely used, on the history of geometry, arithmetic, and astronomy. Spengel has collected the fragments of Eudemus' writings (Berlin, 1870). See A. Th. H. Fritzsche, *De Eudemi Rhodii vita et scriptis* (Regensburg, 1851, in connection with the edition of the ethics). His theological bias likewise appears to some degree in his elaboration of the Aristotelian ethics. His departure from its fundamental political idea is seen in his insertion of economics between ethics and politics.

Aristoxenus of Tarentum was stimulated by the Pythagorean doctrine, which he carried into psychology and ethics. He is especially notable in the field of the history and theory of music. Besides the fragments, there has in particular been preserved his writing, περὶ ἁρμονικῶν στοιχείων, published by P. Marquardt (Berlin, 1868), translated into German, with annotations by R. Westphal (Leipzig, 1883) ; see W. L. Mahne, *De Aristoxeno* (Amsterdam, 1793) ; C. v. Jan (Landsberg a. W., 1870). The fragments of the historical works of the Peripatetics in general have been published by C. Müller, *Fragmenta historicorum græcorum*, II. (Paris, 1848).

Apostasy from the theoretic ideals of Aristotle began to appear already in Dicæarch of Messene, in his preference for the practical life which was of interest indeed to the historian and political theorist. From his numerous works in political and literary history, among which the βίος Ἑλλάδος is the most important, and also from his Τριπολιτικός, only small portions have been preserved. M. Fuhr, *Dicæarchi quæ supersunt* (Darmstadt, 1841) ; F. Osann, *Beiträge*, II. (Cassel, 1839).

The more original genius, Strato of Lampsacus, was called "the physicist," and this shows how actually independent he became of Aristotle. He threw aside all the Platonic immaterialism that Aristotle had retained, — the pure spirituality of God and the supersensible origin and character of the human reason. Even if he thereby threw away the keystone of the Aristotelian teleology, Strato was, on the other hand, opposed to the Democritan mechanical atomism. He found the explanation of the world in the inherent qualities and forces (δυνάμεις) of particular things. He designated the fundamental forces (ἀρχαί) as heat and cold. Of the two, heat plays the more important and creative rôle. The renewal of the old Ionic modes of repre-

sentation is thus completed in the Peripatetic school, and it also
at the same time found expression among the Stoics. It was
a return characteristic of the time of the epigones. G. Rodier,
La physique de Strato d. Lamp. (Paris, 1891).

In the following generations the Peripatetic school became completely absorbed, so far as we know, in the
specialized investigations of Alexandrian erudition, in which
its champions played an important rôle. Under Andronicus
of Rhodes, the eleventh head of the school after the founder,
the school made a great effort for philosophical autonomy.
The publications of Andronicus marked the beginning of a
systematic reproduction, interpretation, and defence of the
original teaching of Aristotle. This activity continued then
through the following centuries, and found in Alexander
of Aphrodisias (200 A. D.) its most distinguished representative. The activity was maintained to later time, until
the Peripatetic school was lost in neo-Platonism.

A great number of names of Peripatetic philosophers have
come down to us from the company around Theophrastus and
Strato, as well as names of some of both the nearer and the
more remote pupils of the latter. These latter have in the
main no longer significance for us: Clearchus of Soli (M.
Weber, Breslau, 1880), Pasicles of Rhodes, who was presumably the author of the second book of the *Metaphysics*, Phanias
of Eresus (A. Voisin, Gant., 1824), Demetrius of Phalerus
(Ch. Ostermann, Hersfeld, 1847, and Fulda, 1857), Hipparchus
of Stagira, Duris of Samos, Chamæleon of Heraclea (Köpke,
Berlin, 1846) ; Lyco of Troas, who succeeded Strato (269–226)
as head of the school, whose successor was Aristo of Ceos ;
Aristo of Cos, Critolaus, who belonged[1] to the embassy to
Rome, 155 B. C. ; and, finally, Diodorus of Tyre.
From the works of the Peripatetics dealing with the history of
literature and the specific history of philosophy, the βίοι of Hermippus and Satyrus (200 B. C.), the Διαδοχαὶ τῶν φιλοσόφων of
Sotion, and the abstract of the last by Heracleides Lembus
(about 150) deserve especial mention. The later writers, who
form our secondary sources, have drawn upon these works.

---

[1] Cicero, *Acad.*, II. 45, 137 ; see Wiskemann (Hersfeld, 1867).

The serviceable work of Andronicus was further carried on
chiefly by his pupil, Boëthus of Sidon, nevertheless in a spirit
akin to that of Strato and the Stoics. The later exegetes,
like Nicolaus of Damascus, and later Aspasius, Adrastus, Her-
minus, Sosigenes, held rather to the logical writings of Aristotle.
A comprehensive, philosophical, and competent appreciation
and exposition of his teaching is first found in the commentaries of Alexander of Aphrodisias, " the exegete." Among his
commentaries those upon the *Analytics prior I.*, *Topics*, *Mete-
reology*, *De sensu*, and especially the *Metaphysics* have been
preserved. The last is in the Bonitz edition (Berlin, 1847).
See J. Freudenthal, *Abhandl. der Berl. Akad. d. Wiss.*, 1885.
In his own writings (περὶ ψυχῆς — περὶ εἱμαρμένης — φυσικῶν καὶ
ἠθικῶν ἀποριῶν καὶ λύσεων, et al.), he defends his naturalistic interpretation of Aristotle, especially against the Stoics.

46. The most important scientific system that the Greek
epigones developed was Stoicism. Its founder was Zeno of
Citium, a man perhaps of Semitic or half-Semitic origin.
Captivated but not satisfied by the Cynic Crates, he listened
in Athens also to the Megarian Stilpo, and the Platonists
Xenocrates and Polemo. After long preparation he opened
his school in the Στοὰ ποικίλη in the last decade of the
fourth century, and from this place his society got its name.
His countryman, Persæus, as well as Cleanthes of Assus,
who was Zeno's successor as scholarch, Aristo of Chios,
Herillus of Carthage, and Sphærus from the Bosphorus, are
named among his pupils. These from a philosophical point
of view stand far behind the third head of the school,
Chrysippus of Soli in Cicilia, who was really the chief
literary representative of the school. Among his numerous
followers there appeared later Zeno of Tarsus, Diogenes of
Seleucia, a Babylonian living in Rome in 155, and Antipater
of Tarsus. In connection with the Stoic school, Eratosthe-
nes and Apollodorus stand among the great scholars of the
Alexandrian epoch.

For a general history of the Stoa, see Dietr. Tiedemann, *Sys.
der stoischen philos.* (3 vols., Leipzig, 1776); F. Ravaisson, *Essai
sur le Stoïcisme* (Paris, 1856); R. Hirzel, *Untersuchungen zu*

304   HISTORY OF ANCIENT PHILOSOPHY

Cicero's philos. Schriften (2 vols., Leipzig, 1882) ; G. P. Wey-
goldt, *Die Philos. der Stoa nach ihrem Wesen und ihren Schick-
salen* (Leipzig, 1883); P. Ogereau, *Essai sur le système philos. du
Stoïcisme* (Paris, 1885). The chief source for the older Stoics,
whose original literature is nearly entirely lost, is found in Diog.
Laert., VII., who breaks off in the midst of an exposition of
Chrysippus. His statements go back in substance to Antigonus-
Carystius (see U. v. Wilamowiz-Möllendorff, Berlin, 1881).

The Stoa was characterized as the typical philosophy of Hellenism, from the fact that it was created and developed in Athens
on the principles of Attic philosophy, and by men that originated
in the mixed races of the East. Likewise, it was of great moment
for the general progress of the world that this particular doctrine
was afterwards extended and most vigorously developed in the
Roman Empire.

Zeno of Cition, the son of Mnaseas, 340–265 — for the difficult chronology see E. Rhode and Th. Gomperz, *Rhein. Mus.*,
1878 f. — was a merchant whose residence in Athens was perhaps
occasioned by a shipwreck. He entered the different schools,
and co-ordinated their teaching with painstaking care. His
writings (see list of Diog. Laert., VII. 4) deal with the most
varied subjects, yet their form is not remarkable. See Ed.
Wellmann, *Die Philos. des Stoikers Zeno* (Leipzig, 1873) ; C.
Wachsmuth, *Commentationes* I., II. *de Zeno Citii et Cleanth.
Assio* (Göttingen, 1874) ; A. C. Pearson, *The Fragments of
Zeno and Cleanthes* (London, 1890).

N. Saal, *De Aristone, Chio et Herillo Carth. commentatio*
(Cologne, 1852); H. Heinze, *Ariston v. Chios bei Plutarch
und Horaz*, and O. Hense, *Ariston v. Chios* (*Rhein. Mus.*, 1890,
497 ff. and 541 ff.).

Cleanthes, who is said to have performed menial work by
night in order to listen to Zeno by day, is in his simplicity,
perseverance, and austerity a type of the Cynic Wise Man, but
he is insignificant as a philosopher. His hymn to Zeus is
preserved and published by Sturz-Merzdorf (Leipzig, 1835).
See F. Mohnike, *Kleanthes der Stoiker* (Greifswald, 1814).

The scientific systematizer of the Stoic doctrine is Chrysippus
(280–206), a copious writer of great dialectic ability. The
titles of his writings are listed in Diog. Laert., VII. 189 ff.
See F. N. G. Baguet, *De Chrisippi vita doctrina et reliquiis*
(Loewen, 1822) ; A. Gercke, *Chrysippea* (*Jahrb. f. Philol.*,
1885). For further information, see Zeller, IV³. 39, 44, 47 f.

A second period of the Stoic philosophy, in which it
made a nearer approach to the Peripatetic and Platonic

teaching, began in the middle of the second century B. C. with Panætius of Rhodes, who introduced Stoicism into Rome. Boëthus of Sidon worked beside him, animated by a similar spirit. After him his pupil Posidonius, of Apamea in Syria, directed the school in Rhodes with great success.

Panætius (180–110) won in Rome the friendship of men like Lælius and Scipio Africanus the Younger, and accompanied the latter on his mission as ambassador, in 143 to Alexandria. He became scholarch in Athens later. He brought the Stoa into great repute and made its success assured in Rome. This success was promoted by his forming Stoicism into a kind of philosophy of universal culture for the needs of the Roman Empire. He ameliorated its original severity, he accommodated it to other great systems, he expressed the system itself in a clever and tasteful way. His chief writing, according to Cicero, was περὶ τοῦ καθήκοντος. See F. G. van Lynden (Leyden, 1802).

His contemporary [1] Boëthus of Sidon partially followed the doctrine of Strato and Aristotle in theology and psychology. The eclectic tendency appeared still stronger in Posidonius (135–150). He was listened to with delight by the aristocratic Roman youth in Rhodes, where after extended journeys he had settled as head of the school. See J. Bake, *Posidonii Rhodii reliquiæ doctrinæ* (Leyden, 1810) ; P. Töpelmann, *De Posidonio Rh. rerum scriptore* (Bonn, 1867) ; R. Scheppig, *De Posidonio Apamensi, rerum, gentium, terrarum scriptore* (Berlin, 1870) ; P. Corssen, *De Posidonio Rhodii. M. T. Ciceronis in libr. I. Tusc. auctore* (Bonn, 1878). In his comprehensive erudition and many-sided interests, Posidonius is the most successful representative of syncretism, that blending of Stoic, Platonic, and Aristotelian doctrines. He is also the most important of those who prepared the way for the Alexandrian philosophy. A thorough examination of his work in detail seems to be the most important and most difficult desideratum for the history of Hellenic philosophy.

For a list of the Stoics of this period, see Zeller, IV[3]. 585 ff. See A. Schmekel, *Die Philos. der mittleren Stoa* (Berlin, 1892).

During the time of the empire, Stoicism became merely a popular moral philosophy ; but even in this condition it joined together the noblest convictions of antiquity in an

[1] Zeller, IV[3]. 46, 1.

impressive form and manner, and it directed the moral feeling along religious paths. Seneca, Epictetus, and Marcus Aurelius appeared as its chief representatives at this time.

Lucius Annæus Seneca, son of the rhetorician M. Annæus Seneca, was born about 4 A. D. in Cordova. He was educated in Rome and called to different offices of state. He was the teacher of Nero, and condemned to death by his pupil in 65 A. D. He has expressed most completely the monitory character of later Stoicism in his sententious writings, — to which the name of scientific researches cannot be unqualifiedly applied. Besides his unimportant *Quæstiones naturales*, there are preserved *De providentia*, *De constantia sapientis*, *De ira*, *De consolatione*, *De brevitate vitæ*, *De otio*, *De vita beata*, *De tranquillitate animi*, *De clementia*, *De beneficiis*, and the *Epistolæ morales*. Also in his strongly declamatory tragedies there is involved this same conception of life. Complete sets of his works are published by Fickert (3 vols., Leipzig, 1842–45) and Haase (3 vols., Leipzig, 1852 f.); German translation by Moser and Pauly (17 vols., Stuttgart, 1828–55), English translation or paraphrase by T. Long (London, 1614); see Holzherr, *Die Philos.*, *L. A. Seneca* (Tübingen, 1858 f.); Alfr. Martens, *De L. A. Senecæ vita et de tempore quo scripta eius philosophica composita sint* (Altona, 1871); H. Siedler, *De L. A. Senecæ philosophia morali* (Jena, 1878); W. Ribbeck, *L. A. Seneca der Philosoph u. sein Verhältniss zu Epicur*, *Plato u. dem Christenthum* (Hannover, 1887). Further in the history of the bibliography, see Ueberweg, 244 f., especially for the writings ✓cited elsewhere about his relationship to Christianity, of which the most important are edited by F. Chr. Baur, *Seneca und Paulus* (1858), printed in three dissertations and published by Zeller (Leipzig, 1875).

The satirical poet Persæus, the erudite Heracleitus, and L. Annæus Cornutus, who systematically developed the allegorical significance of myths in a theological writing, are mentioned among the many names of Stoics, and in particular, C. Musonius Rufus, who confined himself more closely to the practical teaching of virtue. Compare P. Wendland, *Quæstiones musonianæ* (Berlin, 1886).

His pupil is Epictetus, the notable slave of a freedman of Nero. He later became free himself, and lived in Nicopolis in Epirus, when the leaders in philosophy were proscribed by Domitian. His lectures were published by Arrian as Διατριβαί and ’Εγχειρίδιον, and in modern times by J. Schweighäuser (Leipzig, 1799 ; in the appendix is the commentary of Simplicius to the Encheiridion, 1800). See J. Spangenberg, *Die Lehre des Epiktet* (Hanau, 1849) ; E. M. Schranka, *Der Stoiker Epictet u. seine Philos.* (Frankfort a. O., 1885) ; R. Asmus, *Questiones Epicteteæ* (Freiburg, 1888) ; H. Schenkl, *Die epikteteischen Fragmente* (Vienna, 1888) ; A. Bonhöfer, *Epictet u. d. Stoa* (Stuttgart, 1891).

The last significant expression of the Stoic literature is the *Meditations* (τὰ εἰς ἑαυτόν) of the noblest of Roman emperors. Marcus Aurelius Antoninus (121–180). These are edited by J, Stich (Leipzig, 1882), and translated into German by A. Wittstock (Leipzig, 1879) [English translation by G. Long, Bohn’s Library, *The Thoughts of the Emperor, M. Aurelius Antoninus*]. See A. Bach, *De M. Aurelio imperatore philosophante* (Leipzig, 1826) ; M. E. de Suckau, *Étude sur Marc Aurèle, sa vie et sa doctrine* (Paris, 1858) ; A. Braune, *M. Aurel’s Meditationen* (Altenburg, 1878) ; P. B. Watson, *Marcus Aurelius Antoninus* (London, 1884).

The more Stoicism took to moralizing, the more did its Cynic inheritance begin to preponderate. Thus, in the first and second centuries after Christ, Cynicism revived in the persons of those wandering preachers who went from city to city in the costume of the philosopher with obtrusive inconsiderateness and in affectation of beggary. They were eccentric figures, but are of more interest to the student of history than of science. The chief types are Demetrius, a contemporary of Seneca ; Oinomaus of Gadara ; particularly, however, Demonax, concerning whom we have information in a writing, reported under Lucian’s name (see also F. V. Fritsche, *De fragm. Demon. philos.*, Rostock and Leipzig, 1866), and Perigrinus Proteus, whose extraordinary end has been pictured by Lucian. See J. Bernays, *Lukian u. die Kyniker* (Berlin, 1879).

Stoicism, as originally presented, especially by Chrysippus, was a perfectly well-rounded scientific system, which gradually grew lax in some particular doctrines, and finally vanished into a philosophically colorless moralizing. Yet it must be admitted that from the very beginning it was wanting in such organic coherence of its parts as one finds in the separate Greek philosophical systems. In the teaching of Zeno and Chrysippus a number of the elements of the earlier sciences are closely interwoven without making the texture logically necessary and consistent. The Eclectic development, then, which the Stoic school took, was not a fate that came to it from without, but the necessary consequence of its inner constitution.

However many analogous relations may exist between the different parts of the Stoic teaching, yet one must not make the mistake of thinking that its ethical teaching of submission to natural law might not have been as compatible to an idealistic metaphysic as to its materialism. It is, moreover, equally certain that the Stoics' anthropological principle of the identity of the human soul and the divine reason might have been placed at the basis of a rationalistic theory of knowledge, just as well as at the basis of their sensualism and nominalism. The theories of the Stoa are not an organic creation, but woven together with care and cleverness. They make a well-connected system, but are not homogeneous. They could afterwards, therefore, be separated with relative ease.

The scholastic division of philosophy into logic, physics, and ethics was likewise especially distinct among the Stoics. The main point in their teaching lies in their ethics. To teach virtue as the art of living was for them the entire purpose and essence of philosophy. Virtue was conceived by them entirely in its practical meaning of right action. Only so far as this definition of virtue was identical with the Socratic " correct knowledge," did the first division, ethics, need the other two divisions, logic and physics, for its basis.

The development of special sciences corresponded so little with the originally established general relationship of the three divisions, and the Stoic logic and physics stood in such loose connection with its ethics, that it is perfectly conceivable how Aristo, a member of the school standing at first close to pure Cynicism, should estimate these collateral subjects of ethics as useless. It is not remarkable, either, that the physical and logical doctrines of the old Stoa were changed for others and then laid entirely aside. The care with which physics and logic were pursued in the old Stoa in contrast with ethics shows rather that the scientific interest of the school had not been fully lost. To this interest, which was expressed in the numerous special works — particularly the historical — Herillus com-

mitted himself, when he declared science in the Aristotelian
sense to be the highest good.

G. J. Diehl, *Zur Ethik des Stoikers Zeno* (Mainz, 1877) ; F.
Ravaisson, *De la morale du Stoïcisme* (Paris, 1850); M. Heinze,
Stoica ethica ad origines suas relata (Naumburg, 1862) ; Küs-
ter, *Grundzüge der stoischen Tugendlehre* (Berlin, 1864) ;
Th. Ziegler, *Gesch. der Ethik.*, I. 167 ff.

The central point in Stoicism is the Ideal of the Wise
Man. Stoicism drew its picture of the normal man after
the model of Socrates and Antisthenes. It was its fundamental motive to picture the perfect man in absolute freedom from the changes of this world. This ideal was
consequently first defined negatively as the independence of
will and conduct from the passions (*Affekte*). This apathy
(emotionlessness) of the Wise Man consists in his refusal
to submit (συγκατάθεσις) to the excess of natural impulse, from which excess the passion springs. This refusal makes up the judgment of worth and the functioning
of the will. The Wise Man feels impulse, but he does not let
it grow into a passion, and he regards the exciting object as
neither a good nor an evil. For to him virtue is not only the
highest but the only good, and in this he is a true Cynic.

M. Heinze, *Stoicorum de affectibus doctrina* (Berlin, 1861) ;
O. Apelt, *Die stoischen Definitionen der Affekte und Poseido-
nius* (Jahrb. f. Philol. 1885).

One must regard it as a result of the ethical psychology of
Aristotle, that the Stoics so turned the Cynic unity of virtue
and knowledge that they found the essence of passion in the
judgment of worth, inasmuch as this judgment is immediately
identical with feeling and willing. To desire, and to regard
something as a good, are two expressions for the same thing.
The excess of impulse (ὁρμὴ πλεονάζουσα) leads the powers of the
soul (ἡγεμονικόν) into false judgment, and at the same time to a
reasonless and unnatural excitement (ἄλογος καὶ παρὰ φύσιν ψυχῆς
κίνησις), and in this very thing consists the excitement, πάθος (*per-
turbatio*). The Stoa distinguished four fundamental kinds of
unnatural excitement : pleasure, trouble, desire, and fear. They
and their subordinate classes were treated as diseases from
which the Wise Man is free, for he has true health.

Since the passions consist in false judgments and mental disturbance, so the virtue of the Wise Man, positively defined, consists in reasonable insight and the resulting power of will.   Virtue is the reason determining itself theoretically and practically (*recta ratio*).   Whether man will let loose this or that passion in himself, depends on him.   That is to say, the matter is not determined by external events, but through his own inner nature.

" Nature " (φύσις), which, according to the fundamental principle of the Stoics, is identical with reason (λόγος), forms the content of insight, and obedience to insight constitutes virtue.   By " Nature " is meant partly the universal nature of things, partly human nature.   While passion is unnatural and unreasonable, the Wise Man acts naturally and reasonably when he makes his will to agree with the universal law of nature, and when he subordinates himself to that law.   But in this subordination he is only acting as the reason of man requires.   The ethical principle of the Stoa was *obedience to the world law*, and in this way it possessed a religious coloring.

The ethical dualism of the Stoics, with its contrast between nature and what is contrary to nature, and with its identification of reason and nature, goes back to the Sophistic Enlightenment. It avoided, however, the sharpened Cynic antithesis between civilization and nature.   It rather referred what is contrary to nature to the preponderance of the individual impulse, and it characterized the natural as reason dwelling in each and all alike.   The latter thought, which led to the conventional religious principle of subjection to the world-reason, is an obvious revival of the logos doctrine of Heracleitus.

The possibility of unnatural and unreasonable phenomena, as they are supposed to appear in the passions, is absolutely irreconcilable with the metaphysical development of the Stoics' doctrine, and with their idea of fate and providence.   Their ethical dualism and metaphysical monism stand in absolute contradiction.   This difficulty came to the Stoics in the form of the problem of the freedom of the will and the responsibility of conscience.   These are ethical postulates whose union with mechanical necessity made difficulties for them, and difficulties that were solvable only in appearance. In respect to these difficulties they had to defend themselves against the attacks of Epicurus and Carneades.

In designating the ὁμολογουμένως τῇ φύσει ζῆν as the positive content of virtue, and in representing at the same time the cosmic universal law as " Nature," the Stoic lacked a principle of morals that had real content. Consequently, on the one hand in the Stoic school, human nature was substituted for φύσις, — at all events, according to Chrysippus, with reference to its unity with the world reason. On the other hand, the purely formal character of the consistency and of the harmony of the reason was accentuated (simply ὁμολογουμένως). In this sense, suggestive of the " categorical imperative," was Stoicism accepted by the iron statesmen of Rome. Nevertheless, in the Stoic metaphysics, the formula of subjection to the world reason remained an empty form which found its living content first in the Christian doctrine of love.

The Stoics were little able to make theoretically clear their antithesis of the reasonable and the unnatural, yet they rendered the service of introducing into moral philosophy the principle of duty by the accentuation of this antithesis, and by defining virtue as subjection to cosmic law ; and furthermore of having laid a greater stress upon the antithesis between that which is and that which ought to be. Wholly consonant with this is the pessimism which they for the most part held concerning the great mass of mankind and the circumstances of life.

The Socratic concept of virtue, that the Stoa held, concentrated into practical insight (φρόνησις) the whole of moral life, and allowed the existence of a plurality of virtues only in the sense of the application to many objects of this single fundamental virtue of insight. In this way, for instance, the four Platonic cardinal virtues were derived. Yet herein the Stoic clung to the thought of the unity of virtue to such a degree that all the particular forms of virtue exist in inseparable union. They form not only the enduring characteristic (διάθεσις) of the Wise Man, but they also animate his every action.

The unity and perfectness, which the Stoics like the Megarians and Cynics regarded as essential in the concept of virtue, and in the ideal of the Wise Man, led them in the first thoroughgoing statement of their system to say that this ideal is reached either entirely or not at all. In neither goodness nor badness are there degrees of ethical value.

Men are either good (σπουδαῖοι), or bad (φαῦλοι). and to
the latter belong all who do not attain the ideal of wisdom.
It makes no difference whether they be near to it or far
from it. They are all fools, — spiritually sick. Thus for
the older Stoics all virtuous actions (κατορθώματα) were
ethically of equal value, and likewise all sins (ἁμαρτήματα).
With the same rigorism the Stoics declared virtue as the
only good, vice as the only evil, and all between as (ἀδιάφορα) indifferent things.

The last definition led to many serious consequences in applied ethics in which the Stoics agreed with the Cynics, although,
it must be said, in theory more than in practice. Since the
Stoics assessed the disposition ethically, they therefore made the
Wise Man indifferent in principle to external conventional forms
of performance or non-performance. In their theory of goods,
they made a polemic attack, especially against the Peripatetic
recognition of the importance which the goods of fortune were
supposed to have for perfect happiness. Especially prominent
is their treatment of life as an ἀδιάφορον, which theoretically and
practically represented suicide as permissible for the Wise Man.

This rigoristic dualism could not last long, and so the
school gradually inserted the striving, earnest man
(προκόπτων) between the Wise Man and the fool, and the
fitting action (τὸ καθῆκον) between virtue and sin. The
school distinguished in the great interval which lies between
the highest good and the evil, the προηγμένα from the
ἀποπροηγμένα.

On the whole, the Stoics are the most outspoken doctrinaires
that antiquity witnessed. The Stoa was a school of character
building and also a school in reckless stubbornness (Cato). In
the development of the school there entered with the different
individuals many varieties and compromises of doctrine according to impending practical needs. These changes kept pace
with the approach of the school to the teaching of the Lyceum
and the Academy. Thereupon the perfectly unpedagogical
character was gradually stripped off, which the representation
of the ideal of the Wise Man originally had, and in its place in
later times came the reverse and admonitory teaching, how one
should become a Wise Man.

Κατόρθωμα, the conduct of a Wise Man, coming from a good disposition, and καθῆκον, the activity of the ordinary ambitious man adjusted to external requirements, stand somewhat in the relationship which modern ethics marks between morality and legality. The setting up of this distinction shows how the realized ideal of the Wise Man was making way to the more modest ambition of approximating that ideal.

The individualistic tendency expressed in the ideal of the self-sufficient Wise Man, is counterbalanced by the concept of the subordination of the individual to the cosmic law and the society of rational beings. The Stoics recognized, therefore, the social needs of man as natural and reasonable. They saw the realization of those needs simply on the one side in the friendship of individual Wise Men, and on the other in the rational communion of all men. Whatever lies between — that is, the national life in its different political forms — passed for them more or less as of historical indifference (ἀδιάφορον). The Wise Man bows to this as a temporal necessity, but he holds aloof from it as far as possible. Historico-national distinctions vanish before that reason, which gives equal laws and equal rights to all. *The point of view of the Stoic Wise Man was that of the cosmopolitan.*

For the remarkable synthesis of individualism and universalism which characterized the Stoa, it is to be noted that the school soon passed in its social theory from individualism to the most general principle of association. The later Eclectic Stoics in particular were concerned with the theory of the state, and followed Aristotle in many things. But the ideal of the school remained still the citizenship of the world, the fraternity of all men, the ethico-legal equalization of all distinctions of condition and race. From this thought proceeded the beginnings of the idea of natural or reasonable right, which later were laid as fundamental in the scientific theory of Roman right.[1] They reflect in theoretical form the levelling of those

---

[1] See M. Voigt, *Die Lehre vom jus naturale*, etc. *bei den Römern* (Leipzig, 1856) to p. 81 ff.

historical distinctions, which was completed for antiquity about the beginning of this era, and thus show Stoicism to be the ideal philosophy of the Roman Empire.[1]

To this ethical teaching there was joined in a most re-markable manner an outspoken materialistic metaphysics. The monistic tendency, expressed in the metaphysics, was united with the ethical principle, and was developed in an open polemic against the Aristotelian dualism. Uncreative themselves, the Stoics accepted the naïve materialism of the pre-Socratic philosophy in the form of Heracleitanism. They expressly taught that nothing is real except the corporeal. They, however, recognized, in regard to the relationships of individual things, the Aristotelian duality of a passive and an active principle, a moved matter and a moving force ($\pi\acute{a}\sigma\chi o\nu$ and $\pi o\iota o\hat{\nu}\nu$). They give to the unifying cosmic force all the characteristics of the Heracleitan $\lambda\acute{o}\gamma o\varsigma$ and the Anaxagorean $\nu o\hat{\upsilon}\varsigma$. But they emphasize particularly the materiality of this reasonable cosmic force.

In their confessed materialism, the Stoics went nearly to the childish consequence of looking upon all qualities, forces, and activities of bodies as again themselves bodies which were supposed to inhere spatially in the first bodies ($\kappa\rho\hat{a}\sigma\iota\varsigma$ $\delta\iota'$ $\ddot{o}\lambda\omega\nu$). This reminds us in some measure of the homoiomeriai of Anaxagoras. The Stoics also regarded time *quanta* and the like, as bodies — assertions that show nothing more than the doctrinaire wilfulness of the authors. See H. Siebeck on the subject.

The Stoics, like Heracleitus, found in fire the unifying cosmic force, which is God, — which is changed by its own inner rational law into the world. They conceived fully that fire was the identity of the corporeal primeval matter and the rational spirit, and in this way they fell back from

---

[1] Cicero especially (*De rep.* and *De leg.*) developed the Stoic thought of the $\phi\acute{\upsilon}\sigma\epsilon\iota$ $\delta\acute{\iota}\kappa\alpha\iota o\nu$ as the *lex naturæ* born in all men ; but also he has attempted to be just to the historical moments of jurisprudence. See K. Hildenbrand, *Gesch. u. System der Rechts- u. Staatsphilos.*, I. 523 ff.

the dualism of the time of the epigones to the naïvely vague monism of the previous time. Fire is therefore on the one hand the original corporeal substrate, the ἀρχή of the Milesians. On the other it is the primeval spirit, the world-soul, the reason moving and forming all things, permeating and governing, like a divine living breath (πνεῦμα), the entire world of phenomena proceeding from it. It is indeed the creative world-reason, the λόγος σπερματικός.

Fire has differentiated air, water, and earth from itself at the beginning of things, so that the two more volatile elements stand as the active and forming principle, in contrast to the two heavier as matter. In the cosmic development the primitive fire is destined gradually to reabsorb the world of variety into itself, and will finally consume it in a universal catastrophe (ἐκπύρωσις). The complete cosmic cycle is so perfectly determined in all particulars by the divine Being that it is exactly repeated periodically. In so far as the Godhead acts like a body under the law of mechanical necessity, is this absolute determination of the movements of all individuals Fate (εἱμαρμένη). In so far as it acts as a purposeful spirit it takes on the garb of Providence (πρόνοια), and the Stoic evidently means by this that nature can yield only perfect and teleological forms and relationships.

In all this we do not meet new concepts or new ways of stating facts. The Heracleitan principle is combined with the Platonic and Aristotelian concepts without being scientifically more serviceable. No scientific contribution worthy of the name can be found among the Stoics. In particular cases, as in astronomy, the Stoics join themselves in essentials with the Peripatetics. On the whole, in their treatment of these questions, they show a relapse from the inductive science of Aristotle to the old metaphysics.

The pantheistic character of this conception of nature led the Stoic to a nature religion, which at the same time is a religion of reason. A characteristic monument to this is the hymn to

Zeus of Cleanthes (preserved in Stob. *Ecl.*, I. 30). In the same spirit they made the most comprehensive use of the allegorical interpretation of myths. Teleology was so connected with this interpretation, and was so attenuated to a small anthropomorphic spirit in praise of the arrangements useful for human needs, that it anticipated to a great degree the tasteless philosophy of the eighteenth century. The great ethical principles of the Platonic and Aristotelian philosophy diminished in the hands of the Stoics to a miserable utilitarian theory, which was the more characteristic the less it found a point of support in the Stoic doctrine of goods.

It is of particular interest to note how the Stoics began to work a positive religion into their natural religion; for they treated, by the use of the nature-myth interpretation, the gods and dæmons of the popular faith as special forms of the original divine force. They came in this way to a systematic theology of polytheism, and they subjoined to it their widely accepted theory of divination, based on the principle of a universal teleology.

The pantheism and determinism in Stoicism stood finally in absolute contradiction with its ethical dualism. The former was as optimistic as the latter was pessimistic. That everything bad happens παρὰ φύσιν was treated as ethically fundamental, although according to their metaphysical principle it was impossible. This contradiction seems to have come in some measure to the consciousness of some of the Stoics. In response to the sharp attacks of their opponents, particularly of Carneades, it was the occasion for evasions tending toward such questions as the reconciliation of evil with a divine omnipotence, which we have later designated as theodicy. On the one hand, the Stoics attempted to disclaim the reality of evil, and then on the other to make sin and suffering the teleologically indispensable parts of the good and perfectly organized universe.

The anthropology of Stoicism was consistent with its universal physical postulates. The body, teleologically put together out of crass elements, is permeated through and through, and in all its functions ruled by the soul. The soul is the warm breath (πνεῦμα ἔνθερμον), which, as an emanation of the divine soul of the world, forms the unitary, living guiding force of man (τὸ ἡγεμονικόν). It constitutes his reason; it is the cause of his physiological functions, of his speech, of his imagination and desires; and it has its seat in the breast.

Ludw. Stein, *Die Psychologie der Stoa* (2 vols., Berlin, 1886–88).

The essential identity of the human and divine soul (taught also by the pre-Socratics) was carried out by the Stoics, especially on ethical and religious lines. The analogy seemed suitably drawn between the relation of the human soul to its body, and the divine reason to the universe.

The Stoics consistently ascribed to the soul of man no absolute immortality. At the most they gave to it a permanence until the ἐκπύρωσις, the absorption of all things in the divine. Yet some Stoics reserved this last privilege only for the souls of the Wise, while the φαῦλοι were dissipated both in soul and body.

In the Stoic anthropology, as in their entire system, the fundamental contradiction was this : their theoretic doctrine allowed to appear as mechanically necessary that very rationality which according to their ethical postulate was requisite to the formation of the ideal, so that the actual incompleteness of the ideal is inconceivable. From this is explained the fact that the whole theoretic philosophy of the Stoa was subjected to the point of view of that insight which guides the perfectly Wise Man in his conduct. The same contradiction showed itself in the Stoic epistemology, where the emanation from God (ἔμφυτον πνεῦμα) was represented as a *tabula rasa*. The *tabula rasa* does not already possess its rational content, as one would expect from this teaching, but wins its content gradually by the action of the senses.[1]

We must go back to the Cynic opposition to the Academy to understand how the Stoics can combine a sensualistic and nominalistic theory of knowledge with their doctrine of a cosmic reason. The Stoics sought in their nominalism, even as extrinsically as in their ethics, to give to their fundamental principle of individuality the concept of universal validity, — a validity from which they could in neither situation escape. The soul is originally like a tablet of wax, on which nothing is written, and in which ideas (φαντασίαι)

---

[1] There was therefore an easy union possible with Stoic metaphysics, when the later eclectic popular philosophy (Cicero) said that knowledge, particularly that of practical truths, was God-implanted, universal to humanity, and equally innate.

appear through the influence of things.   Every original
idea is an impression (τύπωσις) on the soul, or a change in
it — as Chrysippus said, in order to refine this crude materialism.   On that account this idea always refers to particular things or conditions.   Concepts (ἔννοιαι) are, however,
pictures aroused by memory and the reasoning faculty
rendered possible by the memory.   They are purely subjective, and, therefore, nothing actual corresponds to
them, as in the case of the perceptions.   Yet the Stoa
vaguely tried to find in them the essence of all scientific
knowledge.[1]

Concepts originate in perception, in part involuntarily
from the very necessity of the mental mechanism, in part
with conscious premeditation.   The former are a natural
production, and are common to all alike (κοιναὶ ἔννοιαι).
This class is therefore to be regarded as the norm of rational knowledge, and as the valid *presupposition* (πρόληψις).
In this sense the *consensus gentium* plays a great rôle
in Stoic argumentation, especially in ethics and religion.
For the *consensus gentium* is a common property of concepts
existing for all men with equal necessity.

As regards the scientific construction of concepts, the
Stoics busied themselves with great, and, for the most part,
very unfruitful formalism in their detailed study of the
Aristotelian logic.   They combined this study with that of
grammar.   In treating of the hypothetical character of
logical truth, which they emphasized especially in their
theory of the syllogism, they needed a criterion of truth for
those original Ideas, from which the logical work of thought
is supposed to proceed.   They found such an one only *in
immediate evidence*, according to which single Ideas force
themselves upon the soul and compel its assent (συγκατάθεσις).   An idea of this sort they called φαντασία καταλη-

---

[1] See Zeller, IV[3]. 77 ff.

πτική.[1] They found it either in clear and certain perception or in the κοιναὶ ἔννοιαι.

R. Hirzel, *De logica Stoicorum* (Berlin, 1879); V. Brochard, *Sur la logique du Stoïcisme* (*Arch. f. Gesch. d. Philos.*, V. 449 ff.).

Under the collective name of logic, which they first employed in the study of terms, the Stoics grouped grammatical and rhetorical studies. They — especially Chrysippus — investigated many grammatical problems, and decided a great many of the questions of fact and terminology for more than for antiquity. Compare Lersch, *Die Sprachphilosophie d. Alten* (Bonn, 1841); Schömann, *Die Lehre von den Redeteilen, nach den Alten dargestellt u. beurteilt* (Berlin, 1863); Steinthal, *Gesch. d. Sprachwiss. bei d. Griechen und Römern* (Berlin, 1863).

Concerning the formal logic of the Stoics, see C. Prantl, *Gesch. d. Log.*, I. 401 ff. When the Stoics distinguished studies concerned with the criterion of truth from those concerned with correct syllogistic method, they transmuted the Aristotelian logic into a purely formal science. They were stranded, however, in empty sophistry, which was unavoidable in such a limited conception. The Aristotelian analytic always is the frame on which they stretch out their artificial system with its unnecessary terminological changes. They have added nothing significant. Even in their simplification of the theory of the categories Aristotle himself had preceded them. They recognized only the following four categories: ὑποκείμενον, ποιόν, πῶς ἔχον, πρός τι πῶς ἔχον: substratum, quality, condition and relation. See A. Trendelenburg, *Gesch. der Kategorienlehre* (Berlin, 1846), p. 217 ff.

The distinction of involuntary, universal ideas that enter the mechanism of representation, from those formed with scientific consciousness (Lotze, *Logik*, 1874, § 14), has psychological and logical value, but its epistemological use by the Stoics is an unhappy one. They also, however, according to their ethical principle, first ascribed full certainty to science as a system of fully developed concepts: Diog. Laert., VII. 47; Stob. *Ecl.*, II. 128.

See W. Luthe, *Die Erkenntnisslehre der Stoiker* (Leipzig, 1890).

47. With less philosophical originality, but with a greater degree of unity and compactness, Epicureanism was the

---

[1] Of the difficulty with this term, — the comprehension of the actual from the side of the spirit, or the comprehensibility of the spirit from the side of what is actual, see Bonnhöfer, *Epiktet und die Stoa*, p. 288 ff.

form in which the Cyrenaic conception of life found development just as Stoicism was the development of Cynicism.
In contrast, however, to the multiform eclecticism which
characterized the Stoa in the persons of many of its active
scientific champions through the centuries, Epicureanism
was born mature in its founder as a complete method of
living. Its numberless disciples in all antiquity changed
it scarcely more than in its unessentials.

Consequently, apart from Epicurus himself, who founded
the school in his garden in Athens in 306, there are no
independent thinkers of the school to be named. We may
name some literary representatives: Metrodorus of Lampsacus, the friend of the founder; Colotes of the same city;
Zeno of Sidon (100 B. C.); Phædrus, whom Cicero heard
in Rome about 90 B. C.; Philodemus of Gadara and more
especially the Roman poet Titus Lucretius Carus.

See P. Gassendi, *De vita, moribus et doctrina Epicuri* (Leyden,
1647); G. Prezza, *Epicuro e l'Epicureismo* (Florence, 1877);
M. Guyau, *La morale d'Epicure* (Paris, 1878); P. v. Gizycki,
Ueber das Leben und die Moralphilosophie des Epikur (Halle,
1879); W. Wallace, *Epicureanism* (London, 1880); R. Schwen,
Ueber griech. u. röm. Epicureismus (Tarnowitz, 1881).
As original sources, besides what is left by Epicurus, there
are the didactic poem of Lucretius, *De rerum natura* (edited by
Lachmann, Berlin, 1850, and Jac. Bernays, Leipzig, 1852), and
the writings found in Herculaneum, particularly of Philodemus:.
Herculanensium voluminum quæ supersunt (first series, Naples,
1793–1855, second since 1861). Compare D. Comparetti, *La
villa dei Pisoni* (Naples, 1879); Th. Gomperz, *Herkulanen-
sische Studien* (Leipzig, 1865 f., *Wiener Sitzungsberichte*, 1876,
1879). Secondary antique sources are Cicero (*De finibus* and
De natura deorum), Seneca, and Diogenes Laertius, B. 10.
Epicurus was born 341 in Samos of an Athenian of the deme-
Gargettos. His father seems to have been a school-teacher.
Epicurus grew up in simple circumstances. He had read some
philosophers, especially Democritus, and perhaps also listened
to some of his older contemporaries in Athens. But he had not
at any rate enjoyed a thorough education, when, having tried
his hand as a teacher in Mytilene and Lampsacus, he afterwards

founded his school in Athens, which was later named after the garden in which it was held (οἱ ἀπὸ τῶν κήπων; *horti*). His teaching was opportune, easily understood, popular, and in harmony with the spirit of the time. It is thus explicable how he found wide acceptance equally with the more serious schools of science. Owing to his personal charm, and because he did not make so high and strict demands either upon the life or thought of his auditors as others made, he became greatly esteemed as the head of the school. As such he worked until his death in 270. He wrote much,[1] only a little of which has been preserved. Of the thirty-seven books of περὶ φύσεως only two were found in the Herculanean library ; (published by Orelli, Leipzig, 1818.) In addition three didactic letters and the κύριαι δόξαι, besides many more or less extensive fragments, have been found. H. Usener has published a notably complete and orderly collection, excepting the two books περὶ φύσεως by the name *Epicurea* (Leipzig, 1887).

Epicurus' confidant and celebrated colleague, Metrodorus, died before him. See A. Duening, *De M. Epicurei vita et scriptis, cum fragm.*, Leipzig, 1870, Alfr. Körte, *Metrodori fragm.*, Leipzig, 1890). The headship of the school passed directly then from Epicurus to Hermarchus. From that time on, numerous pupils and heads of the school are mentioned (see Zeller, IV³. 368–378), but seldom in such a way as to lead us to know their distinction as philosophers. We know Colotes from the treatise which Plutarch aims against him, as the champion of the school ; Zeno and Phædrus from the reports of Cicero ; also Philodemus, whose works in part were found in Herculaneum. See the literature in Ueberweg–Heinze, I⁷. 264 f., especially H. v. Arnim, *Philodemea* (Halle, 1888).

Especially at Rome, where C. Amafinius (middle of second century, B. C.) had first naturalized Epicureanism to a considerable degree, the theory found many supporters, and most of all in its poetical presentation in Lucretius (97–54). See H. Lotze, *Quæstiones Lucretianæ* (Philol., 1852) ; C. Martha, *Le poème de Lucrèce* (Paris, 1873) : J. Woltjer, *L. philosophia cum fontibus comparata* (Gröningen, 1877).

Concerning the development of the school, see R. Hirzel, *Unters. zu Cicero's philosophischen Schriften*, I. 98 ff.

The ethics of Epicurus was a reproduction of hedonism (§ 30) in a form riper in so far as the more youthful freshness of the Aristippan doctrine of sense-pleasure made way

---

[1] See Diog. Laert., X. 26 ff.

for deeper reflection, such as already existed among the later Cyrenaics. The limitation of philosophy to *a search for the means of attaining individual happiness* was most boldly expressed by Epicurus, and was developed utterly regardless of every other interest, especially of science. Science and virtue are nothing that should be prized in themselves. They have worth only as indispensable means for the attainment of pleasure, and pleasure is the natural and obvious goal of every desire.

Pleasure is not only positive pleasure in the narrower sense which arises out of a motion that satisfies the need (ἡδονὴ ἐν κινήσει). It is the more valuable pleasure of *painlessness*, which goes with the state of more nearly perfect rest [1] (ἡδονὴ καταστηματική), a state consequent upon the satisfaction of wants. The latter affords doubtless a certain pleasure, but perfect happiness (μακαρίως ζῆν) can be found only in a state in which every want is absent. Happiness is health to the body and repose (ἀταραξία) of the soul: δικαιοσύνης καρπὸς μέγιστος ἀταραξία.[2]

Epicurus showed his deficiency in scientific training in the ambiguity of his expressions, and in his lack of logical clearness. His deficiency also appears in his disdain of all theoretical occupations. He had no appreciation of scientific investigations which serve no use. Mathematics, history, the special natural sciences were closed to him. The theory of pleasure that he called ethics, strictly included his entire philosophy. Physics, which had a determined ethical task to perform, and was pursued only so far as it performed it, was only ancillary; and as a help in preparation for this, a little logic was deemed necessary.

It has given rise to much confusion, because Epicurus considered ἡδονή sometimes as a positive pleasure arising from the satisfaction of all want, and because he sometimes used the word in the more general sense when he meant the more valued ataraxy (ἀταραξία). The introduction of the latter idea probably can be traced back to Democritus. When the πάθη are designated as

---

[1] Olymp. in Plato's *Phileb.*, 274 (also Fr. 416).
[2] Clem. Strom., VI. 2 (also Fr. 519).

storms, and γαληνισμός as tranquillity (Diog. Laert., X. 83), we are reminded of the manner of expression of the great Abderite. This Epicurean ἀταραξία has only an outward resemblance to the Stoic apathy. The former is the virtue of ethical indifference to all passions; the latter is passionlessness, which is based upon the perfect satisfaction of all desire. On this account it was looked upon, both by Epicureans and Cynics, as acquired only through a limitation of desire.

Therefore Epicurus distinguished formally three classes of wants : natural and indispensable; natural and perhaps dispensable ; and finally, imaginary, which are neither natural nor indispensable. Without satisfying the first, man cannot live ; without satisfying the second, he cannot be happy ; the third are to be disregarded. Thus the opposition which the Cyrenaics urged between the natural and the conventional was taken up. Its strenuousness was diminished, however, in so far as the Epicureans gave a place to much in the second category, which the Cyrenaics were compelled to discard, because they recognized only the first category.

Feeling (πάθος) can only decide as to what exists in any particular pleasure. We need, in order to counteract this, to reflect upon the course of life, and to assess the different pleasures so as to bring out also their consequences.[1] Such an estimate is possible only through the rational insight, the fundamental virtue of the Wise Man (φρόνησις). This virtue was developed into different single virtues, according to the different problems to be assessed. Through it the Wise Man is able to estimate the different impulses according to their value for perfect satisfaction. He is able to appreciate expectations and fears at their true value, to free himself from illusionary ideas, feelings, and desires, and to find in the proper balance of enjoyment that serenity of soul which is allotted only to him.

The Epicurean ideal of the Wise Man is represented in nearly the same particulars as the Stoical Wise Man. The Wise Man is to the Epicureans also as free as the gods. By his reflective insight, rising superior to the course of

---

[1] Eus. *Præp. ev.*, 14, 21 (also Fr. 442).

the world and of external fate, he finds happiness only in
himself and in his virtue, which once acquired can never
be lost. Yet the Epicurean description is made in somewhat brighter colors than the Stoic, rather more pleasing
and more joyous. But even if they avoided the sombreness
of the Stoics, they were, on the other hand, rather lacking
in vigor: the Stoic feeling of duty was wanting, as were
both the submission of the individual to universal law and
the consciousness of responsibility. Epicurus prized, it is
true, spiritual above bodily satisfactions, because they are
better qualified to lead to the ideal of rest to the soul. Indeed, he recommended what he himself to a high degree
possessed, — a pure and noble morality, social refinement,
benevolence, and consideration toward all. But all this is
commended to us, because every kind of roughness of deport-
ment must appear to an educated Greek as inharmonious
with the æsthetic enjoyment of existence, which had become
to him a natural want. The wisdom of life of the Epicureans was æsthetic self-enjoyment. Their egoism became
delicate and refined, but nevertheless it was still egoism.

The concept of φρόνησις appeáred in Epicurus's theory almost
exactly as it appeared in that of Aristippus, only the matter of
measuring the consequences of particular pleasures is rather more
emphasized than in Epicurus. Merely upon this distinction of
consequences Epicurus founded his preference for spiritual pleasures over bodily pleasures, and not upon an original distinction
of worth. He insisted, in accordance with his sensualistic psychology, that the spiritual pleasures reduce in their simplest
terms to bodily (σάρξ)[1] pleasures.

The fundamental characteristics of the ethical atomism of
Epicurus are shown most clearly in his treatment of social
relations. He recognized no natural community of mankind, but he treated all the mutual relations of individuals
(1) as those which depend upon the will of the individuals,
and (2) those which depend upon a rational consider-

[1] *Athen.*, XII. 546 (also Fr. 409).

ation of useful consequences. He regarded these human relations not as higher powers, but only as self-chosen means for individual happiness. In this spirit he dissuaded the Wise Man from entering upon marriage, because it threatens him with care and responsibility. So also he recommended avoidance of public life. He regarded the state as a union [1] that has arisen out of the need of mutual protection, and created by the rational reflection of the individuals. The functions of the state are conditioned in their entirety by the point of view of general utility. This purpose of law brings about certain universal principles as everywhere necessary, but law takes a variety of forms of single laws under different circumstances.

Friendship is the only social relationship worthy of the Wise Man. It rests indeed, too, upon the calculation of mutual usefulness. Among wise and virtuous men, however, it rises to a disinterested communion, and in it the happiness of the individual reaches its zenith.

It is thoroughly characteristic of the Epicurean conception of life, for its social ideal to be a purely individual relationship, viz., friendship. Friendship was particularly cultivated in this school, and in connection with its view of the Wise Man friendship easily got an insipid character of mutual admiration. The λάθε βιώσας is the reverse side of it, wherein indifference to political interest and responsibility, the selfish isolation of the individual, decay of national loyalty, is raised to a principle. With this egoistic withdrawal into private life, Epicureanism became the "common sense" philosophy of the Roman world. For the strongest basis of despotism is that desire for enjoyment with which every individual seeks in the quiet of his own life to save as much individual comfort as possible out of the universal confusion.

The utilitarian politics of Epicurus has also its germ in that of the Sophists. Yet Epicurus seems to have been the first to carry politics out consistently, and thus also to have developed

---

[1] Diog. Laert., X. 150 (from the κύριαι δόξαι): τὸ τῆς φύσεως δίκαιόν ἐστι σύμβολον τοῦ συμφέροντος εἰς τὸ μὴ βλάπτειν ἀλλήλους μηδὲ βλά-πτεσθαι.

the leading principle of political compact (συνθήκη). It was by
the use of this theory that the Enlightenment of the seventeenth
and eighteenth centuries tried to conceive the state as the product of the selfish reason of individuals who were without a
state.   There was, therefore, for Epicurus such a thing as right
and wrong only where this sort of agreement about universal
utility takes place between individuals.[1] Lucretius has represented in a typical manner this supposed transition of man
from a state of savagery to a state of society (V. 922 ff.).

If the insight of the reason shall afford peace of soul to
the Wise Man, it accomplishes this principally by freeing
him through correct knowledge from all superstition, erro-
neous representations of the nature of things, and therefore
from all related idle fears and hopes which could falsely
determine the will.   In so far the insight is this φρόνησις,
being not only practical but theoretical in its purpose.   To
this end we need a physical view of the world which excludes all myths and miracles, all transcendent, religious,
supersensible, and teleological aspects. Epicurus finds such
a view in Democritus.

Compare Alb. Lange, *Gesch. des Materialismus*, (2 ed. Iser-
lohn, 1873, I. 74 ff., 97 ff.).   Familiarity with the theory of
Democritus is said to have been made possible to Epicurus
through Nausiphanes.   At any rate, it is the most significant
scientific influence which he experienced.   Yet he is far from
understanding and taking up into himself the body of thought
of the Democritan system.   He selected from the cosmology of
Democritus what appeared useful for his shallow pseudo-enlight-
enment, and he left untouched what was really philosophically
significant.   The identification of his physical and metaphysical
theory with that of Democritus has undoubtedly done the
most to hinder an earlier recognition of the scientific greatness
of Democritus.

The renewal of Atomism by Epicurus is betrayed in the
theory that nothing is real except the void and the atoms,
and that every event consists merely of the motion of the
atoms in empty space. Epicurus refused, however, to ac-

---

[1] κύριαι δόξαι, 32 f.; Diog. Laert., X. 150.

cept the fundamental thought of Democritus of the pure mechanical necessity of all motion. He replaced the originally irregular motion of the atoms in the absolutely directionless and boundless space, such as Democritus taught, by an originally uniform motion *from above* downward, which the senses appeared [1] to represent to him as absolutely given. This is *the rain of atoms*.[2] Since the intermingling of the atoms could not in this way, however, be explained, he asserted that single atoms arbitrarily deviated in a very slight degree from the direct fall. In consequence, collisions and vortices arose, from which the atom-complexes and finally the worlds came. Thus the cosmic theory of Epicurus again blended with that of Democritus and servilely followed it from this point on. Yet he depended on the theory of Democritus only in its most general characteristics of anti-teleology and anti-spiritualism. He took pains to explain that it is a matter of indifference how one answers particular scientific questions.[3]

That this gross representation of an absolute fall of the atoms is not of Democritan origin, but a new theory of Epicurus, can be safely accepted after the researches of Brieger and Liepmann; so also, Lewes, *Hist. of Philos.*, I. 101 ; Guyau, *Morale d'Epicure*, p. 74 ; Plutarch, *Plac.*, I. 3, 26 (*Dox.*, 285) ; Cicero, *De fin.*, I. 6, 17 ff. ; *De fato*, 20, 46 ff. When Lucretius (II. 225 ff.) made a polemic against the view that earlier was held as Democritan, which alleged that the collision of the atoms could be explained by the quicker fall of the heavier ones, he had in mind supposably the hypothesis of other Epicureans. These latter wished to proceed as determinists guided by the fundamental principle of the master, and this seems to have been at one time the inclination in the school. It is not, indeed, impossible that Epicurus in part used also this more mechanical method of explanation side by side with the acceptance of infinitesimal (ἐλάχιστον) declinations. (Cicero, *De fato*, 10, 22.)

Arbitrary self-deviation from the perpendicular fall — a theory with which Epicurus destroyed entirely the theory of Democ-

[1] Diog. Laert., X. 60.   [2] Lucre., *De rer. nat.*, II. 222.
[3] Diog. Laert., X. 87 ff.

ritus — is only the solution of a self-created difficulty.   That
Epicurus prepared for himself this difficulty is to be explained
from his anxious adherence to the truth of the senses.   The
way in which he explained it was suited to his ethical conception
of the metaphysical independence of the individual.   He made
the deviation of the atoms from the perpendicular fall analogous
to the voluntary activity of man.   He showed himself to be in
both cases the opponent of Democritus' leading idea of the
εἱμαρμένη.   (Cicero, *De fato*, 10, 23.)

This anti-teleological conception, which Lucretius especially
developed in details, and extended in an Empedoclean fashion
to the apparently teleological organic forms, seemed to the
Epicureans to be absolute deliverance from superstition.   They
spoke as little of natural religion as of positive religion.   On the
other hand, Epicurus developed a Democritan thought in order
to imagine blissful gods in the intermundia, the empty space
between the numberless worlds.   These gods, undisturbed as
they are in these worlds, appear in the eternal enjoyment of
their self-satisfying peace as a glorified actualization of the ideal
of the Wise Man who does not reach a state of perfection on
earth.

A gross sensualistic epistemology was joined to the
materialistic metaphysics of Epicurus.   The soul, whose
materiality and mortality he especially emphasized, receives
all the content of its ideas from sense perception.   Sense,
therefore, with its immediate evidence (ἐνάργεια) is the
only criterion of truth.   If concepts (προλήψεις) arise
through the aggregation of similar perceptions, and if out
of these upon reflection concerning the causes of phenomena, opinions (δόξαι) and accepted views (ὑπολήψεις) are
developed, the only criterion of their truth is in their repeated confirmation by perception.

The Logic of Epicurus, or, as he called it, the Canonic, is limited to such meagre definitions.   See Th. Tohte, *Epikur's Krite-
rien der Wahrheit* (Clausthal, 1874).   He purposely avoided the
theories of concepts and syllogisms.   In his school Philodemus
accomplished something in the scientific construction of the
hypothesis and the inductive method : see Fr. Bahnsch, *Des
Epicureers Phil. Schrift*, περὶ σημείων καὶ σημειώσεων, Lyck, 1879) ;
R. Philippson, *De phil. libro*, περὶ σημείων καὶ σημειώσεων *et Epi-*

cureorum doctrina logica (Berlin, 1881); P. Natorp, *Forschungen,* 209 ff. In the interest of this methodology which aimed at a theory of empirical knowledge, the later Epicureans merged with the younger Skeptics (§ 48). But in contrast to the outspoken positivism of the latter, the Epicureans held to the conviction that scientific concepts were formed to give us on the one side the probabilities of the imperceptible causes of phenomena (ἄδηλον), and on the other the expectations about the future (προσμένον) through the comparison of facts.

2. SKEPTICISM AND SYNCRETISM.

The strife concerning philosophical truth which waged fiercely between the four great schools, not only in Athens, but also in other intellectual centres, especially in Alexandria and Rome, necessarily presented to unprejudiced minds the skeptical question about the possibility and limits of human knowledge. This would certainly have happened, even if the question had not already come up in the earlier development of Greek philosophy, and if it had not remained a current opinion since the time of the Sophists. It is perfectly comprehensible that the skeptical way of thinking should be consolidated during these school-controversies, and in contrast with them should become more and more systematic. At the same time, however, skepticism succumbed to the universal spirit of the time, when it was brought into most intimate relations with the question of the wise way of living.

K. F. Stäudlin, *Geschichte. u. Geist des Skepticismus* (Leipzig, 1794-95); N. Maccoli, *The Greek Skeptics from Pyrrho to Sextus* (London and Cambridge, 1869); V. Brochard, *Les sceptiques Grecs* (Paris, 1887).

48. The first to perfect the system and ethics of Skepticism was Pyrrho of Elis, whose working years were contemporaneous with the origin of the Stoic and Epicurean schools. He seems to have confined himself essentially to personal instruction, while the literary champion of his

thought seems to have been his pupil, Timon of Phlius.
The doctrine of skepticism was of such a nature that no
school could form around it, and so it vanished with the
next generation from the field of literature.

Ch. Waddington, *Pyrrhon et le Pyrrhonisme* (Paris, 1877);
R. Hirzel, *Untersuchungen zu Cicero's philos. Schriften*, III. 1 ff.;
P. Natorp, *Forschungen*, 127 ff.
Concerning Pyrrho's life little is known. He lived from 365
to 275 approximately. That he was acquainted in his home with
the Elean-Eretrian school, the Megarian Sophism (§ 28), is
probable. It is very doubtful whether or not this happened
through the medium of Bryso, said to be the son of Stilpo.
A safer datum is that he joined the Alexandrian campaign with
the Democritan, Anaxarchus. He later lived and taught at his
home. No writings of his are known.
When one speaks of the school of Skeptics, it lies in the nature of the case that one does not mean an organized society for
scientific work, like the four others. Although moreover the
Greek historians here also speak of diadochi, yet for this as for
later time it must be remembered that only the most distinguished representatives of the skeptical manner of thought
($\dot{\alpha}\gamma\omega\gamma\dot{\eta}$) are meant. Among these Timon is of the first rank,
while the other names in the time succeeding Pyrrho (Zeller,
IV³. 483) are of no importance. Timon lived between 320
and 230 in Athens in his last years, and from his rich literary
activity are preserved particularly fragments of his $\sigma\dot{\iota}\lambda\lambda\omega$, in
which he derides the philosophers. See C. Wachsmuth, *De
Timone Phliasio ceterisque sillographis Græcis* with the fragments (Leipzig, 1859).

The direct derivation of Pyrrhonism from Sophistry
shows itself partly in its reliance on Protagorean relativism,
and partly in its reproduction of the Skeptical arguments
found in the Cynic and Megarian teaching. As regards
the relativity of all perceptions and opinions, Pyrrho asserted that if sense and reason were deceptive singly, no
truth could be expected from the two in combination.
Perception does not give us things as they are, but as
they appear in accidental relations. All opinions, not
excepting the ethical, are conventional ($\nu\dot{o}\mu\omega$), and not

of natural necessity. Therefore any assertion can be maintained against the opposite. Of contradictory propositions one is not more valid (οὐ μᾶλλον) than the other. We should on this account express nothing, but should withhold (ἐπέχειν) our judgment. Since we know nothing of things, things are also indifferent (ἀδιάφορα) to us. He that abstains from judgment is secure against a disturbed condition of mind resulting from mistaken views. The moral worth of the abstinence of judgment (ἐποχή) consists in the fact that it alone can produce equanimity (ἀταραξία), which is likewise the moral ideal of the Skeptics.

The equal emphasis on ἀταραξία by Epicurus and Pyrrho, accompanied by a most distinct disinclination to science, coincides with the idea of a common source of the two theories in the younger Democritans, Anaxarchus and Nausiphanes. But nothing is certain about it. That the Democritan view of the world rather than that of the teleological systems would necessarily further an ethical quietism, is plain. But the hedonistic tendency and the one-sided emphasis of the Protagorean relativism — which was subordinated in Democritus — may be characterized as a falling away from Democritus and a relapse into Sophism.

Even if the so-called ten tropes in which later Skepticism formulated its relativity of perception, should not be stated in this form in Pyrrho, nevertheless the Protagorean principle involved is current throughout his teaching. That he took pains to bring Skepticism into some sort of a system is to be seen from the division which Timon made, to wit, that there is a distinction between the constitution of things, our right relation to them, and the profit that we have to expect from them. That the last is the proper goal of the entire teaching is self-evident. The ἀταραξία is the happiness of the skeptic. The ἐποχή not only in the theoretical, but also in the practical sense is meant as the abstaining from judgment in general, also from judgment of worth, and therefore from desire and feeling. It reminds us of the Stoic apathy which was also a restraint of assent. In either case the ideal of the Wise Man is equally foreign to life, and a denial of life. The ἐποχή (called also ἀκαταληψία) was regarded as the central and characteristic concept of the system. Its adherents were designated on that account ἐφεκτικοί.

In this Skeptical theory it is of importance to note that the will is emphasized as a moment in judgment. The denial of the συγκατάθεσις (see p. 318) is possible only because affirmation or denial, as well in theoretic judgment even as in the approval or disapproval of natural feeling and impulse, is an act of will, and therefore ἐφ' ἡμίν. This is a theory common to Skeptics and Stoics. It is uncertain how far the former philosophers are dependent on the latter.

Skepticism took a scientific and practically more available form at the time when it temporarily succeeded to an ascendency over one of the great schools. Through Arcesilaus, who followed Crates as leader and died 241, it was introduced into the Platonic society, and maintained itself there for perhaps a century and a half, a period which is customarily called that of the Middle Academy. The most significant representative of the school at that time was Carneades of Cyrene, who died 129 B. C. after a long leadership.

From the entire Middle Academy only these two personalities distinctly appear. Neither seems to have left anything in writing. The theory of Arcesilaus was written down by his pupil and successor, Lacydes. Clitomachus, who died about 110, stood in the same relation to Carneades. We know about these two only indirectly, especially through Cicero, Sextus Empiricus, and Diogenes.

Arcesilaus (written also Arcesilas), born about 315 in Pitane in Æolia, had listened to Theophrastus and the Academicians. He also came under the influence of the Megarians, and probably of Pyrrho. He was notable, moreover, as a keen and witty orator. See A. Geffers, *De Arcesila* (Göttingen, 1841) ; *ibid., De Arcesilæ successoribus* (Göttingen, 1845).

In scientific significance and authority, Carneades towers above him. — Carneades, the great opponent of the Stoics, whose writings he had carefully studied, and in his brilliant lectures refuted. He appeared in Rome in the year 155 with the embassy of philosophers, and gave there a deeply impressive example of the *in utramque partem disputare* in his two discourses for and against justice. Compare Roulez, *De Carneade (Ghent,* 1824).

For the names of the above, see Zeller, IV³. 498, 523 ff.

The Academy Skeptics seem to have made the negative part of Pyrrho's theory their own, — and in the main

in unchanged form.   In using this negative doctrine in its
essentials in their polemic against the Stoics, they directed
their arguments chiefly against the theory of a criterion of truth.   In this respect Carneades took the lead
with his destructive dialectic by showing how little the
subjective moment of assent ($\sigma\nu\gamma\kappa\alpha\tau\acute{\alpha}\theta\epsilon\sigma\iota\varsigma$) is a safe
determiner of truth or falseness, and by investigating thor-
oughly the numerous difficulties of the theory of the
$\kappa\alpha\tau\alpha\lambda\eta\pi\tau\iota\kappa\acute{\eta}$ $\phi\alpha\nu\tau\alpha\sigma\acute{\iota}\alpha$ (ideas carrying conviction).   But
he also directed his attack against the guaranty of the
truth in logical reasoning.   He showed how every proof
demands a new proof for the validity of its premises,
which leads to an infinite regress, since there is no immediate certainty.

It is astonishing how little these Platonists seem to have
cared for the rationalism of their original school.   They did not
lead their rationalism into the field against the Stoic sensualism — nay, they even sacrificed it, for their radical Skepticism
holds rational knowledge impossible.   They did not seem expressly to confute rationalism, but they silently neglected it
as *passé*.   When it is said of Arcesilaus (Sextus Empiricus,
Pyrrh. Hyp., I. 234 f.) that he used skepticism simply on
the one side as a polemic and on the other as mental gym-
nastics, but within the innermost circle of the school he
held fast to Platonism, the statement is so far true that the
Academy took the skeptical arguments only as welcome instruments against the continuously pressing competition of the
Stoa.   But in doing so, nevertheless, the Academy became
estranged from its own positive teaching.   It is not impossible,
but perfectly probable, that even if the above were a fact in
regard to the leaders of the school, in the school itself the
Platonic tradition was kept alive as before.   The strength of
the polemic interest among the leaders is shown in Carneades,
who raised with these formal objections many practical ones
against the Stoics.   He combated particularly, and occasionally
with great acumen, their theology, teleology, determinism, and
theory of natural right.

In the Middle Academy the $\dot{\epsilon}\pi o\chi\acute{\eta}$ (see p. 331) is the result-
ant of these views.   Meanwhile Carneades and Arcesilaus

saw that the ἐποχή was impossible in practice.   In order to
act, man must consent to certain ideas, and if he renounces
truth, he must be satisfied with probability (εὔλογον, ἀληθὲς
φαινόμενον).   Neither ethical principles nor the knowledge
of single relations will bring undoubted certainty, but the
will is moved by indistinct and not fully evident ideas.
Therefore everything depends on judging correctly the
degree of probability of different ideas.   There are many
such degrees, three in particular.   The lowest degree of
probability is present in an idea that is plausible in itself
alone (πιθανή) ; the higher in such an idea as without contradictions can be joined to the whole body of ideas to
which it belongs (πιθανὴ καὶ ἀπερίσπαστος) ; the highest
is present in every individual of such a body of ideas when
all the parts have been tested as to their mutual congru-
ence (πιθανὴ καὶ ἀπερίσπαστος καὶ περιωδευμένη).

The content which Carneades gave to this practical probability is thoroughly consistent with the doctrine of goods
in the Older Academy.   The entire system therefore is an
attempt to destroy dogmatism through skepticism and to
found a system of morals for the Academy.

This fact, which indeed accorded with the spirit of the time, is
to be emphasized : — that the theory of probability of the Middle
Academy originated from an ethical, and not from a logical interest.   It was applied only to ethical questions.   This does not,
however, prevent our recognizing that Carneades, to whom we
particularly owe the development of this theory, proceeded in his
work in great part upon the basis of the Aristotelian topics,
and always with great acuteness.   The chief source is Sextus
Empiricus, *Adv. math.*, VII. 166 ff.

Later Skepticism disassociated itself from the Academy,
in which dogmatic eclectic tendencies became ascendant,
and was propagated especially in the circles of the medical empiricists.   The representatives of this theory were
Ænesidemus, Agrippa, and Sextus Empiricus.

Concerning the careers of these men there is little information.

See P. L. Haas, *De philosophorum scepticorum successionibus* (Würzburg, 1875) ; and E. Pappenheim, *Archiv f. Gesch. d. Phil.*, I. 37 ff., who puts the locality of the later Skepticism in " a city of the East, unknown to us." Ænesidemus of Cnossus taught in Alexandria, and wrote Πυρρώνειοι λόγοι, which he dedicated to the Academician L. Tubero, of which Photius prepared an abridgment still extant. If this Tubero was the friend of Cicero, one must put the activity of Ænesidemus at the latest in the middle of the first century, or a little earlier. This is, however, not fully certain. Zeller places him at the beginning of our era, and Macoll at 130 A. D. The calculations according to the Diadochi are doubtful on account of the uncertainty of the duration of the school of Skeptics. See E. Saisset, *Le scepticisme: Enésidème, Pascal, Kant* (Paris, 1867) ; P. Natorp, *Forschungen*, 63 ff., 256 ff.

We know about Agrippa only by the mention of his theory of the five tropes. The names only of many of the other Skeptics are preserved (Zeller, V³. 2 ff.).

Neither the native place nor residence of Sextus Empiricus (200 A. D.) is known. His writings, on the other hand, form the most complete body of skeptical theories. The Πυρρώνειοι ὑποτυπώσεις in three books are preserved, and also two other works, which are usually grouped under the title of *Adversus mathematicos*. Of these works, one (Books 1–6) treats of the science of general culture, of grammar, rhetoric, geometry, arithmetic, astronomy, and music ; the other (Books 7–11) criticises the logical, physical, and ethical theories of philosophers from a skeptical point of view. See E. Pappenheim, *De Sext. Emp. librorum numero et ordine* (Berlin, 1874) ; *ibid., Lebensverhältnisse des Sext. Emp.* (Berlin, 1875). The same author has also translated and annotated the sketches of Pyrrho (Leipzig, 1877); S. Haas, *Leben des Sext. Emp.* (Burghausen, 1883) ; *ibid., Ueber die Schriften des Sext. Emp.* (Freising, 1883).

This later Skepticism moved exactly on the general lines of the older, and it sought in vain to disown dependence upon the Middle Academy. It particularized the Protagorean objections to knowledge based on sensation, and, indeed, as appears first in Ænesidemus, there were considered ten so-called τρόποι. These are badly arranged, but have for their purpose partly the discussion of the relativity of the perceiving subject, partly that of the perceived object, and partly that of the relationship between the two. The five tropes presented by Agrippa are of more importance. To the theory of the relativity of perceptions ($\dot{o}$ $\dot{a}\pi\dot{o}$ $\tau o\hat{v}$ $\pi\rho\acute{o}s$ $\tau\iota$ $\tau\rho\acute{o}\pi os$), and to the conflict among opinions ($\dot{o}$ $\dot{a}\pi\dot{o}$ $\tau\hat{\eta}s$ $\delta\iota a\phi\omega\nu\acute{\iota}as$), he added the thought developed by Carneades, that proof demands either an endless regress from the premises ($\dot{o}$ $\epsilon\dot{\iota}s$ $\check{a}\pi\epsilon\iota\rho o\nu$ $\dot{\epsilon}\kappa\beta\acute{a}\lambda\lambda\omega\nu$), or presupposes unallowed and unproved premises ($\dot{o}$ $\dot{v}\pi o\theta\epsilon\tau\iota\kappa\acute{o}s$). He finally added that scientific method supports its proof upon assumptions which themselves could only be verified by the thing to be proved. These opinions of Agrippa led his followers to the reduction of the skeptical theory to two tropes. Knowledge would be possible either through immediate or mediate certainty; the former is not possible, because the relativity of all representations fails of a criterion, and the second would be possible only if it found its premises in the first.[1]

There is the mooted question whether among all the Skeptics Ænesidemus actually, as Sextus also seems to report, found in the general Sophistic theory of the $\dot{\iota}\sigma o\sigma\theta\acute{\epsilon}\nu\epsilon\iota a$ $\tau\hat{\omega}\nu$ $\lambda\acute{o}\gamma\omega\nu$, that is, that the affirmation and negation of every proposition can be equally well defended, a bridge to the reproduction of the metaphysical opinion of the reality of opposites. This would connect it with the Heracleitan thought, and Zeller seems to be decided (V[3]. 34 ff.) that the ancient reporters have made a mistake. See E. Pappenheim, *Der angebliche Heraklitismus des Ænesidemus* (Berlin, 1889).

The new tropes, which Agrippa introduced in a clever way, are arrayed especially against the Aristotelian theory of the $\check{a}\mu\epsilon\sigma a$, that is, of immediate certainty, and are closely allied to that doubt, which in modern times has been made by Mill against the syllogism. The difficulty is that the particular judgment, which is supposed to be based on the syllogism, is itself necessary for a basis of the general premise. (See Sext. Emp., *Pyrrh. hyp.*, II. 194 ff.; J. S. Mill, *Logic*, II. 3, § 2; Chr. Sigwart, *Logik*, I. § 55, 3.

Connected with the opinions of the empirical schools of physicians, who in denying all causal theories limited themselves entirely to medical observations ($\tau\acute{\eta}\rho\eta\sigma\iota s$), there is the more

[1] Sext. Emp., *Pyrrh. hyp.*, I. 178.

developed treatment, which the Skeptics since Æneseidemus bestowed upon the concept of causality, in discovering many dialectical and metaphysical difficulties. Relativity, the time relation between cause and effect, the plurality of causes for every event, the inadequacy of hypotheses which themselves demand causal explanation, etc., are among these difficulties. See C. Hartenstein, *Ueber die Lehren der antiken Skepsis* (*Zeitschrift f. Philos. u. philos. Kritik*, 1888, vol. 93).

49. The four great schools of philosophy which existed side by side in Athens — the Academy, Lyceum, Stoa, and the Gardens— made violent, nay, passionate war upon each other in the third and second centuries. Long afterward the opposition was so outspoken that after the time of Marcus Aurelius special chairs in the " university " of Athens were endowed by the government for them. Through this mutual contact the different theories were so far reconciled that in the first century before Christ the tendency appeared in these schools to emphasize less their disagreements, to render prominent their points of unity, and to unite them upon that common ground which exists in the most highly generalized ethics. The tendency appeared least of all in the Epicurean school, for that school was relatively stationary.

The Stoa was the first, in conformity to its original nature, to incline to such syncretic views. After the time of Panætius and Posidonius, it adopted into its teaching many Platonic and Aristotelian doctrines, while it tempered its ethical rigorism, and enriched its scientific interests. The teleological principle proved a most efficient cement, and on this account Epicureanism remained to a greater or less degree excluded from this syncretic process.

How far on the other hand the advances on the part of the Aristotelian school could be under the circumstances, the pseudo-Aristotelian writing περὶ κόσμου[1] shows. This

_____
[1] Published in the works of Aristotle, p. 391 ff.

was written probably by a Peripatetic, and supposably at the beginning of this era. It contained the interesting attempt at uniting Aristotelian theism and Stoic pantheism in a way that recognized the transcendence of the divine spirit, and derived the teleologically arranged world from its omnipresent creative power. It is to be noticed that this view gave to power a value independent of the divine spirit.

Compare the literature in Zeller, IV³. 631, 3, as well as the exposition following it; see also the same in *Sitzungs-Berichte* of the *Berlin Akademie*, 1885, p. 399 ff. Zeller regards as a mean between the Peripatetic and Platonic ethics (IV³. 647 f.) the pseudo-Aristotelian treatise περὶ ἀρετῶν καὶ κακιῶν.

To the discrimination between the transcendent essence and the immanent power of God, there is appended, in the writing περὶ κόσμου, a conception related to the Stoic theology. This is concerned with the degrees of divine power in which the peripatetic teaching of πνεῦμα forms the natural and philosophical link.

The union of the teleological systems that existed in later times seems to have been first announced in the Academy. In that school Philo of Larissa (87 B. C. in Rome) went from Skepticism to dogmatism when he asserted that in all the polemic expressions of the school teleology had always remained its esoteric teaching. But his representation of this teleology resembled genuine Platonism only in very slight degree. His more distinguished pupil, Antiochus of Ascalon, to whom Cicero was auditor in Athens in the winter of 79–78 B. C., championed the opinion that Platonism and Aristotelianism were only different aspects of the same thing, and that this thing also definitely reappears with some terminological changes in Stoicism.

J. Grysar, *Die Akademiker Philon und Antiochus* (Cologne, 1849) ; C. F. Hermann, *De Philone Larissæo* (Göttingen, 1851, 55) ; C. Chappe, *De Antiochi Ascalonitæ vita et doctrina* (Paris, 1854) ; R. Hoyer, *De Antiocho Ascalonita* (Bonn, 1883).

The Platonism of this third, or of the fourth and fifth Academies, is only to be found in its ethical teaching. Even Antiochus himself set aside the theory of Ideas, although he was much more energetic than Philo during the breach with the Skeptics of the school. Metaphysics and physics both remained in the background for these two men, and both epistemology and ethics were quite as Stoic as Platonic. The Alexandrians, Eudorus, Arius Didymus, and Potamo, are said to be continuers of the movement of Antiochus.

In their adoption of the Greek philosophy the Romans naturally gave to it a thoroughly eclectic form. When, after conquering their first aversion, they went into the school of Greek science, they went to it in their peculiarly practical way with the need for ethical orientation, and for that general culture in ethics such as a statesman might ask. Undisturbed by the technicalities and hair-splittings of the " controversies of the schools," they selected in the different systems what was suited to their needs. They completed this choice from the point of view that the truth must be found in a practically useful conviction illuminating all with its natural evidence. The probabilism of the Middle Academy and the Stoic teaching of *consensus gentium*, however, for the most part furnished the point of view, which may be called of the " healthy human understanding."

It was Cicero's merit to have given his countrymen a tasteful presentation of Greek philosophy in the above acceptation of the term. His friend Varro and the School of the Sextians, which flourished for a brief period at the beginning of this era, may be mentioned with him. Cicero, who was without independent philosophical significance, had great success in naturalizing the philosophical content of Greek thought in Latin literature, and in thus making it fruitful even beyond Roman civilization.

E. Zeller, *Ueber die Religion und Philosophie bei den Römern* (*Virch. Holtz. Vortr.*, Berlin, 1866); Durand de Laur, *Le mouvement de la pensée philosophique depuis Cicéron jusqu'à Tacite* (Paris, 1874).

The fear which the stricter Romans entertained that the new learning would undermine the traditional morals of society led to a decree of the Senate in 161 B. C. which banished philosophers and rhetoricians from Rome. But in the middle of this century the flow of Greek philosophy into Roman intellectual life began and went on uninterruptedly. At first the philosophic message came through the Greek teachers in Rome, then through the custom among the younger Romans of perfecting their education in the centres of Greek science, — in Athens, Rhodes, and Alexandria; and, doubtless, not the least of these influences was the embassy of Athenian philosophers, Carneades, Critolaus, and Diogenes (156–155 B. C.).

M. Tullius Cicero (106–43) had listened to Greek philosophers of all the schools in Athens and Rhodes, and he had read much, so that in his latter years, when he made Greek philosophy speak the Roman tongue (*römisch reden*), a rich material stood at his command. Out of this, without much scientific discrimination, but with tact for what was suitable for Rome, he brought his books together fairly quickly. Those preserved are: *Academica* (partly), *De finibus bonorum et malorum*, *Disputationes Tusculanœ*, *De officiis*, *Paradoxa*, *De amicitia*, *De senectute*, *De natura deorum*, *De fato* (imperfect), *De divinatione*, *De republica* (partly). Only fragments of *Hortensius*, *Consolatio*, *De legibus* remain. Cicero made no secret that he was essentially setting forth the Greek originals, and in many cases we can determine his sources. From the rich literature (see Ueberweg-Heinze, I⁷. 283 f.) we may mention A. B. Krische, *Forschungen*, Vol. I.; *Die theologischen Lehren der griechischen Denker, eine Prüfung der Darstellung Cicero's* (Göttingen, 1840); J. F. Herbart, *Ueber die Philosophie des Cicero* (1811, Complete Works, XII. 167 ff.); R. Kühner, *M. T. Cicero in philosophiam ejusque partes merita* (Hamburg, 1825); C. F. Hermann, *De interpretatione Timœi dialogi a Ciceronis relicta* (Göttingen, 1842); J. Klein, *De fontibus Topicorum Ciceronis* (Bonn, 1844); Th. Schiche, *De fontibus librorum Ciceronis qui sunt de divinatione* (Jena, 1875); K. Hartfelder, *Die Quellen von Cicero's De divinatione* (Freiburg i. B., 1878); especially R. Hirzel, *Untersuchungen zu Cicero's philos. Schriften* (3 vols., Leipzig, 1877–83).

In his epistemology Cicero adhered to the Middle Academy's teaching as the most moderate, elegant, and important method of philosophizing. Metaphysically he was a Skeptic, and was indifferent in the main to physical problems. Probability however did not satisfy him as an ethical criterion, but he appealed to the Stoic *consensus gentium* both in ethics and in the allied topics of natural religion, — that is, as to immortality, the existence of God, and providence. Nevertheless he conceived the κοιναὶ ἔννοιαι not in the sense of the Stoic προλήψεις (see p. 318), but rather as innate and natural, and therefore immediately certain convictions ; and his strength rests in a noble representation of these.

Likewise his friend, the learned M. Terentius Varro (116–27), made such a profound study of Greek philosophy as to enable him to distinguish two hundred and eighty-eight Greek sects. He found the suitable synthesis of these in the eclecticism of Antiochus of Ascalon, to which he, in the spirit of Panætius, added somewhat more Stoicism. He took in particular from Panætius the distinction between a philosophical, a poetical, and a popular religion. His fragments offer much yet for the history of Hellenistic philosophy. See E. Norden, *Beiträge*, p. 428 f.

Yet nearer to Stoicism stand the Sextians, whose first member, Quintus Sextus, lived as early as in the Augustinian age. His son, who bore his name, and Sotion of Alexandria followed him. The latter was a revered teacher of Seneca and of several others (Zeller, IV[3]. 676 f.). The school soon became extinct, because, as it appears, it rested on the personal impression made by the dignified moral instruction of the Sextians. Some of their *Sentences* are still in a Syrian version (Gildemeister, Bonn, 1873). The Stoic morals form the essential content of these *Sentences*, interspersed, nevertheless, with old Pythagorean precepts, supposedly through the influence of Sotion.

The Eclectic popular philosophy, not as a school, but as the conviction of cultured men, was propagated throughout antiquity nearly in the manner that Cicero had presented it. Its most remarkable later literary representative of this is the well-known physician Claudius Galenus (died about 200). He has immortalized his name in the history of formal logic, through the unfortunate discovery of the fourth figure of the syllogism, named after him. See K. Sprengel, *Beiträge zur Geschichte der Medicin*, I. 117 ff. Ch. Daremberg, *Essai sur Galien considéré comme philosophe* (Paris and Leipzig, 1848) ; a series of discussions by E. Chauvet (Caen and Paris, 1860–82) ; Ueberweg, *Logik*, § 103.

50. It was a result of the Sophistic Enlightenment and its destruction of all belief in the supernatural that Platonic immaterialism could not at first find fast footing in the circles of Greek and Roman civilization; and that, therefore, all the different schools united in laying the whole strength of their convictions in ethics, while cherish-

ing their coldly rational natural religion. In the mean time, however, among the Roman peoples, the religious spirit grew to a mighty desire for a saving faith. It began to invade philosophy also more and more. The masses lost the Hellenic trust in the satisfactoriness of earthly existence. In its place there entered that feverish longing for a higher mysterious satisfaction, which longing showed itself in the groping about after all cults that were foreign and fantastic. In this way belief in the self-sufficiency of the Wise Man vanished from philosophy, and yielded to that expectancy that a higher power would give a blessedness and release from the world, — a thing that virtue could not guarantee. When the consciousness of the old world, broken as it were, thus rose in its longing for supernatural help, philosophy passed out of the sensualism and rationalism, which had governed the post-Aristotelian time, into Mysticism. From its inmost need philosophy seized then upon that conception of the world which contrasted the sensible and supersensible worlds: viz., upon Platonism.

The centre of this movement was Alexandria, where in liveliest intercourse of the people of the Orient and Occident the amalgamation of religions was completed on the grandest scale. Here, at the beginning of our era, two tendencies in mystic religious Platonism became prominent. One of these accorded more with the Greek, the other with the Oriental life. They were the so-called neo-Pythagoreanism and the Judaic-Alexandrian philosophy. Both seem to have gone back to the attempt to develop into a scientific theory, with the help of Platonism, the views which had been fundamental in the Pythagorean mysteries.

J. Simon, *Histoire de l'école d'Alexandrie* (Paris, 1843 ff.); E. Matler, *Essai sur l'école d'Alexandrie* (Paris, 1840 ff.) ; E. Vacherot, *Histoire critique de l'école d'Alexandrie* (Paris, 1846 ff.) ; see W. J. Thiersch, *Politik u. Philos. in ihrem Verhältnis zur Religion unter Trajan, Hadrian, u. den Antoninen* (Marburg, 1853); Th. Ziegler, *Ueber die Entstehung der Alexandrischen Philos.* (*Philologenversammlung*, 1882).

That the so-called neo-Pythagoreanism is only a branch of eclectic religious Platonism is obvious from the content of the theory. It has very little to do with the original Pythagorean philosophy (§ 24), but the more with the religious spirit of the Pythagorean mysteries. But neo-Pythagoreanism shares (Zeller, V³. 325 ff.) this with the Jewish sect of Essenes to such a degree that the origin of the Essenes and their new religious conception may be sought in the contact of Judaism with these Orphic-Pythagorean mysteries. The practical consequence of this contact was in Palestine the origination of the Essenes; the theoretic consequence was in Alexandria the philosophy of Philo.

The Pythagorean band, which in the course of the fourth century b. c. lost its character as a school of philosophy, but, as we may suppose, had always retained its character as one of the Mysteries and as an asceticism, reappeared in the first century b. c. with philosophic teachings. These were, it must be said, essentially of a religious cast, and were developed during the next two centuries in a very large literature, which the band foisted almost altogether upon Pythagoras or other older Pythagoreans, especially Archytas. Among the personalities who represented this direction of thought, and were therefore called neo-Pythagoreans, were P. Nigidius Figulus, a friend of Cicero, Sotion, a friend of the Sextians (§ 49), and particularly Apollonius of Tyana, Moderatus of Gades, and, in later times, Nicomachus of Gerasa and Numenius of Apamea.

See M. Hertz, *De Nigidii Figuli studiis atque operibus* (Berlin, 1845); also dissertations by Breysig (Berlin, 1854) and Klein (Bonn, 1861).

Apollonius was the ideal of neo-Pythagorean wisdom to himself and to others, and he appeared with great *éclat* at the time of Nero as the founder of a religion. His life is oddly embellished by Philostratus (220) (published by Westermann, Paris, 1848, and Kayser, Leipzig, 1870–71). See Chr. Baur, *Apollonius von Tyana und Christus* (in three editions, Leipzig, 1876); Ueberweg-Heinze, 1⁷. 300 f.

Numenius, who lived in the second half of the second century, was already under Philo's influence, and probably also
under that of the Gnostics. The doctrine of the three gods is
characteristic of him: (1) the supreme and supersensible;
(2) the demiurge giving form to material things; (3) the universe thus formed. (See F. Thedinga, *De Numenii philos. plat.*,
Bonn, 1875.) We possess only the arithmetical and musical
works of his younger contemporary Nicomachus. For the spurious literature essentially accounted for by a need of authority
for the school, see in Fr. Beckmann, *De Pythagoreorum reliquiis*
(Berlin, 1844); Zeller, V³. 100 ff.

Neo-Pythagoreanism joined monotheism to its fantastic
cult of gods and dæmons in entirely the same way in which
we meet this in the old Pythagoreans, in Plato, and in a
systematic way among the Stoics. But neo-Pythagoreanism transformed its monotheism with the help of the Platonic-Aristotelian teaching into a reverence for God as a
pure spirit, which man has to serve not by outward sacrifice and act but in spirit, with silent prayer, with virtue
and wisdom. Apollonius travelled about the ancient world
as the proclaimer of this pure knowledge of God and this
higher worship. Pythagoras and he were honored as the
perfect men in whom God had revealed himself. The scientific significance of the school, however, consisted in the
fact that it united with this cult a philosophical point of
view. One finds, indeed, this point of view in all its essentials in Plato, Aristotle, and in part in the Stoa; yet it is
distinguished from the other, one-sided moralizing impulse
of the time by its lively theoretic interests, which, although
dependent and unproductive, extended to logical and physical questions as well.

A sharp dualism of spirit and matter is the fundamental
postulate in this theory in the sense that the former is the
good, pure principle in life, and the latter the bad, unholy
principle. Although God is here likewise pictured in
Stoical fashion as the πνεῦμα immanent in the whole
world, nevertheless he must, on the other hand, be free

from all contact with matter which might pollute him. Consequently he cannot directly act upon matter, but the demiurge for this purpose is introduced as a mediator between God and matter (Timæus). The Ideas according to which God perfects the world passed for the neo-Pythagoreans only as archetypes in the divine spirit. They became, in a similarly fantastic way, partly identified with the Pythagorean numbers, partly set in some secret relationship, as they had begun to be regarded by Plato and his immediate pupils. At the same time they are the forms of matter in the Aristotelian sense. In the graded interval between God and matter, the dæmons and stellar gods find place above men.

The anthropological dualism of the neo-Pythagoreans is consistent with their metaphysical dualism. The spirit is punished by being confined in a corporeal prison, and can free itself again through purification and expiation, through mortification of the flesh, and through godly life. The Platonic theory of the three parts of the soul is blended with the Aristotelian teaching of the $\nu o\hat{v}\varsigma$ (Timæus), and immortality is represented in the (partially conscious) mythical form of transmigration. The moral and religious problem is how to suppress the senses. In the solution of this problem man is helped by mediating dæmons and by divine revelation, which speaks in holy men like Pythagoras and Apollonius.

Pythagoras is said to have revealed such doctrine to his band and to have veiled it in his theory of numbers, Plato to have borrowed it from him. The later neo-Pythagoreans, particularly Numenius, referred the revelation still further back to Moses. This is due to Philo's influence.

The authoritative importance which the fundamental opposition of good and bad has for the neo-Pythagorean idea of the world makes this philosophy appear an offshoot of the Old Academy. Its historical transition is through eclectic Platonism, supposably in the form that Posidonius connected it in Stoicism. See R. Heinze, *Xenocrates*, p. 156.

The divergence of neo-Pythagoreanism from the Platonic
metaphysics consisted essentially in its stripping the Ideas (and
numbers) of their metaphysical independence and in making
them thoughts in the divine mind. This is also the authoritative conception for neo-Platonism. The far-reaching significance of this change consisted in the fact that the immaterial
substance was thought as spirit, as conscious Immanence. The
beginning of this thought is to be found in the Aristotelian
νόησις νοήσεως, its wider preparation in the Stoic doctrine which
contrasted the content of the ideas (τὸ λεκτόν) as incorporeal
to the objects, all of which are corporeal. This tendency
reached its perfect development in Philo's concept of the divine
personality.

Neo-Pythagoreanism was the *first system which expressed the
principle of authority in the form of divine revelation*, and thus
against sensualism and rationalism it initiated the mystic direction of ancient thought. The saints of this philosophical
religion are divinely favored men, to whom the pure doctrine
has in part been given. Theoretically this new source of knowledge was designated still as νοῦς, as the immediate intuition of
the intelligible (νοητόν). It is to be distinguished from the
διάνοια, or the knowledge of the understanding, as also from the
δόξα and the αἴσθησις.

Dæmonology was the theoretic basis for the peculiar amalgamation of this monotheism with the Mysteries. It rested
upon the need of bridging the chasm between God's transcendence and the world. But it offered the possibility of
uniting all the fantastic faiths and cults into one system.
The detailed system of divination which the neo-Pythagoreans
got from the Stoics was united with this theory.

The peculiar blending of Platonism and Judaism was
also closely related to the above neo-Pythagoreanism, and
was completed at the beginning of our era in the so-called
Alexandrian religious philosophy. Philo of Alexandria
was its leader.

A. Gfrörer, *Philo und die alex. Theosophie* (2 ed., Stuttgart,
1835) ; F. Dähne, *Die jüdisch.-alex. Religionsphilosophie* (Halle,
1834); M. Wolff, *Die philonische Philosophie* (2 ed., Gothen-
burg, 1858). Concerning the λόγος doctrine, see F. Keferstein,
Philo's Lehre von dem göttlichen Mittelwesen (Leipzig, 1846) ;
J. Bucher, *Philonische Studien* (Tübingen, 1848) ; Ferd. De-
launey, *Philo d'Alex.* (Paris, 1867); J. Réville, *Le logos d'après*

Philo (Geneva, 1877); Histories of Judaism by Just, Graetz, and Abr. Geiger; Ewald, *Gesch. des Volkes Israel;* Dorner, *Entwickelungsgesch. der Lehre von der Person Christi u. andere dogmengesch. Werke;* see Ueberweg-Heinze, I[7]. 292 f.

Philo (born about 25 B. C. and died 50 A. D.) came from one of the most influential Jewish families in Alexandria. He headed the embassy in 39 and 40 that the Alexandrian Jews sent to Caligula. His writings, among which there is much that is doubtful and spurious, have been published by Th. Mangey (London, 1742), C. E. Richter (Leipzig, 1838 ff.), and stereotyped by Tauchnitz (Leipzig, 1851 ff.). See Ch. G. L. Grossman, *Quæstiones Philoneæ* (Leipzig, 1829, and other editions); Jac. Bernays, *Die unter Philo's Werken stehende Schrift über die Ewigheit der Welt* (published by Berlin Academy, 1877); concerning the writing περὶ τοῦ πάντα σπουδαῖον εἶναι ἐλεύθερον, see K. Ausfeld (Göttingen, 1887) and P. Wendland, *Arch. f. Gesch. d. Philos.*, I. 509 ff.; H. v. Arnim, *Quellen-Studien zu Philo* (Berlin, 1889); J. Drummond, *Philo Judæus* (London, 1888); M. Freudenthal, *Die Erkenntnistheorie Philo's* (Berlin, 1891).

As early as the middle of the second century before this era there can be seen influences of Greek philosophy, especially Platonic, Stoic, and Aristotelian theories, at work in the interpretation of the Jewish scriptures (Aristobulus, Aristeas, etc.). All doctrines of any essential importance are included by Philo.

In the philosophy of Philo, the theory of the transcendence of God is more distinct than in any other form of Alexandrian thought. God is so far beyond all finiteness that he can be defined only negatively through the denial of every empirical quality (ἄποιος), and wholly abstractly, as an absolute Being (τὸ ὄν, — according to the Platonic principle also τὸ γεννικώτατον). This absolute Being is beyond all human ideas of perfectness, even beyond virtue and wisdom. Nevertheless the divine Being is the force that forms the universe by his goodness and rules it with his might.[1] Since God cannot enter into direct relations with impure and evil matter which in contrast to him is passive, potencies (δυνάμεις) go out from him with which

---

[1] The references here are similar to those in the writing περὶ κόσμου.

he forms and directs the world.   These (Stoical) potencies
were identified on the one hand with the Platonic Ideas, and,
on the other, with the angels of the Jewish religion.   Their
unity, however, is the Logos, the second God, the con-
tent, on the one hand, of all original Ideas ($\lambda o\gamma os \, \dot{\epsilon}\nu\delta\iota\acute{a}\theta\epsilon\tau os$
$= \sigma o\phi\acute{\iota}a$), and, on the other, of the teleological formative
forces ($\lambda\acute{o}\gamma os \, \pi\rho o\phi o\rho\iota\kappa\acute{o}s$) that reveal God's presence in
the world.

In man, as the microcosm, the spirit ($\nu o\hat{v}s$) in its eternal
heritage stands in contrast to the body of mortality ($\sigma\acute{a}\rho\xi$).
It is so involved by its own guilt that it can only get
release from the universal sinfulness by divine help.   Its
problem is how to become like the pure spirit of God.   Its
attainment of indifference to all desires, modelled after the
Stoic apathy, and its purification which rises above this
ethical ideal into knowledge (the Aristotelian dianoëtic
virtue) are upward steps toward that highest blessedness
which is only reached in an ecstatic state of absorption in
the divine Being, with the full surrender of one's individu-
ality.   This supra-conscious ecstasy ($\ddot{\epsilon}\kappa\sigma\tau a\sigma\iota s$) is accorded
as a revelation and gift of God only to the most perfect
men.

Platonic and Stoic thories, and incidentally also the Aristotelian, were mingled in the Philosophy of Philo in the most
complicated manner.   With an abundant employment of the
Stoic method of allegorical myth-interpretation he read these
theories into the primitive records of his religion, i. e., into the
teaching of Moses.   He found not only in Moses but in the
teachings of Greek philosophy that revelation of God to which
human knowledge alone can never attain.   In these religious
revelations Philo distinguished the corporeal and spiritual, the
verbal and conceptual sense.   God has to reveal himself to
sensuous man in a manner that man may comprehend.   Therefore it is the task of philosophy (or theology) to reinterpret the
religious records into a system of conceptual insight.   Compare
Siegfried, *Philo von Alex. als Ausleger des alten Testaments*
(Jena, 1875).

The later so-called " negative theology," which in Philo regarded God as the absolutely inconceivable and inexpressible, corresponded to the theory of ecstasy in which also the human spirit was conceived to be lifted out of everything limited and representable, and thereby itself became God (ἀποθεοῦσθαι, deificatio).

The mediation between the neo-Pythagorean transcendence and the Stoic immanence was in the divine potencies. These on the one side inhere in God as Ideas, and on the other work upon matter as independently active potencies. The Logos has also the same specious double aspect of a divine potency and an independent personality. The need of a unifying mediation between God and the world is consistently conceived in the conception of the Logos.

Finally, in a similar manner, the Platonists of the first and second centuries of this era, under the influence of the neo-Pythagorean teaching, perfected a mysticism which substituted a confident faith in divine revelation for the ethical Wisdom of the earlier philosophy. The exponents of this are Plutarch of Chæronea and Apuleius of Madaura.

See Zeller, V³. 203 ff.; Ueberweg-Heinze, 303 ff. To this religious eclectic circle belong the writings current under the name of *Hermes-Trismegistus*. See R. Pietschmann, *Hermes Trismegistus* (Leipzig, 1875).

Plutarch's philosophical writings (Moralia) form, in the edition of Dübner (Paris, 1841), volumes III. and IV. See R. Volkmann, *Leben, Schriften und Philos. des Plutarch's* (2 ed., Berlin, 1872); E. Dascaritis, *Die Psychologie u. Pädagogik des Plutarch's* (Gotha, 1889); C. Giesen, *De Plutarcho contra Stoicos disputationibus* (Münster, 1890); von Willamowitz-Möllendorf, *Zu Plutarch, Gastmahl der sieben Weisen* (in the *Hermes*, 1890). There belongs in the same connection with the philosophical writings of Apuleius (collected by Hildebrand, Leipzig, 1842) his well-known romance, the *Golden Ass*, whose sharp satire seems to be based allegorically upon the neo-Pythagorean mystic view of the world and life.

3. PATRISTICS.

The religious Platonism of the first centuries of our era, in the breadth and variety of its assimilations of the most different religious convictions, showed a change in the

philosophical point of view.   Science as well as philosophy
was placed in the service of a feverish religious need.
Philosophy was no longer to be an ethical art of life but a
religion.   When, on the other hand, science was beginning
to be weary of the problem, the new religion began its triumphant march through the ancient world.

The Gospel originally took no note of science; it was
neither its friend nor foe, and its attitude to the ancient
political state was like its attitude to science.   It had, nevertheless, to assume more of a positive relation to both, the
more it spread, following its own natural impulse among
the people on the Mediterranean Sea.   In both cases the
course of things was as follows : the Church, in its need of
self-justification, found itself in positive contact with the
world, and assimilated gradually the ancient life ; thus
it finally overcame Greek science as well as the Roman
state,[1] — an impossible result unless Christianity reacted
in turn and adopted the essentials of antiquity for its own.

The philosophical secularizing of the Gospel which went
on parallel with the organization and political growth of the
church was called Patristics, and extended from the second
to the fourth and fifth centuries after Christ.

Patristics in the general history of philosophy is usually separated from the development of ancient thought, and then is
afterwards generally treated as the beginning of Christian philosophy.   It is not our purpose to pass judgment upon the
propriety and usefulness of the usual arrangement, when we
make this sketch deviate from that arrangement, or when we
draw the most general outlines of Patristic philosophy.   This
sketch is made, not only because the Patristic philosophy belongs in its time relations to antiquity,[2] but the principal reason

---

[1] See K. J. Neumann, *Der römische Staat und die allgemeine Kirche
bis auf Diokletian*, I. (Leipzig, 1890).

[2] These actual relations show themselves so strong that the present
author develops the arrangement introduced here, in his general *Geschichte der Philosophie;* and he has found them by far the best for the
exposition of scientific development in the first centuries of our era.

is that in it is to be seen a final development of ancient thought corresponding throughout to neo-Platonism. It is obvious that all specific theological moments are left out of account, and the survey is limited strictly within philosophical bounds. There is certainly not much of philosophical originality to be expected in this period. Originality can be found to some extent only among the Gnostics and in Origen. Patristics is only a variation and development of Greek thought, and then only from a religious point of view, — a point of view in which ardent longing has given place to the firm conviction of faith.

With the text-books on the history of philosophy we must compare the following histories of the church and of dogmatics, if we would understand this subject. See Harnack, *Lehrbuch der Dogmengeschichte*, Vol. I. (Freiburg i. B., 1886); Deutinger, *Geist der Christlichen Ueberlieferung* (Regensburg, 1850–51); A. Ritschl, *Die Entstehung der altkatolische Kirche* (2 ed., Bonn, 1857); F. Chr. Baur, *Das Christentum der ersten drei Jahrhunderte* (Tübingen, 1860); Joh. Alzog, *Grundriss der Patrologie* (3 ed., Freiburg i. B., 1876); Alb. Stöckl, *Geschichte der Philosophie der patristischen Zeit* (Würzburg, 1859); Joh. Huber, *Die Philosophie der Kirchenväter* (Munich, 1859); E. Havet, *Le christianisme et ses origines* (2 vol., Paris, 1871); Fr. Overbeck, *Uber die Anfänge der patristischen Litteratur* (in *Hist. Zeitschrift*, 1882). The sources of Patristic literature are most completely collected by J. P. Migne in his collection: *Patrologiæ cursus completus* (Paris, since 1860).

The occasion for Christianity taking some position toward Greek science arose partly out of its polemically apologetic interests, partly out of those that were dogmatic and constructive. With its missionary spirit Christianity stepped out upon a scientifically *blasé* world in which even the less educated people had learned to flee from their religious doubt to philosophy, and in which philosophy was trying to vouchsafe to those in religious need a contentment that had been lost to the world. Christianity entered at the same time into the religious controversies where, under these circumstances, the victory would belong to that party which absorbed most completely the culture of antiquity. It therefore followed that the new religion had to defend its faith theoretically against the mockery and contempt of heathen wisdom, but at the same time it had to vindicate itself as the fulfilment of human need of salvation. The Apologists undertook to accomplish this.

On the other hand, the unity and purity of the Christian conceptions threatened to be lost with the spreading of the community, on account of the many ways in which those conceptions came into contact with the religious elements of the Græco-Roman and Oriental philosophies. The church needed for its inner constitution not only the simple *regula fidei*, but also a fundamentally scientific expression of this formula, a fixed and conceptually developed system of dogmatics. The Gnostics were the first to attempt such a philosophical structure for Christianity. But inasmuch as they at the first step made a striking departure from the rule of faith, the solution of their problem fell into the hands of the Alexandrian School of Catechists, which created for Christianity its scientific dogma from the ripest thought of the Grecian world.

51. To a philosophical vindication of Christianity, naturally only such members of that communion could be called who had a mastery over the thought of Greek and Roman philosophy. But even these men, if their purpose was to rationalize the new religion, would be necessarily inclined to bring the content of the new faith as near as possible to the results of ancient science, and to read into the old philosophy the teachings of the new faith. Unintentionally, therefore, the Gospel was hellenized by the Apologists, the most important of whom are Justin Martyr, Athenagoras, and, among the Romans, Minucius Felix, and, later, Lactantius.

Corpus Apologetarum Christianorum seculi secundi, published by Otto (Jena, since 1842).

Of the predecessors of Justin, we must notice Aristides of Athens especially, whose fragments (published in Venice, 1878) contain a philosophical argumentation for Christianity as a revealed monotheism.

Flavius Justin Martyr of Sichem (Flavia Neapolis), in Samaria, a man of Greek origin and culture, after investigating several contemporaneous systems of science, came to the conviction that only the Christian faith was the true philosophy. He suffered death at Rome (163–166) for defence of this doctrine. Of his writings (see first volumes of Otto's edition) the *Dialogue with the Jew Triphon* and both the *Apologies* are genuine. See K. Semisch, *Justin der Märtyrer* (Breslau, 1840–42); B. Aubé, *St. Justin, philosophe et martyr* (Paris, 1861); M. v. Engelhardt, *Das Christenthum Justin d. Märtyrer* (Erlangen, 1858). Justin's two Apologies have been translated into German and analyzed by H. Veit.

Athenagoras of Athens addressed to Marcus Aurelius (176–177) his πρεσβεία περὶ Χριστιανῶν. There is also preserved his περὶ ἀναστάσεως τῶν νεκρῶν (in Otto's edition, Vol. VII.). See Th. A. Clarisse, *De Athenag. vita scriptis et doctrina* (Leyden, 1819); F. Schurbring, *Die Philosophie des Athenag.* (Bern, 1882).

The conception which Theophilus of Antioch (about 180) embodied in his address to Autolycus in writing (*Corpus*, Vol. VIII.) is related to the above. The *Apology* of Melito of Sardis and Apollinaris of Hierapolis is likewise related.

The apologetic dialogue, *Octavius* (about 200), of Minucius Felix (published in the *Corpus scriptorum ecclesiasticorum latinorum*, by C. Halm, Vienna, 1867) presents Christianity nearly entirely in the sense of ethical rationalism. See A. Soulet, *Essai sur l' Octavius de Min. Fel.* (Strassburg, 1867); R. Kühl, *Der Oktavius d. Min. Fel.* (Leipzig, 1882).

Similar ideas are found in beautiful form, but without philosophical significance in the rhetorician Firmianus Lactantius (died about 325). He undertook in his chief work, the *Institutiones divinæ*, to make a system of Christian morals, whose individual characteristics were to be found strewn in Greek philosophy, which nevertheless in their totality could only be conceived as ultimately grounded through a divine illumination. See J. G. Th. Müller, *Quæstiones Lactantieæ* (Göttingen, 1875).

These hellenizing apologists sought to prove that Christianity was the only "true philosophy," in that it guaranteed not only correct knowledge but also right living and true holiness here and hereafter. They based the pre-eminence of Christian philosophy upon the perfect revelation of God in Jesus Christ. For only through divine inspiration does the rational come to man, who is buried in the wicked sense-world and is in the toils of dæmons. Nevertheless inspiration has been active from the beginning in human life. Everything that the great teachers of Greece — Pythagoras, Socrates, Plato — have known of the truth, they have owed not solely to their own reason. They have, in part, got it directly through divine revelation, and, in part, indirectly through the inspired teaching of Moses and the prophets, whom they were said to have used. But all these revelations are only sporadic and embryonic (λόγος σπερματικός). In Jesus first is the divine Logos perfectly and completely revealed and become man. For the Godhead, who is nameless and inexpressible in itself, has unfolded his entire essence in his Son.

The peculiarity of the teaching of these men, especially of Justin, is the thoroughgoing and detailed identification of reason and revelation. The way was prepared in the Stoic Logos-concept for this and in its transformation at the hands of Philo, in which the materialistic character of the λόγος was stripped off and only the omnipresent character of the divine spirit in nature and history remained. When, therefore, Justin found nearly all the moments of Christian truth, the ethical bearing of which he strongly emphasized, already in ancient philosophy, when he opined that something of the truth of salvation as a natural endowment (ἔμφυτον) has come to all people by divine grace, he was regarding as inspired what is natural and rational according to Greek science. Therefore in that teaching approved by him and sanctioned as Christian, he found partly an immediate revelation, partly an appropriation of the statements of Moses and the prophets, of whom he thought Plato had ample knowledge. Philo had already done this before Justin. On the other hand, in contrast to the indefinite search for a revelation which characterized neo-Pythagoreanism and the other forms of mystic Platonism, the Apologists had the enormous advantage of a faith in a determinate, absolute, positive, and historical revelation in Jesus Christ. In their representing him, they united the Logos conception of Philo with the ethical religious meaning of the Jewish ideal of a Messiah. They designated him, therefore, as the "second God," created by the Father, in whom divine revelation had been incarnated.

The metaphysical dualism of the Apologists stood in intimate relation to their theory of inspiration. They metaphysically set the ἄμορφος ὕλη over against the Godhead, who forms the world through the Logos, entirely in a Platonic and neo-Pythagorean sense. The end of this is to conceive matter as in every way reasonless and bad. Thus results, as their fundamental principle, the following: the Logos, as the content of divine revelation, has appeared in Jesus Christ the man in order to redeem man fallen in sin, and to establish the kingdom of God.

52. The desire to transmute faith (πίστις) and its authoritative content into conceptual knowledge (γνῶσις) began very early in the Christian communion. The Pauline epistles show this. It was completed in a larger way at the beginning of the second century within the Syriac-Alexandrian circles of Christians. Here neo-Pythagorean, Platonic, and Philonic thought met in a heightened fancy, the occasion of which was the Syriac mixture of Oriental and Occidental cults and mythologies. The rivalry of religions was reduced in the presentation of these Gnostics to a Christian philosophy of religion, whose disciples, being chiefly the members of the communion steeped in Hellenic culture, constituted themselves in many localities as unique Mysteries. They perfected an idealism with the fantastic mythological formulæ of the East, and lost, on this account, all sympathy with the majority of the Christian communion, so that they were finally set aside as heretics. The leaders of Gnosticism were Saturninus, Carpocrates, Basilides, Valentinus, and Bardesanes.

A. W. Neander, *Genetische Entwickelung der vornehmsten gnostischen Systeme* (Berlin, 1818); E. Matter, *Histoire critique du gnosticisme* (2 ed., Paris, 1843); F. Chr. Baur, *Die christliche Gnosis oder Religionsphilosophie* (Tübingen, 1835); A. Lipsius, *Der Gnostizismus* (Leipzig, 1860; separately published in Ersch u. Gruber, Vol. 71); H. S. Mansel, *The Gnostic Heresies* (London, 1875); A. Harnack, *Zur Quellenkritik der Geschichte des Gnostizismus* (Leipzig, 1873); A. Hilgenfeld, *Die Ketzergeschichte des Urchristentums* (Jena, 1884); M. Joel, *Blicke in die Religionsgeschichte zu Anfang des zweiten Jahrhunderts* (Breslau, 1880-1883).

Of the conditions of life of the eminent Gnostics but little is known. Only very few fragments of their writings are preserved. Among these is particularly the πίστις σοφία of an unknown author from the circle of Valentinians (published by Petermann, Berlin, 1851). As for the rest, the knowledge we have of the doctrine of these men is limited to what their opponents say about them, especially Irenæus (ἔλεγχος καὶ ἀνατροπὴ τῆς ψευδωνύμου γνώσεως, Leipzig, 1853), Hippolytus (ἔλεγχος κατὰ πασῶν αἱρέσεων, Oxford, 1851), Justin, Tertullian (adversus Valentinianos), Clement of Alexandria, Origen, Eusebius, Augustine, and Saturninus, who came from Antioch and taught in the time of Hadrian. Carpocrates flourished about 130 in Alexandria, and was contemporary to Basilides the Syrian. The career of the most notable of these men, Valentinus, falls somewhat later. Valentinus lived at Rome and died in Cyprus about 160. Bardesanes was born in Mesopotamia and lived 155–225.

See Uhlhorn, *Das basilidianische System* (Göttingen, 1855) ; G. Heinrici, *Die valentinianische Gnosis u. die heil. Schrift* (Berlin, 1871) ; Fr. Lipsius, *Valentinus u. seine Schule (Jahrb. f. prot. Theol.*, 1887) ; G. Köstlin, *Das gnost. System des Buchs* πίστις σοφία (*Theol. Jahrb. Tübingen*, 1854) ; A. Hilgenfeld, *Bardesanes der letzte Gnostiker* (Leipzig, 1864).

The fundamental principle which secures to the Gnostics a permanent place in the history of philosophy in spite of the sensualistic and mythological fancifulness with which they developed this principle, is their plan on a great scale of a philosophy of history. This plan originated in their fundamental religious thought. Since Christianity wished to conceive itself as a victory both over Judaism and Heathenism, the Gnostic interpreted the battle of religions allegorically as a battle of the gods of these religions. They interpreted this battle intellectually also into a theory that upon the appearance of the Redeemer not only the development of the human race but also the history of the universe reached its dénouement. This dénouement, however, is the fundamental part of Christianity : *the redemption of the wicked through the perfect revelation of the highest God through Jesus Christ.*

The transformation of all nature philosophy into ethical-religious categories is consequently the fundamental form of the philosophy of the Gnostics. They undertook at first with a radical one-sidedness to conceive the universe entirely from a religious point of view. They thought of the cosmic process as a strife between good and evil, which is ended in the redemption of the world by Christ, giving the good the victory.

So far as this antithesis was logically conceived, it appeared in the form of a neo-Pythagorean dualism of spirit and matter. In the mythological embodiment of it, however, which took up by far the greatest space in the Gnostic systems, the heathen dæmons and the god of the Old Testament, who had the form of the Platonic demiurge, were considered the powers of this world to be overcome. They were brought into opposition to the true God, who conquered them by the revelation of Jesus, to the same extent as other religions are brought in opposition to Christianity.

The beginnings of the Greek natural sciences were of such a nature that there seemed to be no possibility of giving a satisfactory answer, even in the great teleological systems, to the question of the significance of historical development in its entirety. The science that was wanting to them was the philosophy of history, and of this want the world must needs become conscious when ancient culture was in its senility. The Gnostics are therefore the *first philosophers of history*. Since there stands as the centre of their philosophy of history the Christian principle of the salvation of the world by Jesus Christ, they must be acknowledged as philosophers of Christian history and religion, in spite of their deviation from later orthodoxy.

The conquest of Judaism by Christianity was thus mythologized by men like Cerinthus, the Syrian Cerdo, and particularly Marcion and his pupil Apelles. The God of the Old Testament who formed the world and gave the Judaic law was conceived as a dæmon lower than the highest God, who was revealed by Christ. The former is recognizable in nature and in the Old Testament; the latter is inexpressible and unknowable; the former is only just, the latter is good, — an ethical distinction emphasized by Marcion particularly.

This way of representing things led the Gnostics into a dualism between good ar d bad, spirit and matter. The dualism between spirit and matter was developed in a true Hellenic fashion with a most decided leaning to neo-Pythagorean syncretism by Carpocrates, but by Saturninus, and particularly by Basilides (see Irenæus), by means of Oriental mythology. According to the astronomical dualism of the Pythagorean and Aristotelian thought, the space between God and the world is filled by whole races of dæmons and angels that are arranged according to numerical symbols. The lowest of these is far enough distant from the divine perfectness so that the lowest can have relationship with the impure material, and as demiurge form the world. In this world then, as already in the spirit world, the battle of the perfect and imperfect, of light and darkness, waged until the λόγος, the νοῦς, Christ, the most perfect of the æons, came down to the world of the flesh to release the spirit shut up in matter. This is the fundamental idea of Gnosticism, and its different mythological shadings are of no philosophical importance.

Their anthropology in a corresponding manner distinguished in man the material of sense (ὕλη), the dæmonic soul (ψυχή), and the divine spirit (πνεῦμα). According, then, to the prevalence of one of these three elements man is either spiritual, psychic, or material, — a distinction which was incidentally identified by Valentinus with that between Christianity, Judaism, and Heathendom.

This dualism originated apparently in the Alexandrian, that is, the Hellenic, circle, and assimilated later some analogies from Parseeism. Manichæism arose later (third century) from the influence of the Gnostics upon the religions of the East. It was an extreme dualistic religion, and played an important rôle in the intellectual controversies of the following centuries (F. Chr. Baur, *Das manichäische Religionssystem* (Tübingen, 1831); O. Flügel, *Mani u. seine Lehre* (Leipzig, 1862); A. Geyler, *Das System des Manichäismus* (Jena, 1875).

This dualism accorded with the Christian's ethical convictions as well as with those growing out of his need of redemption; but not with his metaphysical principles, which could recognize no other power in the world besides the living God and be consistent with its Jewish traditions. The monistic feeling naturally turned away from the dualism of Greek thought and tried to overcome it. Later forms of Gnosticism approached Monism, which predominated among the orthodox churchmen. At the same time it sought to explain dualism by a theory of emanation from the divinity, and it had as its model the Stoic theory of the change of the cosmic fire into its elements. It itself in turn thus became the model for neo-Platonism. The school of Basilides, if the statement of Hippolytus refers to it, followed out this motive, and it was perhaps influenced by the notable Gnostic, Valentinus.

Valentinus undertook first to transfer the antithesis to the original divine being (προπάτωρ). He called it the eternal Depth (βυθός), which created out of its underived and unspeakable content (σιγή — ἔννοια) in the first place the πλήρωμα, the world of Ideas. From this world, one Idea, σοφία, falls on account of its unbridled longing for the Father and creates the sense world[1] through the demiurge. There was here attempted for the first time in entirely mythical form the conquest of Greek dualism and the establishment of an idealistic monism, which was a fantastic precreation of neo-Platonism.

In their teaching and their cult the Gnostic mysteries were so far distant from the Christian Church which had been continuously developing its organization, that Gnosticism was placed under the ban as heresy. Its bold philosophy of religion called forth on the one hand an extreme reaction against turning faith into a science, and on the other a polemical limitation of dogma to the simplest content of the *regula fidei*. Tatian and Tertullian are to be named here: the one as the radical champion of Orientalism, which beheld in all Greek culture the work of the Devil; the other as the ingenious and narrowminded opponent of rationalism. Tertullian pushed the anthropological dualism so far as to maintain that the truth in the Gospel is confirmed just because it contradicts human reason. *Credo quia absurdum.* Contemporaneously with Tertullian and Tatian, Irenæus (140–200) and his pupil Hippolytus combated the anti-Judaic philosophy of history of the Gnostics with the Pauline theory of a divine method of education. According to this theory the Judaic Law was " our schoolmaster to bring us to Christ." They also formulated a religious philosophy of history in that

[1 Windelband, *History of Philosophy*, 251, n. 2. — Tr.]

they conceived the historical process as a teleological series of acts of divine redemption, which expresses in the conception of the church (ἐκκλησία) the ideal community of mankind. This anti-Gnosticism was not able to maintain itself without help from Greek philosophy (Stoicism in Tertullian, Philonism in Irenæus and Hippolytus) and even from Gnosticism itself, especially in Tatian, who later went over entirely to Valentinian Gnosticism.

Tatian was an Assyrian. His treatise, πρὸς Ἕλληνας, which used the Justinian reflections for a polemic against all philosophy and set up against the Greek pretended wisdom the faith of the barbarians, is to be found in Otto's collection, Vol. VI. (Jena, 1851), printed lately by E. Schwartz (Leipzig, 1888). See Daniel, *Tertullian der Apologet* (Halle, 1837).

Tertullian (160–220), in his last years champion of the Montanists, is the Christian Stoic. His strict, relentless morality and his abrupt contrast of sensationalism and morality is conjoined with a fantastic materialism and sensualism. His numerous writings, partly apologetic, partly polemic, partly hortatory, are published by F. Oehler (Leipzig, 1853 ff.). Compare A. W. Neander, *Antignosticus ; Geist des Tertullian und Einleitung in dessen Schriften* (2 ed., Berlin, 1849); A. Hauck, *Tertullian's Leben und Schriften* (Erlangen, 1877) ; G. R. Hauschild, *Tertullian's Psychologie und Erkenntniss-Theorie* (Leipzig, 1880).

This same spirit, but without the paradoxical originality of Tertullian, occurred later in the African Rhetorician, Arnobius, who wrote his thesis *Adversus gentes* about 300 (published by A. Reifferscheid in the *Corpus scriptorum eccl. lat.*, Vienna, 1875). He and Tertullian uphold in a typical way the theory that orthodoxy, intending to demonstrate authority, grace, and revelation to be absolutely necessary for men, suppresses the natural intelligence as far as possible, and makes common cause with sensualism and its skeptical consequences.

Excepting some fragments, the writings of Irenæus exist only in Latin translations. See Böhringer, *Die Kirche Christi* (Zurich, 1861), I. 271 ff. ; H. Ziegler, *Irenaeus, der Bischof von Lyon* (Berlin, 1871); A. Gouilloud, *St. Irenæus et son temps* (Lyon, 1876). The work of Hippolytus, whose first book was earlier than the φιλοσοφούμενα of Origen, is published by Duncker and Schneidewin (Göttingen, 1859). See Bunsen, *Hippolytus und seine Zeit* (2 vols., Leipzig, 1852 f.).

53. The scientific statement of the religion of the Christian church likewise took final form in Alexandria in the use of the Gnostic and the Apologetic theories by the School of Catechists. Clement of Alexandria (about 200) and Origen, the founder of Christian theology, were the leaders of this school.

Guerike, *De schola, quæ Alexandriæ floruit catechetica* (Halle, 1824 f.) ; C. W. Hasselbach, *De schola, quæ Alexandriæ floruit catechetica* (Stettin, 1826); further the writings of E. Matter, J. Simon, I. Vacherot.

The three chief writings that are preserved of Clement are λόγος προτρεπτικὸς πρὸς Ἕλληνας, παιδαγωγός and στρωματεῖς. The last has especial significance in the history of philosophy. Clement's dependence on Philo appears clearly in his teaching. It is *mutatis mutandis* the application of the principles of Philo to Christendom, and it is related to Christendom in exactly the same way as Philo's teaching to Judaism. Although therefore not throughout philosophically independent, Clement has the great significance that through him and the more original form of his theory in Origen, eclectic Platonism, strongly mixed as it was with Stoical elements, was definitely crystallized into Christian dogma. See Dähne, *De γνώσει Clementis Alex. et de vestigiis neoplatonicæ philosophiæ in ea obviis* (Leipzig, 1831); J. Reinkens, *De fide et γνώσει Clementis* (Breslau, 1850) and *De Clemente presbytero Alexandrino* (Breslau, 1851); Lämmer, *Clement Alex. de λόγῳ doctrina* (Leipzig, 1855); Hébert-Duperron, *Essai sur la polémique et la philosophie de Clément* (Paris, 1855); J. Cognat, *Clément d'Alexandrie sa doctrine et sa polémique* (Paris, 1858); H. Treische, *De γνώσει Clementis Alex.* (Jena, 1871).

Origen (185–254), whose surname was the Adamantine, appeared early as teacher in the School of Catechists that had been directed by Clement. He attended afterward the lectures of Ammonius Saccus (§ 54). He had to endure much persecution on account of his teaching, and, driven from Alexandria, he spent his old age in Cæsarea and Tyre. The most important philosophical writings of his are περὶ ἀρχῶν and κατὰ Κέλσου. Celsus, a Platonic philosopher, wrote between 170 and 180 his ἀληθὴς λόγος, which was partly a reconstruction of the opposing thesis of Origen, and contained an arsenal of verbal weapons against Christianity. See Th. Keim, *Celsus's wahres Wort* (Zurich, 1873); E. Pélagaut, *Étude sur Celse* (Lyon, 1878); Origen's thesis concerning *Principles* is preserved almost exclusively in

the Latin version by Rufinus. See Migne, vol. 11–17; G. Tho-
masius, *Origenes* (Nürnberg, 1837); Redepenning, *Origines,
eine Darstellung seines Lebens u. seiner Lehre* (2 vols., Bonn,
1841–46); J. Denis, *De la philosophie d'Origène* (Paris, 1884);
A. Harnack, *Dogmengeschichte*, I. 512 ff.

Anticipated thus by Clement, Christian theology was
founded by Origen as a scientific system. For if the church
then and later took offence at some of Origen's doctrines
and supplanted them, yet his philosophical point of view
and his conceptual structure remained in a manner authoritative for the permanent foundation of Christian dogma in
the shape into which he had developed it from the ideas of
the Alexandrian school. Origen has the significance that
in trying to transform πίστις into γνῶσις (he called it also
σοφία), he was not carried away from the Christian fundamental principles by mythical speculation or by philosophical theories. So far as its purpose is concerned, his
teaching is then wholly parallel to Gnosticism. But while
the Gnostic boldly and deliberately created a separate and
individual form of Christianity, the Alexandrian school of
Catechists gradually began a scientific organization of the
universal Christian faith from within itself, and Origen
drew with steady hand the fundamental outlines within
whose limits later detailed developments were made.

The *regula fidei* and the canon accepted by the church of the
Holy Writ of the Old and New Testament were therefore for
Origen the source and measure of religious knowledge. The
science of faith is the methodical explanation of the Gospel.
After the manner of Philo, Origen said this method consisted in
the translation of historical into conceptual relations. The
historical element in revelation is only the " somatic " meaning
of revelation, and is intelligible to the masses. The " psychic "
meaning of revelation is its moral interpretation, and is especially
applicable to the Old Testament. Above both is the " pneumatic " meaning of the philosophical teaching expressed in Holy
Writ. If thereby an esoteric is distinguished from an exoteric
Christianity (χριστιανὸς σωματικός), Origen justified himself by
claiming that revelation, equal everywhere in its content, is

suited in its form to the different endowments and stages of development of the mind. As, therefore, the true spirit of the Old Testament was first revealed in the Gospel, so ever behind the New Testament is the eternal pneumatic gospel to be sought, which is now, for the first time, revealed only to a few, by the grace of God.

As the leading principle of the teaching of Origen, stands the concept of God as the pure spirit, who in perfect changelessness and unity (ἑνάς — μονάς) above all Beings (ἐπέκεινα τῆς οὐσίας) is recognizable as the everlasting author of all things, but in his entire fulness transcends all human knowledge. His essential characteristic is *the absolute causality of his will.* Creativeness is an essential element of his being, and therefore his creative activity is as eternal as himself. On account of his unique unchangeableness, nevertheless, his creative activity cannot deal directly with ever-changing individual things, but only with the eternal revelation of his own essence, with his image the Logos (ὁ λόγος). The Logos is expressly conceived by Origen as a person, as an hypostasized being. He is indeed not ὁ θεός, but still θεός, a δεύτερος θεός, and the Holy Spirit stands related to him as he is related to the Father. The λόγος is related to the world as the ἰδέα ἰδεῶν, the archetype according to which the divine will creates all things. Creation then is also everlasting, and made up of the endless number of spirits who are destined to participate in divine blessedness, and all of whom shall finally become part of the divine essence (θεοποιούμενοι). They are endowed, however, with freedom, to which is due the fact that they each to a greater or less degree, in his own manner, fall away from the divine essence. For their purification God created matter, and thus do the spirits in heaven become materialized and graded according to their worth: the angels, the stars, mankind, and evil dæmons.

In a characteristic and specifically Christian way, and in opposition to Hellenic intellectualism, Origen emphasized the

will and the metaphysical meaning attached to it. The will of
God appears here as the eternal necessary development of his
being, but the wills of the spirits, as free temporal choice. *The
two stand in a mutual relation that in the Platonic system
obtains between οὐσία and γένεσις.* In contrast to the unchangeableness and unity of the divine will, the freedom of will of the
spirits includes the principle of variety, of change, in a word,
of nature processes. Freedom is the ground both of sin and
of materiality. So Origen made it possible to join with his
conception of the absolute causality of God, which conception
forbids the originality of matter, the existence of wickedness,
sense, and imperfection. He reconciled ethical transcendence
with physical immanence, — God as creator, but not creator of
evil. Faith in divine omnipotence and the consciousness of sin
are the two fundamental antithetical principles of Christian
metaphysics. Origen mediated between them by his conception
of freedom.

Eternal creation involves the acceptation of an endless series
of æons, and of world systems, wherein fall and redemption
are continually repeated in new individuals. Yet this difficult
point is not further treated by Origen, but is avoided on account of the concentration of his attention upon the realm of
spirits.

The fallen spirits strive to rise from matter, to which
they are condemned for purification, and to return to their
divine source. In their own freedom do they aspire on
account of the divine essence within them, which is never
entirely lost, however deeply they may be abased. But
they do not have to act without the help of grace, which
was always active in man as a revelation from heaven, and
is revealed perfectly in the person of Jesus. One recognizes that a propedeutic value was given by Origen here,
after the manner of the Apologists, to the heathen philosophy, especially to Platonism and Stoicism. The eternal
λόγος has connected itself with the blameless ψυχή of Jesus
in a divine-human unity. Through his suffering he has
presented redemption as a temporal fact for the whole
body of believers, but through his essence the true illumination has been brought to those especially chosen (the pneu-
matically inspired). With his help, the eternal spirit has

attained different grades of redemption : faith, — the religious understanding of the perceptual world, — knowledge of the λόγος, and finally absolute absorption in the Godhead. Through the conjoined action of freedom and grace, all souls shall finally be redeemed, material existence shall vanish, and salvation of all things be perfected in God (ἀποκατάστασις).

These are the conceptual principles of Christian theology, as Origen developed them. They show that Christianity seized the ideas of ancient philosophy and revised it with its own religious principle. The changes which dogmatic development made in the system pertain especially to eschatology and Christology. As to Christology, Origen emphasized more the cosmological than the soteriological aspect of the λόγος, and neither is fully developed. The battles waged over his theory in the third and fourth centuries until the perfect consolidation of the Catholic dogma, are attributable to specific theological motives, and change none of his fundamental philosophical principles.

4. NEO-PLATONISM.

The Hellenistic thought that ran parallel to Christian scientific faith was neo-Platonism. Out of the same circles of Alexandrian culture, in which all the forms of Greek science and all religions met, arose two contemporaneous theories, — the theory of Origen and that of Plotinus. As we can see in Gnosticism a kind of precreation of Christian theology, so in the eclectic Platonism influenced by Philo (particularly in Numenius) can we also see a preparation for neo-Platonism.

Neo-Platonism and Christian theology had a community of purpose and a common origin. Both were scientific systems that methodically developed a religious conviction and sought to prove that this conviction was the only true source of salvation for the soul needing redemption. But there is a great difference between the two. Christian theology was not only supported, but also gradually regulated, by the religious consciousness of a community organizing itself into a church. Neo-Platonism was a doctrine thought out and defended by individual philosophers, which spread to associations of scholars, and then sought to profit by contact with all kinds of mysteries. Christian theology was the scientific external form of a faith that had already mightily developed. Neo-Platonism was an erudite religion, which tried incidentally to assimilate all the then existing cults. Although the scientific strength of neo-Platonism was certainly not less than that of Christianity, this attempt at assimilation was the cause of its downfall.

The historical unfolding of neo-Platonism was in three stages. In the first stage it was essentially a scientific theory. In the next it was a systematic theology of polytheism, and in this it was in pronounced opposition to Christianity. After it had gone to pieces in this way, it sought in its third stage to become a scholastic recapitulation of the entire Greek philosophy. We are accustomed to designate these different phases as the Alexandrian, the Syrian, and the Athenian schools, and to place, as the head of each respectively, Plotinus, Jamblichus, and Proclus.

See E. Matter, J. Simon, and Vacherot; Barthélemy Saint-Hilaire, *Sur le concours ouvert par l'académie*, etc., *sur l'école d'Alexandrie* (Paris, 1845) ; K. Vogt, *Neoplatonismus u. Christentum* (Berlin, 1836) ; K. Steinhart (in Pauly's *Realencyklopädie des klass. Altertums*) ; R. Hamerling, *Ein Wort über die Neuplatoniker* (with examples translated into German, Triest, 1858) ; H. Kellner, *Hellenismus u. Christentum oder die geistige Reaktion des antiken Heidentums gegen das Christentum* (Cologne, 1866) ; A. Harnack, *Dogmengeschichte,* I. 663 ff.

54. The founder of neo-Platonism was Plotinus, born 204 A. D. in Lycopolis in Egypt. He received his philosophical education in Alexandria, especially at the hands of a certain Ammonius Saccus. He took part in the expe-

dition of the Emperor Gordian in his Persian campaign in order to pursue scientific studies in the Orient. About 244 he appeared with great éclat as a teacher in Rome, and died in 269 at a country estate in Campania. Among his pupils were Amelius, and especially the publisher of his documents, Porphyry.

Ancient traditions designate the porter Ammonius (175–242) as the founder of neo-Platonism. He abandoned Christianity for Hellenism, and held impressive lectures in Alexandria. Among his pupils were said to be, besides Plotinus and the Christian Origen, Herennius (Erennius), Origen the Platonist, and the rhetorician and critic Longinus (213–273). Nothing is, however, at all certain about the teaching of Ammonius, and these so-called pupils travel such theoretically different ways that there is no good reason to speak of Ammonius as the founder of the specific philosophy of Plotinus. See W. Lyngg, *Die Lehre des Ammonius* (publication of *Gesellschaft d. Wissenschaft* at Christiania, 1874).

The Platonist Origen is not the Patristic, as G. A. Heigl supposes. See *Der Bericht des Porphyrius über Origenes* (Regensburg, 1835); G. Helferich, *Untersuchungen aus der Gebiet der klass. Alterthumswissenschaft* (Heidelberg, 1860). He asserted (probably in opposition to Numenius) the identity of God with that of the world-builder. See his writing ὅτι μόνος ποιητὴς ὁ βασιλεύς. Compare Zeller, V³. 461, 2.

Εἰς τὰ μεταφυσικά is the name of a document transmitted under the name of Herennius, but it is a compilation of much later origin. See A. Mai, *Classicorum Auctorum*, IX.; E. Heitz (Berlin *Sitzungsberichte*, 1889).

Longinus, who taught in Athens, held fast to the pure Platonic teaching of the reality of Ideas independent of the Spirit, and was opposed to Plotinus' interpretation. In spite of many doubters on the point, he is presumably the author of a treatise under his name, περὶ ὕψους (published by J. Vahlen, 1887). The rhetorical phases of the subject seem to have been of chief interest to the author; yet the treatise has real value beyond this, for it developed in the highest spiritual and intellectual manner the æsthetic concept of the sublime as not only independent of the idea of the beautiful and co-ordinate with it, but also in its numerous variations and applications. This treatise had a very great influence on the æsthetic theory and criticism of later time.

If, in comparing the great systems of Origen and Plotinus, one wishes to draw a conclusion as to the doctrine of their common teacher, one meets only the most universal principles of the Alexandrian religion-philosophies, and even then perhaps only the fundamental principles of overcoming metaphysically the dualism which forms the presupposition of that philosophy. There is not even a hint that would let us trace these philosophies back to Ammonius. He existed rather in the air, so far as the development of Alexandrian thought was concerned. The form of Ammonius is historically as colorless as perchance the view ascribed to him that Aristotelianism and Platonism are in essential agreement. See Zeller, V³. 454 ff.

Plotinus found so great recognition in the highest circles of Rome that he desired to found a city of philosophers in Campania, with the help of the Emperor Gallienus. It was to be called Platonopolis. It was to be arranged after the model of the Republic, and would be a retreat for religious contemplation, an Hellenic cloister. But it came to naught. Plotinus was active in a literary way only in his old age, and he wrote his doctrine in single treatises and groups of such. They were classified by his pupil, Porphyry, in six enneads, and published. They were translated into Latin by Marsilius Ficinus (Florence, 1492), and into Greek and Latin (Basel, 1580); new publications of them are: Oxford, 1835, Paris, 1855; Leipzig (by Kirchhoff), 1856; Berlin (by H. Müller), 1878–80. There is also a German translation of them (Leipzig, 1883–84) by Volkmann.

See K. Steinhart (in Pauly's *Realencyklopädie*); H. Kirchner, *Die Philosophie des Plotin's* (Halle, 1854); A. Richter, *Neuplatonische Studien*, five volumes (Halle, 1864–67); H. v. Kleist, *Plotinische Studien* (Heidelberg, 1883).

Porphyry, probably born and certainly brought up in Tyre, became the true disciple of Plotinus in Rome. Besides presenting and defending the doctrine of Plotinus, he busied himself especially with making commentaries on the Platonic and Aristotelian writings, and particularly on the logic of the latter. His Εἰσαγωγὴ εἰς τὰς κατηγορίας is preserved. It is published by Busse (Berlin, 1887). This became exceedingly important for the Middle Ages, as was also his biography of Plotinus (see Kirchhoff and Müller's publication of the works of Plotinus) and his smaller single writings. See bibliography in Ueberweg-Heinze, I⁷. 313. See also the Parisian Plotinus edition.

The problem of the Alexandrian philosophy of religion was the same for the Hellene as for the Christian. In the development of ancient thought, the individualization and the contemplativeness of the spiritual life kept equal pace, and created finally the burning desire to conceive the divine essence immediately and wholly with the innermost activity of the soul, — to unite oneself entirely and undividedly with that essence. But the more that confidence in the ancient forms of mythical representation vanished, the farther off, the more unknown, and the more incomprehensible appeared the divine essence. The Christian faith overcame this difficulty by the principle of love ; the mythical religion by the interpolation of countless grades between God and matter ; science, by attempting to conceive the totality of things as a series in diminishing perfection from the one all-creative divine power, and, conversely, by looking upon the entire cosmic life as the similarly graded returning series of things completed in God. The neo-Pythagorean dualism was to be overcome both ethically and metaphysically and therein Plotinus and Origen agreed. But while the latter, absorbed in the mysteries of the fall into sin and the redemption, analyzed the entire physical existence in ethical and religious terms, the former strove to make conceptual in the terms of sense the spiritual unity of the universe. Whereas the return to God according to the conception of Origen formed a tremendous historical cosmic process for the entire spiritual realm, it was limited by Plotinus to the mysterious ecstasy of the individual.

Metaphysics and ethics to Plotinus were, then, in inverted parallelism : ethics teaches the way of salvation to be the same series of stages of development toward an end, which is known in metaphysics as the process of origination from a beginning.

To Plotinus the Godhead is the original Being ($\tau\acute{o}$ $\pi\rho\tilde{\omega}\tau ov$) superior to all oppositions, inaccessible to all definitive characterization, wholly unspeakable ($\check{a}\rho\rho\eta\tau ov$). As absolute unity it is superior to all oppositions, especially to those of thought (νόησις) and Being (οὐσία). Only by relative determinations can it be conceived as a cosmic final cause (τὸ ἀγαθόν) and a cosmic force (πρώτη δύναμις), as pure, substratum-less (*substratlos*), creating activity. As such, it creates the world out of itself in an eternal, timeless, and necessary process. It is present in all creatures, yet it is separate and distinct from plurality. Itself eternally finished, it lets the fulness of things proceed from itself without division of itself or losing anything of its essence. The emanation of the world from the Godhead is an Overflowing in which the Godhead is as unchanged as light when it throws its gleam into the depths of the darkness. But as its gleam becomes less and less strong with the increase of distance from its source, so the creations of the Godhead are only a reflection of its glory, which reflection becomes less and less bright and finally ends in darkness.

The attempt to reconcile the monistic causality of God with the fact of the imperfection of individual things, and on the other hand of reconciling (religious) transcendence with (Stoical) pantheism, became also very prominent in Plotinus. His " dynamic pantheism " completed an abstract monotheism which sought to regard the Godhead neither as spirit, soul, nor matter, nor in fact under any category. Yet the theory conceived the Godhead, though entirely contentless, as the origin of all determinations and as superior to them all. The light in the darkness is an illustration; yet this simile defines also the thought of the philosopher from his point of view.

There are three particular steps in which emanation proceeds from the divine being: spirit, soul, matter. Spirit (νοῦς) as the image (εἰκών) of the One bears in itself the principle of duality. For all thinking, even consciousness of self, involves the opposition of subject and object, of thought-activity and thought-content (νοητόν). The νοῦς having its source in the Godhead is indeed a unitary, self-related, intuitive function. Nevertheless it includes within itself the entire manifold of objects, the Ideas which are the archetypes of individuals. These are then designated as single spiritual potencies (νοî). They are in the νοῦς and form in it the κόσμος νοητός, but as efficient powers they are at the same time the particular causes of events.

From reflection upon the essential duality of the activity and the content of thought, there resulted the fact that the neo-Platonists were the first to formulate and investigate with exactness the psychological conception of consciousness (συναίσθησις). The Aristotelian theory of αἰσθητήριον κοῖκον gave them a point of departure which they happily further followed out. The distinction between the unconscious content of an idea and the activity to be directed upon that content is current in their psychology and was their most important service. See H. Siebeck, *Gesch. der Psych.*, I. b, 331 ff.

This distinction naturally ceases to apply to the divine νοῦς in so far as it thinks its entire content of ideas as eternally actual. In Aristotelian Phraseology, Plotinus said that the duality (ἑτερότης) within the Spirit's essence presupposes the antithesis of thought-form (νόησις) and thought-content (ὕλη νοητική), — a content which is distinguished nevertheless from sense-content by the fact that it is formed without residuum and in timeless ἐνεργεία.

"Matter" is here the principle of plurality, and Plotinus followed this thought also so far as to develop the manifold of Ideas in a Pythagorean number-speculation. In this the Idea is however no longer the Platonic class-concept, but the (Stoic) archetype of the particular thing.

In respect to the intelligible world the Aristotelian categories were cast aside in so far as they refer to spatial and temporal relations and especially empirical events. For these Plotinus substituted five fundamental conceptions which were experimentally treated in the dialogue *Sophist* (254 b) as κοινωνία τῶν ἰδεῶν : ὄν, στάσις, κίνησις, ταὐτότης, ἑτερότης.

So far as Ideas are causes of events, they are called λόγοι, as for that matter the νοῦς of Plotinus has throughout to take the place of the λόγος of the Philonic and Christian philosophy. See M. Heinze, *Die Lehre vom Logos*, p. 306 ff.

The Soul (ψυχή) stands in the same relation to the Spirit as the Spirit to the ἕν. Since, although it belongs to the world of light, it stands on the bounds of the world of darkness, there is a duality in it: (1) unity and (2) divisibility, the higher and the lower souls. This duality is predicated in the first place of the world-soul, which Plotinus divided into two potencies, and the lower part, the φύσις, as a directly formative power (θέαμα) creates the body of the world and enters into it. It is the same with the individual souls into which the world-soul has discharged itself. There exists also in mankind the supersensible soul, to which were ascribed the functions of the Aristotelian νοῦς. (See above.) This has pre-existed, and shall after death undergo metempsychosis according to its deserts. This soul is to be distinguished from the lower soul which has built up the body as an instrument of its working power and is present in all its parts as well as in its sensational and functional activities.

As the light gradually fades away into darkness, the streaming out of the divine essence degenerates finally in matter. Plotinus regarded matter expressly as μὴ ὄν in the sense that it has no metaphysical dualistic independence in relation to the Godhead. It is the absolute στέρησις, the πενία παντελής, and as ἀπουσία τοῦ ἀγαθοῦ it is also πρῶτον κακόν. Plotinus founded his theodicy upon these negative determinations. Whatever is true, is divine and good : the bad is only what belongs to the μὴ ὄν. By the same necessity with which the gleaming of light is lost in the darkness, souls were supposed to create matter out of themselves and enter into it as formative powers. The world of sense phenomena has an existence that is just as eternal as the soul. In a circular process of mechanical development it unrolls the archetypes of Ideas. Then follows not merely a teleological conception of nature, but a downright magical one. Every event is an activity of the soul : the pure world-soul creates gods, star-spirits, and the φύσις-dæmons out of itself. In the mysterious co-operation of the whole is the individual sympathetically bound and prophetically to be foreseen. All investigation of nature was here annulled, but the door to all forms of faith and superstition was opened.

This comprehensive view of nature, however, was under these premises cleft in two. The entrance of the soul into the matter created by it is its fall into the darkness, its alienation from the divine source of light. The world of sense is bad and irrational. Yet, on the other hand, the world of sense is formed by the soul which enters into it as λόγος σπερματικός, and to that extent is it reasonable and beautiful. In this respect Plotinus, in spite of the dualistic point of departure made necessary by his religious problem, held distinctly to the Greek conception of the beauty of the world of sense, and he knew how to connect it in the most happy way with the fundamental outlines of his picture of the world. When he enthusiastically praised, in opposition particularly to the Gnostic disdain of nature, the harmony, soulfulness and perfection of the world, and proved this out of his idealistic construction of the world, he gave us a metaphysical æsthetic. Beautiful is the object of sense when it makes its λόγος, its ideal form, its εἶδος, appear in a perceptible form. Beautiful is the world because down to the lowest deeps it is permeated and illuminated by the divine essence.

Like a last farewell to the Grecian world was this theory of the beautiful which Plotinus brought into close connection with the ultimate principles of his system, and which he used for the first time as an integral part of a system of philosophy. To be sure, he strongly used Platonic and Aristotelian thoughts in it. But even the theory of the beautiful was not so fully developed by Plato, nor was it so essential a moment of Plato's as of Plotinus's system. The celebrated *Ennead*, I. 6, is doubtless the most original scientific achievement of Plotinus. The distinction of bodily and spiritual beauty, the contrast between the beauty of nature and of art, the organic insertion of æsthetics partly into his metaphysical system and partly into the development of his ethics and psychology — all these are great points of view which Plotinus is the first conceptually to define. See Ed. Müller, *Gesch. der Theorie der Kunst bei den Alten*, II. 285 ff. (Berlin, 1837) ; R. Zimmermann, *Gesch. der Æsthetik* (Vienna, 1858), 122 ff. ; R. Volkmann, *Die Höhe der antiken Æsthetik oder Plotin's Abhandl. vom Schönen* (Stettin, 1860) ; E. Brenning, *Die Lehre vom Schönen bei Plotin* (Göttingen, 1864), A. J. Vitringa, *De egregio, quod in rebus corporeis constituit Plotinus pulcri principio* (Amsterdam, 1864) ; J. Walter, *Gesch. der Æsthetik in Alterthum* (Leipzig, 1893), pp. 736–786.

Plotinus set out from the opposite point of view in his ethics, when he designated the share that men have in the divine life and their independence of the world as their goal ; and also when he conceived of the freeing of the soul from the body and its purification from sense — in a word, the turning away from the material — as the fundamental ethical task. There is not lacking a positive supplement to this negative morality although only in small measure did the philosopher indeed find such positive supplementation in ethical or, as he called it, political virtues. Conduct was of little value to him, for it binds the soul to the material world. Social and political integrity is only a preparation by which the soul learns how to become free from the power of sense. Therefore the teaching of Plotinus was also without significance for political life. His attempt to realize the Platonic Republic seemed to be not a political experiment but the realizing of a condition in which chosen men could live their true lives of " contemplation."

The return of the soul to God consists in its soaring to the νοῦς from which it came. Pure sense-perception offers little help to the soul for this return ; reflection affords rather more. The most potent incentive is found in love for the beautiful, the Platonic ἔρως, when the soul turns from sense impressions to the illuminating Idea. He who has an immediate recognition of the pure Idea, is pressing

on to higher perfection. Yet true blessedness is nevertheless attained only when man in an ecstasy (ἔκστασις) tran-
scending thought for a more complete contact and union
(ἁφή, ἅπλωσις) with the divine unity, forgets himself and
the objective world and becomes one with the Godhead in
such moments of consecration.

Plotinus regarded this highest holiness as a grace which
comes only to few, and to these but seldom. · He granted that
the culture of positive religion is a help to the attainment of this
ecstatic condition, although in other respects he opposed positive religion. This help, however, had earlier seemed essential
to Porphyry, and among the later members of the school it became the all-important thing.

55. A pupil of Porphyry, the Syrian Jamblichus, used the
philosophy of Plotinus as the groundwork of a speculative
theology of polytheism, which co-ordinated all the cults of
ancient religions in a systematic whole, and while excluding Christianity attempted to consider the religious movement as complete. Among the enthusiastic supporters of
this speculative theology are Theodorus of Asine, Maximus
of Ephesus, the Emperor Julian, his friend Sallustius, and
the martyr Hypatia.

Jamblichus came from Chalcis in Cœle-Syria, and listened to
Porphyry and his pupil Anatolius in Rome. He himself went
to Syria as a teacher and religious reformer, and had very soon
a numerous school, which exalted him as a worker of miracles.
Nothing further is known of his life, and his death also is only
approximately set about 330. His literary activity was limited
almost entirely to commentaries on Plato and Aristotle, as well
as on the theological works of the Orphics, Chaldæans, and the
Pythagoreans. Portions of his exposition of Pythagoreanism
are preserved : περὶ τοῦ Πυθαγορικοῦ βίου (published by Kiessling,
Leipzig, 1815 f., and Westermann, Paris, 1850) ; λόγος προτρεπτικὸς εἰς φιλοσοφίαν (Kiessling, Leipzig, 1813) ; περὶ τῆς κοινῆς
μαθηματικῆς ἐπιστήμης (Villoison, Venice, 1781) ; περὶ τῆς Νικο-
μάχου ἀριθμητικῆς εἰσαγωγή and τὰ θεολογούμενα τῆς ἀριθμητικῆς
(Fr. Ast, Leipzig, 1817). Related (and probably erroneously
ascribed to him) is *De mysteriis Ægyptiorum* (by Parthey, Ber-

lin, 1857) ; see Harless, *Das Buch von den ägyptischen Myste-rien* (Munich, 1858); H. Kellner, *Analyse der Schrift des Jamblichus De Mysteriis* (in *Theol. Quartalsschrift*, 1867).

Ædesius, Chrysanthius, Priscus, Sopater, Eusebius, Dexippus are other members of the school. A writing of Dexippus concerning the Aristotelian categories is preserved (edited by Spengel, Munich, 1859). Some of the biographies of philosophers of the time by Eunapius of Sardis are also preserved (edited by Boissonade, Amsterdam, 1822). Maximus played a great rôle at the court of Emperor Julian, whose short reign marks the zenith of the power of this Syrian school. Precisely these same court connections drove the school into its hopeless war with Christianity. Julian himself was a devoted follower of Jamblichus. The letters published under his name are spurious. His views appear in his speeches and in the fragments of his thesis against the Christians. *Juliani contra Christianos quæ supersunt* (E. J. Neuman, Leipzig, 1880 ; translated into German, Leipzig, 1880); other editions of his writings by E. Talbot (Paris, 1863) and F. C. Hertlein (2 vols., Leipzig, 1875 ff.). See A. W. Neander, *Ueber den Kaiser Julian u. seine Zeitalter* (Leipzig, 1812); W. S. Teuffel, *De Juliano Imp. Christianismi contemtore et osore* (Tübingen, 1844); D. Fr. Strauss, *Julian der Abtrünnige, der Romantiker auf dem Thron der Cäsaren* (Mannheim, 1847) ; Auer, *Kaiser Julian* (Vienna, 1855) ; W. Mangold, *Julian der Abtrünnige* (Stuttgart, 1862) ; C. Semisch, *Julian der Abtrünnige* (Breslau, 1862) ; Fr. Lübker, *Julian's Kampf u. Ende* (Hamburg, 1864) ; A. Mücke, *Julian nach den Quellen* (Gotha, 1866–68) ; A. Naville, *Julien l'Apostat et sa philos. du polytheisme* (Neufchatel, 1877) ; F. Rode, *Gesch. der Reaction Julian's gegen die christliche Kirche* (Jena, 1877). A compendium by Sallust of the theology of Jamblichus is preserved (published by Orelli, Zurich, 1821).

Concerning Hypatia, see Rich. Hoche (in *Philol.* 1860); St. Wolff (Czernowitz, 1879) ; H. Ligier (Dijon, 1880). Her pupil was the bishop Synesius, who tried to unite Neo-Platonism to Christianity in a unique way. See R. Volkmann, *Synesios von Kyrene* (Berlin, 1869).

The theology of Jamblichus included no new point of view for philosophy. His metaphysics and ethics were entirely those of Plotinus so far as the treatment is conceptual. But this was exactly what did not satisfy the theologian. Born in a land of the greatest religious eclecticism, a land where Christian Gnosticism had arisen, he wished to transform this philosophy into an amalgamation of all religions. Since he regarded the ordinances of the Mysteries and the activities of all their fantastic cults as indispensable for sinning man in solving moral and religious problems, he used the neo-Platonic metaphysic only for inserting by allegorical interpretation the forms of gods of all religions in the intermediate grades which Plotinus had supposed to lie between the human soul and God. In order to find place for this fantastic pantheon, he had to increase considerably the number of these intermediaries; and in order to bring the entire world of gods into a system, he had nothing better to use than the Pythagorean number-scheme.

The passing success that this theory had in the cultured and political world shows only the obstinacy with which the Hellenic, as opposed to the Christian world, held fast to the hope of solving the religious problem from within itself; and Julian also, who gave historical significance to this fantastic theory, can only thus be understood.

The details of this polytheism, and indeed those of the theurgic undertakings of Jamblichus and his pupils, are philosophically unimportant. Even his fancy of setting the πάντῃ ἄρρητος ἀρχή over the ἕν of Plotinus, which, bare of qualities, must not also be identified with the ἀγαθόν, is still only aimless sophistry. Plotinus set up the opposition of subject and object in the νοῦς, and Jamblichus made out of this opposition the κόσμος νοητός and the κόσμος νοερός. These are two worlds which are peopled with their own gods, and are again trebly divided. Some of his pupils further developed these divisions, and in this showed a preference for the triad schema, as did Jamblichus also to a certain extent.

56. The failure of this philosophical restoration of the old religions frightened neo-Platonism back to erudite studies, the centre of which again appeared finally at Athens. Through the influence of Plutarch of Athens and his pupils Syrianus and Hierocles, the school turned back to the study of Plato and Aristotle. In the person of its leader Proclus (410–485) it tried to systematize in a

dialectic way the entire historical content of Greek philosophic thought.

The commentators stand out advantageously against the background of fantastic theories of the time. As Themistius previously, so Simplicius and Philoponus now, transmitted their learned compilations of the works of Aristotle, which became of value to subsequent time. But when the pupils of Proclus — Marinus and Damascius — undertook to develop the system of their master, then they fell victims to unfruitful quibbling. The effect of this was unfortunate in proportion as the diction was bombastic and assertive.

The power of Greek thought was extinguished. The simple magnificent spirit of Greek philosophy had, to speak after the manner of Plotinus, grown so weak through all the Hellenic emanations that it passed away into its opposite, into ostentatious vapidity.

The edict by which the Emperor Justinian in 529 closed the Academy, confiscated its property, and prohibited lectures on Greek philosophy in Athens, was the official certification of the death of ancient philosophy.

Plutarch was called "The Great" by his pupils after the neo-Platonic manner of excessively admiring the leaders of their school. By this title he is generally distinguished from his really more significant namesake. He died soon after 430. He seems to have been particularly interested in psychological questions, and he further developed a theory of consciousness, defining it as the activity of the reason in sense perception.

Of the Syrian commentaries on Aristotle's writings, that upon a part of the *Metaphysics* is preserved and published in the fifth volume of the Berlin edition of Aristotle (p. 837 ff.). The commentary of Hierocles on the *Golden Poem* of the Pythagoreans is in Mullach's *Fragments* (I. 408 ff.) ; Photius has preserved extracts from Hierocles' writing, περὶ προνοίας. Hierocles and his pupil Theosebius worked in Alexandria, and Syrianus was scholarch in Athens.

Proclus was the intimate pupil and follower of Syrianus. He was of Lycian family, born in Constantinople, educated in Alexandria under Olympiodorus the Aristotelian, and was re-

vered as head of the school by his pupils with extravagant devotion. His life was written by his pupil Marinus (*Cobet's
Edition of Diog. Laert.*). Among the works of Proclus (see J.
Freudenthal in the *Hermes*, 1881, and Zeller, V. 778 ff.), especially noteworthy is περὶ τῆς κατὰ Πλάτωνα θεολογίας; and there
are also the commentaries on the *Timæus*, *Republic*, and *Parmenides*. These are collected by V. Cousin (Paris, 1820–25),
with Supplement (Paris, 1864). See A. Berger, *Proclus, exposition de sa doctrine* (Paris, 1840); H. Kirchner, *De Procli
metaphysica* (Berlin, 1846); K. Steinhart, article in *Pauly's
Realencyclopädie*.

Of the pupils of Proclus there are mentioned, besides his
successor Marinus, Hermias, who wrote a commentary on the
Phaedrus; the son of Hermias, Ammonius, who edited the
writings of Aristotle; the mathematician Asclepiodotus, and
further, Isidorus, Hegias, and Zenodotus. The biography of
Isidorus by Damascius is partly preserved in the writings of
Photius.

The last scholarch of the Academy was Damascius, who,
like Isidorus, returned to the fantastic theories of Jamblichus.
He was born in Damascus and studied in Alexandria and
Athens. After the closing of the school he emigrated with
Simplicius and other neo-Platonists to Persia. They returned
soon, however, after some hard experiences. Of his writings we
possess, besides fragments of various commentaries and his
biography of Isodorus, also a portion of his writing περὶ τῶν
πρώτων ἀρχῶν (published by J. Kapp, Frankfort on the Main,
1826, with details of his personality), and also the conclusion of
his commentary on the *Parmenides*. This commentary shows
markedly the influence of Proclus. See Ch. E. Ruelle, *Le
Philosophe Damascius* (Paris, 1861, and also in *Arch. f. Gesch.
d. Ph.* 1890); E. Heitz (particularly), *Der Philos. Damascius*
(in Strassburger *Abhandl. zur Philos.*, Freiburg i. B. und Tübingen, 1884).

Among the commentators who occupied a position of greater
independence toward the neo-Platonic theory was Themistius,
called ὁ εὐφραδής on account of his remarkable manner of presentation. He lived about 317–387, and taught in Constantinople.
Those of his preserved paraphrases upon Aristotle are upon
the second *Analytics*, the *Physics*, and the *Psychology* (published by Spengel, Leipzig, 1866). The paraphrase erroneously
ascribed to him on the first *Analytics* can be found in the Berlin edition of commentators (M. Wallies, Berlin, 1884). See
V. Rose (in the *Hermes*, 1867).

Of the commentaries of Simplicius the Cilician, who, next to

Alexander of Aphrodisias, was the most notable expounder of Aristotle and the contemporary and companion of Damascius, there are preserved those upon the first four books of the *Physics* (published by H. Diels, Berlin, 1882), and his commentary on *De cœlo* (published by S. Karstein, Utrecht, 1865), on *De anima* (published by M. Hayduck, Berlin, 1882), on the *Categories* (Basel, 1551), and on Epictetus' *Encheiridion*.

By the side of Priscianus and Asclepius there was the younger Olympiodorus, whose commentaries on the *Gorgias*, *Philebus*, *Phœdo*, and first *Alcibiades* (with the life of Plato) are preserved. There was also John Philiponus, of whose numerous commentaries (Venice, 1527 f.) those on the *Physics* have been published in the Berlin collection by Vitelli (1887).

Of still greater significance than these men for our present knowledge of ancient philosophy there was a neo-Platonist, who, a contemporary to them, came out of the movement in the East. This was Boëthius, who was condemned in 525. Although calling himself a Christian, he recognized only the arguments of ancient science in his treatise, *De consolatione philosophiæ* (published by R. Peiper, Leipzig, 1871). His translations and expositions of Aristotle's *Logic* and of the *Isagoge* of Porphyry belong among the important writings on philosophy in the early Middle Ages. See F. Nitzsch, *Das System des Boëthius* (Berlin, 1860); H. Usener, *Anekdoton Holderi* (Bonn, 1877); A. Hilderbrand, *Boëthius u. seine Stellung zum Christenthum* (Regensburg, 1885).

The peculiarity of the work of Proclus was his union of mythological fancifulness with barren formulism, of his insatiable desire for faith with the gift of dialectic combination. He was a theologian to the same extent as was Jamblichus, but he constructed for his teaching a philosophical schematism which was carried out with exactness even to the smallest detail. He got the content of his teaching from authority : from the barbarian and Hellenic religions, and in addition from the great philosophers, especially Plato, Plotinus, and Jamblichus. He had himself initiated into all the mysteries, and no superstition however childish was so bad as to be rejected by him. He did not rest until he had given a place in his universal system to every such significant thought; and he was the true systematizer of Heathendom and the scholastic of Hellenism.

The fundamentally constructive thought in his system was its abstract expression for the universal problem of neo-Platonism : the problem to make comprehensible the development of the One into the Many and the return of the Many into the One. The manifold effect is similar to the unitary cause, and yet different from it ; and this contradiction is reconciled by the fact that the effect strives by means of that very similarity to return to the cause from its state of separation from the cause. Hence these three moments, *permanence*, *going-forth*, and *return* (μονή, πρόοδος, ἐπιστροφή), are essential in every event. This is the leading idea of the conception of nature of Plotinus, who had also added the further principle that the return is through the same phases as the going-forth. Proclus, however, applied this triadic schematism with a powerful dialectic to every distinct phase of development in nature, and repeated it again and again even in treatment of the finest details. Every form of his metaphysical theology divides into three parts, each of which is again subjected to the same dialectic fate *ad infinitum*.

A certain formal likeness is obvious between this method of Proclus and the thesis, antithesis, and synthesis of Fichte, Schelling, and Hegel. It must not be overlooked, however, that by the latter the relationship is considered as between concepts, by the former between mythical potencies. But Hegel and Proclus are particularly alike in striving to systematize a very large given content of ideas in a dialectic way. (W. Windelband, *Gesch. der neueren Philos.*, II. 306 ff.)

The development of the world out of the Godhead was, then, represented by Proclus as a system of triadic chains, in which the descent is from the universal to the particular, from the simple to the complex, from the perfect to the imperfect. At the apex stands the original *One*, the original Good, which is raised above all determinations, entirely inexpressible, and only figuratively represented as the One, the Good, the αἴτιον. Out of this One emanate (even before the νοῦς) a limited, but, for our knowledge, an indeterminable number of unities (ἑνάδες) which are also unrecognizable. These are above Being, life, and reason, and are gods having power over the world.

These Henades had this theological significance for Proclus, that they place at his disposal a great number of supernatural incognizable gods. Metaphysically these appear in place of the second ἕν of Jamblichus. Another " Somewhat " accordingly perhaps plays a part here. Proclus is, like Porphyry, an outspoken realist in the spirit of the Middle Ages. The universal stands over against the particular as a higher and more nearly primitive actuality. Cause is identical with the universal, and the highest cause, the ἕν, is identical with the highest, most nearly characterless abstraction. One might, accordingly, suppose these simple abstract concepts to be the Henades, over and above which conceptions only the " Somewhat " remains. They have then a meaning similar to the Spinozistic attributes of the divine substance.

The Spirit is divided, in the scheme of Proclus, into the νοητόν, the νοητὸν ἅμα καὶ νοερόν, and the νοερόν. The Plotinian distinction between thought content and thought activity is fundamental here, but it is, however, at once disregarded on account of the theological construction. For here the νοητόν is divided into three parts, in which the concepts of πέρας, ἄπειρον, and μικτόν are combined respectively with πατήρ, δύναμις, and νόησις. Further, the concepts of οὐσία and ὕπαρξις, of ζωή and αἰών are combined in so multifarious a relationship, and with so many interchangeable meanings that a whole army of gods results. This same play repeats itself in the second sphere, and in part with the same categories. In the third sphere there are the seven Hebdomades of intellectual gods, among which, for example, the Olympians appear.

This entire construction, which in accordance with the same scheme is carried in the psychical world to gods, dæmons, and heroes, has no real intellectual motive at its basis. It is a kind of philosophical "mummification" of

Hellenism. This is partly due to the dialectic architectonic, and partly to the need of giving to every form of polytheism its place in the hierarchy of mythological formulæ into which Proclus had translated the Greek conceptual world.

The physics and ethics of Proclus show little individuality. He stood far off from the first, and adduced only this new thought that the material is not derived from the psychical, but directly from the ἄπειρον of the first intelligible triad, and that it is fancifully formed by the lower world-soul, the φύσις. His attempt in ethics is to lower the metaphysical dignity of the human soul and to make it appear thereby the more needy of the help of positive religious exercise and of divine and dæmonic grace. Proclus thinks, therefore, that the characteristic of the soul is its freedom, and therefore its guilt. The steps of its redemption are here also "political" virtue, scientific knowledge, divine illumination, faith, and finally ecstasy (μανία) for which a peculiar power of the soul is presupposed.

The two great streams of theosophy which burst forth from Alexandria, on the one hand, into Christian theology, on the other into neo-Platonism, were not long separate from each other. Although neo-Platonism was destroyed by scholasticism, it sent its thought through a thousand channels into the orthodox as well as the heterodox development of Christian thought after Origen. Both systems of thought found their perfect reconciliation in an original thinker, who was the philosopher of Christianity, — Augustine. The doctrine of Augustine, however, was much more than a receptacle for the confluent streams of Hellenic-Roman philosophy. It was rather the living fountain of the thought of the future. His was an initiating rather than a consummating work, and therefore he does not belong to the history of ancient philosophy.

BIBLIOGRAPHY

(A list of works on Ancient Philosophy for English readers.)

[Histories of Philosophy: by Stanley, London, 1655; Tenne-
mann, *Grundriss der Geschichte der Philosophie*, English tr. in
Bohn Library, 1833, 1852; *Ueberweg*, 3 vols., 8th ed., tr. by
G. S. Morris, New York, 1872–74; Hegel, *Vorlesungen über die·
Geschichte der Philosophie* (vols. XIII.–XV. of the Complete
Works), tr. by E. S. Haldane, 3 vols., London, 1892–96;
Schwegler, tr. by Seelye, New York, 1856 ff., and by J. H.
Sterling, 7th ed., Edinburgh, 1879; Cousin, tr. by O. W.
Wight, 2 vols., New York, 1889; Lange, *Geschichte des Ma-
terialismus*, 3 vols., tr. by E. C. Thomas, London, 1878–81;
Erdmann, 3 vols., tr. edited by W. S. Hough, London, 1890;
Lewes, 2 vols., 3d ed., London, 1863; Windelband, tr. by
J. H. Tufts, London and New York, 1893; Weber, tr. by F.
Thilly, New York, 1898.

Histories of Greek Philosophy: by Zeller, 5 vols., in 3 parts,
5th ed., tr. by S. F. Alleyne and O. J. Reichel, London and
New York, 1876–1883; *ibid.*, *Grundriss*, tr. by S. F.
Alleyne and Evelyn Abbot, New York, 1890; Ferrier, *Lectures
on Greek Philosophy*, 2 vols., Edinburgh and London, 1866,
London, 1888; Burnet, *Early Greek Philosophers*, London and
Edinburgh, 1892; Mayor, *A Sketch of Ancient Philosophy
from Thales to Cicero*, Cambridge, 1881 ff.; Benn, *The Greek
Philosophers*, 2 vols., London, 1883; Marshall, *A Short History
of Greek Philosophy*, London, 1891; Butler, *Lectures on the
History of Ancient Philosophy*, 2 vols., London, 1866; Ritter,
History of Ancient Philosophy, tr. by J. W. Morrison, Oxford,

1838–46; Anderson, *The Philosophy of Ancient Greece Investigated in Origin and Progress*, Edinburgh, 1791.

Histories of Greece, Greek Literature, etc.: Grote, *History of Greece*, 6th ed., 10 vols., London, 1888; Mahaffy, *History of Classical Greek Literature*, 2d ed., 3 vols., London, 1892; Laurie, *Historical Survey of pre-Christian Education*, London, 1895; Sidgwick, *History of Ethics*, London and New York, 1892; Flint, *History of the Philosophy of History*, New York, 1894; Bosanquet, *History of Æsthetics*, London and New York, 1892; Wundt, *Ethics*, vol. II., tr. by M. F. Washburn, New York, 1897; Cushman, *History of the Idea of Cause*, Harvard College Doctorate Thesis, Harvard Library; Botsford, *History of Greece*, New York, 1899; Holm, *History of Greece*, English tr., 4 vols., Boston, 1894; How and Leigh, *History of Rome to the Death of Cæsar*, New York, 1896; Bury, *History of the Roman Empire*, New York, 1893; Mommsen, *History of Rome*, 5 vols., New York, 1869–70; Peter-Chawner, *Chronological Tables of Greek History*, New York; Kiepert, *Atlas Antiquus*, Berlin and Boston, 1892; Kiepert, *Manual of Ancient Geography*, New York, 1881; Teuffel, *Geschichte der römischen Literatur*, tr. by G. C. W. Warr, New York, 1891; Jebb, *Primer of Greek Literature*, New York, 1878; A. S. Wilkins, *Primer of Roman Literature*, New York, 1890; Mahaffy, *History of Classical Greek Literature*, 2 vols., New York, 1891; Cruttwell, *History of Roman Literature*, New York, 1878; Middleton and Mills, *The Student's Companion to Latin Authors*, New York, 1896; J. W. Mackail, *Latin Literature*, New York, 1895.

The pre-Socratic Greeks: Burnet, *Early Greek Philosophy with translations*, London and Edinburgh, 1892; Patrick, *Heracleitus on Nature*, Baltimore, 1889; Bohn's Classical Library, translations; *Encyclopædia Britannica*, especially article by H. Jackson on *Sophists;* Davidson, *The Fragments of Parmenides*, in *Jour. of Spec. Phil.* IV., 1, St. Louis, Jan. 1870.

Works on Socrates: Plato, *Apology, Crito, and Phædo, Phædrus, Meno, Theætetus*, etc.; Xenophon, *Memorabilia* and *Symposium;* Aristotle, *Metaphysics*, I., 6 ff.; Grote, *History of*

Greece, vol. VIII., ch. 68 ; Potter, *Characteristics of the Greek Philosophers, Socrates and Plato*, London, 1845; R. D. Hampden, *The Fathers of Greek Philosophy*, Edinburgh, 1869 ; see also articles in *Encyclopædia Britannica.*

Works on Plato: Jowett, Translation of the *Dialogues*, with introductions and analyses, in 5 vols., 3d ed., New York and London, 1892; Grote, *Plato and Other Companions of Socrates,* 3 vols., London, 1865; Pater, *Plato and Platonism*, New York and London, 1893; Van Oordt, *Plato and His Times*, Oxford and the Hague, 1895 ; Bosanquet, *A Companion to Plato's Republic*, New York, 1895; Hartmann, *Philosophy of the Unconscious*, tr. by E. C. Thomas of the chapter *On the Unconscious in Mysticism ;* Martineau, *Types of Ethical Theory*, London and New York, 1886 ; see also *Essays ;* Campbell, in *Encyclopædia Britannica*, article *Plato ;* Nettleship, in *Hellenica, The Theory of Education in Plato's Republic;* Mill, J. S., *Essays and Discussions.*

Works on Aristotle, Translations: *Psychology* in Greek and English, page for page, with introduction and notes, by E. Wallace, Cambridge, 1882 ; *Nicomachœan Ethics*, tr. with analysis and notes by J. E. C. Welldon, New York and London, 1892 ; also by Williams, 1876, Chase, 1877, Hatch, 1879, Peters, 1881, Gillies, 1892; *Politics*, tr. by Welldon, Cambridge, 1888, also by Jowett, 2 vols. 1885–88, Ellis, with introduction by Morley, 1892 ; *On the Constitution of Athens*, tr. with notes by Kenyon, London, 1891; *Politics*, tr. by Wharton, Cambridge, 1883; *Rhetoric*, tr. by Welldon, London and New York, 1886 ; *Metaphysics, Organon*, and *History of Animals*, tr. in the Bohn Library ; Lewes, *Aristotle*, London, 1864; Grote, *Aristotle*, 2 vols., incomplete, 3d ed., London, 1884 ; E. Wallace, *Outlines of the Philosophy of Aristotle*, 3d ed., Oxford, 1883; A. Grant, *Aristotle*, in *Ancient Classics for English Readers*, Edinburgh and London, 1878 ; Davidson, *Aristotle and Ancient Educational Ideals*, New York, 1892 ; Th. H. Green, *Works ;* Bradley, in *Hellenica*, on *Aristotle's Theory of the State ;* Taylor, *Dissertation on the Philosophy of Aristotle*, London, 1813; Bain, *Senses and Intellect*, supplement by Grote, London, 1869.

The post-Aristotelian period: W. Wallace, *Epicureanism*, London, 1880; Grote, *Aristotle* (see Aristotle); Jackson, *Seneca and Kant*, 1881; Bryant, *The Mutual Influence of Christianity and the Stoic School*, London, 1866; Capes, *Stoicism*, London, 1880; Lightfoot, *St. Paul's Epistle to the Philippians*, 4th ed., London, 1878.

For Epictetus, the Διατριβαί and Ἐγχειρίδιον, tr. by T. W. Higginson, Boston, 1865; for Marcus Aurelius, τὰ εἰς ἑαυτόν, tr. by G. Long; Watson, *Life of Marcus Aurelius*, London, 1884; Drummond, *Philo Judæus*, London, 1888; Schürer, *History of the Jewish People*, 5 vols., New York, 1891; Munro, tr. of Lucretius' poem, *De Natura Rerum*, London, 1886; Masson, *The Atomic Theory of Lucretius*, London, 1884; Courtney, in *Hellenica*, subject, *Epicureanism;* Maccoll, *The Greek Sceptics*, London, 1869; Owen, *Evenings with the Sceptics*, London, 1881; A. Seth, in *Encyclopædia Britannica*, article *Scepticism;* Cicero, Translations of, in the Bohn Library; Tredwell, *Life of Apollonius of Tyana*, New York, 1886; Pater, *Marius the Epicurean*, London and New York, 1888; Yonge, tr. of *Philo*, 4 vols., Bohn Library, London.

Works on neo-Platonism and Patristics: *Plotinus*, tr. of parts of works of, by Th. Taylor, London, 1787, 1794, 1817; Harnack, *Neo-Platonism* in *Encyclopædia Britannica;* St. Paul, *Epistle to Corinthians*, I., XV. ; *ibid.*, *Philippians*, I.; Gale, *Life of Protagoras, of Plotinus, and Epistle to Anebo*, by Porphyry, Oxford, 1678 ; Taylor, *Life of Pythagoras*, London, 1818; Chiswick, *Egyptian Mysteries*, 1821, also by Taylor; Schaff and Wace, Library of Nicene and post-Nicene Fathers, New York, 1890 ; Mansel, *The Gnostic Heresies*, London, 1875; Allen, *Continuity of Christian Thought*, Boston, 1884 ; Donaldson, *Critical History of Christian Literature and Doctrine;* Neander, *Expositions of the Gnostic Systems*, tr. by Torrey, Boston, 1865 ; *ibid.*, *Antignosticus*, tr. in Bohn Library ; Bigg, *Christian Platonists of Alexandria*, Oxford, 1887 ; Harnack, *Encyclopædia Britannica*, article *Origen ;* Taylor, tr. of works of *Proclus*.

INDEX

A CATALOGUE OF SELECTED DOVER BOOKS
IN ALL FIELDS OF INTEREST

A CATALOGUE OF SELECTED DOVER BOOKS
IN ALL FIELDS OF INTEREST

WHAT IS SCIENCE?, *N. Campbell*
The role of experiment and measurement, the function of mathematics, the nature of scientific laws, the difference between laws and theories, the limitations of science, and many similarly provocative topics are treated clearly and without technicalities by an eminent scientist. "Still an excellent introduction to scientific philosophy," H. Margenau in *Physics Today*. "A first-rate primer . . . deserves a wide audience," *Scientific American*. 192pp. 5⅜ x 8.
60043-2 Paperbound $1.25

THE NATURE OF LIGHT AND COLOUR IN THE OPEN AIR, *M. Minnaert*
Why are shadows sometimes blue, sometimes green, or other colors depending on the light and surroundings? What causes mirages? Why do multiple suns and moons appear in the sky? Professor Minnaert explains these unusual phenomena and hundreds of others in simple, easy-to-understand terms based on optical laws and the properties of light and color. No mathematics is required but artists, scientists, students, and everyone fascinated by these "tricks" of nature will find thousands of useful and amazing pieces of information. Hundreds of observational experiments are suggested which require no special equipment. 200 illustrations; 42 photos. xvi + 362pp. 5⅜ x 8.
20196-1 Paperbound $2.00

THE STRANGE STORY OF THE QUANTUM, AN ACCOUNT FOR THE GENERAL READER OF THE GROWTH OF IDEAS UNDERLYING OUR PRESENT ATOMIC KNOWLEDGE, *B. Hoffmann*
Presents lucidly and expertly, with barest amount of mathematics, the problems and theories which led to modern quantum physics. Dr. Hoffmann begins with the closing years of the 19th century, when certain trifling discrepancies were noticed, and with illuminating analogies and examples takes you through the brilliant concepts of Planck, Einstein, Pauli, Broglie, Bohr, Schroedinger, Heisenberg, Dirac, Sommerfeld, Feynman, etc. This edition includes a new, long postscript carrying the story through 1958. "Of the books attempting an account of the history and contents of our modern atomic physics which have come to my attention, this is the best," H. Margenau, Yale University, in *American Journal of Physics*. 32 tables and line illustrations. Index. 275pp. 5⅜ x 8.
20518-5 Paperbound $2.00

GREAT IDEAS OF MODERN MATHEMATICS: THEIR NATURE AND USE, *Jagjit Singh*
Reader with only high school math will understand main mathematical ideas of modern physics, astronomy, genetics, psychology, evolution, etc. better than many who use them as tools, but comprehend little of their basic structure. Author uses his wide knowledge of non-mathematical fields in brilliant exposition of differential equations, matrices, group theory, logic, statistics, problems of mathematical foundations, imaginary numbers, vectors, etc. Original publication. 2 appendixes. 2 indexes. 65 ills. 322pp. 5⅜ x 8.
20587-8 Paperbound $2.25

THE MUSIC OF THE SPHERES: THE MATERIAL UNIVERSE — FROM ATOM TO QUASAR, SIMPLY EXPLAINED, *Guy Murchie*
Vast compendium of fact, modern concept and theory, observed and calculated data, historical background guides intelligent layman through the material universe. Brilliant exposition of earth's construction, explanations for moon's craters, atmospheric components of Venus and Mars (with data from recent fly-by's), sun spots, sequences of star birth and death, neighboring galaxies, contributions of Galileo, Tycho Brahe, Kepler, etc.; and (Vol. 2) construction of the atom (describing newly discovered sigma and xi subatomic particles), theories of sound, color and light, space and time, including relativity theory, quantum theory, wave theory, probability theory, work of Newton, Maxwell, Faraday, Einstein, de Broglie, etc. "Best presentation yet offered to the intelligent general reader," *Saturday Review*. Revised (1967). Index. 319 illustrations by the author. Total of xx + 644pp. 5⅜ x 8½.
21809-0, 21810-4   Two volume set, paperbound $5.00

FOUR LECTURES ON RELATIVITY AND SPACE, *Charles Proteus Steinmetz*
Lecture series, given by great mathematician and electrical engineer, generally considered one of the best popular-level expositions of special and general relativity theories and related questions. Steinmetz translates complex mathematical reasoning into language accessible to laymen through analogy, example and comparison. Among topics covered are relativity of motion, location, time; of mass; acceleration; 4-dimensional time-space; geometry of the gravitational field; curvature and bending of space; non-Euclidean geometry. Index. 40 illustrations. x + 142pp. 5⅜ x 8½.   61771-8 Paperbound $1.35

HOW TO KNOW THE WILD FLOWERS, *Mrs. William Starr Dana*
Classic nature book that has introduced thousands to wonders of American wild flowers. Color-season principle of organization is easy to use, even by those with no botanical training, and the genial, refreshing discussions of history, folklore, uses of over 1,000 native and escape flowers, foliage plants are informative as well as fun to read. Over 170 full-page plates, collected from several editions, may be colored in to make permanent records of finds. Revised to conform with 1950 edition of Gray's Manual of Botany. xlii + 438pp. 5⅜ x 8½.   20332-8 Paperbound $2.50

MANUAL OF THE TREES OF NORTH AMERICA, *Charles Sprague Sargent*
Still unsurpassed as most comprehensive, reliable study of North American tree characteristics, precise locations and distribution. By dean of American dendrologists. Every tree native to U.S., Canada, Alaska; 185 genera, 717 species, described in detail—leaves, flowers, fruit, winterbuds, bark, wood, growth habits, etc. plus discussion of varieties and local variants, immaturity variations. Over 100 keys, including unusual 11-page analytical key to genera, aid in identification. 783 clear illustrations of flowers, fruit, leaves. An unmatched permanent reference work for all nature lovers. Second enlarged (1926) edition. Synopsis of families. Analytical key to genera. Glossary of technical terms. Index. 783 illustrations, 1 map. Total of 982pp. 5⅜ x 8.
20277-1, 20278-X Two volume set, paperbound $6.00

IT'S FUN TO MAKE THINGS FROM SCRAP MATERIALS,
Evelyn Glantz Hershoff
What use are empty spools, tin cans, bottle tops? What can be made from
rubber bands, clothes pins, paper clips, and buttons? This book provides
simply worded instructions and large diagrams showing you how to make
cookie cutters, toy trucks, paper turkeys, Halloween masks, telephone sets,
aprons, linoleum block- and spatter prints — in all 399 projects! Many are easy
enough for young children to figure out for themselves; some challenging
enough to entertain adults; all are remarkably ingenious ways to make things
from materials that cost pennies or less! Formerly "Scrap Fun for Everyone."
Index. 214 illustrations. 373pp. 5⅜ x 8½.   21251-3 Paperbound $1.75

SYMBOLIC LOGIC and THE GAME OF LOGIC, *Lewis Carroll*
"Symbolic Logic" is not concerned with modern symbolic logic, but is instead
a collection of over 380 problems posed with charm and imagination, using
the syllogism and a fascinating diagrammatic method of drawing conclusions.
In "The Game of Logic" Carroll's whimsical imagination devises a logical game
played with 2 diagrams and counters (included) to manipulate hundreds of
tricky syllogisms. The final section, "Hit or Miss" is a lagniappe of 101 additional puzzles in the delightful Carroll manner. Until this reprint edition,
both of these books were rarities costing up to $15 each. Symbolic Logic:
Index. xxxi + 199pp. The Game of Logic: 96pp. 2 vols. bound as one. 5⅜ x 8.
                                             20492-8 Paperbound $2.50

MATHEMATICAL PUZZLES OF SAM LOYD, PART I
selected and edited by M. Gardner
Choice puzzles by the greatest American puzzle creator and innovator. Selected
from his famous collection, "Cyclopedia of Puzzles," they retain the unique
style and historical flavor of the originals. There are posers based on arithmetic,
algebra, probability, game theory, route tracing, topology, counter and sliding
block, operations research, geometrical dissection. Includes the famous "14-15"
puzzle which was a national craze, and his "Horse of a Different Color" which
sold millions of copies. 117 of his most ingenious puzzles in all. 120 line
drawings and diagrams. Solutions. Selected references. xx + 167pp. 5⅜ x 8.
                                             20498-7 Paperbound $1.35

STRING FIGURES AND HOW TO MAKE THEM, *Caroline Furness Jayne*
107 string figures plus variations selected from the best primitive and modern
examples developed by Navajo, Apache, pygmies of Africa, Eskimo, in Europe,
Australia, China, etc. The most readily understandable, easy-to-follow book in
English on perennially popular recreation. Crystal-clear exposition; step-by-
step diagrams. Everyone from kindergarten children to adults looking for
unusual diversion will be endlessly amused. Index. Bibliography. Introduction
by A. C. Haddon. 17 full-page plates, 960 illustrations. xxiii + 401pp. 5⅜ x 8½.
                                             20152-X Paperbound $2.25

PAPER FOLDING FOR BEGINNERS, *W. D. Murray and F. J. Rigney*
A delightful introduction to the varied and entertaining Japanese art of
origami (paper folding), with a full, crystal-clear text that anticipates every
difficulty; over 275 clearly labeled diagrams of all important stages in creation.
You get results at each stage, since complex figures are logically developed
from simpler ones. 43 different pieces are explained: sailboats, frogs, roosters,
etc. 6 photographic plates. 279 diagrams. 95pp. 5⅝ x 8⅜.
                                             20713-7 Paperbound $1.00

PRINCIPLES OF ART HISTORY,
H. Wölfflin
Analyzing such terms as "baroque," "classic," "neoclassic," "primitive," "picturesque," and 164 different works by artists like Botticelli, van Cleve, Dürer, Hobbema, Holbein, Hals, Rembrandt, Titian, Brueghel, Vermeer, and many others, the author establishes the classifications of art history and style on a firm, concrete basis. This classic of art criticism shows what really occurred between the 14th-century primitives and the sophistication of the 18th century in terms of basic attitudes and philosophies. "A remarkable lesson in the art of seeing," *Sat. Rev. of Literature.* Translated from the 7th German edition. 150 illustrations. 254pp. 6⅛ x 9¼. 20276-3 Paperbound $2.25

PRIMITIVE ART,
Franz Boas
This authoritative and exhaustive work by a great American anthropologist covers the entire gamut of primitive art. Pottery, leatherwork, metal work, stone work, wood, basketry, are treated in detail. Theories of primitive art, historical depth in art history, technical virtuosity, unconscious levels of patterning, symbolism, styles, literature, music, dance, etc. A must book for the interested layman, the anthropologist, artist, handicrafter (hundreds of unusual motifs), and the historian. Over 900 illustrations (50 ceramic vessels, 12 totem poles, etc.). 376pp. 5⅜ x 8.   20025-6 Paperbound $2.50

THE GENTLEMAN AND CABINET MAKER'S DIRECTOR,
Thomas Chippendale
A reprint of the 1762 catalogue of furniture designs that went on to influence generations of English and Colonial and Early Republic American furniture makers. The 200 plates, most of them full-page sized, show Chippendale's designs for French (Louis XV), Gothic, and Chinese-manner chairs, sofas, canopy and dome beds, cornices, chamber organs, cabinets, shaving tables, commodes, picture frames, frets, candle stands, chimney pieces, decorations, etc. The drawings are all elegant and highly detailed; many include construction diagrams and elevations. A supplement of 24 photographs shows surviving pieces of original and Chippendale-style pieces of furniture. Brief biography of Chippendale by N. I. Bienenstock, editor of *Furniture World.* Reproduced from the 1762 edition. 200 plates, plus 19 photographic plates. vi + 249pp. 9⅛ x 12¼.   21601-2 Paperbound $3.50

AMERICAN ANTIQUE FURNITURE: A BOOK FOR AMATEURS,
Edgar G. Miller, Jr.
Standard introduction and practical guide to identification of valuable American antique furniture. 2115 illustrations, mostly photographs taken by the author in 148 private homes, are arranged in chronological order in extensive chapters on chairs, sofas, chests, desks, bedsteads, mirrors, tables, clocks, and other articles. Focus is on furniture accessible to the collector, including simpler pieces and a larger than usual coverage of Empire style. Introductory chapters identify structural elements, characteristics of various styles, how to avoid fakes, etc. "We are frequently asked to name some book on American furniture that will meet the requirements of the novice collector, the beginning dealer, and . . . the general public. . . . We believe Mr. Miller's two volumes more completely satisfy this specification than any other work," *Antiques.* Appendix. Index. Total of vi + 1106pp. 7⅞ x 10¾. 21599-7, 21600-4 Two volume set, paperbound $7.50

THE BAD CHILD'S BOOK OF BEASTS, MORE BEASTS FOR WORSE CHILDREN, and A MORAL ALPHABET, *H. Belloc*
Hardly and anthology of humorous verse has appeared in the last 50 years without at least a couple of these famous nonsense verses. But one must see the entire volumes — with all the delightful original illustrations by Sir Basil Blackwood — to appreciate fully Belloc's charming and witty verses that play so subacidly on the platitudes of life and morals that beset his day — and ours. A great humor classic. Three books in one. Total of 157pp. 5⅜ x 8.
20749-8 Paperbound $1.00

THE DEVIL'S DICTIONARY, *Ambrose Bierce*
Sardonic and irreverent barbs puncturing the pomposities and absurdities of American politics, business, religion, literature, and arts, by the country's greatest satirist in the classic tradition. Epigrammatic as Shaw, piercing as Swift, American as Mark Twain, Will Rogers, and Fred Allen, Bierce will always remain the favorite of a small coterie of enthusiasts, and of writers and speakers whom he supplies with "some of the most gorgeous witticisms of the English language" (H. L. Mencken). Over 1000 entries in alphabetical order. 144pp. 5⅜ x 8.
20487-1 Paperbound $1.00

THE COMPLETE NONSENSE OF EDWARD LEAR.
This is the only complete edition of this master of gentle madness available at a popular price. *A Book of Nonsense, Nonsense Songs, More Nonsense Songs and Stories* in their entirety with all the old favorites that have delighted children and adults for years. The Dong With A Luminous Nose, The Jumblies, The Owl and the Pussycat, and hundreds of other bits of wonderful nonsense. 214 limericks, 3 sets of Nonsense Botany, 5 Nonsense Alphabets, 546 drawings by Lear himself, and much more. 320pp. 5⅜ x 8.   20167-8 Paperbound $1.75

THE WIT AND HUMOR OF OSCAR WILDE, *ed. by Alvin Redman*
Wilde at his most brilliant, in 1000 epigrams exposing weaknesses and hypocrisies of "civilized" society. Divided into 49 categories—sin, wealth, women, America, etc.—to aid writers, speakers. Includes excerpts from his trials, books, plays, criticism. Formerly "The Epigrams of Oscar Wilde." Introduction by Vyvyan Holland, Wilde's only living son. Introductory essay by editor. 260pp. 5⅜ x 8.   20602-5 Paperbound $1.50

A CHILD'S PRIMER OF NATURAL HISTORY, *Oliver Herford*
Scarcely an anthology of whimsy and humor has appeared in the last 50 years without a contribution from Oliver Herford. Yet the works from which these examples are drawn have been almost impossible to obtain! Here at last are Herford's improbable definitions of a menagerie of familiar and weird animals, each verse illustrated by the author's own drawings. 24 drawings in 2 colors; 24 additional drawings. vii + 95pp. 6½ x 6.   21647-0 Paperbound $1.00

THE BROWNIES: THEIR BOOK, *Palmer Cox*
The book that made the Brownies a household word. Generations of readers have enjoyed the antics, predicaments and adventures of these jovial sprites, who emerge from the forest at night to play or to come to the aid of a deserving human. Delightful illustrations by the author decorate nearly every page. 24 short verse tales with 266 illustrations. 155pp. 6⅝ x 9¼.
21265-3 Paperbound $1.50

THE PRINCIPLES OF PSYCHOLOGY,
William James
The full long-course, unabridged, of one of the great classics of Western literature and science. Wonderfully lucid descriptions of human mental activity, the stream of thought, consciousness, time perception, memory, imagination, emotions, reason, abnormal phenomena, and similar topics. Original contributions are integrated with the work of such men as Berkeley, Binet, Mills, Darwin, Hume, Kant, Royce, Schopenhauer, Spinoza, Locke, Descartes, Galton, Wundt, Lotze, Herbart, Fechner, and scores of others. All contrasting interpretations of mental phenomena are examined in detail—introspective analysis, philosophical interpretation, and experimental research. "A classic," *Journal of Consulting Psychology*. "The main lines are as valid as ever," *Psychoanalytical Quarterly*. "Standard reading . . . a classic of interpretation," *Psychiatric Quarterly*. 94 illustrations. 1408pp. 5⅜ x 8.
20381-6, 20382-4 Two volume set, paperbound $6.00

VISUAL ILLUSIONS: THEIR CAUSES, CHARACTERISTICS AND APPLICATIONS,
M. Luckiesh
"Seeing is deceiving," asserts the author of this introduction to virtually every type of optical illusion known. The text both describes and explains the principles involved in color illusions, figure-ground, distance illusions, etc. 100 photographs, drawings and diagrams prove how easy it is to fool the sense: circles that aren't round, parallel lines that seem to bend, stationary figures that seem to move as you stare at them — illustration after illustration strains our credulity at what we see. Fascinating book from many points of view, from applications for artists, in camouflage, etc. to the psychology of vision. New introduction by William Ittleson, Dept. of Psychology, Queens College. Index. Bibliography. xxi + 252pp. 5⅜ x 8½.   21530-X Paperbound $1.50

FADS AND FALLACIES IN THE NAME OF SCIENCE,
Martin Gardner
This is the standard account of various cults, quack systems, and delusions which have masqueraded as science: hollow earth fanatics. Reich and orgone sex energy, dianetics, Atlantis, multiple moons, Forteanism, flying saucers, medical fallacies like iridiagnosis, zone therapy, etc. A new chapter has been added on Bridey Murphy, psionics, and other recent manifestations in this field. This is a fair, reasoned appraisal of eccentric theory which provides excellent inoculation against cleverly masked nonsense. "Should be read by everyone, scientist and non-scientist alike," R. T. Birge, Prof. Emeritus of Physics, Univ. of California; Former President, American Physical Society. Index. x + 365pp. 5⅜ x 8.   20394-8 Paperbound $2.00

ILLUSIONS AND DELUSIONS OF THE SUPERNATURAL AND THE OCCULT,
D. H. Rawcliffe
Holds up to rational examination hundreds of persistent delusions including crystal gazing, automatic writing, table turning, mediumistic trances, mental healing, stigmata, lycanthropy, live burial, the Indian Rope Trick, spiritualism, dowsing, telepathy, clairvoyance, ghosts, ESP, etc. The author explains and exposes the mental and physical deceptions involved, making this not only an exposé of supernatural phenomena, but a valuable exposition of characteristic types of abnormal psychology. Originally titled "The Psychology of the Occult." 14 illustrations. Index. 551pp. 5⅜ x 8. 20503-7 Paperbound $3.50

FAIRY TALE COLLECTIONS, *edited by Andrew Lang*
Andrew Lang's fairy tale collections make up the richest shelf-full of traditional children's stories anywhere available. Lang supervised the translation of stories from all over the world—familiar European tales collected by Grimm, animal stories from Negro Africa, myths of primitive Australia, stories from Russia, Hungary, Iceland, Japan, and many other countries. Lang's selection of translations are unusually high; many authorities consider that the most familiar tales find their best versions in these volumes. All collections are richly decorated and illustrated by H. J. Ford and other artists.

THE BLUE FAIRY BOOK. 37 stories. 138 illustrations. ix + 390pp. 5⅜ x 8½.
21437-0 Paperbound $1.95

THE GREEN FAIRY BOOK. 42 stories. 100 illustrations. xiii + 366pp. 5⅜ x 8½.
21439-7 Paperbound $1.75

THE BROWN FAIRY BOOK. 32 stories. 50 illustrations, 8 in color. xii + 350pp. 5⅜ x 8½.
21438-9 Paperbound $1.95

THE BEST TALES OF HOFFMANN, *edited by E. F. Bleiler*
10 stories by E. T. A. Hoffmann, one of the greatest of all writers of fantasy. The tales include "The Golden Flower Pot," "Automata," "A New Year's Eve Adventure," "Nutcracker and the King of Mice," "Sand-Man," and others. Vigorous characterizations of highly eccentric personalities, remarkably imaginative situations, and intensely fast pacing has made these tales popular all over the world for 150 years. Editor's introduction. 7 drawings by Hoffmann. xxxiii + 419pp. 5⅜ x 8½.
21793-0 Paperbound $2.25

GHOST AND HORROR STORIES OF AMBROSE BIERCE,
edited by E. F. Bleiler
Morbid, eerie, horrifying tales of possessed poets, shabby aristocrats, revived corpses, and haunted malefactors. Widely acknowledged as the best of their kind between Poe and the moderns, reflecting their author's inner torment and bitter view of life. Includes "Damned Thing," "The Middle Toe of the Right Foot," "The Eyes of the Panther," "Visions of the Night," "Moxon's Master," and over a dozen others. Editor's introduction. xxii + 199pp. 5⅜ x 8½.
20767-6 Paperbound $1.50

THREE GOTHIC NOVELS, *edited by E. F. Bleiler*
Originators of the still popular Gothic novel form, influential in ushering in early 19th-century Romanticism. Horace Walpole's *Castle of Otranto*, William Beckford's *Vathek*, John Polidori's *The Vampyre*, and a *Fragment* by Lord Byron are enjoyable as exciting reading or as documents in the history of English literature. Editor's introduction. xi + 291pp. 5⅜ x 8½.
21232-7 Paperbound $2.00

BEST GHOST STORIES OF LEFANU, *edited by E. F. Bleiler*
Though admired by such critics as V. S. Pritchett, Charles Dickens and Henry James, ghost stories by the Irish novelist Joseph Sheridan LeFanu have never become as widely known as his detective fiction. About half of the 16 stories in this collection have never before been available in America. Collection includes "Carmilla" (perhaps the best vampire story ever written), "The Haunted Baronet," "The Fortunes of Sir Robert Ardagh," and the classic "Green Tea." Editor's introduction. 7 contemporary illustrations. Portrait of LeFanu. xii + 467pp. 5⅜ x 8.
20415-4 Paperbound $2.50

EASY-TO-DO ENTERTAINMENTS AND DIVERSIONS WITH COINS, CARDS, STRING, PAPER AND MATCHES, *R. M. Abraham*
Over 300 tricks, games and puzzles will provide young readers with absorbing fun. Sections on card games; paper-folding; tricks with coins, matches and pieces of string; games for the agile; toy-making from common household objects; mathematical recreations; and 50 miscellaneous pastimes. Anyone in charge of groups of youngsters, including hard-pressed parents, and in need of suggestions on how to keep children sensibly amused and quietly content will find this book indispensable. Clear, simple text, copious number of delightful line drawings and illustrative diagrams. Originally titled "Winter Nights' Entertainments." Introduction by Lord Baden Powell. 329 illustrations. v + 186pp. 5⅜ x 8½. 20921-0 Paperbound $1.00

AN INTRODUCTION TO CHESS MOVES AND TACTICS SIMPLY EXPLAINED, *Leonard Barden*
Beginner's introduction to the royal game. Names, possible moves of the pieces, definitions of essential terms, how games are won, etc. explained in 30-odd pages. With this background you'll be able to sit right down and play. Balance of book teaches strategy — openings, middle game, typical endgame play, and suggestions for improving your game. A sample game is fully analyzed. True middle-level introduction, teaching you all the essentials without oversimplifying or losing you in a maze of detail. 58 figures. 102pp. 5⅜ x 8½. 21210-6 Paperbound $1.25

LASKER'S MANUAL OF CHESS, *Dr. Emanuel Lasker*
Probably the greatest chess player of modern times, Dr. Emanuel Lasker held the world championship 28 years, independent of passing schools or fashions. This unmatched study of the game, chiefly for intermediate to skilled players, analyzes basic methods, combinations, position play, the aesthetics of chess, dozens of different openings, etc., with constant reference to great modern games. Contains a brilliant exposition of Steinitz's important theories. Introduction by Fred Reinfeld. Tables of Lasker's tournament record. 3 indices. 308 diagrams. 1 photograph. xxx + 349pp. 5⅜ x 8. 20640-8 Paperbound $2.50

COMBINATIONS: THE HEART OF CHESS, *Irving Chernev*
Step-by-step from simple combinations to complex, this book, by a well-known chess writer, shows you the intricacies of pins, counter-pins, knight forks, and smothered mates. Other chapters show alternate lines of play to those taken in actual championship games; boomerang combinations; classic examples of brilliant combination play by Nimzovich, Rubinstein, Tarrasch, Botvinnik, Alekhine and Capablanca. Index. 356 diagrams. ix + 245pp. 5⅜ x 8½. 21744-2 Paperbound $2.00

HOW TO SOLVE CHESS PROBLEMS, *K. S. Howard*
Full of practical suggestions for the fan or the beginner — who knows only the moves of the chessmen. Contains preliminary section and 58 two-move, 46 three-move, and 8 four-move problems composed by 27 outstanding American problem creators in the last 30 years. Explanation of all terms and exhaustive index. "Just what is wanted for the student," Brian Harley. 112 problems, solutions. vi + 171pp. 5⅜ x 8. 20748-X Paperbound $1.50

SOCIAL THOUGHT FROM LORE TO SCIENCE,
H. E. Barnes and H. Becker
An immense survey of sociological thought and ways of viewing, studying, planning, and reforming society from earliest times to the present. Includes thought on society of preliterate peoples, ancient non-Western cultures, and every great movement in Europe, America, and modern Japan. Analyzes hundreds of great thinkers: Plato, Augustine, Bodin, Vico, Montesquieu, Herder, Comte, Marx, etc. Weighs the contributions of utopians, sophists, fascists and communists; economists, jurists, philosophers, ecclesiastics, and every 19th and 20th century school of scientific sociology, anthropology, and social psychology throughout the world. Combines topical, chronological, and regional approaches, treating the evolution of social thought as a process rather than as a series of mere topics. "Impressive accuracy, competence, and discrimination . . . easily the best single survey," *Nation*. Thoroughly revised, with new material up to 1960. 2 indexes. Over 2200 bibliographical notes. Three volume set. Total of 1586pp. 5⅜ x 8.
20901-6, 20902-4, 20903-2 Three volume set, paperbound $9.00

A HISTORY OF HISTORICAL WRITING, *Harry Elmer Barnes*
Virtually the only adequate survey of the whole course of historical writing in a single volume. Surveys developments from the beginnings of historiography in the ancient Near East and the Classical World, up through the Cold War. Covers major historians in detail, shows interrelationship with cultural background, makes clear individual contributions, evaluates and estimates importance; also enormously rich upon minor authors and thinkers who are usually passed over. Packed with scholarship and learning, clear, easily written. Indispensable to every student of history. Revised and enlarged up to 1961. Index and bibliography. xv + 442pp. 5⅜ x 8½.
20104-X Paperbound $2.75

JOHANN SEBASTIAN BACH, *Philipp Spitta*
The complete and unabridged text of the definitive study of Bach. Written some 70 years ago, it is still unsurpassed for its coverage of nearly all aspects of Bach's life and work. There could hardly be a finer non-technical introduction to Bach's music than the detailed, lucid analyses which Spitta provides for hundreds of individual pieces. 26 solid pages are devoted to the B minor mass, for example, and 30 pages to the glorious St. Matthew Passion. This monumental set also includes a major analysis of the music of the 18th century: Buxtehude, Pachelbel, etc. "Unchallenged as the last word on one of the supreme geniuses of music," John Barkham, *Saturday Review Syndicate*. Total of 1819pp. Heavy cloth binding. 5⅜ x 8.
22278-0, 22279-9 Two volume set, clothbound $15.00

BEETHOVEN AND HIS NINE SYMPHONIES, *George Grove*
In this modern middle-level classic of musicology Grove not only analyzes all nine of Beethoven's symphonies very thoroughly in terms of their musical structure, but also discusses the circumstances under which they were written, Beethoven's stylistic development, and much other background material. This is an extremely rich book, yet very easily followed; it is highly recommended to anyone seriously interested in music. Over 250 musical passages. Index. viii + 407pp. 5⅜ x 8.
20334-4 Paperbound $2.25

THREE SCIENCE FICTION NOVELS,
John Taine
Acknowledged by many as the best SF writer of the 1920's, Taine (under the name Eric Temple Bell) was also a Professor of Mathematics of considerable renown. Reprinted here are *The Time Stream*, generally considered Taine's best, *The Greatest Game*, a biological-fiction novel, and *The Purple Sapphire*, involving a supercivilization of the past. Taine's stories tie fantastic narratives to frameworks of original and logical scientific concepts. Speculation is often profound on such questions as the nature of time, concept of entropy, cyclical universes, etc. 4 contemporary illustrations. v + 532pp. 5⅜ x 8⅜.

21180-0 Paperbound $2.50

SEVEN SCIENCE FICTION NOVELS,
H. G. Wells
Full unabridged texts of 7 science-fiction novels of the master. Ranging from biology, physics, chemistry, astronomy, to sociology and other studies, Mr. Wells extrapolates whole worlds of strange and intriguing character. "One will have to go far to match this for entertainment, excitement, and sheer pleasure . . ."*New York Times.* Contents: The Time Machine, The Island of Dr. Moreau, The First Men in the Moon, The Invisible Man, The War of the Worlds, The Food of the Gods, In The Days of the Comet. 1015pp. 5⅜ x 8.

20264-X Clothbound $5.00

28 SCIENCE FICTION STORIES OF H. G. WELLS.
Two full, unabridged novels, *Men Like Gods* and *Star Begotten*, plus 26 short stories by the master science-fiction writer of all time! Stories of space, time, invention, exploration, futuristic adventure. Partial contents: *The Country of the Blind, In the Abyss, The Crystal Egg, The Man Who Could Work Miracles, A Story of Days to Come, The Empire of the Ants, The Magic Shop, The Valley of the Spiders, A Story of the Stone Age, Under the Knife, Sea Raiders,* etc. An indispensable collection for the library of anyone interested in science fiction adventure. 928pp. 5⅜ x 8.

20265-8 Clothbound $5.00

THREE MARTIAN NOVELS,
Edgar Rice Burroughs
Complete, unabridged reprinting, in one volume, of Thuvia, Maid of Mars; Chessmen of Mars; The Master Mind of Mars. Hours of science-fiction adventure by a modern master storyteller. Reset in large clear type for easy reading. 16 illustrations by J. Allen St. John. vi + 490pp. 5⅜ x 8½.

20039-6 Paperbound $2.50

AN INTELLECTUAL AND CULTURAL HISTORY OF THE WESTERN WORLD,
Harry Elmer Barnes
Monumental 3-volume survey of intellectual development of Europe from primitive cultures to the present day. Every significant product of human intellect traced through history: art, literature, mathematics, physical sciences, medicine, music, technology, social sciences, religions, jurisprudence, education, etc. Presentation is lucid and specific, analyzing in detail specific discoveries, theories, literary works, and so on. Revised (1965) by recognized scholars in specialized fields under the direction of Prof. Barnes. Revised bibliography. Indexes. 24 illustrations. Total of xxix + 1318pp.

21275-0, 21276-9, 21277-7 Three volume set, paperbound $8.25

HEAR ME TALKIN' TO YA, *edited by Nat Shapiro and Nat Hentoff*
In their own words, Louis Armstrong, King Oliver, Fletcher Henderson, Bunk
Johnson, Bix Beiderbecke, Billy Holiday, Fats Waller, Jelly Roll Morton,
Duke Ellington, and many others comment on the origins of jazz in New
Orleans and its growth in Chicago's South Side, Kansas City's jam sessions,
Depression Harlem, and the modernism of the West Coast schools. Taken
from taped conversations, letters, magazine articles, other first-hand sources.
Editors' introduction. xvi + 429pp. 5⅜ x 8½.   21726-4 Paperbound $2.00

THE JOURNAL OF HENRY D. THOREAU
A 25-year record by the great American observer and critic, as complete a
record of a great man's inner life as is anywhere available. Thoreau's Journals
served him as raw material for his formal pieces, as a place where he could
develop his ideas, as an outlet for his interests in wild life and plants, in
writing as an art, in classics of literature, Walt Whitman and other contemporaries, in politics, slavery, individual's relation to the State, etc. The
Journals present a portrait of a remarkable man, and are an observant social
history. Unabridged republication of 1906 edition, Bradford Torrey and
Francis H. Allen, editors. Illustrations. Total of 1888pp. 8⅜ x 12¼.
                    20312-3, 20313-1 Two volume set, clothbound $30.00

A SHAKESPEARIAN GRAMMAR, *E. A. Abbott*
Basic reference to Shakespeare and his contemporaries, explaining through
thousands of quotations from Shakespeare, Jonson, Beaumont and Fletcher,
North's *Plutarch* and other sources the grammatical usage differing from the
modern. First published in 1870 and written by a scholar who spent much of
his life isolating principles of Elizabethan language, the book is unlikely ever
to be superseded. Indexes. xxiv + 511pp. 5⅜ x 8½. 21582-2 Paperbound $3.00

FOLK-LORE OF SHAKESPEARE, *T. F. Thistelton Dyer*
Classic study, drawing from Shakespeare a large body of references to supernatural beliefs, terminology of falconry and hunting, games and sports, good
luck charms, marriage customs, folk medicines, superstitions about plants,
animals, birds, argot of the underworld, sexual slang of London, proverbs,
drinking customs, weather lore, and much else. From full compilation comes
a mirror of the 17th-century popular mind. Index. ix + 526pp. 5⅜ x 8½.
                        21614-4 Paperbound $2.75

THE NEW VARIORUM SHAKESPEARE, *edited by H. H. Furness*
By far the richest editions of the plays ever produced in any country or
language. Each volume contains complete text (usually First Folio) of the
play, all variants in Quarto and other Folio texts, editorial changes by every
major editor to Furness's own time (1900), footnotes to obscure references or
language, extensive quotes from literature of Shakespearian criticism, essays
on plot sources (often reprinting sources in full), and much more.

HAMLET, *edited by H. H. Furness*
Total of xxvi + 905pp. 5⅜ x 8½.
                    21004-9, 21005-7 Two volume set, paperbound $5.25

TWELFTH NIGHT, *edited by H. H. Furness*
Index. xxii + 434pp. 5⅜ x 8½.   21189-4 Paperbound $2.75

LA BOHEME BY GIACOMO PUCCINI,
translated and introduced by Ellen H. Bleiler
Complete handbook for the operagoer, with everything needed for full enjoyment except the musical score itself. Complete Italian libretto, with new,
modern English line-by-line translation—the only libretto printing all repeats;
biography of Puccini; the librettists; background to the opera, Murger's La
Boheme, etc.; circumstances of composition and performances; plot summary;
and pictorial section of 73 illustrations showing Puccini, famous singers and
performances, etc. Large clear type for easy reading. 124pp. 5⅜ x 8½.
20404-9 Paperbound $1.25

ANTONIO STRADIVARI: HIS LIFE AND WORK (1644-1737),
W. Henry Hill, Arthur F. Hill, and Alfred E. Hill
Still the only book that really delves into life and art of the incomparable
Italian craftsman, maker of the finest musical instruments in the world today.
The authors, expert violin-makers themselves, discuss Stradivari's ancestry, his
construction and finishing techniques, distinguished characteristics of many
of his instruments and their locations. Included, too, is story of introduction
of his instruments into France, England, first revelation of their supreme
merit, and information on his labels, number of instruments made, prices,
mystery of ingredients of his varnish, tone of pre-1684 Stradivari violin and
changes between 1684 and 1690. An extremely interesting, informative account
for all music lovers, from craftsman to concert-goer. Republication of original
(1902) edition. New introduction by Sydney Beck, Head of Rare Book and
Manuscript Collections, Music Division, New York Public Library. Analytical
index by Rembert Wurlitzer. Appendixes. 68 illustrations. 30 full-page plates.
4 in color. xxvi + 315pp. 5⅜ x 8½. 20425-1 Paperbound $2.25

MUSICAL AUTOGRAPHS FROM MONTEVERDI TO HINDEMITH,
Emanuel Winternitz
For beauty, for intrinsic interest, for perspective on the composer's personality,
for subtleties of phrasing, shading, emphasis indicated in the autograph but
suppressed in the printed score, the mss. of musical composition are fascinating
documents which repay close study in many different ways. This 2-volume
work reprints facsimiles of mss. by virtually every major composer, and many
minor figures—196 examples in all. A full text points out what can be learned
from mss., analyzes each sample. Index. Bibliography. 18 figures. 196 plates.
Total of 170pp. of text. 7⅞ x 10¾.
21312-9, 21313-7 Two volume set, paperbound $5.00

J. S. BACH,
Albert Schweitzer
One of the few great full-length studies of Bach's life and work, and the
study upon which Schweitzer's renown as a musicologist rests. On first appearance (1911), revolutionized Bach performance. The only writer on Bach to
be musicologist, performing musician, and student of history, theology and
philosophy, Schweitzer contributes particularly full sections on history of German Protestant church music, theories on motivic pictorial representations
in vocal music, and practical suggestions for performance. Translated by
Ernest Newman. Indexes. 5 illustrations. 650 musical examples. Total of xix
+ 928pp. 5⅜ x 8½. 21631-4, 21632-2 Two volume set, paperbound $4.50

THE METHODS OF ETHICS, *Henry Sidgwick*
Propounding no organized system of its own, study subjects every major methodological approach to ethics to rigorous, objective analysis. Study discusses and relates ethical thought of Plato, Aristotle, Bentham, Clarke, Butler, Hobbes, Hume, Mill, Spencer, Kant, and dozens of others. Sidgwick retains conclusions from each system which follow from ethical premises, rejecting the faulty. Considered by many in the field to be among the most important treatises on ethical philosophy. Appendix. Index. xlvii + 528pp. 5⅜ x 8½.
21608-X Paperbound $2.50

TEUTONIC MYTHOLOGY, *Jakob Grimm*
A milestone in Western culture; the work which established on a modern basis the study of history of religions and comparative religions. 4-volume work assembles and interprets everything available on religious and folkloristic beliefs of Germanic people (including Scandinavians, Anglo-Saxons, etc.). Assembling material from such sources as Tacitus, surviving Old Norse and Icelandic texts, archeological remains, folktales, surviving superstitions, comparative traditions, linguistic analysis, etc. Grimm explores pagan deities, heroes, folklore of nature, religious practices, and every other area of pagan German belief. To this day, the unrivaled, definitive, exhaustive study. Translated by J. S. Stallybrass from 4th (1883) German edition. Indexes. Total of lxxvii + 1887pp. 5⅜ x 8½.
21602-0, 21603-9, 21604-7, 21605-5 Four volume set, paperbound $11.00

THE I CHING, *translated by James Legge*
Called "The Book of Changes" in English, this is one of the Five Classics edited by Confucius, basic and central to Chinese thought. Explains perhaps the most complex system of divination known, founded on the theory that all things happening at any one time have characteristic features which can be isolated and related. Significant in Oriental studies, in history of religions and philosophy, and also to Jungian psychoanalysis and other areas of modern European thought. Index. Appendixes. 6 plates. xxi + 448pp. 5⅜ x 8½.
21062-6 Paperbound $2.75

HISTORY OF ANCIENT PHILOSOPHY, *W. Windelband*
One of the clearest, most accurate comprehensive surveys of Greek and Roman philosophy. Discusses ancient philosophy in general, intellectual life in Greece in the 7th and 6th centuries B.C., Thales, Anaximander, Anaximenes, Heraclitus, the Eleatics, Empedocles, Anaxagoras, Leucippus, the Pythagoreans, the Sophists, Socrates, Democritus (20 pages), Plato (50 pages), Aristotle (70 pages), the Peripatetics, Stoics, Epicureans, Sceptics, Neo-platonists, Christian Apologists, etc. 2nd German edition translated by H. E. Cushman. xv + 393pp. 5⅜ x 8.
20357-3 Paperbound $2.25

THE PALACE OF PLEASURE, *William Painter*
Elizabethan versions of Italian and French novels from *The Decameron*, Cinthio, Straparola, Queen Margaret of Navarre, and other continental sources — the very work that provided Shakespeare and dozens of his contemporaries with many of their plots and sub-plots and, therefore, justly considered one of the most influential books in all English literature. It is also a book that any reader will still enjoy. Total of cviii + 1,224pp.
21691-8, 21692-6, 21693-4 Three volume set, paperbound $6.75

THE WONDERFUL WIZARD OF OZ, *L. F. Baum*
All the original W. W. Denslow illustrations in full color—as much a part of
"The Wizard" as Tenniel's drawings are of "Alice in Wonderland." "The
Wizard" is still America's best-loved fairy tale, in which, as the author expresses
it, "The wonderment and joy are retained and the heartaches and nightmares
left out." Now today's young readers can enjoy every word and wonderful picture of the original book. New introduction by Martin Gardner. A Baum
bibliography. 23 full-page color plates. viii + 268pp. 5⅜ x 8.
20691-2 Paperbound $1.95

THE MARVELOUS LAND OF OZ, *L. F. Baum*
This is the equally enchanting sequel to the "Wizard," continuing the adventures of the Scarecrow and the Tin Woodman. The hero this time is a little
boy named Tip, and all the delightful Oz magic is still present. This is the
Oz book with the Animated Saw-Horse, the Woggle-Bug, and Jack Pumpkin-
head. All the original John R. Neill illustrations, 10 in full color. 287pp.
5⅜ x 8. 20692-0 Paperbound $1.75

ALICE'S ADVENTURES UNDER GROUND, *Lewis Carroll*
The original *Alice in Wonderland*, hand-lettered and illustrated by Carroll
himself, and originally presented as a Christmas gift to a child-friend. Adults
as well as children will enjoy this charming volume, reproduced faithfully
in this Dover edition. While the story is essentially the same, there are slight
changes, and Carroll's spritely drawings present an intriguing alternative to
the famous Tenniel illustrations. One of the most popular books in Dover's
catalogue. Introduction by Martin Gardner. 38 illustrations. 128pp. 5⅜ x 8½.
21482-6 Paperbound $1.00

THE NURSERY "ALICE," *Lewis Carroll*
While most of us consider *Alice in Wonderland* a story for children of all
ages, Carroll himself felt it was beyond younger children. He therefore provided this simplified version, illustrated with the famous Tenniel drawings
enlarged and colored in delicate tints, for children aged "from Nought to
Five." Dover's edition of this now rare classic is a faithful copy of the 1889
printing, including 20 illustrations by Tenniel, and front and back covers
reproduced in full color. Introduction by Martin Gardner. xxiii + 67pp.
6⅛ x 9¼. 21610-1 Paperbound $1.75

THE STORY OF KING ARTHUR AND HIS KNIGHTS, *Howard Pyle*
A fast-paced, exciting retelling of the best known Arthurian legends for young
readers by one of America's best story tellers and illustrators. The sword
Excalibur, wooing of Guinevere, Merlin and his downfall, adventures of Sir
Pellias and Gawaine, and others. The pen and ink illustrations are vividly
imagined and wonderfully drawn. 41 illustrations. xviii + 313pp. 6⅛ x 9¼.
21445-1 Paperbound $2.00

Prices subject to change without notice.

Available at your book dealer or write for free catalogue to Dept. Adsci,
Dover Publications, Inc., 180 Varick St., N.Y., N.Y. 10014. Dover publishes more
than 150 books each year on science, elementary and advanced mathematics,
biology, music, art, literary history, social sciences and other areas.